T0366410

The Dry Years

PROHIBITION AND SOCIAL CHANGE IN WASHINGTON

THE

DRY

YEARS

Prohibition and Social Change in Washington

Revised Edition

NORMAN H. CLARK

Foreword by John C. Burnham

University of Washington Press

Seattle and London

Library of Congress Cataloging-in-Publication Data

Clark, Norman H.
The dry years.

   Bibliography: p.
   Includes index.
   1. Prohibition—Washington (State)—History—20th
century. 2. Washington (State)—Social conditions.
3. Washington (State)—Politics and government,
I. Title.
HV5090.W2C58 1988   363.4'1'09797   86-26741

ISBN 0-295-96466-9 (pbk.)

For Kathy, Karen, and Kenneth

Foreword

THE appearance of a new edition of *The Dry Years* is an important scholarly event. Norman Clark's study of prohibition in Washington has always set a high standard for works that use regional events to cut through and enlarge our understanding of the history of all of the United States. Clark is in fact one of the most interesting social historians of the United States, with his works on both local and regional history as well as his classic general interpretation of American Prohibition, *Deliver Us from Evil* (1976). But it was in *The Dry Years* that most of us came to know and admire his scholarship.

This new edition appears in a scholarly context that is in one way quite different from that of the first. Temperance and alcohol history has expanded dramatically in recent years, and there is now even a small journal devoted exclusively to the subject. Numerous historians have added greatly to our knowledge of the ways in which various societies in their own contexts have attempted to cope with the existence of alcoholic beverages. In this lively research arena, Clark's work continues to hold an honored place, and for good reason, as readers of this new version will discover.

Perhaps the most subtle aspect of the distinctive quality in Clark's work is his ability to maintain an objective tone in dealing with even the most controversial matters. In *The Dry Years*, all parties who took sides, whatever the issues, receive respectful and understanding treatment. His delightful but not destructive sense of irony aids Clark in cultivating and fostering detachment, regardless of whether dry, wet, or bootlegger is the subject, and Clark's perspective therefore has a dimension above just fairness and respect.

A second special characteristic of Clark's approach is his ability to sense and explicate the symbolic nature of events. In his narrative, an election is not just an election; rather it represents historical forces. He is not afraid to talk about what it meant to be respectable and middle class and have dreams, nor also to have a business and good business sense. It is insight as well as vivid prose that leads him, for example, to show that the change in generations in the First Presbyterian Church embodied a whole shift in temperance movements.

Clark brings in national and universal considerations without invoking the theoretical or ideological discussions that have burdened other scholars' work in careful local history. His portrait of recent events in the state provides a fresh perspective on the history of Washington. But all of *The Dry Years* evokes the impact on American history in general of specific occurrences and, more importantly, relationships that developed in this corner of the Northwest.

In both the first edition and this second edition the story of temperance and prohibition in Washington provides a telling contrast to the general accounts of American dry crusades that have depended upon interpretations of provincial journalists in the East. The importance of Clark's work in the substantive materials of a single state not only continues but is reemphasized in recent works, particularly a comparable account of Kansas by Robert Smith Bader and Austin Kerr's recent new history of the Anti-Saloon League.

I well remember my own reaction to the original version of this work. It was the first time that I had a sense that any author had created a realistic, three-dimensional portrait of prohibition in the United States. In 1965 Clark opened up for many scholars a new possibility, the possibility that one could maintain with confidence that Prohibition was a reform and that it was neither an aberration nor a mistake. This updated, second edition will help yet another generation of historians underline the fact that Prohibition was a revealing and profoundly important event in history. It is not enough to observe that *The Dry Years* will show that good local history is just localized history and that what happened in Washington teaches us what happened in the United States, from the place of churches in everyday life to the changes in newfangled lifestyles. In an age when public figures are debating the "new temperance movement" and Neoprohibitionism, Clark's findings are, in fact, of more than historical interest.

Yet this second edition of *The Dry Years* goes even further than illuminating current questions in their own terms. Once again, Clark has pioneered in introducing perspective that permits a new inquiry into a difficult, confused, and misled history. What happened, he asks again, after 1933? For the story, it turns out, was not a simple one. What were the issues and who were the contenders? The same fair-minded approach that tells so much about events during formal prohibition has now illuminated the commercial and business interests and the baffling ambivalence of voters and drinkers. Even factoring in specific population changes, Washingtonians of the mid-twentieth century, Clark shows, approached alcoholic beverages with consistent and persistent interests. Clark has, in short, overcome the confusion and propaganda that have frustrated earlier attempts to explore the recent history of temperance, intemperance, reform, privatism, and greed as each one interacted with changes in American society.

The colorful figures of the temperance and prohibition efforts in Washington and elsewhere are still evoking anxiety about the forces that contend on either side of the drink question. That there is less color among the recently contending parties, Clark points out, does not change the fact that moral questions as well as social concerns are still at issue.

JOHN C. BURNHAM
Ohio State University

Preface

THE search for order in American life that began shortly after the American Revolution led many citizens to demand of their state governments what the churches, in their total disestablishment, could no longer provide—a source of strong moral stewardship. Laws against robbery and murder were never in question, but many people wanted protection also from slavery, dueling, gambling, adultery, prostitution, and drunkenness. They met with both failures and triumphs, and the list of moral-social priorities was revised by each generation. In the early twentieth century, the list included protection from predatory monopolies, child-labor practices, and the twelve-hour day. But at a critical point, many voters lost hope that their legislators could or would respond honestly to their needs, and they then demanded access to political tools—the initiative measure was the most potent—that allowed them to create the circumstances in which they themselves could say Yes or No to the most vital moral and social questions.

In the state of Washington, the first such question on the ballot addressed the traffic in intoxicating liquors, and, most pointedly, the licensing of saloons. Looking eagerly toward a momentous beginning, the Reverend Mark Matthews, moderator of the nationwide Presbyterian General Assembly and in 1912 pastor for the First Presbyterian Church of Seattle (then the largest such congregation in the world), hoped to galvanize latent political power into a revolutionary force for social change. The saloon, he cried, was "the most fiendish, corrupt, and hell-soaked institution that ever crawled out of the slime of the eternal pit." It takes "your sweet innocent daughter, robs her of her virtue, and transforms her into a brazen, wanton harlot." It was "the open sore of this land." To protect their homes and children, voters of the state should rise up in righteous anger and go forth with their newfound strength to crush this evil, because, he assured them, "the two great political parties are rum-soaked, saloon-cursed, and without conscience on the abolition of this great enemy."

Lurid as these images may seem today, and even slightly ludicrous, they are an integral part of American political history, in every way as substantial as the haunting images of black slavery, of mothers bonded in wage slavery to textile mills, of stunted children in coal mines, of families robbed of dignity by a railroad, of ragged individuals cowering in bread-lines untouched by charity, justice, or human grace. Taken singly, such images are easily open to rhetorical inflation. Yet they signal coordinates, as it were, with which we chart an American conscience. Taken collectively, they define the American reform tradition by illuminating the disorders and abuses against which reform energies have always been directed.

Because of our melancholy experiences with such matters, few Americans today can study the role of alcohol, or the efforts to control its use, without first discarding some comfortable prejudgments. When I set out to understand the Prohibition Movement in the state of Washington, I supposed my subject to be the antithesis of reform, a history, in a way, of the failure of repression. I thought I might spend an interesting year reading and writing about a bizarre misalignment of booze and politics that, I had learned, had brought into prominence some odd people and odd confrontations that usually amused historians. The most alluring part, of course, was the "dry decade" of the 1920's, which is where I began. My first efforts yielded a chapter about enforcement of the Volstead Act, which in my reading meant the dry squads' often comic pursuit of a sort of folk hero, Roy Olmstead, the former policeman who became Seattle's most affable and reliable chief executive officer in the bootlegging business. It was, I believed, a good story. But my pleasure in it was diminished by a realization that it contributed nothing to my understanding of why the state had passed laws that allowed Olmstead his enviable wealth and social position. Nothing happened to rumrunners or to their fumbling pursuers that could clarify why so many Americans had wanted laws that clever men like Omstead found so many Americans pleased to see violated. To understand why there were such laws, I would have to look beyond the bootleg booze, fast boats, big money, and adventurous women—beyond what seemed to be all the good stories and ask serious questions about why prohibition came to the state and the nation.

While trying to know why, years before anyone had heard of Roy Olmstead or the Volstead Act, people in many states were voting for state prohibition, I was learning much that I had not known about American priorities. The antisaloon movement in Washington was not, I came to realize, an impulsive gathering of perversely repressive lunatics or fanatics. For reasonable people, the case against the saloon, the drunkard, and the liquor traffic seemed both urgent and obvious in the social statistics of alcohol-related crime, delinquency, poverty, prostitution, disease, and political corruption that careful observers of these problems had been publishing for four generations. Reasonable people had directed the movement through a sequence of preeminently rational achievements in political reform that actually changed fundamental democratic procedures. Early in this century, Direct Primary laws opened the selection of political candidates to the influence of antisaloon leaders, who could then identify the dry candidates. In a few years a largely dry legislature could approve constitutional amendments that, first of all, allowed women to vote, then allowed all voters to use the initiative measure, which then allowed a vote of all the people on the question of abolishing the saloon. To many people, there was no more important question. By 1916, twenty-three states, including Washington, had prohibition laws. When in 1919 the nation ratified the Eighteenth Amendment to the Constitution, most of the states had been dry for years, some for decades. To most people in the United States, the Volstead Act, passed by Congress to empower the state and national agencies to enforce prohibition, was a belated confirmation of their early wisdom.

I followed the record of antisaloon sentiment that led to the "bone-dry" sentiment that moved reasonable people to embrace the Eighteenth Amendment. I wanted to go on to learn how that astonishing achievement itself so soon became a threat to dominant social values, and how, in an achievement equally astonishing, voters after a decade's experience would decide that they could countenance neither the old-time saloon nor prohibition. Beyond this remained a most intriguing question: what would be the character of the anti-prohibition laws written for a steadfastly antisaloon state? At the time—because books must end somewhere—I had no careful answers. I concluded in *The Dry Years* when it was published in 1965 that such laws were but tentative steps toward the solution of a problem in American society that may always have an open end.

This present expansion of that work moves the open end forward about fifty years. I have taken up the study and writing again at the point of repeal in 1933 (the end of chapter 15), revising some thoughts, reorganizing others, and adding a substantial body of new material. What the reader now has is a history in one region of attempts through nearly two hundred years to make the use of alcohol compatible with the American view of social progress.

The most recent half-century presents surprising conceptual challenges. It is, for example, easy to accept a common assumption that voters of the more recent period, in contrast to the antisaloon crusaders, have learned painfully from the prohibition experience that society "can't legislate morality." Yet the record shows clearly enough that voting No on the question of whether or not the beer-wine taverns should be licensed to sell "spirituous liquors" (an initiative measure on the ballot in 1960) was a rather calculated act of moral legislation.

Even so, it is true that ways of thinking about alcohol as a social problem during the post-repeal period have become less and less morally explicit. Many, and probably most, voters have rejected the notion that alcohol is without qualification an evil substance, an addictive poison relentlessly threatening ruin for innocent men, women, and children— the controlling idea of prohibitionists since their work first began. And though most voters seem to have accepted the possibilities that alcohol will always be with us and that it may even have a few redeeming virtues, they clearly do not share the early Puritans' full confidence that alcohol is the "water of life," the "good creature of God," a blessed refreshment abused only by the eternally degenerate.

Such uncertainty fosters a reluctance to condemn either the substance or the abuser, and it projects, paradoxically, several social imperatives. If the substance does indeed present measurable hazards to public and private health, an informed awareness of these hazards is a state obligation. (Alcohol information should flow from the laboratories to the classrooms, to the posters in liquor stores, to the billboards, to the television programs; a declining figure of per-capita consumption and the recent movement of tastes toward light wines and beers are good signals.) If for some people alcohol is indeed a blessing, it is surely for others a ubiquitous enticement to self-destruction toward which society cannot stand either remote or indifferent. (The increasing visibility across the state of alcohol rehabilitation centers and the rising number of weekly meetings of units of Alcoholics Anonymous are good indications of social sophistication and concern.) If, as most people seem to believe, the circumstances under which public drinking takes place can indeed determine the character of public drinking, then the competitive commerce in pro-

viding drink demands severe regulation. (The administrative codes written by the Washington State Liquor Control Board since 1934 now list
hundreds of discrete constraints). If alcohol is a terrifying factor in highway fatalities, then the state must make drunken driving less attractive.
(Heavy fines and mandatory jail sentences seem now to be more effective
than earlier penalties.)

This same uncertainty seems more likely to unite voters than to divide
them and finds its clearest expression in the language of accommodation.
Historians describe the sequential victories of the antisaloon movement
as sternly measured steps toward sternly unambiguous goals: the death of
the drunkard-making business, the saloon-free state, the bone-dry nation. To explain them, they use the abrasive words that spring easily from
metaphors of war, or crusade, or revolution—words such as *triumph*, or
prohibition, or *abolition*. But in the period beyond repeal such analogues
quickly distort perception. The goals of post-repeal voters have been
softly and deliberately ambiguous, often unverifiable, even ineffable.
They suggest no easy metaphorical conversion. To explain them, one re-
sists the images of measurable conquest or destruction and seeks instead
the language of functional interrelationships, words that in a social-
political context can suggest situations that are often unmeasurable and
even equivocal: words such as *stability, equilibrium, equity, negotiation,
harmony*, and *prudence*. After a history of fear and conflict, these are
liberating words, and somewhere in their tone and meaning is the legacy
of the antisaloon, anti-prohibition experience.

Of the several books about prohibition published since 1965, at least a
couple would have influenced *The Dry Years* if they had been earlier
available. Austin Kerr's fine study, *Organized for Reform: A New History
of the Anti-Saloon League* (Yale University Press, 1983), would have
shown me how the ASL quickly lost its impressive strength after 1920
and was totally disarmed before the battle against the repeal movement.
Many ASL supporters believed that revising the Constitution was for them
victory enough, and that enforcing the law was an every-day obligation of
the federal government. Churches wanted their money for other purposes,
and they denied the ASL its essential funding. Then ASL leaders, state
and national, fell into divisive disputes over strategy: to work for effective
enforcement of state laws and the Volstead Act or to devote diminishing
funds and energies to the goals of long-term education. Using Kerr's insights and sources to detail the collapse of the state ASL would be fasci-

nating research. A second book, *Alcohol and Public Policy: Beyond the Shadow of Prohibition*, Mark Moore and Dean Gerstein, eds. (National Academy Press, 1981), presents thoughtful essays that would have given me a more sensitive approach to the problems of liquor control after 1933.

In the 1965 edition of this book, I was happy to thank my parents, Leigh W. Clark and Sadie O. Clark, for the trust and generosity that made my graduate work possible. I also tried to express my enduring gratitude to Robert E. Burke, who first suggested this topic to me and whose critical judgment and friendship have benefited all of my work since. I acknowledged debts to John Broussard, Thomas Pressly, Edwin Bingham, and Richard Berner, and I am happy to renew them. I want also to thank several men whose experiences and insights figure largely in the last two chapters: Don Eldridge, Robert Seeber, Malachy Murphy, Lewis Holcomb, George Scott, John Martinis, and Representative Dick King. And I am especially grateful for the help of Leroy Hittle and James Hoing, whose advice was distinguished by its courtesy, scope, and precision.

NORMAN H. CLARK
October 1987

Contents

The Dry Years

PROHIBITION AND SOCIAL CHANGE IN WASHINGTON

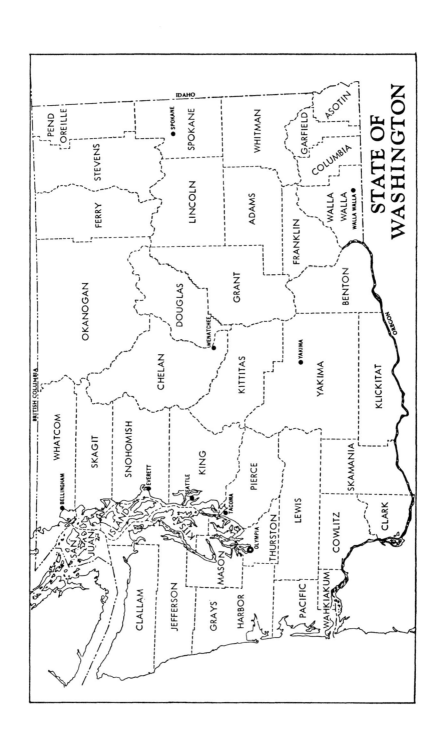

STATE OF
WASHINGTON

1

The Nefarious Trade

WHEN Captain Meriwether Lewis reached the mouth of the Columbia River in 1805, he found the natives there to be a "mild and inoffensive" people who "uniformly behaved to us with great friendship." They lived in houses, provided well for their children, their
women, and their old people. They enjoyed a benign, harmonious
society "scarcely ever interrupted by disputes." The remarkable tran-
quillity of their private lives, their aversion to violence and warfare,
Lewis thought, had been secured by "their ignorance of spiritous
liquors, the earliest and most dreadful present which civilization had
given to the other natives of the continent."[1]

In this regard the Indians of the Pacific Northwest Coast were indeed unusual. Unlike most Stone-Age peoples, they had never known
the techniques of brewing or distilling, nor had they had any experience at all with liquor before it came to them through the maritime fur trade, which did not begin on the Northwest Coast until after
the American Revolution. In 1778, Captain James Cook first sighted
Vancouver Island and dropped his anchor in Nootka Sound. A year
later, his men learned that sea otter pelts which they had acquired
casually from the natives at Nootka would bring 120 silver dollars
each from the merchants of Canton. News of this fabulous exchange
quickly spread through Europe and the United States, and the great
fur rush to the Northwest Coast began.[2] Among the axioms of the
trade was the assumption that the easiest way to trap a pelt was with
a bottle of rum.

By 1790, most of the Indians of the coastal regions—with the exception of those on the Columbia River, where no whites had yet been
—were familiar with intoxication. The Northwest natives, however,
were curiously insusceptible to its persuasions. For example, when the
Boston trader Robert Gray equipped the *Columbia* for his second

voyage to the Northwest Coast in 1790—after he had traded with the Indians for several years and knew what they wanted—liquor was still not a significant item in his trading supplies. Others, like Gray, found to their chagrin that among these people real addiction did not come easily. This, at least, was the experience of traders with the natives of the lower Columbia, whose reaction to alcohol was probably typical.[3]

Liquor first came to these groups from Canadians of the Northwest Company, probably between 1807 and 1810. It is probable, too, that the employees of John Jacob Astor's Pacific Fur Company were trying to use liquor when they competed with the Northwest Company near the mouth of the Columbia after 1810.[4] Both, however, met with firm resistance from the natives themselves. One of Astor's clerks, a Canadian named Gabriel Franchère, noted in his journal that "these savages are not addicted to intemperance" as were other American Indians, and that they regarded liquors "as poisons, and drunkenness as disgraceful." He recorded an incident in which "some of the gentlemen" of Astor's company had amused themselves by making the son of a local chief drunk on wine. "The old chief came to reproach us," Franchère related, "saying that we had degraded his son by exposing him to the ridicule of the slaves."[5]

The same attitude was recorded by Ross Cox, of the Northwest Company. "All the Indians on the Columbia entertain a strong aversion to ardent spirits," Cox wrote. "They allege that slaves only drink to excess; and that drunkenness is degrading to free men."[6]

This aversion must have persisted until about 1820, for Sir George Simpson, of Hudson's Bay Company, reported to London that until then "the use of Spiritous Liquors was unknown among the Natives of the lower Columbia and nothing gave them such a contemptible opinion of the Whites as seeing them deprive themselves of reason thereby." For a good ten years, then, these natives of the Columbia regarded alcohol as a threat to the integrity of their own culture and possessed the moral strength to refuse it.

Sir George, however, banefully recorded the unhappy change. By 1824, he wrote, these Indians were "getting as much addicted to Drunkenness as the tribes of the East side of the Mountain." The habit arose, he said, from the traders' practice of giving a free dram every time they bought furs. At last, he said, the gift became agreeable, and "they were allowed a present of a Bottle of Rum for every 10 skins."[7]

Sir George thus witnessed a massive breakdown of group morality

and a major step in sociocultural disintegration. The most convincing
account of what had happened to these Indians has been written by an
anthropologist, Edwin M. Lemert, who has studied this breakdown in
some detail. In his book *Alcohol and the Northwest Coast Indians*,
Lemert showed that the fur trade, first of all, brought to these natives
what was really an embarrassing profusion of riches—"increments of
wealth without precedent"—which precipitated a grave social and
cultural crisis. This was a society, as Ross Cox had observed, in which
the individual commanded respect, status, and prestige "in proportion
to the number of wives, slaves, etc., which he may keep." The greater
the wealth, the greater the individual's status. Because this was a society with strong taboos against violent or aggressive conduct, the
delicate fabric of social control was supported entirely by the prestige
of its leaders. Thus this prestige, based on wealth, was the very heart
of a complex culture. The crisis came with the *nouveaux riches* created
by the fur trade, whose wealth brought chaos to the traditions of social status and, consequently, insoluble problems to the traditions of
social control.[8]

The decline of these traditions was accelerated by the overwhelming grief the Indians knew as their groups succumbed to European
diseases. The number of deaths in itself might have created status
problems of a devastating magnitude. In the course of one short generation, the Chinooks of the Lower Columbia whom Lewis saw were
reduced from an integrated society of five thousand to a demoralized,
disintegrated band of twenty-five hundred. By 1850 there were probably no more than one hundred Chinooks left to be counted. The
Indians of the Chehalis, Owilapash, and Cowlitz groups in the area
north of the Columbia River probably numbered about four thousand
in 1800. The fevers which struck them in the 1820's left maybe two
hundred of them alive. In a pattern of destruction that even today
staggers the imagination, the other Indians of the Northwest Coast
were similarly decimated during the first three decades of the nineteenth century.[9] In their sorrow, in their social disorientation, and in
their moral confusion, the Indians finally reached for the bottle of
rum which the fur traders had for years been offering them. In the
white man's liquor they found a source of ecstasy and a release from
their grief that their native culture had neither provided nor demanded. Their pathos is expressed poignantly in an old drinking
song:

I am afraid to drink, but still I like to drink.
I don't like to drink, but I have to drink the whiskey.
Here I am singing a love song, drinking, drinking, drinking.
I didn't know that whiskey was no good, and still I was drinking it.
I found out that whiskey is no good.
Come, come closer to me, my slaves,
And I'll give you a drink of whiskey.
Here we are drinking now.
Have some more, some more of my whiskey.
Have a good time with it.
Come closer to me, come closer to me, my slave.
We are drinking now, we feel pretty good.
Now you feel just like me.[10]

After the fall, drunkenness probably became in part the evidence of status which allowed the Indians to identify themselves in some degree with the power and the prestige of the whites, and when the Indian turned to whiskey, he turned all the way. "One of the outstanding characteristics of Indian drinking in the coast areas from early times to the present," Lemert writes, "has been the very rapid consumption of liquor"—that is to say, drinking until the supply is gone or the drinkers fall. And drinking was always a group activity, never a solitary one, with entire adult populations, sometimes, given to excess.[11]

Most significantly for whites, these massive losses of self-control released the aggressive tendencies which the social values of the native culture had so successfully restrained. Drunkenness encouraged an ugly streak of natural viciousness at the very time when cultural decay had weakened the methods for controlling it. Such behavior was, in fact, furthered by social confusion, apathy, remorse, and bitterness. Thus it was that the Indians, who had shunned violence before they knew whites, began to take up the techniques of bloodshed in orgies of terror.[12] In the late 1820's, for example, the brig *William and Ann* struck a spit at the mouth of the Columbia River, and her captain and crew of twenty-six landed in small boats at Clatsop Point. The natives, whom Meriwether Lewis had found "mild and inoffensive" people, butchered the twenty-six to the last man.[13]

In 1821, the British government belatedly expressed alarm over the indecencies which competition between the London-owned Hudson's Bay Company and the Northwest Company had brought to Indians and to whites alike all across British North America. Not only had it debauched the Indians with trickery and liquor when traders employed any means open to them to further the end of trade; by

1820, the rivalry had passed beyond even superficial morality as the whites themselves expressed it in the naked use of force—in robbery, kidnaping, and murder. It became a bloody business indeed at the Seven Oaks Massacre, near present-day Winnipeg, where a band of Northwest Company men attacked and killed twenty-one members of the Hudson's Bay Company's Red River Colony. When news of this horror reached London, Parliament acted decisively.

The government forced the two companies to merge, with the result that the Northwest Company totally disappeared. The Hudson's Bay Company took the properties and most of the personnel of its competitor and assumed complete jurisdiction over all the disputed territories, including the "Empire of the Columbia," which it entered with a license of exclusive trade.

The act of Parliament which granted this license made it "incumbent [upon the HBC] to take measures for the amelioration of the condition of the Indians and to discourage the use of Spirits among them." The governor and committee of the company in London made it clear to Simpson, their "Governor of Northern Department of Rupert's Land," that a complete withdrawal of liquor from the fur trade should be accomplished in a period of two or three years, and that higher prices for furs should go to the Indians in lieu of gifts of liquor.[14]

Sir George began immediately, reducing the amount of liquor distributed to the Indians by one half during 1822 and 1823. When he arrived at the Columbia River in 1824, he prohibited the traffic in that area altogether. With the first stern measure of liquor control in the region's history, he limited imports "to a very small quantity barely sufficient to give an occasional treat to the Servants." One should note in passing, however, that Simpson was a businessman, not a moralist, and that his restriction of the trade in spirits was prompted by his fear that if the Indians "were allowed to drink the Value of the Furs they bring, they would not have the means of continuing the Barter and we should be the sufferers in the long run."[15]

When Simpsom gave the management of the Columbia River Department to Dr. John McLoughlin, he insisted that this policy of prohibition for the Indians and lean rations for the "servants" of the company be vigorously pursued. McLoughlin—his title was chief factor—eagerly complied. To protect the Indians, McLoughlin on several occasions even purchased the liquor stocks aboard American vessels that came into the river.[16] These incidents, however, indicate that the company's policy was subject to serious frustrations. In fact, they anticipated another epoch of debauchery.

It began in the late 1820's, when there were several American ships trading up and down the Northwest Coast challenging the discipline under which the Hudson's Bay Company held the Indians. In 1829, Simpson was more disturbed by the nature of this competition than he was by its magnitude. He wrote to London that the principal articles of trade with the Americans were "Guns, Ammunition, Cloth, Blankets, Slops, Liquor," and he ominously underlined a new and to him a frightening evil for which the Americans were responsible—participation in the Indian slave trade. They were buying slaves from the natives at Cape Flattery, he said, and bartering them to "the Northern tribes at about 30 Beaver each, and some good looking female slaves as high as 50. In this unhuman traffic . . . they deal largely in Guns Ammunition & Liquor . . . and to the imminent danger of all who are connected with the trade."[17]

Nevertheless, Hudson's Bay Company, London, in 1831 forbade the sale of rum to all Indians. Shortly thereafter, Chief Factor McLoughlin wrote to Simpson that the competition was growing more intense and that the company was suffering from this prohibition. The Americans were making gains with liquor along the coast, he warned, and he concluded that "We must do the same or abandon the trade." At about that time, too, American fur companies were pushing westward across the Rocky Mountains, challenging the Snake River trade. They used liquor without restriction.[18]

Threatened from the coast and from the mountains, McLoughlin began with some reluctance to use liquor where he felt he must. Apparently he interpreted the rule against selling rum to Indians as not applying to gifts, and the stores of alcohol at Fort Vancouver were again opened to the traders. McLoughlin told his lieutenant Peter Skene Ogden that if the Russians complained, "you will tell them that you are obliged to do so in consequence of its being done by the Americans."[19]

In 1832 he reported to London that he did not have enough rum in stock to supply the Snake River brigades and that the "expenditure of Liquor on the coast" had been "much greater than anticipated." By 1837, Simpson admitted that his prohibitions of the previous decade had all been abandoned. "So inseparable is drunkenness or

the abuse of spiritous liquor from the opposition in the Indian
trade," he said, "that on the north-west coast, where we contend with
the Americans and Russians . . . I am sorry to say that our utmost
efforts to check it have been unavailing."[20]

This was a time of anxious concern for Dr. McLoughlin, for he
was threatened not only by the economic competition but by the ruin
of the relationship with the Indians which he had so carefully culti-
vated for more than ten years. He apparently did all he could to protect at least those Indians in the area of Fort Vancouver by continuing his prohibition of the liquor traffic there and reinforcing it with
restrictions on the use of liquor by the whites within the fort. To prevent drinking from "degenerating in the long run into Intemprance,"
he even found it at times wise "to Limit the use of Liquor at Dinner."[21]

The nights, however, were damp and cold, and there is no reason
to believe that his efforts were always successful. But if one looks for
the beginnings of the temperance movement among white people in
the Pacific Northwest, he will find it in the correspondence of Sir
George Simpson and Dr. John McLoughlin. Their attitudes toward
liquor had been conditioned by the Hudson's Bay Company's experience with Indians since 1670, by their own knowledge of the habits
of the white traders, and by their understanding of the company's
economic best interests. These attitudes, then, were already something of a tradition when the first American missionaries found their
way to the Columbia River in 1834.

The small group of Methodists from New England who settled in
the Willamette Valley that year were of the generation of reformers
that was directing American temperance sentiment into a vital and
compelling movement during the 1830's. Their church had resolved
against the distilling of grain as early as 1780. In the 1820's, members of their faith had supported a movement toward total abstinence, and in 1826 they had assisted in the organization of the
American Society for the Promotion of Temperance. They were also
active in the Board of Commissioners for Foreign Missions. It was
during this decade that the movement assumed a clearly evangelical
character, and pledge-signing, songs, verse, and temperance revivals
began to spread across the country.

Between 1831 and 1834, membership in the American Society increased by 500 per cent to a total membership of one million, and there were local organizations in every state and territory. Though the society was sometimes torn by doctrinal disputes between those who believed in total abstinence and those who believed in abstinence from "ardent spirits" only, it served to marshal the emotions of all those who saw liquor as a darkening threat to the American dream. Like other social movements of this generation—the antislavery cause, prison reform, educational reform, egalitarian passions, and religious revivals—the temperance crusade moved on the conviction that its work could ennoble that dream and bring it into practical reality. As its principal historian has said, the movement was based upon a philosophy whose "central idea was the perfectibility of man."[22]

This idea was the core of faith for the missionaries who came to the Oregon Country in 1834. Responding to what they understood to be the Indians' desire for Christianity, they came west to perfect "the savage." The leader of the party, the Reverend Jason Lee, kept a journal of his travels westward. "O how I long to erect the standard of my master," he wrote, "in these regions which Satan has so long claimed for his own." Lee, as a New Englander and as a Methodist, felt that he knew Satan, and he came to know that Satan's claim on these regions included whites as well as Indians. Traveling across South Pass in the summer of 1834 with the trader Nathaniel Wyeth and his party, Lee was deeply saddened when the mountain men took their whiskey rations and "quarreled in the night" from the effect of it. "Would to God," Lee wrote in his diary, "that the time may come soon when its use shall be entirely abandoned except as a medicine."[23] (Bernard DeVoto called this prayer "the first known sigh of a prohibitionist in Oregon."[24])

When Reverend Lee met Dr. McLoughlin at Fort Vancouver, then, the two leaders already shared certain significant concerns. McLoughlin encouraged Lee and his party to settle in the Willamette Valley. Lee shortly came to feel that the colony of whites there could become a more "extensive and valuable field of usefulness" for his talents than could any group of depraved Indians, who, Lee observed, were "dirty and naked," having "fallen a sacrifice to the fever and ague."[25] It was here—also with McLoughlin's encouragement—that Lee organized the Oregon Temperance Society in 1836.

This was no routine matter. Nathaniel Wyeth, Lee's benefactor from Cambridge, Massachusetts, had come to the Columbia with carefully planned and well financed intentions of cracking McLoughlin's monopoly in the Indian trade. At the trading post he called Fort William, near the mouth of the Willamette, Wyeth showed no reluctance to sell liquor to whites or Indians. The consequent revelry and disorder rocked the stability of McLoughlin's moral domain and distressed Jason Lee even more than it had in the mountains. Both men, then, were relieved when Wyeth admitted defeat in his efforts to win the Indians' commercial loyalty. He broke up Fort William early in 1836 and returned to the East.

The peace, however, was only momentary. During the liquidation of Wyeth's holdings, a mountain man named Ewing Young, recently from California, obtained a large caldron which, he announced, he would convert into a distillery. This Ewing Young was a man of bold character and determination who was destined to leave a broad mark as a leader in Oregon's colonial society. At this juncture he was enraged at Dr. McLoughlin and had shrewdly and sullenly resolved to humble him in an extremely painful manner.

This vendetta had sprung from events which followed Young's arrival in the valley with a herd of horses he hoped to sell. Because McLoughlin had been falsely advised by Mexican officials that Young was a horse thief, Young found himself unwelcome at Fort Vancouver and at the Willamette Mission. Denied his trade and branded as something of a social leper, Young released his mountain-man's fury upon McLoughlin. He had harsh words for the chief factor, words which he coupled with a severe invective against the presumptions of British influence in all of Oregon. Young knew well that a distillery would challenge this influence at a most sensitive point, and when he saw the opportunity, he took it. Young's grievances were reinforced by another anti-British settler named Lawrence Carmichael, and the two set to work with a vengeance.

Lee's temperance society addressed itself to this problem immediately. It worded a petition to Ewing Young which appealed to his American dignity, pleaded for the general welfare of the colony, and urged him to give up his plans for the liquor trade. There were twenty-four petitioners, nine Americans and fifteen Canadians, the latter, surely, acting under instructions from Dr. McLoughlin. They all indicated their sincerity by pledging themselves to purchase Young's equipment should he comply with their prayers. Ewing Young, responsive to pride as well as dignity, agreed to abandon his project, but he refused to accept any payment. He used the occasion to heap more abuse upon McLoughlin. But for a while, at least, this threat to the security of the valley from mountain men had ended.[26]

The Temperance Society, however, continued as a going concern. Its efforts were mostly those of pledge-signing and speaking; in general, activities of the temperance movement no different from those in Massachusetts or New York. Because McLoughlin cooperated, these efforts met with some initial success among both whites and Indians. In 1838, another group led by Reverend Henry Spalding and Dr. Marcus Whitman, both Presbyterians from the United States, formed a temperance society at the Protestant Mission near Fort Walla Walla. The Americans prevailed upon Pierre Pambrun, the Roman Catholic, French-Canadian chief trader for the Hudson's Bay Company at the fort, to become the society's first president. Their hope, plainly, was to encourage Pambrun to restrict the use of alcohol among the Indians of the area. It is not clear that their conversion of the chief trader was a complete success, but Spalding began taking pledges of total abstinence from the illiterate Nez Perces, who would make their marks on the papers and allow the missionary to write in their Indian names.[27]

Such an impermeable faith that the conventions of temperance evangelism were meaningful to a Stone-Age people was possible only because the goals of the missionaries in this matter were shared by the Hudson's Bay Company. The survival of the Columbia River Department depended upon sober and dependable whites and upon industrious and peaceful natives. After several years of disruptive rivalry, much of it conducted with liquor, the economy of the fur trade was entering a period of decline and relative calm. The American Fur Company and Hudson's Bay Company had finally defined the limits of their jurisdictions, and, in 1834, the fierce competition from the Rocky Mountain Fur Company collapsed. As the competitive pace slackened, McLoughlin was able to abolish "the use of Spiritous Liquors among the trappers of the Snake Country" by 1840. In 1842, the Hudson's Bay Company entered an agreement with its principal competitor, the Russian American Fur Company, to withdraw all liquor from the Indian trade. Having done this, Sir George Simpson felt that the only way to keep liquor from the Indians was to keep it from the whites. He therefore instructed McLoughlin to dry up the Northwest Coast. He forbade the sale or gift of liquor by company employees there to anyone, white or Indian, and he cautioned McLoughlin that "remonstrances may be made against this measure, on the ground that the moisture of the climate of the N.W. Coast renders the moderate use of Spiritous Liquors necessary to the preservation of health." Such complaints, he announced imperially, "are totally unworthy of notice and must not be regarded."[28]

Employees may still have been able to import small quantities from London each year for their own use, though this loophole was probably no threat to the objectives of Simpson's pronouncement. In the following year, McLoughlin wrote to London that "if no spiritous liquors are used by Whites or Indians, it is to the Hudson's Bay Company alone, that the Country owes this blessing."[29]

If he had been disappointed with the missionaries in this matter, it was probably because of their inability to control the Americans who came into the river from the sea. Surely the missionaries had more influence over the captains of trading vessels from the United States than he did, but it was not enough. In 1842, the *Blanche*, out from Boston, entered the river loaded with whiskey for the Indians, and it was the Reverend J. H. Frost from the Willamette Valley, not McLoughlin, who boarded the ship and extracted a promise from the captain that he would neither give nor sell any liquor. But the promise was quickly ignored. Both the Clatsops and the Chinooks got the whiskey, and there followed a night of bedlam during which three Indians were shot and several more were stabbed.[30]

On the other hand, the missionaries, for a while at least, probably had more influence in the Valley than McLoughlin was willing to admit. In these last years of the fur trade, more and more trappers were leaving the mountains to settle near the Willamette, and these were men notoriously unsympathetic to the temperance movement. Shortly after the temperance society had been formed, one such fellow made it known that he intended to construct a distillery and make his living in ways more pleasant than grubbing in the soil. With the announcement, temperance advocates called a general meeting of all whites in the Valley. In an atmosphere of crisis similar to

that of the Ewing Young affair, almost everyone—even those who
had ignored the pledges—signed a petition condemning the proposed
whiskey factory. The dejected distiller, wrote one of the missionaries,
"acceeded to the voice of the people." Thus the temperance society
provided a structure through which the settlers could work on problems of this nature, and it must have functioned reasonably well in
the late 1830's and early 1840's. When Lieutenant W. C. Slacum
made his report to Congress after a tour of the Northwest in 1836-
37, he complimented Jason Lee on his temperance work, which, Slacum thought, had brought a remarkable degree of sobriety to a
group of old mountain guzzlers.[31]

Lee's work was rather abruptly pre-empted in 1842 by Dr. Elijah
White, a physician from New York State. Dr. White had been in the
Valley in 1837, but he had returned to the United States after quar-
reling with Reverend Lee. (The issues of the quarrel are vague, interpretations ranging from the account of a struggle for power to the
hint that White had taken pleasure in the Indian girls around the
Methodist Mission.) Upon his reappearance in 1842, White presented
papers issued him by officials of the United States, which commissioned him a "sub-Indian agent" for the Oregon country. His duties
and authorities in such a capacity, however, were extremely confusing to the settlers because the United States had no clear power to
appoint officials to serve in territories the United States did not own.
Jesse Applegate, one of the most distinguished of the pioneers of the
1840's, thought that White was probably a spy in the pay of the
United States Secret Service. Others regarded him as "a great syco-
phant" and an intruder. At any rate, White contended that his being
the only official of the United States in the Willamette Valley made
him the de facto "governor of the colony." This was a contention
which, perhaps, influenced one pioneer's evaluation of White as "not
very bright; slow of perception, but able to jump at a conclusion."
With such a jump behind him, White set himself to the task of controlling the Indians and enforcing American law.[32]

Acting under the United States Indian Intercourse Act of 1834,
which forbade liquor in Indian territory, Dr. White attempted to
search an American ship for liquor. In this endeavor, however, he
was summarily refused by the captain. Back in the Valley, he carried
his alleged powers to their limit by placing one man "under bonds in
the sum of one thousand dollars" for possessing wine and brandy in

his own home for his own personal use. The individual concerned was probably not unduly disturbed, inasmuch as White had no judge, no marshal, and no jail. Dr. White's career as a prohibitionist took him even deeper into humiliation: an Englishwoman prevented him from confiscating a barrel of whiskey by protesting loudly "in the name of Great Britain, Ireland, and Scotland." In this matter, clearly, he had gone far beyond his limits.[33]

In the minds of many settlers, he had also gone beyond his limits in trying to establish himself as a one-man government. White's failure in this regard served to emphasize the necessity of some authority more legitimate than his pretensions and more solid than the diminishing disciplines of prestige and commerce. By 1843, many of the newcomers were afraid that unless they formed a government themselves, they would be ruled entirely by the missionaries. Others saw a great urgency in the validation of their land claims, which were yet without any official recognition. Some feared the insolence of the Indians. Before the year was out, these anxieties prompted a majority of the settlers to organize the provisional government of Oregon.[34]

This unique body did not interfere in any way with the settlers' allegiance to the United States or to Great Britain, but it did provide them with a governor, a judge, a jail, militia, and—some may have hoped—protection from Dr. White. In the same year, though, about a thousand immigrants came into the Valley from the United States, and among these were a number of experienced moonshiners.

When the legislative assembly of the provisional government met in May, 1844, its members gave attention to the problem of "illicit" stills. Peter Burnett, who had led one of the emigrant parties of 1843, introduced a prohibition law, which passed easily. The preamble read in part:

> . . . the introduction, distillation or sale of ardent spirits under the circumstances in which we are placed, would bring withering ruin upon the prosperity & prospects of this interesting and rising community by involving us in idle and dissolute habits, inviting hither swarms of the dissipated inhabitants of other Countries . . . bringing upon us the swarms of savages now in our midst. . . .[35]

The legislators set fines of fifty dollars for the importation with intent to sell, twenty dollars for the sale, and one hundred dollars for the manufacture of "ardent spirits." Physicians were excepted from the rule and were allowed to sell in the generous quantity

of one gallon at a time. This measure has been called the first prohibition law in the United States. However, as scholars have tried to
point out, Oregon was not then a part of the United States.[36]

The law itself—if seen as part of a century of liquor legislation—
was a good example of a "temperance" law. It sought to abolish the
liquor traffic, but not drinking. There was no provision against the
possession or use of liquor, none against importing for personal use,
and there was nothing said about fermented beverages, for "ardent
spirits" meant hard liquor. The purpose of the law was only to effect
the aims of the preamble—to provide the community with a comfortable measure of protection against drunken Indians and dissolute
whites.

In the 1840's, both of these problems grew apace. Because it could
evoke the lurid visions of murder, rape, and mayhem, Indian drinking was always a strong motive in liquor legislation. The problems of
drinking white men, on the other hand, intruded upon certain class
and religious distinctions, upon concepts of personal freedom which,
by 1845, had already sharply divided the growing community. The
migrants of the 1830's had established the nucleus of a pious Victorian society whose highest values were modesty, self-control, dignity,
sobriety, and family responsibility. These values rested easily upon a
glowing, romantic faith in the perfectibility of man and the quick
triumph of God's kingdom on earth.[37] The missionaries nurtured
these values and this faith, reinforced them, and, of course, protected
them. The partisans of Jason Lee and Elijah White may have known
their struggles for power, but they could unite immediately when
their values and achievements were challenged by the presence of the
mountain men—some of them obstreperous, boozy, amoral, and in-
dolent—and the waves of uninitiated Oregon Trail migrants who
swept into the Valley after 1842, upsetting by their numbers the
power which the missionaries had for a decade held without opposition.

When the Methodist community found that its prestige was no
longer adequate to the tasks of social discipline, it quite naturally
tried to legislate the values which before had been upheld by moral
suasion. The provisional government of Oregon was a convenient instrument for this purpose. One important dimension of the political
in-fighting of the provisional legislature was this conflict between the

followers of the missionaries and those who resisted their efforts to legislate their romantic ideals. There were, of course, other dimensions, and they became more complex each year as the thousands of newcomers took land around the Willamette River: Whig against Democrat, Catholic against Protestant, American against Britisher. A problem that contributed to all of these rivalries, and especially to the oldest one, was how the new society would regulate the manufacture and sale of liquor.

Even while the legislature voted on the prohibition law of 1844, two moonshiners named Richard Macray and James Conner were at work in a canyon below Oregon City. They distilled something from "the offal of shorts, and wheat and molasses" which, possibly with charity, was referred to locally as "blue ruin." They sold to both races without prejudice. The social consequences of their business, in the words of an observer, was to cause "many a staid and upright looking man" to "stagger a little." In June, Dr. White called for war: "Liquor was in our midst . . . as was but too manifest from the noisy, vulgar, obscene, and even diabolical expressions of those [who got it] . . . ."[38]

With ten "noble volunteers," White smashed the still and all of its inventory. James Conner, in a state of rage and emotional shock from his loss, challenged Dr. White to a duel. White took the challenge to court, where Conner was fined five hundred dollars and disfranchised. The two manuscript accounts of this episode agree that in all of this, White had the sanction of most of the settlers.[39]

If this were true, then public sentiment changed rapidly indeed during the next few months. In 1845 a new constitution was drawn for the provisional government, one which abrogated all the old laws, including prohibition. The new organic laws gave the legislature the power to "regulate" but not to prohibit "the introduction, manufacture, and sale of ardent spirits."[40] According to the historian H. H. Bancroft, the people gave this power to the lawmakers because the supplies of liquor at Fort Vancouver were open once again and were washing down into the Valley.

Shortly before this time, Dr. McLoughlin had left the company—he resigned in 1845 and moved to Oregon City—and the new chief factor, James Douglas, felt that he could not refuse liquor to the British Navy. The sloop of war *Modeste* entered the Columbia

River early in 1845 to press forward British authority in the impending boundary settlement, or war, in the Oregon country between the
United States and England. The officers and men of this ship, un-
bound by the codes of the provisional government, used the Hudson's
Bay Company's rum to lubricate themselves and all those whom they
chose to favor with their hospitality. Even after the *Modeste*'s departure, apparently, thirsty settlers continued to find some satisfaction
around Fort Vancouver. In response to this situation, the legislature
in the Willamette Valley passed a licensing act in 1846.[41]

The first retail license went to a man named Sydney W. Moss who
had come to the Valley in 1842 with Dr. White. He paid two hundred
dollars for his privilege, and he bought liquor from licensed distillers
at six dollars a gallon.[42] The opening of Moss's saloon was a dramatic
indication that the missionaries, in their struggle to fix their own
values upon the community and to perpetuate their own power, had
lost the battle. (The Reverend Jason Lee did not have to suffer this—
he had returned to the East, where he had died the year before.)

The License Act proved, if anything, easier to violate than the old
prohibition law had been. By 1847, "blue ruin" was flowing illicitly
in the valleys and in the hills, much of it going to the debauched natives. Moss, the saloonkeeper, wrote down a song which the Indians
sang as they staggered, arm in arm, through the streets of Oregon
City:

> Nah! six, potlatch blue lu
> Nika ticka, blue lu
> Hiyu blue lu
> Hyas olo
> Potlatch blue lu[43]

The "blue lu" of the song was clearly the "blue ruin" from the illegal stills, and the potlatch, among the coastal Indians, was a cere-
mony for validating status claims. The other words have to do with
"thirst" and "friends."[44] The song itself is a fascinating bit of evidence that the Indians of the valley had integrated liquor and drunkenness into the hazy structure of their decaying culture. This "potlatch blue lu" must have been what Edwin M. Lemert called the
"whiskey feast," a ritual of excessive drinking through which a host
might confer upon himself a high degree of prestige. According to
Lemert, the whiskey feast was a response by the coastal Indians to

the deterioration of their traditional institutions for achieving status. From the 1840's on, excessive group drinking assumed a deep and abiding significance to their culture.[45]

This may have been a factor in the reconsideration of liquor laws in the Valley toward the end of the decade. More important, probably, was the acquisition of the Oregon country by the United States in 1846 and the coming of thousands of migrants who wanted not only to share the new land but also to insure the blessings of sobriety for the new society. In 1848 the provisional legislature, acting on petitions submitted by groups of temperance evangelists, authorized a general referendum on a proposal which would allow the provisional government to prohibit the manufacture and sale of ardent spirits. The measure passed, but those who supported it did not yet control the legislature. In 1849, during the very last session of the legislature of the provisional government of Oregon, a prohibition law was tabled on a motion by Jesse Applegate.[46]

Applegate anticipated the formation of Oregon Territory by the United States and the coming of a formal territorial government which would sweep away the provincial concerns of an isolated colony. The problems of Oregon, he thought, should be those of the United States. Later called the "sage of Yoncalla," he had consistently been an overwhelming conservative force in Oregon. As a major intellect and leader, he had, apparently, controlled the provisional government almost singlehandedly, writing most of the laws, wording the resolutions, marshaling the votes. Probably the best-read man on the Pacific Coast and certainly the most articulate, he stood solidly for order, form, precedent, racial segregation, the rights of property, a limited franchise, and, above all, the power and dignity of the federal Constitution. He opposed states' rights, missionaries—whom he regarded as men more "sectarian than Christian" and primarily interested in economic gain—and prohibition.[47] In tabling the motion on liquor control, he had, in a sense, sustained most of his convictions and affirmed their predominance in the new society.

Two weeks later, Applegate's wish became a reality. General Joseph Lane arrived to organize a government, and he immediately brought the authority of the United States into the affairs of the people of Oregon. He solved the Indian problems not with legislation but with force, and the purges that followed did much to alleviate the

old fears, for the Indian problem thereafter was in the hands of the
United States government. As the drums rolled and the soldiers
marched, the new government brought with it the authority and stability around which a new society could find security and confidence.
Then the gold fever, burning across the West, brought prosperity and
more people. As the territory began to fill with farmers, lumbermen,
and merchants, the Oregon frontier, as Applegate had known it
would, blended into the churning social and political movements of
mid-century American life.

2

Whigs and Indians

In 1849, the territorial legislature of Oregon passed a licensing act to regulate the manufacture and sale of "ardent spirits." Though it forbade the sale or gift of alcohol to Indians, it was a liberal act which allowed just about anyone with two hundred dollars to open a saloon.

There were many in Oregon who objected to the coming of the saloon, but they rejoiced at the news of organized temperance action from the state of Maine, action which in 1851 achieved a law prohibiting the manufacture and sale of liquor throughout that state. Under their famous leader Neal Dow, the temperance forces of Maine won a democratic victory after years of inspired campaigning. Anti-saloon workers everywhere cheered their accomplishment. In 1852, a Temperance Convention assembled in Salem to discuss and devise ways of bringing the Maine law to Oregon. This meeting generated a marked degree of heat in territorial politics, and in the next election some candidates identified themselves as "Maine Law Whigs." The election of a few of these gentlemen colored the character of legislative proceedings almost immediately, for in 1852 one member of the opposition moved to "amend the resolution inviting ministers to serve the legislature as Chaplains by adding 'Except such ministers as are known to be in favor of the enactment of a Maine liquor law.' "[1] The amendment was defeated.

The enthusiasms of the Salem convention were spread through the settled regions of the territory and were kept burning by the arrival of more and more wagon trains, each of which was almost sure to have its dedicated group of Maine Law advocates from Indiana, Illinois, Missouri, or New York. Many of these were attracted to the new settlements north of the Columbia River, and when, in 1853, Congress organized Washington Territory, this new political unit almost immediately had its temperance society. The Reverend George F. Whitworth, a Presbyterian missionary recently from Indiana and the Oregon Trail, called the first meeting and pledged his followers to total abstinence and to work for the passage of a Maine Law for this far northwest corner of the United States.[2]

Whitworth drew up a petition for the first territorial legislature of Washington Territory, which had just then convened. This petition proposed a territorial referendum on a prohibitory law, a matter which the legislature debated and then tabled in April, 1854. It was, however, very much alive in the 1854-55 session, and in 1855 the legislature referred to the four thousand people of Washington Territory a law to prohibit the manufacture and sale of liquor. This referendum precipitated the first prolonged battle over the liquor problem in the future state of Washington.[3]

The campaign was a polite one—at least one can find in it none of the fiery invective that seasoned most territorial political discussions. Neither of the two newspapers of the territory approved the measure. The Whig *Puget Sound Courier* actively opposed it, but the Democratic *Washington Standard* was silent. The *Courier* editorials were models of genteel Whiggery:

> We are all agreed upon one thing, that intemperance is an evil and should be suppressed; the only question is, how can it best be accomplished? . . . Is it not better to bring about a social revolution by a proper preparation of the public mind and a gradual approach to the change desired? We certainly believe so, and whilst we shall advocate the cause of temperance in our zeal. . . .

The editor would support a law, he said, that would keep liquor out of the country, but he had no confidence that such a law could be designed. On the other hand, the Territorial Temperance Committee stressed the economic advantages sure to accrue with the passage of the law: for example, there would be no poorhouses for the territory to support.

The ballots decided the issue with 564 votes for, 650 votes against. A cry of "fraud" went up shortly after the official announcement—one that would echo through almost every election on the liquor question in territorial and state history—when temperance supporters claimed that in some precincts the ballots not marked on the prohibition vote were counted "against."[4]

Though the evidence here is scanty, there were a number of things about this election that invite closer examination. Most importantly, what was the voting really for or against? Undoubtedly there were endless orations and debates on the prohibition law, and it is curious that in the newspaper accounts, the campaign was rather lifeless: no drunkard's laments, no weeping women or children, no ringing defenses of individual rights. It is, in fact, difficult to find any evidence of widespread temperance sentiment, and there is, on the other hand, plenty of evidence that the territorial founding fathers enjoyed their cups. Arthur A. Denny was said to be "the only member of the Legislature who consistently lives up to the principles of the Maine liquor law," and George N. McConaha, president of the first legislative council, was an alcoholic who allegedly drowned in Puget Sound as a result of the riotous drinking that closed the first legislative session. A writer to the editor of the *Courier* noted that drunkenness was so common in Olympia that the territory was developing a reputation for intemperance which was discouraging migrants from crossing the Columbia River. The editor himself, who was against the prohibition law, regretted that in the Northwest "everyone who has the least ill or trouble runs to the maddening bowl to drown it."[5]

For example, the territorial governor, Isaac I. Stevens, was angered by the insolence of an Indian chief who presented himself in an intoxicated condition to the Governor at the Walla Walla Indian Conference in 1855. This was perhaps just as well for the Indians, for Governor Stevens himself—according to the *Washington Republican* (formerly the Whig *Courier*)—had been drinking heavily at Walla Walla, where his treaties produced an Indian war. The same paper accused Stevens not only of taking too much at Walla Walla but of indulging himself freely all over the territory and of suspending Captain A. A. Denny from the command of a company of volunteers because Denny had called the Governor a drunk. While Stevens was campaigning as a Democrat for election as delegate to Congress, the *Republican* reported that Governor Stevens was a "confirmed inebriate," and that, furthermore, he had lately obtained "a certificate of his suspension of that habit, until he had deceived the people into a belief that he had reformed."[6]

However skeptical one may be of journalistic ethics during this period, it is clear enough that the 564 people who voted for prohibition in 1855—less than 90 short of victory—might have had something to vote against in the boozy condition of their neighbors. Nevertheless, the absence of any real temperance propaganda makes it difficult to believe that the issue was so simple. The other aspect of the campaign—the economic argument stressing the costs of poor-houses—was probably superficial, for the territory was without experience with such institutions at the time.

The fears that motivated these 564 votes were, most likely, not so much about poorhouses or besotted citizens as they were the more historic concern for wild Indians. Much evidence suggests that in 1855 in Washington Territory, the Indian problem and the liquor problem were still very much the same. The correspondence to the *Courier,* for example, included a letter from a writer who noted that a popular topic of discussion in the territory was "what can we do to rid ourselves of the mean-spirited and filthy-minded white scoundrels who cowardly deal out liquid damnation to the poor 'Siwashes' . . . keeping the community in complete ferment."[7] In the phrases "better portion of the community" and "mean-spirited and filthy-minded white scoundrels," one hears finally the ring of class-consciousness which so often marked the rhetoric of the American temperance movement. The same concern with "white scoundrels" was noted by the German traveler Richard Oberländer, who toured the Pacific Northwest during these years and whose account included a condemnation of "Die Squaw männer" who corrupted the Indians with whiskey and guns. Even booster literature of the time advised emigrants that the Indians were peaceful except when they were drunk and if they killed anyone it was usually he "who gave them liquid fire." That the selling of liquor to the Indians by one class of whites was basic to the liquor problems of 1855 is made even more clear by the fact that other settlers were defending the practice in letters to newspapers: the argument was that Indians could not be degraded any lower than they already were.[8]

Governor Stevens had begun making Indian treaties in 1854, and shortly thereafter there were rumors of war. In 1855 the people voted down prohibition, but the legislature passed a law against selling intoxicating drink to Indians. The legislature did not provide a jail sentence for this offense, an oversight which strongly suggests that some significant part of the economy was involved in the liquor traffic.

That this was true is abundantly clear. The traveler Theodore Winthrop, in his book about the Northwest, made much of the Indian chief Chetzemoka, better known as "the Duke of York":

> The Duke of York was ducally drunk. His brother, King George, was
> drunk—royally Royalty may disdain public opinion and fall as low as
> it pleases. . . . Courtiers had done likewise. Chamberlain Gold Stick,
> Black Rod, Garter King at Arms, a dozen high functionaries, were
> prostrate by the side of prostrate majesty. Courtiers grovelled with
> their sovereign. Sardanapalus never presided, until he could preside no
> longer, at a more tumble-down orgie.[9]

In Port Townsend, Ezra Meeker found Indians drunk, having celebrated the sale of their fish. He also recorded the prices current in
Olympia during the same year, 1853: whiskey was one dollar a gallon, while farmers could get three dollars a bushel for potatoes and a
dollar a pound for butter, and Indians could sell fish for ten cents a
pound. The lumber camps paid four dollars a day for common labor
and occasionally hired Indians; a person could chop wood for himself
and sell it at four dollars a cord.[10] This boom economy, caused by
insatiable California markets, had a drastic effect on the Indians,
shattering, as the fur trade had done, the old ecology and further
disintegrating the traditional patterns of prestige and status based on
individual wealth. United States territorial law, which abolished slavery among the Indians, became another factor in cultural disintegration. All of this enhanced the function and desperation of the whiskey
feast.

During the 1850's Indians frequently camped near the mill towns,
where their tendency to steal caused trouble. At Port Gamble in 1855,
for example, the Indians were driven away from the town by a
cannon shot which killed their leader. This same group of Indians
returned to the area in 1856 and murdered Colonel Isaac Ebey on
Whidbey Island in revenge. They cut off Ebey's head. They were
drunk at the time—or at least most of the whites thought so.[11]

It is in regard to the Indian problem, then, that the thin statistics
of the prohibition vote in 1855 become at all significant. Settlers in
the Puget Sound counties (Jefferson, Pierce, King), where Meeker
and Winthrop noted so much drunkenness among Indians, voted for
the law. In Thurston County, where the legislature met and where
there were probably the fewest Indians, the voters were against prohibition. The few whites in Walla Walla, Skamania, Chehalis, Sa-
wamish, Clallam, and Whatcom counties were probably engaged in
the liquor traffic and thus opposed to the law. And possibly—though

there is no evidence for such speculation—those in the border counties (Wahkiakum, Clark, Skamania, Walla Walla, Whatcom) voted
against prohibition because their Indian trade in liquor might have
moved quickly to Oregon or to Canada without affecting the Indian
problem against which the law was aimed.

TABLE 1

PROHIBITION AND THE INDIAN PROBLEM: THE REFERENDUM OF 1855*

County	For prohibition	Against
Walla Walla	1	27
Skamania	0	9
Clark	54	132
Cowlitz	55	19
Wahkiakum	4	10
Pacific	18	14
Chehalis	8	14
Lewis	39	65
Thurston	75	159
Sawamish	1	12
Pierce	54	64
King	81	44
Island	20	40
Jefferson	46	5
Clallam	5	14
Whatcom	1	22
Total	564	650

* Steilacoom *Puget Sound Courier*, Sept. 7, 1855.

The problem was aggravated by other, more inexorable forces, and
it exploded into four years of war just after the election of 1855. The
clashes which followed Governor Stevens' Walla Walla conference
grew into a series of bloody engagements after General Newman S.
Clarke came to Fort Vancouver to conduct campaigns against the Indians of Washington Territory who were resisting the white invasion.
Whatever threat there had been to white society from drunken Indians disappeared in the further decimation of the natives and in the
restrictive clauses of the reservation treaties pressed upon them by
the United States soldiers. It was all over by 1860, and selling whiskey to the Indians was never again a major territorial issue.

Then during the Civil War, the eastern reaches of the territory were open to the tens of thousands of gold miners who came to exploit the land. These men settled in loose and rather unruly mobs along the tributaries of the Columbia and the Snake and across the Continental Divide, and few of them gave much thought to the temperance movement. (The founding of Slaterville, high on the Clearwater River in 1862, was marked by the raising of two tents and a saloon.[12]) For several years there were more miners milling around the eastern regions than there were settlers west of the Cascade Mountains, and public discussions of legal prohibition among whites were unlikely until the potential power of the gold seekers could be cut out of territorial politics. Not until after 1863, when Congress organized Idaho Territory, did the farmers, merchants, and lumbermen of Washington Territory feel enough social and political security to bring the temperance issue again before a legislative forum.

3

The Cry of Abolitionists

FROM THE TIME of its organization, Washington Territory was receptive to the sentiments of American reform. The ideologies of freemen and free soil, for example, which were debated with such anguish in other parts of the country during that decade, were already principles rather than issues in the new territory. In fact, the people north of the Columbia River were, in these respects, even more liberal than their neighbors of the Willamette Valley, for they welcomed Negroes (forbidden by law from settling in Oregon), and they moved quickly toward extending the franchise to women.

These were popular causes, sturdy enough to survive the emotional upheavals of the Civil War. After 1865 there were vigorous and widespread public discussions of the problems of controlling the liquor traffic and enfranchising women, and well-organized efforts to secure these goals for Washington had their beginnings in this period. For example, the International Order of Good Templars became active around Olympia and other Puget Sound communities in the late 1860's. This organization attracted young men who "banded together to do good." They favored women's suffrage, and they attacked the liquor traffic as "one of the greatest menaces to mankind." Their foremost champion in Washington later claimed that the work of the order was educational rather than political: "but out of Good Templary and its educational propaganda came the Prohibition Party . . . the W.C.T.U. . . . and the Anti-Saloon League."[1]

The order enlisted leaders like the Reverend George F. Whitworth, who had led the temperance movement through the previous decade, and David Denny, a founding father of the new community of Seattle. In the Good Templar lodges—which were really nonalcoholic saloons—the order attempted a masculine appeal through an emphasis on companionship, ritual, "wholesome" entertainment, and "clean

28

manhood," on pool tables, reading rooms, and good talk.[2] Members pledged themselves to complete abstinence from intoxicating drinks.

By 1867, large audiences around Olympia were turning out to hear the professional temperance lecturers sent to the territory by the national offices of the International Order of Good Templars (IOGT). These orators were quick in borrowing from the prestige of medical science, for they took the title of "doctor" and held their listeners in attitudes of shock and dismay by employing visual aids to illustrate "the progress of decay of vital organs . . . shown by charts, drawn from nature, and embracing the results of patient research of eminent medical men. . . ."

The lecturers became more militant after 1874, when the WCTU organized in the territory and brought a new strength and enthusiasm to the movement against liquor. A lecturer for the IOGT might then share the stage with men and women who would pray for pledges of abstinence; and in the lectures, the pledge-signing, and the songs, the movement found its distinctly evangelical tone.[3]

This was happening all over the United States in the 1870's. The national Prohibition party organized in 1869, the WCTU in 1873. A State Temperance Union of those who favored legislative prohibition had been formed in Oregon in 1873, and praying women marched against the saloons in Portland in 1874. In that same year there was a "siege against the saloons" in Olympia. The street preaching and praying was intense enough to drive the editor of the *Washington Standard* to comment that the only apparent effect of the crusade "has been to increase the use of liquor." The novelty of the proceedings attracted a crowd in front of the saloons, he said, and as soon as "the singing and praying ceases the drinking and dissipation commences. Sunday bids fair to become a fashionable day for spreeing."[4]

The Washington Territorial Temperance Alliance, formed in 1874 with George F. Whitworth as president, was a combination of temperance forces in the territory which attempted to enlist the churches in a drive for a territorial prohibition law. To John Miller Murphy, editor of the *Washington Standard*, Whitworth's alliance against liquor was a public nuisance. He insisted that church-goers were also saloon patrons, and that "intemperance" was not confined to the use of alcohol. He was especially sensitive, however, to the excesses of evangelical preaching, and he noted with distress that the wilder temperance preachers had used racist terms to condemn the Irish and the Germans because they liked beer. This outrage, said Murphy, revived the passions of Know-Nothingism. The leaders of the prohibitionists, he wrote with some Irish belligerency, should "don petticoats and open a fish market."[5]

Quite naturally, it seems, as the prohibitionists developed their antisaloon vocabulary they also groped among the techniques of popular appeal and struck, from time to time, the nativist propaganda that so irritated John Murphy. This technique was not uncommon in the United States after 1865, for hundreds of thousands of immigrants were coming from Europe and the Orient to feed the factories of American industry. Anglo-Saxons, fearful for their racial purity, were beginning to complain. They were heard in many voices in the Pacific Northwest when the Irish and Chinese who had worked on the Central Pacific and the Union Pacific railroads began to move north from California. The completion of the Northern Pacific, which would bring more, was imminent. There was, indeed, a rising chorus of protest after the panic of 1873. The immigrant laborers, the usual argument went, were dirty, maybe diseased, heathen or Popish, and emotionally dedicated to their antecedents more than they were to the American future. They undercut wages and might upset political balances. They frequently drank to excess and encouraged the growth and the power of the saloon.

The disadvantage to the temperance leaders of such demonology was that it drew its advocates into the increasingly complex tensions of class-consciousness that expanded in American life with the progress of industrialization. In Washington Territory, as elsewhere, most of the men of wealth, most of the solid citizens of finance and business—in short, the upper class—did not share this hostility to immigrants. It was, of course, not in their economic interest to do so, and many of them felt that racism contributed to the class-consciousness which, they hoped, the society they were building from a wilderness might somehow avoid. For example, Judge Thomas Burke of Seattle, an Irishman himself and a prominent spokesman for the wealthy and the economically powerful, was an eloquent defender of the Chinese and a pleader for peace and good feelings among all social classes.[6] The Knights of Labor, on the other hand, opposed both him and his class and fanned anti-Chinese hostilities into hatred and on toward riot and even toward class revolt. If the temperance forces were to play with nativist emotions, they would tie themselves to a set of working-class values and turn away from their cause the group of people represented by Judge Burke. Furthermore, the working class, as it existed at that time, liked its saloons.

This was made quite clear in 1878, when Governor Elisha Ferry called delegates to a convention in Walla Walla to draft a constitution for the proposed state of Washington. When the fifteen delegates assembled to discuss the problems of boundary, finance, and corruption in government, they were beset by two strong lobbying groups, the prohibitionists and the suffragettes.[7] After days of talking, pleading, and pressuring, it was obvious that while some delegates might have been sympathetic toward these reforms, they were not going to risk the proposed instrument of state by committing it to either. They finally agreed to compromise by submitting to the voters separate articles on each reform, to be approved or rejected on the same ballot with the constitution.

The prohibitionists were somewhat more severely compromised than were the suffragettes, for their article was not a prohibition law at all. It was, rather, a local option provision:

> It shall be lawful for the Electors of any County, municipal corporation, or precinct, not included within the corporate limits of any municipality, at any general election to prohibit, by a majority vote, the sale or disposal of spiritous liquors in less quantities than one gallon, except for medical or mechanical purposes.[8]

This was antisaloon local option, a proposal of modest proportions. It was in no sense a no-drink option. It protected the cities from any moral dictation from the rural areas. For the dedicated temperance crusaders, there was no triumph in the article, and there was even less in the returns of October, 1878.

The constitution approved by the voters got nowhere: the bill to admit Washington as a state was never debated in the House of Representatives because most congressmen felt that the population of the area was too low and because they did not wish to upset the political balance of power at the time.[9]

Though local option was easily more popular than women's suffrage, of the total vote cast (9,773), the liquor reformers won less than 30 per cent. After this poor showing, it is not remarkable that the prohibitionists changed the tenor of their appeal. The major change seems to have been that their racist propaganda rapidly disappeared in the late 1870's. Apparently the prohibitionists probed beyond anti-Chinese and anti-Irish hatreds to a reality which even Judge Burke could not deny: the saloon was much more than a symptom of racial pollution; it was a citadel of debauchery and of anti-middle-class sentiments and hence a threat to the deepest values of polite society. The reformers never said this in so many words, but two legislative acts, one in 1877 and the other in 1879, help clarify the new character of the movement.

TABLE 2

TEMPERANCE AND WOMEN'S SUFFRAGE: THE REFERENDUM OF 1878*

	For	Against
The Constitution	6,537	3,226
Local Option	2,874	4,151
Women's Suffrage	1,827	5,117

* Wilfred J. Airey, "A History of the Constitution and Government of Washington Territory" (Ph.D. thesis, University of Washington, 1945), p. 420.

The first was a law prohibiting the sale of liquor to minors; this pointed to but one way in which the saloons threatened the world of Judge Burke. The second law created the first prohibition territory in Washington—a strip two miles wide along the construction route of the Northern Pacific Railroad in several eastern counties—to be observed throughout the period of construction.[10] It was probably urged by people who remembered the "hell on wheels," the tent towns of saloons, prostitutes, gamblers, and hooligans that had afflicted the Central Pacific and the Union Pacific during the previous decade.

This first prohibition law, then, was an effort to protect workers from the saloonkeepers, who were as eager to debauch the railroad gangs as they had been to debauch the Indians. Unlike the Indians, though, the workers were coming with the potentials of political power and social ambition. Many of them would stay to use both. The territory was just beginning the transition from a frontier society to an industrial one, and the legislature was saying that if Washington were to have a working class, it should be sober and industrious. The new society, if it were to be more perfect, must set itself resolutely against the evils of the old.

This was the kind of movement that touched the heart of John Miller Murphy of the *Washington Standard*. Early in 1879, a great change came over his editorials, and he began to write with some sympathy about the temperance lecturers and the temperance rallies. He began to wish them "abundant success." However unarticulated were the reasons for this change, Murphy made it clear that liquor reform was becoming more and more respectable. "Open temperance meetings" were popular in Seattle. Murphy reported that these meetings featured speeches and songs, and brought out physicians, lawyers, and clergymen, citizens as highly regarded as Judge Burke himself. "Prominent citizens," he wrote, "are promiscuously called out upon the floor to tell the people what they know about the great evil of the American people. . . ."

Murphy himself was shortly on the wagon. "Among all the advertized remedies for drunkenness," he noted piously, "nothing has been found to compare with total abstinence. . . ." The temperance cause, he glowed, was "a great reformation which is at this moment convulsing the land."

And there were other developments, too, which might have brought Murphy and others like him to the temperance movement in the late 1870's. One of these was the widespread interest in the theories of evolution, as Murphy's own newspaper clearly attests. Something close to horror must have been inspired by the "brute nature" of man which, according to the lecturers, liquor could so easily release. The brute was close to the surface, and the good society would have to prevent it from breaking through. A place to begin was in the saloons.

Parallel to this concern was a public worry about "liberal" religion, especially Unitarianism, and its ministers who did not believe in Hell. This was a factor in the revival undertaken by the evangelical churches in 1879, and revivalism was usually the herald of temperance reform. A week of prayer was declared in January, 1879, and this was the week that John Murphy first declared himself for temperance.

One of the most fascinating aspects of this revival was the class of people who had recently associated themselves with the movement against saloons. Judge Burke's presence at a temperance rally was significant, as was John Murphy's. But also among those who joined the crusade in late 1870's were William Newell, appointed territorial governor by President Rutherford B. Hayes, and the even more august dignity of Roger S. Greene, chief justice of the territorial Supreme Court. The Reverend Daniel Bagley of Seattle, president of the board of commissioners of the territorial university and a leading divine as well as a prominent businessman, also gave assistance. These days were markedly different from those in which John Murphy had ridiculed the street preachers and their followers who prayed on the sidewalks in front of saloons. And in October, 1880, Murphy became the secretary of the Territorial Temperance Alliance.[11]

This organization called delegates to Olympia to consider proposals for a more ambitious campaign. Murphy, Newell, Greene, Bagley, and Whitworth were all there.[12] The alliance was among the WCTU, the Templars, and the more militant churches, and it sought political action. It was clearly abolitionist in intent, for it was committed heart and soul to the destruction of the saloon.

The first year of the new organization was marked by a pair of solid achievements: one was a law requiring saloons to close on Sundays; the other was legislation making the owners of saloon property—as well as the saloonkeeper himself—liable for any injuries attributable to intoxicating drinks sold in the saloon.[13] Enforcing these provisions, of course, was another matter, but the Alliance could view them with some pride. They were the first antisaloon laws in Washington.

The Alliance also moved aggressively to enlarge its following. A week in July, 1883, was declared "Temperance Week," and the WCTU and the churches carried the cause to platforms all across the territory. The work was done so thoroughly that when Governor Newell addressed the biennial session of the legislative assembly in October, 1883, he could speak directly to the point:

> Intemperance in the use of intoxicating liquors is engaging the attention of philanthropists, political economists, deluded votaries, victims, and all tax-paying citizens, as a question of the highest magnitude and importance.
>   The fearful destruction of property and happiness which it occasions in its march of desolation, disease, and death . . . the vice, degeneration and crime which it engenders . . . all these, with no

redeeming or compensating influences for good, may well cause it
to be a subject of greatest solicitude to our race.

The right of society to protection by suitable legislation from the
effects of evils so manifest will not be denied. . . . The right to abate
an evil clearly argues a right to effect its prohibition. . . .[14]

Newell had just spoken when the first issue of the *Mirror* was published in Seattle. This was a militant IOGT paper, edited and written
by a group of Templars and preachers who wanted prohibition and
women's suffrage. The first editorial struck the metaphor that steeled
many a reformer—the battle is nigh, we have seen the fearful light-
ning of His terrible swift sword: "The Temperance war. It is coming.
It is here. . . . The question at issue involves the sanctity of home,
the chastity of youth, the moral and political purity of voters. . . ."
The war was against "saloonacy," and the sword was to be equal
suffrage.[15]

The women's suffrage movement, too, had been thirty years in the
making. During the first session of the legislature in 1853, Arthur
Denny, the prohibitionist, had introduced legislation to enfranchise
white women. This failed by one vote, and thereafter the agitation
"persisted with wavering vehemence." The first women's suffrage
convention met in 1871. That year Susan Anthony and Abigail Duniway, both nationally famous suffragettes, spoke throughout the territory. During the 1870's, the politics of equal suffrage and of prohibition were clearly the same, for the following of Mrs. Duniway could
not be distinguished from that of the Washington Territorial Temperance Alliance. Both causes found a warm friend in Governor
Newell, who in 1883 signed a law which declared the equality of
women and allowed those in Washington Territory to vote, hold
office, and serve as jurors.[16]

This victory served the prohibitionists exactly as they had anticipated, for their additional political power began to produce some
real abolitionist legislation. The 1885-86 session of the assembly
passed an Alcohol Education Act, requiring that the "effects" of alcohol and narcotics be taught in the public schools. Under the law,
the county treasurer was to withhold county funds from those schools
that did not comply. Pressure for this law came largely from the
WCTU, and the intent was to institutionalize abolitionist propaganda.[17] From this time on, antialcohol indoctrination was administered

by the public school teacher, who was one of the most vivid symbols of authority in American life. The results are difficult to estimate, but when the people of Washington voted for antidrink measures in 1914, 1916, and 1918, they had been exposed to over three decades of formalized, official antidrink instruction.

And the Alcohol Education Act was but the beginning. The same session of the legislature, in January, 1886, passed a local option law which meant certain death to a number of saloons. According to its provisions, the cities and towns were separate voting units, and the precincts outside of incorporated cities and towns also had the authority to hold local option elections.[18] County commissioners could receive petitions from as few as fifteen voters and schedule elections every two years.

The campaigns which followed were really neighborhood battles. Some precincts had fewer than thirty voters, and some were quite naturally sparked with unneighborly emotionalism. The WCTU was active in every county, and in Snohomish, at least, the Knights of Labor sponsored the local option petition. In one Whatcom County precinct, only five people voted (Lake Precinct—two votes for, three votes against), though at least fifteen must have petitioned for the election. Perhaps the campaign had caused the other ten voters to regard personal relationships more highly than the issue at stake. In Snohomish County, where most precincts voted out the saloons, one leading capitalist irately announced that he was moving all of his logging, merchandising, and hotel business out of dry territory. He founded the community which bears his name, Cathcart, across the river from the town of Snohomish. After the elections, the unhappy situations of dry precincts next to wet precincts, and the fact that bootlegging went mostly unchecked, served to increase the many hostilities already sharply provoked.[19]

The prohibitionists, though, were heady with success, and in 1886 they seriously advanced the radical aims of the Alliance: William A. Newell, former governor, announced his candidacy for territorial delegate to Congress on the Prohibition ticket. Nationally and locally, the IOGT and the WCTU had fallen in with the Prohibition party. In Seattle the extremists were in control, filling the *Mirror* with inflammatory prohibitionist prose. One editorial praised William Lloyd Garrison and Wendell Phillips and urged its readers to bring the holy zeal of fanaticism to Washington Territory, where the Lord's work would soon be done.[20]

Those citizens who were offended by this attitude could ignore Newell—the voters gave him less than three thousand votes out of about fifty thousand. However, it was the Supreme Court of Washington Territory, not the voters, that hurt the reformers most seriously. In February, 1887, the court declared (*Harlan* v. *Washington*) that a technical error in the title of the women's suffrage law rendered that act invalid. Prohibitionists and suffragettes claimed that Harlan was a "henchman" of Harry Morgan, the "boss gambler of Tacoma," and that the saloon interests had really designed this defeat of the suffrage law.[21] The legislature responded by rewording the act and passing it again in January, 1888.

The saloon owners moved quickly. During the election in April, 1888, they arranged to have authorities of a Spokane precinct refuse to register a saloonkeeper's wife whose almost incredible name was Mrs. Nevada Bloomer. Mrs. Bloomer then brought a damage suit against the election officials, and the women's suffrage law was again in the courts. In *Bloomer* v. *Todd,* the Supreme Court of the territory held that Mrs. Bloomer had sustained no injury because she really had no right to the franchise. Congress, the justices said, had not authorized United States territories to enfranchise women.[22] In this decision the sword of the antisaloon cause was broken, with some irony, by a woman. (She may not have known that in Iowa at this moment there lived another Mrs. Bloomer, the wife of a Quaker and a friend of Susan B. Anthony. Amelia Jenks Bloomer edited and published the *Lily,* a journal for ladies interested in temperance, women's rights, and the reform of women's clothing.)

There have been at least two interpretations of *Bloomer* v. *Todd.* The Seattle historian Clarence R. Bagley, without being specific, said that the behavior of certain women during the anti-Chinese riots of 1886 had turned public opinion against equal suffrage.[23] These women could have been the wives of wealthy citizens who supported the Home Guard, the pseudo-military band of upper-class citizens who in this year of violence and bloodshed faced the mobs of workers in a futile effort to protect the Chinese. Or they could have been working-class women whose presence in the mobs caused some to regret that women had any rights at all.

Mrs. Abigail Scott Duniway, in a second interpretation, asserted
that the local option elections really killed equal suffrage because
women had allowed themselves to become identified with the crusade
of the prohibitionists. Wet or dry, the results of the local option elections were blamed on women, said Mrs. Duniway. Prohibition, she had decided, was a fad led by a bunch of fanatics. She
held the WCTU responsible for Washington's women losing the franchise. Churches in Washington Territory thereafter refused Mrs. Duniway an audience.

Others blamed the judges, if not the WCTU, but with the same
reasoning. In Sultan, a town on the Snohomish River, Mrs. W. H.
Illman wrote to her county newspaper that the judges decided as they
did on women's suffrage because women had defeated the whiskey
interests. "By this infamous decision of Judges Langford and Tur-
ner," she said, "the white women of Washington Territory have been
put on an equality with Chinese, insane, and full-blooded Indians."[24]

Each of these interpretations ignored the possibility of an honest
judicial decision honestly arrived at, which may indeed have been
the case. However, each in its way illustrates the social complexities
of the reform movement in the 1880's. The causes of prohibition and
equal suffrage were both inextricably enmeshed in the conflicts between capital and labor, between lower and middle class, between
"the interests" and "the people"—conflicts which had come to Washington with the railroads and with which the new society was having
its first grievous experiences.

The judges of the territorial court may have felt these more keenly
than did most men of the time. That same year they struck even
more deeply into the antisaloon movement by declaring that the local
option law also was unconstitutional. Their opinion held that the precinct, because it was not a municipal corporation, could not constitutionally exercise the authority granted to it by the local option law.
They found the legislature delinquent in granting such authority in
the first place, because it moved toward a degree of democracy
which, the court feared, might go "unchecked in its impulses."[25]
This seems to have been the decision of men who feared the rum-
blings of class protest.

The temperance movement, however, was not often demoralized by
either legislative or judicial defeats when its leaders felt that most of

the people were with them. There were barriers to liquor reform, but these could be broken; there were setbacks in the great crusade, but the ground could always be recovered, usually with an increment. The movement was driven by sentiments that had grown steadily in the United States since the 1820's, and though it might from time to time lack leadership or direction, its vitality did not wane.

4

Liquor Fanaticism
and Agrarian Discontent

AFTER THEIR DEFEAT in the courts by men who feared too much democracy, members of the Temperance Alliance turned again to their
friends in the territorial legislature. In 1888 the Governor signed a
license law which served as a sort of crippled local option arrangement until 1909. Under it the county commissioners had the power,
through licenses with fees varying from three hundred to one thousand dollars,[1] to regulate the flow of liquor in those parts of their
counties which were outside cities and towns. Municipalities had the
same regulatory power, and in areas where the prohibitionists were
strong, licenses could be revoked or refused. In Wenatchee, for example, when dry councilmen were in a majority, they voted to issue
no more saloon licenses and to revoke all existing ones; the election
for city councilmen was in effect a vote on saloons.[2]

At about the same time, the territorial Prohibition party found a
new candidate. Roger S. Greene, chief justice of the territorial court,
stepped from the bench to become the party's nominee for delegate to
Congress. His platform had caught the extremist tone: "The liquor
power is the mightiest instigator of political iniquity, the most fertile
source of political corruption, the unfailing promotion of social disorder, and the element of extreme danger to American civilization
and freedom."[3]

This platform was also a fairly clear reflection of western unrest
on the eve of the Populist Revolt, and it shows to what forces the prohibitionists had appealed in their bid for political power. They called
for women's suffrage and the direct election of United States senators
(to broaden the base of democracy), for restricted immigration and
improvements in the conditions of labor (to raise the living stand-

40

ards of urban laborers), and for the forfeiture of unearned railroad land grants (to open new areas to homesteading). Prohibition candidates would shortly pledge themselves just as seriously to free silver (to raise farm prices and lower interest rates), low tariffs (to reduce the costs of farm machinery), and government arbitration in labor disputes (to curb the power of monopolists in railroads and mines).[4]

This was strong medicine indeed for an area still popularly regarded as a frontier of individual freedom and opportunity for self-made men. Events of the next few years, however, would make clear just how distorted the popular image was and how eager were the farmers of the American West to buy such remedies in large quantities. The prohibitionists, sensitive to the rising fevers of economic malaise, were shrewd enough to articulate the growls of protest into their own distress over saloon "iniquity." Thus they elevated their own cry into a general wail of pain that demanded relief from a comprehensive inventory of social and political evils. But unfortunately for the drys, the many people who felt strongly about free silver, railroads, and immigration were just as strongly set against the doctrine of prohibition.

In the face of this misfortune, the prohibitionists sought professional help. Answering the call of Everett Smith, a Seattle lawyer, and Mrs. Lucy Switzer of Cheney, Edward B. Sutton, a full-time organizer and prohibition speaker, arrived just before the election of 1888 and made his home in Seattle. Sutton was a Methodist, a Templar, a temperance missionary, and an organizer for the Prohibition party of the United States. He was a key personality in the Washington temperance movement for the next twenty years. His own account of these years is the best description available of the motives and actions of the prohibition movement from the time of his arrival until the end of the century, for one sees in E. B. Sutton a case study of the energies and the antecedents of an uncompromising and indefatigable saloon fighter.

His father was from England, his mother from Vermont. He wrote with pride that both his parents had been antislavery "fanatics" who worked on the Underground Railroad in Michigan. Born in 1847, Sutton fought in fifty-two battles during the Civil War, including marching gloriously with Sherman to the sea. "Converted to God in his twentieth year" and ordained in his thirtieth, his great passion after the war was to help abolish the saloon. He was a man who

could tell a joke, mimic a drunkard's incoherence, burst into a fiery
wrath at the evils of drink, and deliver a thousand speeches a year.
The words flowed from his lips with an easy rhythm that fascinated
the more tongue-heavy farmers:

> Ladies and Gentlemen: We find four things necessary or four corner
> stones which must be laid in order to succeed in building up a sys-
> tem of Christian civilization: First, good morals; second, good edu-
> cation; third, good business principles; fourth, the spirit of love. We
> propose, ladies and gentlemen, to show and prove conclusively that
> the American liquor traffic, both in theory and practice, is opposed
> to each and all of these fundamental principles, and that we cannot
> arrive at the highest climax of Christian civilization while this strong
> and powerful oligarchy is allowed to exist and have a hand in shaping
> legislation. . . .

He spoke hundreds of times, traveled across the territory to organize
county committees and hold conventions, sometimes in the face of
considerable resistance. He took much pride in Whatcom County,
for example, where he found only one man initially interested in his
message; but with hard work and evangelical zeal he soon drummed
up a good meeting and a county committee. He helped to organize
county newspapers, headed the drives for funds, and, generally, coordinated the affairs of the party.[5]

As an organizer of prohibitionist sentiment, Sutton was superb,
but political fortune did not immediately follow. Roger Greene polled
1,137 of about 50,000 votes cast in the election for delegate to Congress.[6] E. B. Sutton, however, was not discouraged. The defeat of
Greene he regarded as a challenge to the energy and determination
of the temperance leaders, for more people were coming to Washington each month, and he knew the movement would grow.

In 1888, the whole territory was surging with excitement and activity; one transcontinental railroad had arrived, another was
coming and so was statehood. Landholders who had waited out the
depression of 1873 now had visions of great wealth. The population
had been 75,000 in 1880 and would reach 357,000 by 1890, and still
there were more jobs than workers. Farmers found greater markets
than they could supply. Business was "splendid." These were the
great days of change, optimism, and prosperity.[7]

When the Democrats and Republicans called for conventions, in
December of 1888, to select delegates for a state constitutional con-

vention, E. B. Sutton sent out invitations to a proposed Washington State Temperance Alliance which would work against the "deadly influence of the liquor traffic," he said, and seek to "annihilate the drunkard-making business of the future State of Washington." The new Alliance would welcome "every citizen, male or female, black or white, rich or poor, of any and all religious and political beliefs to be present and help in this effort for 'God and Home and Native Land.' "[8] The new Alliance had the same leadership as the old—David T. Denny, Everett Smith, Mrs. Switzer—but its platform, adopted under Sutton's direction, reflected the experience of 1888: it resolved its members to support candidates of either major party who supported prohibition, rather than nominate candidates for a Prohibition ticket.

The ambitions of the new Alliance were frustrated by time and disaster. Sutton and his co-workers had really not expected a constitutional convention for at least another two years, and though their response to the call was immediate, they were caught without adequate funds for a major campaign. Sutton traveled, worked, spoke, and solicited at a tremendous pace, selling shares in WSTA at ten dollars, even on the installment plan, so that the Alliance might print and distribute literature. Then in June the great fire of Seattle burned them out—the organization lost its headquarters, its records, and its funds. When the constitutional convention convened in July, Sutton had committed only five of the seventy-five delegates to prohibition.[9]

Members of the convention that assembled in Olympia were mostly wealthy men with political experience, and their mood reflected the western reform spirit of the 1880's—a distrust of government and of large business corporations. But they had serious doubts about the two reforms of immediate concern to the WSTA. Unfortunately, the texts of speeches and arguments of the conventions have been lost to history because the delegates neglected to appropriate any money to preserve them: reform sentiment is sometimes difficult to distinguish from niggardliness in the nineteenth century. But the Secretary of State did keep the minute book. This document shows that the Committee on Miscellaneous Subjects and Future Amendments considered "certain petitions and memorials from E. B. Sutton and others, representing many thousands of citizens, of a clause forever prohibiting within the limits of the state the manufacture and sale of alcoholic and malt liquors as a beverage. . . ."[10] A majority of the committee quickly recommended that these prayers not be granted.

Meanwhile, in the Committee for Elections and Election Rights, a motion to strike the adjective "male" from the prescribed qualifications for voting failed by an "overwhelming vote." The minute book here illuminates the motive:

> Dunbar said he personally favored women's suffrage but when voting in a representative capacity had to vote against it. He preferred leaving the entire question to the Legislature. Cosgrove took exactly the same ground. He and Griffitts were afraid the Constitution would be defeated if women's suffrage were in it. . . .[11]

The weight of this opinion easily prevailed among the delegates. (R. O. Dunbar became justice of the state Supreme Court immediately after statehood, and S. G. Cosgrove became governor of the state in 1909. Thomas C. Griffitts conducted a highly successful criminal-law practice in Spokane.) It is likely that most of the delegates were moderates in these matters, favoring—as did Dunbar and Cosgrove—equal suffrage and probably some measure of liquor control, and that they were disturbed by the extremists who, the delegates felt, threatened statehood itself with their reforms. Most were willing, as a reasonable compromise, to ask the people to vote on these matters. The delegates finally approved a ballot in four parts:[12]

1. For the Constitution_____
   Against the Constitution_____

2. For Women's Suffrage Article_____
   Against Women's Suffrage Article_____

3. For Prohibition Article_____
   Against Prohibition Article_____

4. For the permanent Location of the
   Seat of Government (Name of Place voted for)_____

The placing of Article 3 on the ballot clarifies a number of aspects of the prohibition movement in 1889. First of all, the movement had rejected the soft local option provisions of the previous decade—Ar-

ticle 3 was aimed at "alcoholic, malt, or spiritous liquors" throughout the state and was a true prohibition measure. Second, there was
enough support among the elected delegates to get the article on the
ballot. (A motion on August 5 to postpone the article indefinitely,
lost on the convention floor, fifty-two to ten.[13]) The delegates probably recognized that there was a substantial popular sentiment in
favor of such a provision and were quite willing to let the people
have their say on the matter. (The delegates were responding, according to the election returns, to 37 per cent of the voters.) Third,
one sees in the documents of the convention no evidence of any organized liquor forces. Political death-struggles with the saloon barons were yet in the future.

The achievement of leadership reflected in Article 3 was largely
E. B. Sutton's, and one wonders about the territorial temperance leaders of 1878, many of whom were not in Sutton's company. Newell and
Greene, to be sure, were staunch antidrink men and close to the
cause, but although both had political ambitions, neither was among
the delegates at Olympia. On the other hand, John M. Murphy, former secretary of the Washington Temperance Alliance and still editor
of the *Washington Standard* in Olympia, had abandoned his earlier
enchantment with reform. He advised his readers in July, 1889, that
"experience in other states proves prohibition to be a failure." There
is no evidence—in obituaries or biography—that Murphy was proud
of his career as a temperance worker, and no indication of why he
committed this apostasy. The same is true of the Reverends George
Whitworth and Daniel Bagley, who when they made themselves
available to subscription historians in a later decade, failed to mention their activities for the old temperance cause.[14]

Thus a deep split must have occurred within the forces of the territorial temperance movement sometime before Murphy left it. One
can only surmise that—as was the case in the 1870's—the character
of the movement, not the men, had changed, and that the change had
attracted some but offended others. Murphy had attached himself to
the cause in 1879 because the territorial middle class had felt the saloon to be a threat to the security of its values and to the society it
wished to establish; gentlemen of position had set their prestige
against the instruments of dissipation and debauchery. Within the
next ten years, though, the movement had fused with the campaign

for equal suffrage and splashed again in the mud and sweat of the class conflict.

After the bitter local option elections of 1886 and the blow to the movement by the Supreme Court, the extremists, under E. B. Sutton, took over the machinery of the Temperance Alliance and committed it to fanaticism. Even more, they ignored the polite social discipline offered by the prestige of former leaders; they turned deliberately to professional agitation and power politics. Here certainly was enough to alienate the older temperance advocates like Murphy, Whitworth, and Bagley. It is conceivable, too, that these men suffered from various degrees of shock when they saw the temperance standard blend in with the angry banners of railroad hatred, labor unionism, direct legislation, low tariffs, and free silver. If there was to be a "holy war" against the oligarchy, they wanted no part of it.

Even before the constitutional convention adjourned, this "holy war" had begun. The *Leader,* a weekly Seattle prohibition paper which printed the official communications of the IOGT, the WCTU, and the Washington Equal Suffrage Association, was on the streets by late August, 1889. The lead editorial paraded "Reasons Why You Should Vote For Prohibition." The tone was extremist, the appeal was to fear. It focused upon the rough and unlovely margins of a territorial society in boom-time and attributed every offense against middle-class decency to the evils of drink—a perceptive attack in so far as the movement toward statehood was also a movement toward respectability:

> If you are ashamed of the brothels that are found in all our cities and desire to see them closed forever, vote for prohibition.
> If you are ashamed of the bloated-faced staggering drunkards along our streets every day insulting decency and purity, vote for prohibition.
> If you are ashamed of the spider-legged tin horn gamblers that hang around the principle (*sic*) street corners in the afternoon gazing insultingly at the respectable women of our town as they pass, vote for prohibition.
> If you are ashamed of the bloated, loud-mouthed saloon keeper or his patron that peddles tickets and works for the whisky candidate at your polling place. . . .
> If you would save your boy and your neighbor's boy from becoming a drunkard, vote for prohibition.[15]

The early issues of the *Leader* are an interesting catalog of the prohibitionist party line. The paper stated flatly, for example, that no one in the liquor business claimed to be a Christian; that the saloons controlled state politics and that they had been responsible for the 1888 court decision against precinct local option; that 50 per cent of the young men in Pacific Coast cities spent their Sunday evenings in saloons; that Mrs. Abigail Scott Duniway, the suffragette who criticized the WCTU, was being paid by the liquor interests; and that those who held for "temperance" were traitors to the cause. "When a minister or a teacher refuses to speak out on this question," the editor told his readers, "he is ruled by the liquor interests." The emotions were also set to music: one of the many spirited songs printed for prohibition workers was called "We are Going to the Polls, Boys," to the melody of the popular Civil War song, "The Battle Cry of Freedom." ("Temperance forever, hurrah, boys, hurrah!")[16]

The *Leader* frequently reiterated the political position of the WSTA—that the Prohibition party would stand aside in this election so that neither Democrats nor Republicans could have an excuse for not supporting prohibition. All of this—the issues, the propaganda, the crusade—was well received by a broad element of the farm population of Washington.

The Washington State Grange was organized in September to protest the actions of the constitutional convention and to oppose the constitution submitted to the people as "an instrument fraught with so much peril to the public welfare." The perils, specifically, were too many public officials with salaries too high, an invitation in the constitution to foreign capital, and an insensitivity to the evils of monopoly in transportation and finance. In addition, the Grange proposed to stop all candidates for the state legislature who would not support the separate articles, "for temperance and equal rights were cardinal principles of the farmers' organization."[17]

The Grange Convention, however, met a short two weeks before the constitutional election called for October 1. It was impossible for the Grange to become a significant political force between the middle of September and the first of October; it could hardly get itself organized. The returns of October 1, then, did not measure the potential power of the Grange, and they probably did not test very accurately the power of the WSTA, which was burned out and broke. But nevertheless, here was a referendum of high purity: interest was strong, and practically everyone who voted (52,031) also voted on

TABLE 3

PROHIBITION AND THE CONSTITUTION, 1889*

For the Constitution:	40,152
Against the Constitution:	11,879
For Women's Suffrage:	16,527
Against Women's Suffrage:	35,613
For Prohibition:	19,546
Against Prohibition:	31,487

* The vote on the Constitution and on Women's Suffrage is from the "First Report of the Secretary of State of Washington," *Washington Public Documents* (Olympia, Wash., 1890). The secretary was remarkably indifferent to history—his report does not mention the prohibition vote, nor did he break the vote down by county. Figures cited here are from Ernest H. Cherrington, *The Evolution of Prohibition in the United States of America* (Westerville, Ohio, 1920), p. 236, and Sutton, *Prohibition Seed Thoughts*, p. 10.

prohibition (51,033). A clear 63 per cent of the people in the new sovereign state did not want prohibition as it was defined in Separate Article 3.

There was, however, immediate and violent disagreement with such an evaluation. Sutton and the Temperance Alliance cried that over one hundred thousand Republican ballots had been fraudulently printed so that "For Women's Suffrage" and "For Prohibition" had been blurred out in a "corrupt and shameful political trick."[18] Because this cry of fraud followed, almost without exception, every defeat of a prohibition measure both before and after 1889 and was clearly a basic part of prohibitionist doctrine, one cannot accept its validity without caution. In this instance, though, the most credible account of what actually happened exposes a degree of malicious political knavery and polished seduction seldom achieved in the history of any state.

Mrs. Adella M. Parker, in 1910 president of the Washington College Suffrage League and a graduate of the University of Washington Law School, wrote that just before the statehood election a wholesale liquor house in Seattle had offered to print the Republican ballots without cost. Concealing their iniquitous purpose, the conspirators hired the printing office of the Prohibition Press (which published the *Leader*) for the ballot job, insisting that their own printers do all the work. The shop was under lock and key during the printing; even the owners of the press were excluded by the terms of the contract. The product—if the facsimile shown in Mrs. Parker's report is an accurate one—was a ballot with an unmistakable line printed through the phrase "Against the Constitution" and a similar one through "For Women's Suffrage." The words "For Prohibition" were corrupted with a blur which made them almost illegible. Mrs. Parker wrote that "large numbers" of the ballots were returned, but that "thousands" were used.[19]

If this is true, sentiment in Washington for prohibition and for women's suffrage may have been more extensive than the official returns suggest. The affair was never investigated, probably because such a question would have challenged the integrity of the winning party and even the validity of President William H. Harrison's proclamation of statehood. George Cotterill later wrote that "reverence for the dead prompts silence as to the name of the man who was guilty of perpetrating this contemptible deed." Sutton told the prohibitionists that they had been cheated and that they were not to be deterred from the crusade. He said that three fifths of the voters in Washington favored prohibition, and he rejoiced that the recorded prohibition vote was larger than that cast for the Democratic party.[20]

Sutton also saw great hope in the Seattle vote, where prohibition won three of the eight precincts, though it lost by a vote of 2,286 to 1,604. This vote, he felt, in the "stronghold of rum," was not a defeat, but a triumph.[21] He thought it most significant that in Seattle the prohibition vote was not drawn on party lines. The conclusion Sutton drew from this fact was that neither party could afford to support his cause, and therefore the cause must have its own party.

He attempted to rally the faithful by asking, "Who shall rule the nation—the saloon keepers or the sober people? We fought a grand fight for Prohibition on non-Partisan lines and were sold out . . . our only hopes lies in the growth of a party pledged to our principles." "We have," Sutton told a newspaper man, "washed our hands of this non-partisan nonsense." With the authority of the WSTA, he went out to organize county clubs for the Prohibition party and to harass

the saloonkeepers with endless speeches. His favorite refrain became
an iambic blast at the nonpartisan principle:

> Behind each bar within the state
> Stands a bruiser sleek and fat;
> Who is a true Republican
> Or a trusted Democrat.

Or more sweetly (to "In the Sweet By-and-By"):

> In the sweet by-and-by,
> We shall welcome that beautiful day;
> In the sweet by-and-by
> When all Christians will vote as they pray.

But defeat at the polls—and the belief that he had been cheated—
gave an edge to the rising fanaticism that Sutton encouraged within
himself and others. It became a shriek during the next decade: he
compared himself to William Lloyd Garrison and preached that "To
license sin is sin . . . on this rock we rest."[22]

In June of 1890, after a lecture at Almira—and after a warning that
he should not lecture—Sutton was viciously beaten by a saloonkeeper
and consequently bedridden for three weeks. Publicity, sympathy, and
financial help flowed to him; one group gave him a gold-headed cane
for "defense as well as support."[23] Here was the martyrdom which,
perhaps, he had sought. He was then signing his letters with dedicated
militancy: "Yours for the war, E. B. Sutton."[24]

The *Leader* followed Sutton through the emotions of abolitionism.
The paper was the printed word, the record of Sutton's lectures for
the faithful to treasure and the weak to admire. On political revolution:

> The question is not, "is public sentiment ready for prohibition," but
> "is prohibition right." Public sentiment was not ready for the ten com-
> mandments when they were first given. . . . To say that public senti-
> ment is not ready for it, is simply to admit the necessity of that very
> education which such legislation can alone give.

On the nature of individual liberty:

> If your liberty to take a glass of beer when you want it means the sub-
> jugation of a nation to the worst enemy man ever had, then I would
> dash your beerglass into a thousand pieces. When the liberty of one
> man means the subjugation of a hundred, let his liberty cease then
> and there.

On class exploitation: "The revenue from the liquor traffic is raised and paid in by the dealers. They do not create any wealth, but simply gather it in. Most of revenue comes from the poorer class. This, of course, lets out the large property holders [from taxation]."[25]

The *Leader* became the official organ of the Prohibition party, the International Order of Good Templars, and the Women's Christian Temperance Union. The old Washington State Temperance Alliance was broken up, and in its place stood the Washington State Prohibition Alliance. The nonpartisan unity of 1889 was gone.

The Grange, for example, could not bring itself to a partisan stand, even though it shared the impatience of the Prohibition party. The Grange approach to prohibition in the 1890's was to stand aloof from party politics and whip up the froth of fear and discontent:

> We have pledged ourselves to labor for the development of a better manhood and womanhood among us, but how can we hope to succeed if we allow Satan's stronghold to flourish. . . . What has caused the women of our land to come knocking at the door of justice asking for the right of franchise but this wide-spread desolation, this misery, and destruction that is settling like a great black pall down upon our people . . . they have seen the husband who pleaded for the right to love and protect, lured from the home . . . a man, but returned to it a demon to . . . murder the wife he promised to protect and the helpless offspring he is accountable for to the laws of both God and man, all destroyed by that mighty desolator, liquor.[26]

Thus in the 1890's, prohibition was both a partisan and a nonpartisan matter. In 1892 the "Prohibs," as Sutton called them, ran a full ticket in Washington, from President right down to state printer. It was a year of economic and social unrest, and the party tried to strengthen its identity with the "common people's" war against "the interests." The platform of 1892 was not only a hard statement of uncompromising hatred of liquor; it was again an appeal for the votes of the discontented. On state issues the party stood for "abolishing the sweating systems as practiced in some of the mining districts," for tax reform, and for women's suffrage.[27]

The Prohibs ran Roger S. Greene for governor. Sutton distributed over two hundred thousand pieces of printed material, made scores of speeches, and spent over three thousand dollars. His Prohibs, including Greene, polled about 4 per cent of the popular vote, striking-

ly smaller than the Prohibition Article had received in 1889.[28] The
Populist party received about 23 per cent. It was clear that the thou-
sands who had supported prohibition earlier would not vote for the
Prohibs.

But Sutton's faithful marched onward, trying to push their way
against the facts of their existence. Their newspaper found a verse
for their cry:

> By votes we run the devil's still!
> By votes we kill God's living grain!
> By votes the drunkard's cup we fill,
> And doom him to eternal pain!
>
> Who casts these votes? Thou, voter, thou!
> Thy ballot damns these drunken souls!
> Thy brother's blood is on it now,
> Dropped, red and reeking, at the polls![29]

Nationally, the party stood at the end of its line—twenty-five years
of poor show. In Washington, it had barely survived a decade during
which just about every other movement prospered. John Murphy of
the *Washington Standard* was openly contemptuous: "Prohibition is
too big a word for such a small party to wear. The Dewdrop party
would sound better and conform more fully to the eternal fitness of
things. Dew is evanescent; it comes early, goes soon and leaves no
trace of its presence. By all means let it be Dewdrop."[30]

The party was indeed small, but it did not evanesce. It disintegrated, and the pieces were lying around the political landscape for
many years. It disintegrated partly because of the pressures of its
own fanaticism, which turned the more moderate reformers away
from it, and partly because of its futile attempt to wade into the
mainstream of agrarian discontent, which embarrassed both the
Populists and the urban middle class.

The panic of 1893 began a long and painful depression in Washington, especially in the lumber economy, and energies and emotions
were directed to concerns more urgent than liquor control. Thus a
local option law failed in the legislative session of 1895, and there is
plenty of evidence to indicate that the Sunday closure law was openly
violated and that sales to minors were common during the 1890's.
The People's party arose out of the grievances of the depression to
overwhelm the state, absorbing all the Prohibition party's policies

except prohibition itself. Nationally, the Populists could not afford to offend any sector of their support, especially the German farmers who drank beer. In Washington, the Populist governor, John R. Rogers, never spoke on prohibition, and the Populist legislature of 1897 never seriously considered it.

By this time, the Prohibition party was severely disoriented. In 1896, the Prohibs at their national convention had argued bitterly over the stand they should take on the currency issue, and they had split into bickering groups of hard-money and soft-money crusaders. The search for panaceas had produced too many for the movement to sustain. The antidrink crusade would go on, of course, but under different leadership and in a different direction.

One can follow the disintegration of the Prohibs in the career of Austin F. Griffiths, a "temperance lawyer," as he called himself, who settled in the lumber town of Montesano in 1889. A reform-minded young man full of ambition and optimism, he joined the Chautauqua Circle, practiced law, and took the Prohib nomination for county attorney. The depression hit Montesano with disastrous blows: in December, 1892, the local paper had to give 132 column inches to notices of land to be sold by the sheriff. Griffiths, eager to advance himself, waited impatiently until 1897, then took an opportunity to join a Seattle law firm. In leaving Montesano, he found it convenient to leave the Prohibition party as well. The currency squabble among the Prohibs had irritated him, and he was simply no longer interested in Prohib politics. He remained a temperance advocate, but he was joining the urban middle class where Republicanism was a matter of form and style.[31]

In Seattle, Griffiths joined the First Presbyterian church where a few years later the Reverend Mark Matthews became nationally famous for his lurid attacks on vice, sin, and saloons. In 1905, this church found room on its staff for the Reverend E. B. Sutton, the saloon-fighter with the gold-headed cane, and employed him as a street preacher, a jail worker, and a teacher of Bible classes.[32] The old abolitionists had ceased to lead.

5

The "Hell-Soaked Institution"

THE Prohibition party passed quickly into the shadows where the political crankiness of each generation seems to languish for a decade or two before it is forgotten. The prohibition sentiment, on the other hand, did not. It awaited only good times and new leadership, for the "wave" theory of prohibition sentiment, besides presenting obvious inadequacies as a liquid metaphor (waves of dry sentiment?), is simply not accurate. Antidrink feeling grew with the progress of industrialization in Washington, in the United States, in the western world. What to do about the saloon was one of the problems of progress and poverty.

The saloon was for centuries an honorable institution. In colonial times, well-meaning legislators made its presence mandatory in certain townships and defined its purpose as the "refreshment of mankind in a reasonable manner," and this same happy regard for a necessity of life was probably close to the American consensus at least until after the Civil War.[1] The saloon of the early nineteenth century was dedicated to the values of fellowship, equality, and euphoria. It was a warm and quiet retreat where men could explore the pleasures of friendship away from the nagging cares of creditor or clerk, wife or clergyman. It was a place where one could lift the burdens of caste, of status, and of the more restrictive social inhibitions, and thus freed, could grasp for the dim image of his own individuality. The saloon was also a glittering release from the drab and gray monotonies of an agrarian reality, a momentary refuge from worry or trouble, humiliation or shame. It offered an honest and felicitous distinction between relief and abandon to a grateful clientele. In a society not yet oppressed by the god of precision—when a man could spell his own name differently every day of the week if he wanted to and when no one measured the trueness of a furrow in millime-

54

ters—a reasonably soft cloud of alcoholic haze was a luxury one could hardly afford to be without. Until the agrarian America that produced the saloon no longer existed, the saloon sustained many an honorable man.

Even after the industrial age began, the saloon, at its best, still had a distinct social function. This was clarified in the 1890's by a national committee of fifty tolerably objective clergymen, lawyers, and educators who surveyed a variety of watering places and concluded that the saloon was "meeting the thirst for fellowship, for amusement, and for recreation," and that, furthermore, many communities had given to the saloon a "monopoly of the social life of a majority of American wage-earners."[2]

There were many such communities in the state of Washington, a political unit which, in terms of industrialization, urbanization, immigration, and class structure, was at this time probably representative of most of the American western states. In the nature and the quality of its saloons—and in what its people did about the saloons—it may have been typical of a significant American experience.

At the turn of the century, Washington could show both the good and the bad. A newspaper reporter named Jim Marshall, who had gained a detailed and intimate knowledge of Washington's saloons during the first two decades of statehood, later defended them as places of refuge where men gathered simply because saloons were the only places where they could congregate in working clothes, "with grimy hands and faces, and where they could think and talk uninhibitedly." The saloon, he said, "was a place where all men were equal and where every man was a king." Women, he noted, were admitted only in low-class bars, and only then through side doors, and they were not allowed in the main drinking room. Thus the saloon was a "bulwark against national drunkenness," he claimed, for as long as women were not allowed there, at least half the population stayed sober.

But drunkenness, he recalled, was not really a problem. The saloon was a place where a man informed himself about the social and political matters of the day. In Spokane in the 1890's, the saloons kept the newspaperman close to the miners from the Coeur d'Alene, the wheat growers from the Palouse, the "apple knockers" from the big orchards, and the mayor and councilmen from city hall. "We learned our social and political fundamentals bellied up to the bar," he wrote. "I cannot recall that we ever got drunk, but upon occasion we were moderately stimulated and inspired to create and announce improvements in government, or denounce social inequities. . . ."

Marshall also remembered a saloon in Aberdeen that doubled as a natural museum, full of Indian artifacts, stuffed birds, and photographs of early logging scenes. The bartender served as banker for the loggers, and he allegedly never gave a man his money unless the depositor was sober. One might suspect that behind the romance, there must have been at least some reality.[3]

The saloon was often defended, with varying success, as a "poor man's club" and a center of charity. It is a fact that during the winter of 1894, in the cold depths of the depression, the saloons of Spokane were lodging and feeding at least 650 unemployed men from the mines, ranches, and logging camps. The saloonkeepers thought this was a reasonably secure investment. The saloons of Washington, at their most gracious, may actually have been a contribution to basic human dignity.[4]

But for every decent saloon that filled a real social need, there were too many others that increased poverty, crime, and degradation. All the evidence points to the truth that the saloon as an institution never made a satisfactory transition into the industrial age. Reformers, who were trying to make the industrial age humane, would strike down the saloon in the same way they struck down child labor, rotten food, and the great trusts—except, perhaps, that striking the saloon was to them much more important. When in 1895 Edmond S. Meany of the University of Washington wrote a bill which prohibited the sale of intoxicating drinks within two miles of the University, what he and his colleagues feared was the debauchery of their most cherished values through drunkenness, prostitution, narcotic addiction, gambling, and violence. They heard, all too plainly, the rumble of a distant revelry—or more precisely, they heard the rumble of steel rails, and they saw that the immediate future would bring a great increase in the number of saloons. And the more saloons there were, the worse they would become.

The coming of the transcontinental railroads changed the entire character of regional social history. They brought such great increases in population and industry that continuities between the pre-railroad epoch and the next period are difficult, and sometimes impossible, to trace. Under the impact of the enormous population growth, regional traditions shifted, leadership changed, and most social and economic problems took on vastly different proportions. In 1880 there were but 289 miles of track in Washington and few saloon problems. During the next decade two thousand miles of track were made operative in the state, and transcontinental connections were completed; and the legislature passed the local option law of 1886, which was an antisaloon measure. In the 1890's almost another thousand miles of track were laid, and by 1903, an additional five hundred. By that time the Anti-Saloon League was a significant political force.[5]

The relationship between the miles of railroad track and the increasing antisaloon sentiment had to do with something more than just the growing population. Before the railroads came to Washington, the saloon was almost entirely an urban institution because the art of brewing was impractical beyond the centers of population. Draught beer was never pasteurized, and it had to be handled quickly. But when the Northern Pacific came in the 1880's, the city brewers began to look eagerly beyond the limitations of beer wagons. Even though refrigeration cars were few and shipping arrangements were hazardous, the brewers saw the opening of a great world and began, with unseemly haste, to encourage the cultivation of saloons in the small communities that were sprouting along the Northern Pacific right-of-way. Sales of beer in Washington increased by 33 per cent between 1889 and 1890, and the resentment of the rural population toward this saloon empire-building was measured, however inaccurately, by the ballots of 1889.

This situation underwent a marked change because of the truly extraordinary developments of the early 1890's. At the very time when refrigeration cars were coming into general use, the "crown" bottle cap was patented, and Washington brewers began shipping bottled beer in quantity. Thus a technological revolution immediately opened vast new areas for saloon planting, and competition among urban brewers for this new territory became a serious consideration.

Then the Great Northern tied its tracks across the state in January, 1893, thus completing the second transcontinental railroad to Puget Sound, and the competition took on entirely new dimensions. The big brewers in St. Louis and Milwaukee began establishing district sales offices in the Pacific Northwest, and even foreign investors began buying up brewery properties. For example, a London corporation called the Portland and Seattle Breweries, Ltd., was organized in 1891 with a capital investment of £370,000. It amalgamated under one management and control the City Brewery of Portland, the Clausen-Sweeney Brewery of Seattle, the Bay View Brewery of Seattle, and the Star Brewery of Walla Walla. Other Washington State brewers then came to understand the nature of survival in the industrial wilderness, and the competition became frenzied.[6]

The principal feature of the brewing business in the 1890's was the great rush to open new saloons or to capture old ones. Brewers, national and local, found it convenient to loan money for licenses, fixtures, and stock at easy terms as they hurried to stake out new ground, and they undoubtedly encouraged many irresponsible men to become saloonkeepers. For those already in the business, there were attractive offers—polite bribes, actually—for exclusive contracts. The brewers soon found it necessary to include hard liquor in the equipment they extended to saloons, and this phase of competition brought the brewers and distillers into the same flood of excesses.[7]

When almost anyone could become a saloonkeeper, almost anyone who did was in debt to a brewery. And the brewery barons were harsh taskmasters. The debt slaves had to hustle to attract the customers to pay their bills, or they had to get out. And therein lay the catalyst of saloon indecencies. As always in the state's history, unrestrained business competition was the excuse for ruthless and stupid exploitation—of furs, of fish, of timber, of human flesh.

In 1914, just after the people voted for state-wide prohibition, the editor of the Seattle *Argus* drew this sober conclusion:

> There are saloons in which fights are of nightly occurrence. There are saloons where drunks are "rolled." There are saloons where the man who gets his check cashed stands mighty little show of getting away with any of the coin. There are saloons where liquor is sold to boys. And against these saloons the prohibition law is aimed.

In 1933, following the repeal of prohibition, the State Advisory Committee on Liquor Legislation gravely warned the voters against the active promotion of liquor sales; the committee remembered such sales as the most objectionable feature of the open saloon.[8]

One can understand, then, that when the Master of the Grange called the saloon a "putrid fester spot," there were even antiprohibitionists who could agree. For example, in 1902 the Secretary of the Navy found the city of Bremerton "infested" with saloons and threatened to move the navy yard to San Francisco unless they were rooted out. The chambers of commerce of both Seattle and Bremerton—groups not usually among the saloon fighters—hurriedly retained Austin Griffiths, the "temperance lawyer," to find a way to satisfy Secretary Moody. Griffiths got rid of the Bremerton saloons, but only temporarily.[9]

One of the milder protests against the saloons in Washington around the turn of the century was that they customarily stayed open for business twenty-four hours a day, seven days a week. Because of the saloon men's power in local politics, the Sunday Closure Law was openly violated, and Sunday debauchery was paraded in defiance of middle-class morality. An investigator for the *Leader* found, by his calculation, more people in Beede's Music Hall in Seattle one Sunday than had attended church in the city that day. He found three shifts of bartenders working around the clock, and he reported that prostitutes were all over the place. Though the state Supreme Court upheld the Sunday closing laws in 1899, Seattle saloons did not close on Sundays until 1907. In Walla Walla they defied the law even longer.[10]

Even more seriously, the very nature of the saloon seemed to encourage brutality and violence. Dr. Louis Banks, who founded a prohibition newspaper in Vancouver, was shot by a saloonkeeper in 1881. E. B. Sutton, the prohibitionist speaker, was almost killed by a saloonkeeper in the 1890's. In Yakima in 1902, the Chief of Police brawled with a city councilman in a local saloon. In 1906 in Meadowdale, on Puget Sound, a saloonkeeper who had been a part-time teamster and wood-chopper before he got his license, callously ridiculed a woman who pleaded that her drunkard husband not be served. The husband was killed by a train a few nights later as he staggered toward his wife and children. In Wapato, residents complained that "decent" women were afraid to walk the streets on Sunday because of the hell-raising of drunken workers who washed in and out of the saloons. The small community of Kiona may have been representative. Kiona had only one saloon, and four hundred railroad workers came in every night and all day Sunday to drink. The saloon was so crowded that citizens of Kiona could hear the noise all over town. There was standing-room-only in the saloon, and the dead-drunks were thrown into the back yard like so many soggy sacks to retch there in full view of the townspeople.[11]

In communities where saloons were not so crowded, the behavior of customers was concealed by screens and various other obstructions on doors and windows. Virtuous citizens could imagine the worst, and they were usually correct. When the railroads came into Snohomish, for example, the Knights of Labor tried to close the saloons because a grand jury reported that children were being served there. In Wenatchee the Salvation Army sent a young boy into a saloon to prove that the saloonkeeper was selling to minors, and the evidence came easily. The saloons of Spokane in 1888 were the worst "low slum dives" in the nation, according to one alderman who found seven boys in a single saloon.[12]

But the screens concealed even more than sales to minors. In 1901 in Spokane, forty saloons had "wineroom" attachments that left little to the imagination: private boxes with couches, according to a group of Protestant and Catholic leaders, permitted "immorality in its most depraved form."[13] Civic groups and organizations of businessmen condemned the winerooms, and the wholesale brewers and liquor men fought back. The Mayor refused to ban the boxes.

When Austin Griffiths became chief of police in Seattle, he found saloons where girls "more or less in their natural attire" would leave the music platform to mingle with the guests and make engagements. "Saloons prospered, dice rattled, fig leaves were scarce, evil flourished, crime festered. . . ." Besides prostitution, as Griffiths noted, gambling was usually a common adjunct to liquor. And according to Jim Marshall—the newspaper man who in later years was so romantic about saloons—the hustling for a quick dollar even led some saloon men to use morphine, chloral hydrate (a depressant), and cantharides (Spanish fly). It was common for saloons to be the hangouts for prostitutes, pimps, and criminals. In 1909, a saloonkeeper in Aberdeen sold out and devoted his efforts to local option. He quit, he said, because the sixty-nine men who had been murdered in Aberdeen in 1907 were the responsibility of Aberdeen bartenders and their women friends.[14]

Earlier in Seattle, solid citizens like Dexter Horton, W. R. Ballard, Henry Yesler, and R. H. Thomson signed petitions to keep a saloon from opening next door to the post office, protesting that the sights and sounds of a saloon should not be made a necessity for women and children who would have to pass by. These men were not hypersensitive. But as the competition increased, the saloon was indeed omnipresent. Everett soon had forty saloons for twenty-four thousand people. Pasco in 1909 had sixteen for two thousand men, women, and children. Walla Walla in 1915 had forty-six for a population of sixteen thousand. Even the Yakima Indians pleaded with the government to keep saloons off their reservation.[15]

And the political power of the saloons was also obvious. In Olympia in 1908, voter registration in one ward controlled by the saloons went up 50 per cent when the saloons made their effort to defeat Governor Albert E. Mead, who sought re-election. Mead had raised the issue of local option during the campaign; he lost the saloon vote and the governor's mansion. Before leaving office, he addressed the legislature on the matter that had caused him considerable pain:

> The policy of the state should be to encourage temperance. Under present legislation, competition among those engaged in the liquor traffic results in the practical ownership of many saloons in this state by brewers and distillers. This competition is so marked that in many instances drunkenness is encouraged as a popular pastime. . . . Effective regulation of the liquor traffic by cutting off the cause of the crime would tend to lessen the number of inmates of the penitentiary, insane asylums, almshouses, hospitals. . . .[16]

In 1911, Governor Marion E. Hay spoke to the lawmakers about the same excesses: "Every opportunity has been afforded the better element in the saloon business to effect the necessary reforms from within, but, since they have utterly failed to achieve any substantial betterment, the people are determined that . . . the reforms must come from without."[17]

Governor Hay was referring to the futile activity of a group of liquor men and cigar dealers who had belatedly welcomed reform. The organization was the Knights of the Royal Arch, whose spokesman in 1908 discovered that the public image of the saloon was not what it should be:

> The most powerful argument the prohibitionist can present is the drunk man reeling from the doors of a saloon. . . . Let us put ourselves right as a business before our fellow men. Let us cut off, root and branch, the minors, the drunkard, the tramp, the criminal, the dance hall, the vicious of every class and kind. . . . I strongly urge . . . the restriction of licenses to respectable men, who will raise the sale of drink to a po-

sition of such respectability that saloons will become something like clubs for men of small means. . . .

The exhortation itself was damning: in other words, the saloons were terribly far from middle-class standards. The Knights hoped that "in time" the reforms would take place. But they had no power to discipline their members, and time was running out. There remains the strong suspicion, too, that the organization of the Knights was either a political subterfuge, or that its leaders were given to incredible political bungling. The Tacoma chapter of the Knights of the Royal Arch pledged fifteen hundred votes to the opponent of Governor Mead.[18]

The Knights had no measurable effect on the saloon business. In 1914, in the lengthening shadow of the Prohibition Initiative, the Olympia Modern Tavern League took up the cause of saloon reform. Its purpose was to stop sales to drunks, to divorce saloons from gambling, and to drive out prostitution.[19] But in that year the people of Washington passed a measure which gave the saloon only two more years to live.

The only way the liquor interests might have disciplined their own members was through effective consolidations in brewing and distilling which would have allowed the producer to escape his concern with competition. There is some evidence that such consolidation was a strong trend in the 1890's and the early 1900's. Andrew Hemrick of Seattle, for example, was president of Seattle Brewing and Malting Company in 1893, after the company had absorbed three competing breweries. The depression of 1893 caused the Portland and Seattle Breweries, Ltd., to dissolve its holdings, all to Hemrick's advantage. By 1916, Hemrick was president of Seattle Brewing and Malting Company and of the Claussen Brewing Association, all of these consolidated companies.[20] But if Hemrick had the authority to clean up saloons, he did not use it. And by this time, consolidation worked for the prohibitionists by allowing them to use all the highly polished propaganda of the antitrust cause in their attack.

The reasons for antisaloon sentiments were, of course, not strictly local or regional. The antisaloon movement in Washington was but a part of the national reform. The railroads brought the saloons in numbers, and they also brought to the state people who were already keyed to a high pitch of abolitionist emotion. They brought, among others, E. B. Sutton, the professional prohibitionist, and they brought the Reverend Mark Matthews, a Presbyterian minister who had the will and the power to turn the eyes of the middle class toward saloon evil. These men found in their new home a rich field for their work. In Washington State one sees the microcosm: there was hardly an evil in the chronicle of American saloon history that could not be illustrated there.

6

House Divided

THE MEN and women who joined together to fight the saloon had varied motives. Historically, the antisaloon sentiment had not consistently been the antialcohol sentiment. When, for example, the United States Temperance Union in 1836 split into groups of "total abstainers" from alcoholic drinks and "total abstainers" from "ardent spirits" only, it was clear that the Union as well as the English language was undergoing a significant change.[1] The word *temperance* thereafter became practically synonymous with *prohibition* and sheltered the full range of reform proposals and reformers, from the "radicals" who wanted to abolish both the liquor traffic and the liquor industry to the "moderates" who were primarily concerned with the social evils attributable to the saloon.

The "radicals" at the hard core of the Washington prohibition movement were dedicated alcohol fighters, absolutely convinced of the evil of all intoxicating drink. To these men and women, the saloon was evil institutionalized, at once a symbol and an instrument of Satan's work among God's unfortunate creatures. This attitude was graphically illustrated by a Spokane minister who solemnly decorated the window of a saloon with the image of Satan over a background of sable black as a stern warning to all who might approach.[2] Many of the radicals, like E. B. Sutton, even felt that they had been called from On High to do holy battle, to swing the might of the Lord against the Devil's machinations. As true millenarians, they would be satisfied with nothing short of world-wide prohibition.[3]

There was a striking kinship between these radicals and the antislavery radicals of another generation. That his parents had been "fanatical abolitionists" was a source of considerable pride to E. B. Sutton. Roger S. Greene, Prohibition candidate for governor in 1892, had been a captain of colored infantry in 1863, and before that, proba-

64

bly, an abolitionist. Stephen P. Willis, another Prohib candidate, had as a younger man been an abolitionist. So, perhaps, had many others, for most of them shared common passions and a common background: they came from the states of Indiana, Illinois, Ohio, or from New England.[4]

The Prohibs lashed out at the saloonkeepers with the same zeal with which their fathers had lashed out at the slaveowners. And their ranks bristled with members of the Protestant clergy. Like their fathers, they could not form a successful political party and were for years generally regarded as somewhat disreputable. But also like their fathers, they saw themselves as unselfish and God-inspired. "Are we not," one of them asked, "repeating the experience of a half century ago in our attitude toward the great moral question forced upon our attention? For years, earnest, devoted men have been pleading with our people for the abolition of a greater curse than negro slavery in its worst days."[5]

They drew strength from this parallel. Indeed, two prominent abolitionist writers associated with the temperance movement before the Civil War were George H. Shirley and William Lloyd Garrison. The extremism of the latter particularly impressed E. B. Sutton, who was at times so seized by his mission that he almost saw himself as The Liberator. Thus he could underscore with pious abandon that "Like William Lloyd Garrison, *I am in earnest; I will not equivocate; I will not retract a single inch; and I will be heard.*"[6]

Like the antislavery radicals, the prohibition radicals were usually people with no personal experience with the evil which they pledged themselves to abolish. Perhaps because this was true, they could unleash the rhetoric of fanaticism for which the only discipline is the rhythm of words. This was the battle of "Heaven against hell," as Billy Sunday told the saloon fighters in the state. The WCTU told them that the saloon was "everything that is vile and evil":

> In Washington West we do our best
> To help drive out tobacco and rum!
> Just see us come!
> Do you hear us yell?
> We are the Washington L. T. L. [Loyal Temperance League]
> Saloons must go, must go![7]

Such exuberance was stiff and fragile, and it must have caused snickers even in 1909. But one must pair it with the dark suggestions in Sutton's "annihilate," "destroying intruder," "gigantic crime," and "monster of cruelty." Some of the radicals were artless, to be sure, but their historic achievement was that they did in fact abolish the saloon. In doing so they manipulated the obvious reality of the institution into a symbol of evil and so controlled the connotations of the word *saloon* that even today the state forbids the use of the word in public advertising. To comprehend the endurance of their victory, one must know the verbal terror of a sermon by the Reverend Mark A. Matthews:

> The liquor traffic is the most fiendish, corrupt and hell-soaked institution that ever crawled out of the slime of the eternal pit. It is the open sore of this land. . . . It takes the kind, loving husband and father, smothers every spark of love in his bosom, and transforms him into a heartless wretch, and makes him steal the shoes from his starving babe's feet to find the price for a glass of liquor. It takes your sweet innocent daughter, robs her of her virtue and transforms her into a brazen, wanton harlot. . . . [He gives an example of a drunkard who killed his wife and child.]
> But perhaps you, like thousands of foolish co-conspirators, will say that the saloon is a necessary institution. You never uttered a more blasphemous lie on earth. . . . The open saloon as an institution has its origin in hell, and it is manufacturing subjects to be sent back to hell. . . .[8]

The hyperbole included the use of statistics. Matthews threw out to his congregation that "over a thousand wives were murdered last year in the United States by drunken husbands."[14] A Baptist preacher in Spokane said that in 1904 the saloons in that city were destroying two hundred boys and girls annually. In 1916, the Grange reported that if liquor were authorized in hotels, the law would make a brothel of every hotel in the state. Antidrink passions were so intense that the Washington State Grange resolved in favor of jailing anyone who took any intoxicating beverages. (In other states, proposals were made that the government forbid drinkers to marry, or that it execute them and their posterity to the fourth generation.)[9]

Such hatreds flowed from a reservoir of fear which the radicals, in the pre-Freudian age, made no effort to obscure. A part of it was expressed in Mark Matthews' view of wine and women. "Combine the two," he said, "and we get the lowest admixture of human vileness. Man is bad enough in himself, but he is a thousand times worse when assisted in him immoralities by the active cooperation of feminine auxiliaries and whiskey." He concluded that "the virtue or chastity of an intoxicated woman is worthless." He urged the press of the country to spend a week "exposing the domestic infidelity to be seen in cafes, restaurants, and beer gardens where liquor is sold." Matthews had a committee from his congregation survey the saloons and brothels of Seattle, and the long and lurid reports of this fascinating field work provided constant fuel for his sermons.[10]

Such were the anxieties, in part, of the nineteenth-century middle class, whose values were rural, Protestant, and Anglo-Saxon, about the changing character of American life. Sometimes they spoke explicitly: "Where else shall we look but to the farmer to counteract the venality and corruption of the slums of our cities' population, that seem to be so rapidly increasing by the aggregation of alien voters, anarchists and saloon influences?"[11]

The root of it all lay in the threat of alcohol to middle-class American mores. Alcohol caused an individual to lose his self-control, and loss of self-control—physical, intellectual, sexual, financial, political—was the cardinal sin. Drunkenness, prostitution, miscegenation, venereal disease, poverty, bossism—these were the darkest threats to the values through which the American middle class had established its identity. These were the challenges to what the prohibitionists liked to call "clean, wholesome manhood."

These were also the fears that inspired fanaticism. When a New York Anti-Saloon League leader was questioned about his undemocratic attempt to force prohibition upon cities that clearly did not want it, his reply defined his enthusiasms: "There is one thing greater than democracy . . . and that is the will of God." And when the "radicals" were in control of the Washington State Senate, Senator Oliver Hall of Whitman County took the floor to answer the charge that the prohibition forces in the legislature, in passing a bone-dry law, were unfairly setting aside a law enacted by the people:

> Our opponents seem to think that a prohibitionist must be fair; that isn't the definition of a prohibitionist. He is a man who always hits whisky a blow, whether above the belt or below the belt. He isn't expected to be fair. In the past year we didn't get fair treatment. Now we've got the votes, don't ask us to be fair for we are not built that way. . . .[12]

In this open arrogance and antidemocratic heresy lay the strength and the terror of the radicals which pushed them toward excesses sometimes nearly as sordid as those of the saloonkeepers. This was clear to some people long before Senator Hall spoke, for in 1911 the Reverend E. B. Sutton, the aging street preacher for Mark Matthews' church, was tried and convicted for fraudulent registration of voters. As an election clerk, he had registered a woman "unable to come to the registration office." An editorialist commented then that "the only possible excuse that might be offered, but has not been, is that he thought the end would justify the means." Before he could be sentenced, Sutton was pardoned by a fellow saloon hater, Governor Marion E. Hay.[13]

Thus one can see in what the radicals did and in what they said many of the tensions in American life at the end of the nineteenth century which became driving forces in the prohibition movement: the nativist-immigrant tension which intruded into the temperance agitation and so outraged John Miller Murphy as early as the 1870's and reappeared from time to time; the rural-urban cultural tension which was a source of so much anxiety within the Grange movement; the class-consciousness apparent in the earliest antisaloon laws; and, basic to all of this, the sharp strains of opposing moral codes competing in the same society, so clear in Dr. Matthews' speeches and sermons.

All of these tensions have been illuminated recently by a sociologist, Joseph R. Gusfield, whose study of the Women's Christian Temperance Union suggests a synthesis. His study stresses that social status and social mobility have been significant and unexplored motives in temperance enthusiasms. Gusfield shows that temperance reform to the WCTU in the nineteenth century was part of a broad concern with environmental reform which tried to assimilate lower groups into the middle class. It was sensitive to labor problems, to slum conditions, and to saloon evils. One of Gusfield's contributions has been to illustrate how solidly established in the "secure" middle class the WCTU leaders were in the 1880's—their husbands were doctors, lawyers, prosperous merchants, and wealthy farmers. The leaders were women anxiously concerned with the effects of industrialization upon middle-class America, and their goal was to reform the conditions which seemed to threaten their way of life. Their hope was to elevate the lower classes economically, socially, and morally. The WCTU was extending, through temperance reform, a ladder for those who wanted to climb into the middle class.[14]

This invitation is illustrated beautifully in the attempt of some temperance leaders to encourage the "coffee house" substitute for the saloon. In Seattle, Dr. Matthews led the movement, hoping that the coffee house would satisfy all the functions of a saloon except drunkenness and depravity—hoping, in short, that saloon patrons might really share the aspirations of members in good standing of the First Presbyterian church. He described his proposals with an unmistakable emphasis on class values:

> The coffee house substitute for the saloon is not intended as a hoboes' resort nor a pauperizing institution. It is a legitimate, respectable place for any man who desires to enter, read the papers, study the magazines, inform himself on current literature and write a letter home to his aged mother, who anxiously watches the footsteps of the coming and going postman for some tidings of her lost boy.

Thus the temperance cause might bring the rural, Protestant, Anglo-Saxon values of sobriety, thrift, industry, and responsibility to the lower classes.[15]

Gusfield's most significant work, however, has been to show the changing character of temperance leadership after 1885. Leadership in the WCTU at the local level, he says, began to "shift toward lower areas of the socio-economic scale."[16] In 1885, for example, 53 per cent of the husbands of WCTU leaders in thirty-eight representative cities were "professional and semi-professional . . . managers and officials." In 1910, this figure had fallen to 37.1 per cent, while the number of leaders whose husbands were clerks and skilled laborers had increased markedly. In other words, leadership was shifting toward the lower-middle class.

If this was true, then a corollary should follow: those individuals who were most vocal and active in their temperance convictions in the 1890's and early 1900's would most likely have been those on the margins of middle-class identification to whom status had a high urgency. Their backgrounds should reflect a high degree of class mobility.

This corollary holds up well against the backgrounds of the "radical" temperance leaders in Washington in 1892. Most of these leaders came to Washington in the 1880's with the railroads, and their geographic mobility was probably an expression of social mobility as well. Most of them had been born in the upper Midwest or in New England, though some were immigrants from Great Britain and

Sweden. Most of them, so far as the records can reveal, spent their childhood and adolescence in a marginal type of farm life or in the working class environments of towns and cities, then moved through frequently heroic efforts of self-education into the middle class. Their occupations in 1892 reflected their newly achieved status, for they were teachers, real estate salesmen, preachers, self-educated "engineers," clerks, "builders," bookkeepers, grocers, printers. Only a few were in the secure middle class of college-educated professionals and really prosperous farmers and merchants. Most of them came to the Prohibition party at about the same time they came to Washington, when they were pulling themsleves into the middle class. They gave the party its strength in the 1880's.[17]

This motive of status identification can also help explain the diminution of the Prohibition party during the 1890's. In the first place, secure middle-class status came to demand membership in one of the middle-class political parties, and those who looked beyond their status achievements of the 1880's were drawn to the Republicans or the Democrats. In the second place, the Prohibition party—because it wanted to win votes and because strong prohibition sentiment first arose in the rural areas—was so deeply soaked in agrarian grievances and antibusiness passions that it could not hope to attract the urban middle class. Before the decade was out, the more astute Prohibs had come to realize that E. B. Sutton had been absolutely wrong when he had announced in 1889 that the wets could prevent either of the major parties from making any antisaloon commitment and that prohibitionists must wash their hands of "non-partisan nonsense." Just the opposite was true: to most of the drys, the status values of being Republicans or Democrats had become more important than being a partisan Prohib. Their dryness was disoriented, awaiting a nonpartisan outlet. Thus Austin Griffiths, Prohibition candidate for prosecutor of Chehalis County in 1892, slipped quietly into the Republican party when he joined a big-city law firm.[18]

The Prohibs might have joined with the Populists in 1892 or 1894 and found in fusion a graceful exit from the political scene, but the Populists would not have them: the people's party needed the German farmers more than it needed the beer-haters. The Populists got the discontented, both wet and dry; the Republicans and Democrats got the urban middle class, both wet and dry; and the Prohibs were left with only the most wooly fanatics. The prohibition movement was forced, in a real sense, to become nonpartisan. At about the same time, devout and intelligent reformers of many persuasions—direct legislation, direct primary, direct election of United States senators, women's suffrage—were responding to the same pressures. They discovered that they must sow their seeds on both political fronts and then cultivate them with patience and precision. For example, the reformer William S. U'Ren of Oregon turned nonpartisan and became the "fourth branch of the state legislature." In the rewarding phases of his drive to achieve direct legislation, he traded votes, gave promises, and developed into a lobbyist par excellence. It is in many such changes that one can chart the transition between the Prohibition party and the nonpartisan Anti-Saloon League at a time when the "radicals" were seeking new moorings.

One of the "radicals" who encouraged the revisionists to leave the Prohibition party—and to accept evolution rather than revolution as the new posture of the prohibition movement—was Ernest H. Cherrington, an early leader of the Washington Anti-Saloon League and later the historian of the national organization. He wrote this obituary for the orthodox: "The Prohibition party was a demand to right a great wrong by political revolution rather than by political evolution. Strictly speaking, the Prohibition party was a political party in name only. It was not a party; it was a crusade."[19]

The career of another radical, James Duncan, illustrates how widely diffused throughout the middle class the enthusiasms of temperance actually were. Duncan, for years secretary of the Seattle Central Labor Council and a principal leader during the Seattle General Strike, was a hard-core prohibitionist who was convinced that workers would never achieve their proper position in American industrial society until they learned the virtues of abstinence. He was a deeply religious Presbyterian who never touched a drop of liquor in his life, and he was a good friend of E. H. Cherrington. Even though he worked closely with solid Republican capitalists like Robert Chase Erskine, Laurence Colman, and J. R. Justice on plans to make the state dry, at the same time he was attacking them for their attitudes toward organized labor.[20]

Of all the radicals, however, none was more representative than Duncan's friend, George F. Cotterill. Born in England in 1865, Cotterill was the son of a gardener. The family migrated to New Jersey when he was seven years old. He graduated from high school and

went on to become a self-educated engineer. After arriving in Tacoma in 1884 with twenty-five cents to his name, he was, progressively,
a housekeeper, a bookkeeper, a transit man on a survey crew, then
assistant city engineer of Seattle and a partner of R. H. Thomson,
who was a college-educated, middle-class temperance worker. Cotterill had been a Republican, then a Prohibitionist, a Populist, then a
Democrat. In 1900 he was active in the hopeless campaign against
prostitution in Seattle. His convictions included strong beliefs in municipal ownership and the single tax, and as a state senator he wrote
the women's suffrage amendment to the constitution. He sponsored
the drive to get the initiative and referendum in Washington. His
friends included William Jennings Bryan and William S. U'Ren.
When he was the leading Democratic state senator, he cooperated
closely with a Republican governor and Republican legislators to get
a local option bill in 1909.

Cotterill became Seattle's reform mayor in 1912 after a campaign
which stressed that he stood for "No Surrender to Private Monopoly
Brokers' Conspiracy." The future of Seattle, he had said, must not be
shadowed by the "dollar mark, but brightened by an increasing de-
votion to the ideals of Human Helpfulness and Human Happiness."
During his tenure he outraged many civic leaders as well as many
common citizens with his antifornication squads from the police department which swept through downtown hotels. And he tried
once—during the "Potlatch Riots" of 1913 between members of the
Industrial Workers of the World and sailors from a United States
battleship—to close down the saloons. Probably the state's leading
prohibitionist and one of the most highly regarded of the more extreme reformers, he considered the Prohibition Initiative of 1914 the
greatest achievement of his life. He was assisted in this victory by
business leaders, many of whom thought of him as a single-tax, Socialist, red-flag mayor.[21]

The motif in liquor reform most muted among the "radicals" was
that of economic self-interest. To hear the economic notes most clearly, one must move toward those who can conveniently be called the
"moderates" of the prohibition movement. The "moderates" were
those who could not be whipped into frenzied visions of devils, and
who did not find in the antidrink crusade any release from personal
fears and tensions. They could, however, find some solid satisfactions

in the movement against the saloon. Austin Griffiths, who helped the chambers of commerce of Seattle and Bremerton clean out their saloons on two different occasions, remarked that "nothing raises public morality so quickly as a loss of business."[22]

There were many parts of the state's business community whose position was the moderate one. Most simply and directly, there were those men in the restaurant business who resented the competition of saloons and whose efforts were first directed toward laws which would prohibit free lunches in saloons, then toward the saloon itself. For other groups of businessmen, the issue was somewhat broader. A newspaper editor put it this way: "The saloon man realizes that if he is to stay it will be because he convinces a majority of the voters that his presence is essential to the city's development. . . . His opponent knows that if the saloon is to be ousted he must convince the majority that the saloon does not help the city's growth."[23]

This position was a popular one during the local option elections, when the economic arguments always paralleled the moral ones. The Anti-Saloon League leaders always had statistics to "prove" that the cost of saloons, measured in hard dollars and cents, was more than the saloons were worth to any community. The standard ASL analysis took this pattern:

> The city of North Yakima, Wash., has twenty-two saloons. These saloons pay to the city in license fees, $22,000; rent, $30,000; by labor . . . $79,200; by labor in brewery, $25,000; total, $156,200.
> The saloons cost the people of the city: By drinks sold, $275,440 (for a year of 313 days, which leaves out Sundays.)
> Last year the police department cost the city $9,691.12 and its receipts were $6,478.45, leaving a net cost of $3,212.67. The total arrests of the year were 1,559, and of these 904 were for drunkenness. This gives a percentage of drunkenness of 57. This percentage of the net cost is $1,831.32. It represents what the saloon cost the city through the police department. Added to the approximate cost of drinks it brings the total to $277,271.32.
> This makes the saloons an expense to the city each year of at least $121,071.32.
> This does not include the cost of county jail and hospitals.[24]

Other approaches to businessmen stressed the cost of state institutions traceable to drink, the increase in bank deposits allegedly enjoyed by communities when they went dry, and the more favorable tax rates in such communities. Still another emphasized the costs of saloons as measured by the inefficiency of labor. A Portland editori-

alist, commenting on the prohibition movement in Washington, reported that "the great pressure for restricting or eliminating the evil
is coming from the employers of labor, to whom the economic feature of the question has appealed in a forcible manner."

The writer noted the unsentimental stand taken by the Farmers'
Union of Lind, Washington, which resolved that "farmers, in this
immediate community have experienced serious and expensive results
to the loss and damage of our crops from the unreliability of harvest
hands on account of a too free use of intoxicating liquors during the
harvest season."[25] This had been a common temperance argument
for a hundred years, but the rapidly changing character of employment, on the farm and in the city, had given it new force.

A related but somewhat more subtle and complex drive in the anti-
saloon movement among certain businessmen was the threat that saloon interests presented to the power structure of many small towns
and cities. As the number of saloons increased, their owners were increasingly tempted to use their influence among the working class,
whose thirsts they served, to attack the dominance of the entrenched
group of business leaders who had traditionally directed the affairs
of their communities without challenge. The attacks must have been
frequent after 1900. To businessmen who lost out in such power
struggles, the antisaloon sentiment could approach the passions of a
personal vendetta. This was the case with Marion E. Hay, later governor of the state, whose power in the small town of Wilbur, near
Spokane, had been taken from him in a miniature revolution. He described it to a friend in 1909:

> For years and years Wilbur has been absolutely in the grasp of the
> liquor element. From the time the town was incorporated up to about
> ten years ago, the affairs of the city were handled by Mr. Farnsworth,
> Mr. Parrish, Mr. Alexander and your humble servant with a few of the
> others of the leading businessmen of the town. We only maintained
> control so long as we allowed the liquor interests to have a certain
> amount of freedom. In 1898 or '99 we raised the saloon license . . .
> to $1000. At the next election they put us completely out . . . and from
> that time on they held absolute sway in Wilbur. . . . During all the
> years the town's affairs were handled by businessmen, our tax levy
> never reached five mills . . . the tax rate now has been up to ten
> mills. . . .[26]

In Wenatchee, a friend of Hay's named John A. Gellatly (later
mayor of the city and for one term the lieutenant governor of the

state) had a similar experience. A depression refugee, Gellatly came to Wenatchee in 1900 where he did well during the next decade in apples and land. About 1907, from his desk in his real estate office, he observed that the saloons were controlling the town while "certain social conditions" were getting worse. The city jail, in fact, could not hold all the drunks that reeled from the booze dens along Wenatchee Avenue. His account of his feelings comes rather close to defining the reform impulse among men of his class:

> I had been a farmer nearly all my life and had never given much thought to social conditions. For some reason which I do not yet fully understand I suddenly got the conviction that perhaps I was as much to blame as anyone else for this sordid social condition, and that if a city had to maintain its civic expenses by such debauching means [saloons paid annual license fees of $1,000] we had better do something about it or disband our corporate responsibility. I also had a family of several children who were being constantly forced to encounter this morally depraving situation. There were many fine people here who felt as I did, and the upshot developed whereby an organization of similarly minded men got together in an effort to remedy the condition.[27]

The "upshot" was that Gellatly ran for mayor on a "no-license" ticket and won.

There is no way, of course, to measure with any precision the extent of moderate thinking among the state's business leaders. Some were but passive participants in the antisaloon movement—like Rufus Woods, editor of the Wenatchee *Daily World* and a significant leader of opinion in central Washington, who was personally a dry, never accepted liquor advertising, but, on the other hand, never campaigned against liquor. Others entered the movement without inhibitions. Robert Chase Erskine, a prosperous real estate developer in Seattle during this period and an active moderate, said that the antisaloon cause became an important movement in Washington only when "the substantial business people" of the state gave it their support.[28]

What is remarkable is that most of them came forward with their support at about the same time, i.e., during the first ten years of the twentieth century. This was the decade of the state's most rapid growth, the decade when the population shot from about five hundred thousand in 1900 to over a million by 1910. It was the time of great social thrust and shift, a time when—as a Prosser home-

steader named William Guernsey remembered it—"the pioneer
days seemed to end and the modern days begin." "Before," said
Guernsey, "we seemed as one family, sharing our joys and sorrows,
but now [after 1910] there began to be a division. It is a difficult
thing to explain. It seemed to come when money became the yard-
stick for measuring men and women."[29]

It was also a time of growing power for the state's labor unions,
and there were many moderates among laboring groups. James Duncan marshaled antisaloon sentiment in the Washington State Federation of Labor, and that organization was bitterly divided on the liquor question until 1916, when the bartenders' and brewery workers'
locals were broken by state-wide prohibition. For years after 1916,
the State Federation was solidly prohibitionist, and it criticized Samuel Gompers of the American Federation of Labor for his opposition
to the Eighteenth Amendment.[30]

Antisaloon sentiment was also strong in the most radical of the
labor unions. Leaders of the Industrial Workers of the World detested saloons because they "robbed the workers" and made them unfit
for the class struggle. IWW dogma held that capitalists used saloons
to tranquilize and humiliate the proletariat. The IWW on some occasions suppressed bootleggers and closed down drinking places when
its members were on strike.[31] Thus antisaloon sentiment might promote both radical and conservative labor leadership: it might be a
protest against a threat to class solidarity, as with the IWW, or a
protest against an obstacle to mobility into the middle class.

Another "moderate" group were those clergymen who opposed the
saloon but would not follow their evangelical colleagues all the way
to an antidrink war. These men—some Catholic, some Lutheran, some
Episcopalian—were part of the prohibition movement against the
evils of the saloon. They represented the social conscience of the
many middle-class citizens who had no direct economic interest in
the prohibition movement but who were eager to see the saloon go.[32]

A definition of the moderates, then, should accommodate all those
who believed the saloon to be an evil institution and, in an age of reform, were willing to do something about it. But their ambivalence
toward the use of alcohol restrained them from any commitments to
the antidrink crusade. Moderate solutions proposed for the problems
of the saloon, therefore, lacked unity, and until the ASL welded to-

gether all the antisaloon sentiments, there was no coherent moderate program.

Before 1900, some held for "high license," feeling that a reasonable solution might be to tax the worst saloons out of existence. The radical response was to insist that license fees could never distinguish between good saloons and bad ones, and that the crimes of the saloons bore no relationship to high or low license.[33] Fees did go up, though, from about three hundred dollars in 1890 to around a thousand dollars by 1910. This probably drove some of the independent saloons into the arms of the brewers, who could easily afford the increase.

Among other moderates, there was enthusiasm for the Swedish solution called the Gothenburg System, which was a system of state-owned dispensaries. This would eliminate private profit from the liquor business and thus strike at the root of all evils. The solution was championed in the United States by Governor Ben Tillman of South Carolina and was seriously debated in the Washington State House of Representatives in 1901. However, Ernest Cherrington, who could not tolerate moderation, called this an attempt "to clothe the traffic with a garment of respectability vouched for by the state itself . . . the most insidious and dangerous aspect of the liquor problem to date."[34] He and the other radicals prevented any prolonged consideration of this system after the turn of the century.

The proposal which finally unified the moderates was one upon which the radicals were willing to compromise while prohibition evolved. The solution was popular sovereignty, or local option. Under local option laws, each community could decide for itself whether or not to abolish its saloons. Local option proposals did not include abolishing liquor from private homes, and for the moderates this proposal had all the blessings of individual dignity, democracy, and local control. For the radicals, it was the first step toward drying up the state piecemeal, toward gradually isolating the wet areas, toward shattering any unified opposition to prohibition into small geographical fragments. Proposals for local option drew to the prohibition movement many who would otherwise not have been there. The Seattle *Post-Intelligencer*, for example, opposed state prohibition laws but favored local option.[35] It was a cause which could attract reformers from all political parties.

Governor Marion E. Hay, under whom the local option law was finally enacted, was a politician who inspired the confidence of most moderates. A Republican, a reformer of sorts, he favored more democracy and more local control. He stood sternly against the saloon, but he was not willing to force prohibition upon any community that did not want it. To Governor Hay, the old-line radicals were cranks. He wrote to one of them:

> We are both, I think, trying to arrive at the same goal. You want to force people into prohibition whether they are educated up to it or not. . . . As soon as I feel that the people of the State by a decisive majority are ready to banish saloons then I am willing to support such a measure . . . but there are certain localities in this state that are decidedly in favor of saloons. For instance . . . Walla Walla. . . . I feel it would be an injustice to force that community to go upon a dry basis at this time.

To the president of Washington State College, who objected to the fact that even with antisaloon local option, people could still buy intoxicating drinks for home consumption, Governor Hay wrote out his belief in individual liberty in an incisive statement of the moderate position:

> The object of these anti-saloon laws is to prohibit the indiscriminate sale of liquor and to remove temptation from the rising generation. The old toper who has created the appetite is bound to have the liquor if it is possible for him to get it. If a man wishes to buy liquor and take it home with him, that is his right, but what we wish to prevent is the open sale of liquor and the maintenance of the saloon where young men are invited to spend both money and time.[36]

Governor Hay and his friends in the Anti-Saloon League did much to make the antisaloon cause thoroughly respectable. The cause drew to it the middle-class energies that would shortly sweep over the social and political life of the state and the nation. Local option, like the secret ballot, the initiative, the referendum, women's suffrage, was an instrument sharpened for the work of reform which the middle class could use in good conscience.

The defenders of the status quo worked under grievous handicaps. Few men, for instance, were brazen enough to defend the saloon as a positive good at a time when its evils were so well published. Few of the "conservatives" had the courage of their platitudes about the necessity of evil in the affairs of men, though some insisted that whatever followed the saloon would be as bad or worse. Others objected

to what they saw as an attack upon the institution of private property. But these thoughts were the antithesis of the reformists' faith that
all evil could be obliterated by intelligent pieces of legislation.

Conservatives also suffered from an embarrassing inability to organize into effective political opposition. Though their points of view
sometimes prevailed in the state legislature, it was only around the
brewing and distilling industries that they could rally, and most conservatives resisted being labeled tools of the "drunkard-making business." Even today it is difficult to distinguish in that period between
what was disinterested philosophical persuasion and what was a
sophistical attempt to justify self-interest.

And the nature of local option crusades also made conservative action extremely awkward. Opposing democracy was not very graceful,
and few of the urban conservatives, other than the individually concerned brewers and wholesalers, would bother themselves with what
the voters in the towns and the rural areas wanted to do with the saloons. Probably a strong factor in this reluctance was the primitive
reactions of some brewers and saloon men when they were endan-
gered by local option: they sometimes threatened communities with
economic ruin or herded in colonies of transients to stuff ballot boxes.
In short, they made it rather distasteful for men of good will to rise
in their defense. Consequently, even those actually facing disaster
from prohibition—the saloonkeepers, the industry, the hotel owners,
the hop growers, the laboring groups in the industry—did not co-
alesce. The Anti-Prohibition Labor League, for example, which drew
the bartenders, waiters, brewery workers, and beer wagon drivers,
refused to accept money from the saloon or liquor interests in their
campaign against state prohibition in 1914.[37]

The businessmen who stood to suffer in the tax loss consequential
to an antisaloon measure had no effective leadership until Seattle was
aroused by Initiative Measure Number 3. Then Judge Thomas Burke,
formerly of the temperance cause, and Henry Broderick, who, like
Burke, was a leader in the highest financial circles, opposed the
movement. Their Anti-Prohibition Association employed Erastus
Brainerd, former editor of the *Post-Intelligencer* and probably the
most brilliant and accomplished publicist in the state, to argue the
case for saloon taxes. In his speeches and in his literature, Brainerd
elaborated the cherished wet contentions: drinking is a consequence
of evil, not a cause; if the saloons go, the "blind pigs" will be worse

for their freedom from control; abolishing saloons will force drinking into the homes and make drunkards of the women; thus the saloons support both taxes and morals. These ideas found an easy reception in the German-American societies, in some labor groups, and
in various anonymous "Good Government" leagues.[38]

The most philosophical of the conservative attacks on prohibition,
however, came from the center of the state's hop industry. Weaving
through the controversy, the Puyallup *Valley Tribune* groped for the
tragic concept of life and politics:

> The world is not perfect. It is very imperfect. But our contention is
> that it is impossible to make men good by acts of legislation. . . .
> It is high time that over-zealous reformers learned that it is a danger-
> ous thing to interfere with the workings of man's nature. . . . A re-
> former, or deformer, as we shall some day learn to call him, of the
> type which desires to make everybody good by acts of legislation, is a
> hater of Nature, and must be. He has no faith in the laws that govern
> the world. . . .
> The need of genuine reform is frankly admitted. Man must grow; he
> must develop strength and character. But the fact that he needs to grow
> and needs to develop strength and moral fibre is sufficient proof that
> he will . . . man shall attain unto the majesty of himself, through the
> natural working of the law that dwells within the soul.

This Emerson-on-the-Puyallup was quoted in full and supported by
the Seattle *Argus,* whose editor, H. A. Chadwick, was from the beginning to the bitter end the most intelligent spokesman for the opponents of prohibition in the state. To Chadwick, there were the
strong and the weak, for men were not equal: "Shall those who are
strong eschew all the pleasures and good things of life because they
are harmful to men and women of weak mentality who have not the
moral stamina to withstand temptation?"

If so, he said, then let us have a law against sexual intercourse too.
Prohibition, he wrote almost weekly, denied human nature. He had a
consistently caustic contempt for the prohibitionists, and he said of
George F. Cotterill when the reformer left the mayor's office in 1914:
"Mayor Cotterill is a rabid prohibitionist—one of those men who
would reform the world and cause all people to be good by force. He
has given a wonderful exhibition of the utter impracticability of this
class when given power. Mr. Cotterill, good-bye."

He described for his readers the president of the Farmers' Union:
". . . one of those intolerant prohibitionists who, because he has some

weak-minded relative who cannot or does not want to control his appetite . . . would place the burden of doing so on society."[39]

Chadwick was a classic conservative. He was against labor leaders, Billy Sunday, direct legislation, and municipal ownership, against Theodore Roosevelt, against Woodrow Wilson. Thoroughly oriented toward big business, books, music, art, and automobiles, he wrote only for the urban sophisticates and had no power at all in any local option election. When prohibition threatened Seattle, he was too late. The failure of Chadwick, and of those for whom he wrote, to affect the course of the antisaloon movement measured the slight influence of their class.

The real strength of any "conservative" opposition, of course, lay in the great army of saloon patrons whose thirst and fellowship provided a livelihood for the state's 4,824 liquor dealers before local option in 1909. (According to ASL figures, only six states had higher numerical ratios of liquor dealers to customers.)[40] Even though there was no vocal "vote as you drink" campaign, this army formed the sullen core of resistance to the prohibition movement whose pro-saloon votes held out pockets of wet territory until 1914. Occasionally one of the more articulate captains would enter a local option campaign to defend the saloon as one of the natural rights of man, but seldom with much persuasion. The argument did not stand well against the talk of tax cuts, vice, evil, and corruption.

The antisaloon forces had the big guns—local option, women's suffrage, initiative, organized political power—and all on the crest of middle-class reform enthusiasms. In the end they even convinced many of the saloon regulars to vote not as they drank but as they dreamed the good middle-class dream of a polite and sober society.

7

The Irrepressible Conflict, 1900-14

WHILE THE RAILROADS were bringing thousands and thousands of families to the state of Washington during the 1890's, a small group of "prohibs" in Oberlin, Ohio, formed the first Anti-Saloon League in the United States. Their efforts in that state were so successful that in 1895 they organized the Anti-Saloon League of America, which in turn organized its Washington State Anti-Saloon League affiliate in 1898.

In the Anti-Saloon League, the emotional power of the Protestant evangelical churches was being disciplined for militant secular action. The League used the individual congregation as the basic organizational unit, and the individual minister acted as a sort of precinct whip under the direction of professional organizers tied together under a highly centralized authority. Within each state organization, a board of trustees represented the various congregations. The board "appointed" a state superintendent who had been nominated by the national office to direct programs of education, propaganda, and political coercion which would advance the cause and the crusade.

The very name of the organization reflected an accurate appraisal of the national temper. While the stiff-necked Prohibition party was sinking into disrepute because of its extremism, the star of the ASL was rising. The national temper was increasingly antisaloon but not yet antidrink, just as it was, say, antitrust but not antibusiness. This does not mean, however, that the ASL was in any way a front organization for conspirators, for the real intent of its leadership was never deeply concealed. Peter Odegard's study emphasized this point:

> During the early days the league trained its guns on the saloon, going so far as to disavow any desire for complete prohibition. Its literature, however, made no such distinction but depicted the entire liquor traffic

as the enemy of society, the home, the individual, the church, law, order, and humanity.[1]

In Washington, the evolution of the movement the League hoped to lead was painfully slow in these early years. In 1900, for example, the Good Templar leader George F. Cotterill ran for mayor in Seattle on the Fusion ticket (Democrat, Silver Republican, Populist) and had many forces immediately in his favor. The city was beginning to react to the excesses of commercial sin which it had so willingly provided the gold seekers of 1898, and Cotterill wanted to clean up the town. Even "Col." A. J. Blethen, publisher of the Seattle *Times* and a man who prided himself in his "realistic" view of human nature, stood for Cotterill, the reformer and prohibitionist. Blethen soothed the anxieties of Seattle businessmen by saying that Cotterill could not close the saloons if he wanted to because he would be violating the law if he tried. Blethen felt that a good mayor could and should, however, "relegate bawdy houses and all their connections to such portions of the town as would not disturb honest people."[2]

The Seattle *Post-Intelligencer,* on the other hand, caricaturized Cotterill as a villain who concealed a knife (labeled "theories"), a blackjack (labeled "single tax"), and a bomb ("prohibition").[3] And the paper had good fun with the spectacle of the state's Democrats supporting a prohibitionist.

The *P-I,* however, had little to sell but the status quo, and Blethen had fashioned an image of his man as a vigorous and dashing, yet honest and safe, reform candidate. Cotterill had many friends in the newly organized Anti-Saloon League of Seattle, and that group was quick to endorse him. Then on election day a "forged circular" was distributed widely across Seattle—allegedly by the Republican campaign committee—which appeared to be an ASL publication. The circular promised voters that Cotterill could and certainly would close the saloons.[4] He lost the election, 3,669 to 5,182. It may well have been that the ASL endorsement, reinforced by the circular, contributed a great deal to his defeat.

However this may be, the weakness of the state ASL in these early years was apparent on all sides. After the Seattle election, it had neither the agility nor the strength for an effective counterattack. Under the leadership of a Dr. J. C. Thoms, the League conducted a rather moderate campaign of education until 1905 when, according to the research of Peter Odegard, Dr. Thoms absconded to Alaska with the League's treasury.[5] Thoms was succeeded by Ernest Cherrington, an Ohio born and trained ASL professional saloon fighter who was also a talented and energetic writer and editor. While serving as state superintendent of the ASL, Cherrington edited the League's paper, the *Citizen*, in Seattle, built up a strong organization of churches, solicited funds, and began the investigation of every candidate for state office to determine his worthiness for an ASL endorsement. It was Cherrington who gave structure and power to an organization which would soon be strong enough to manipulate the state legislature.

He knew how to direct the increasingly strong antisaloon sentiments of the state into channels where political power could be generated. His *Citizen* was immediately for local option on the liquor question, for recall, for the direct primary, for initiative and referendum—i.e., thoroughly reformist in tone and content. It printed Edwin Markham's "The Man with the Hoe" at a time when the poem was being quoted by farm and labor leaders. It urged Sunday closures. In a state where reform sentiment was gaining momentum—the railroads and the big party bosses were the public villains—the *Citizen* was only slightly ahead of the public mind. This was just where Cherrington wanted to stay, moving slowly toward a full campaign at the most opportune time.[6]

In the early 1900's there were signs that this time was not too far in the future. The Grange resolved to expel any member who had had anything to do with the sale of liquor. More and more cities were enforcing Sunday closure laws, increasing saloon license fees, and passing ordinances against the free lunch. The State Criminal Code even included a law which made the possession of cigarettes a misdemeanor, a law which was passed in 1907 with only two votes against it. The sentiments to which prohibition might be harnessed were indeed evolving.[7]

Certain headlines from the Spokane *Spokesman-Review* during these years provide an interesting chronicle of this evolution:

Ministers Condemn Wineroom Attachments of Many Saloons (1901)
Prominent Citizens Condemn Winerooms (1901)
Chief of Police Orders Couches Taken Out of Winerooms (1901)
City Council Says Remove All Boxes and Winerooms (1901)
Charter Revision Committee Votes to Raise License Fee (1903)

Mayor Says Boxes and Curtains Can Stay But Establishments Can't
Serve Refreshments to Less than 4 Behind a Door (1903)
Justice Hinkle Rules Bartenders Guilty When They Serve Minors (1904)
J. H. Wilmot Asks for Ban on Free Lunches—
Unfair to Restaurants (1905)
WCTU in Mass Meeting, Discuss Sunday Closure (1906)
Kid Scaler's Saloon Transformed Into Rescue Mission (1909)
Police Commissioner Orders All Screens That Obstruct View
of Bars Removed (1909)
Police Ban Sleepers from Saloons (1911)
Commissioners Revoke License of Mecca Saloon After Hearing Evidence
That It Is A Hangout for Immoral Men and Women (1911)
Spokane Has 183 Saloons, Had 239 Three Years Ago (1914)[8]

Cherrington began to apply the political pressure of his organization by having the member churches send memorials to the legislature on local option. About the same time the *Citizen* started publishing pictures of saloons owned by politicians. Cherrington claimed
that the *Citizen's* technique was measurably effective, that it had, for
example, caused the defeat of Henry Beck, candidate for the legislature whose normal majority of fifteen hundred votes was cut to a minority after photos of his saloon were sent to every voter in Beck's
district.[9]

In 1907, both the *P-I* and the *Times* endorsed local option as a
reasonable solution to the liquor question. When a local option bill
was killed in the House of Representatives in Olympia, forty-three to
forty-four, the ASL publicized the names of dissenting legislators
and set itself to end their political careers. The Grange publicly condemned those legislators who were "too sick" to vote.[10]

By 1908, neither of the major political parties in the state could
afford to ignore the significance of the antisaloon movement and the
power of the Anti-Saloon League. Indeed, the league had its stand-
ard-bearers in the ranks of both parties. When the Republicans met
in May, their convention endorsed, among other things, the policies of
Theodore Roosevelt, child labor laws, an employers' liability act, and
local option on saloons. "We believe," the delegates wrote, "that the
issue of local option is purely a local one and this convention records
itself in favor of a reasonable local option bill to be enacted by the
next legislature."[11] This plank was aligned perfectly with Cherrington's principle of evolution, and if the state ASL had a timetable, the

plank probably met its most optimistic expectations. It was clear to everyone that the Republicans would win in 1908 and that the legislature would be bound to "reasonable" local option.

The unenviable task of encouraging Democrats to think dry thoughts fell upon George F. Cotterill, a principal ASL figure and a party leader, inasmuch as he was one of only three Democrats in the state Senate. Cotterill was treated less kindly, perhaps, than a party leader of his stature has a right to expect. Meeting in Spokane, the Democrats ignored local option by voting 530 to 116 in favor of a referendum on state-wide prohibition by constitutional amendment, thus throwing Cotterill a blanket when he wanted only a napkin.[12] At such a time, the referendum would have done more harm than good to the ASL cause, but there was really no danger that the Democratic platform would receive any legislative attention.

In 1908, one seedbed of reform came into full bloom in Washington when the state changed from the old method of nomination by party convention to the more progressive system of state-wide primary elections. The experiment that year was with the preferential primary, a complex scheme for avoiding the corrupting influence of party conventions, and, at the same time, for making impossible the selection of a gubernatorial candidate who did not enjoy the support of a majority from his own party. In practice, the preferential primary election allowed the voter two votes in the gubernatorial race—one for his first preference and another for his second preference among the names on his party's slate. According to the law, the candidate with the highest combined total of first and second preference votes was declared the nominee. The theory behind such arithmetic was that in a field of six candidates, for example, the two-vote ballot would produce a nominee who had more votes for him than against him—a condition not at all guaranteed by the old one-vote machinery. If the reasoning was devious, the motive was at least honorable, and voters must have marveled at a reform which brought them such a bounteous harvest of democracy in the first season.

One of the contenders was Henry McBride, a reform-minded Republican supported by many of the wheat-growing counties, who had been governor of the state from 1901 to 1905. The party convention had dumped him in 1904, largely because of his stand against the railroad lobby. He had been succeeded by Albert Mead, an old-style Republican more suitable to the directors of the Northern Pacific.[13]

Both of these men wanted to return to Olympia in 1909, despite the perils of a state-wide popularity contest.

Another man who welcomed the chance to campaign among the people was Samuel G. Cosgrove, a wealthy lawyer and wheat farmer from Garfield County. Cosgrove had been a delegate to the convention of 1889; he had always wanted to be governor but had never been able to command the attention of a nominating convention.[14]

All of these men were pledged, of course, to the "reasonable" local option plank of the Republican platform. Mead, however, first raised the issue in Republican politics (perhaps to compensate for his reputation as a railroad governor), and the saloon forces set themselves solidly against him. It was then that the Knights of the Royal Arch, the organization of saloon men and liquor dealers, pledged votes to Henry McBride and began their own campaign of voter registration.

The ASL backed Mead because of his stand on local option and probably because they thought him to be the antisaloon candidate most likely to win. The League gave its second preference to Samuel Cosgrove. Because he had been a local option man at least as long as Albert Mead had been, Cosgrove was somewhat disturbed by the ASL endorsement. He campaigned with a desperation which, according to Edmond Meany, probably ruined his health. He may have hoped to verify the prediction of the Portland *Oregonian* that "a majority of the people [of Washington] want a local option law but that there is a good percentage of such people who will not sacrifice their personal preference for Governor at the dictation of the radicals."[15]

Cosgrove won the Republican nomination, but it was a curious and confusing election. His combined total of first and second-choice votes was greater than the total of any other candidate, but both Mead and McBride had more first-choice votes than did Cosgrove. The ASL endorsement given Cosgrove as a second-choice candidate probably had a great deal to do with his victory. (Voters made the first-choice race a lively contest, giving McBride 33,507 votes, Mead 32,357, and Cosgrove 25,519. In the second-choice voting, however, Cosgrove had a clear majority with 32,148 to Mead's 17,054 and McBride's 14,085.)

The legislative races were an even more impressive index of ASL strength. Of the forty-four men marked wet by the ASL because of their position in 1907, only fifteen survived the elections of 1908. In

King County, eight were marked and six survived; in Pierce County, six were marked and one survived; in Spokane County, five were marked and two survived; in Walla Walla County, none of the three marked were returned to the legislature.[16]

In January, 1909, when Albert Mead made his final remarks to the legislature, he placed a pointed emphasis on what would become the major political issue of the year: "The promise to enact a reasonable local option law," he said, "should receive your earnest and early attention. . . . This and other pledges should be sacredly kept."[17]

Then Samuel Cosgrove, who would never be able to perform the duties of his office and who was at the very moment close to death, admonished his colleagues like a stern father:

> There are some matters of legislation that I would like also to mention to you now, because I may not be with you again. I would like to see a good, strong local option law enacted in this state—and I want no foolishness about it either. It is fair to the men who manage the saloons; it is fair to the people who don't want them. . . .[18]

Cosgrove left for California, where he would soon die. In Olympia, there would be a great deal of foolishness.

Petitions on local option reached the legislature from church groups in all parts of the state. George F. Cotterill, the single Democrat in the state Senate in 1909, fulfilled the obligations of his party by introducing a bill to provide a referendum on state-wide prohibition. Even Cotterill's friends gave it small attention. The ASL bills were the Falconer Bill (S.B. 28, J. A. Falconer, Everett) and the Mc-Master Bill (H.B. 29, W. C. McMaster, Kenmore), both of them "county unit" bills, and it was over this provision that the legislature began to bleed.

The county unit was the immediate goal of the antisaloon forces. It would allow the rural areas to overwhelm the cities and towns in county local option elections. Under the county unit, the farmers could very possibly vote out most of the state's saloons. The "reasonable local option" phrase in the Republican platform, of course, encouraged the legislature to reflect all shades of opinion, and the county-unit proposal was opposed bitterly by most of the legislators who represented cities, some of whom favored the principle of local option but could not accept the county unit. The issue was really the degree of dictation to be allowed the rural areas. The Grange, the

WCTU, and the ASL pushed their people hard in what became a showdown battle.

In this supreme test of power, Ernest Cherrington was faced by the personification of all that he hated: the saloon lobby was led by former state senator Andrew Hemrick, president of the Seattle Brewing and Malting Company. He was the state's leading liquor capitalist, and he had been the "beer king" in the Senate until 1905. Debate opened in late January and continued vigorously and vehemently through twelve-hour days for more than a month. Probably no legislative session in the history of the state, not even the Populist fights of 1897, had been so heated with sustained clamor, with dedication and sincerity, and with pure hate. The Reverend Billy Sunday came trumpeting into the field, having enlisted one hundred business and professional men in Spokane who held prayer sessions in a chartered railroad car while they rolled toward Olympia, where they would march for the county-unit bill. Andrew Hemrick also had his marchers, and around and within the capitol, the battle began.

Early in February, Acting Governor Marion Hay broke precedent by appearing on the floor of the House.[19] Hay, the merchant who had fought saloon men for political power in the town of Wilbur, had never sought the governorship. He had always regarded himself as a weak speaker, one whose party service and sound business principles qualified him at most for the lieutenant governor's role.[20] But when it was clear that he would indeed be governor, he did not hesitate to use the office. The small-town merchant uncovered a flair for leadership that distinguished him at once as a reasonably open-minded reformer. Hay was convinced that the state should have a local option law, but when he appeared on the floor of the House, it was to listen as well as to influence.

There were speakers who said that the ASL bill was not the "reasonable" bill to which Republicans had pledged themselves. They called the bill, variously, "anti-saloon," "anti-drugstore," and "anti-people." It was clear that many observers—including Governor Hay himself—held with one representative who concluded that he was "in favor of local option, but . . . not in favor of prohibition."

Those legislators opposed to the county unit for whatever reason began the tedious business of amending the ASL bills to death. There followed, then, many long arguments over what percentage of alcohol should be defined as intoxicating, and, to corrode the patience of the ASL legislators, roll-call votes on every proposed amendment. One such proposal would have added the word "water" to the painfully drawn list of prohibited beverages, and it had to be voted down by roll call. These wet techniques were continued until all hope for the county unit had disappeared.[21]

The compromise was introduced by Senator Ralph Nichols of Seattle, a rather wet and very conservative Republican. Its most significant feature was that it made all incorporated towns and cities legal voting units. The possibilities of compromise were made more attractive to the hard county-unit men when the chairmen of the House and Senate appropriations committees—both men were wets—offered to restore certain meaty budget cuts to various districts if the representatives of these districts could find some pleasure in the Nichols Bill. When the spirit of compromise finally brought both wets and drys together, George Cotterill and an attorney from the governor's office assisted in the final draft.[22] The bill, which passed easily through both branches, made voting units of any city of the first, second, third, or fourth class; counties exclusive of the cities were also voting units. Petitions for local option elections required the signatures of 30 per cent of the registered voters and could be received every two years. "This," Cotterill wrote later, "was a compromise bill for all pending and cannot be considered as any man's bill. It was supported by the wets and represented the largest amount of local option they were willing to concede to the temperance forces."

Though Cotterill had worked on the Nichols Bill, he voted against it in the end when he knew that his vote was not needed to pass the bill and that his "no" would leave him in a "strategic position for future action in behalf of temperance." He sent to the desk a written denunciation of the bill which became the keynote for ASL disgust: the law, he wrote, was "temperance legislation with brewery modifications." At the same time the Master of the state Grange accused the Republican party of having "betrayed its pledge."[23]

This disgust bespeaks their radicalism, for the local option law of 1909, in each of its provisions, was a triumph of moderation. It was not an antidrink bill. Though it allowed voting units to prohibit the sale or the "giving away" of intoxicating drinks, it was explicitly not a challenge to private drinking. Druggists in antisaloon territory could sell on written orders for "medical or sacramental purposes."

The law gave individuals an almost total protection against drought by permitting them to carry into dry territory, in their personal baggage, a gallon of liquor and a case of beer. The law did not allow any local interference with the manufacture of liquor or beer —conceivably a saloonless town might include several breweries. But it was an antisaloon law insofar as it offered the machinery for the abolition of saloons to communities that did not want them. An instrument of popular sovereignty, it did not allow the rural areas to dictate to the urban centers. In short, the law gave a measure of control and a type of control that, to judge from the elections that followed, was what the people wanted in 1909. Saloon competition could be halted. The people of the state could experiment with antisaloon laws at a local level before they were asked to consider statewide prohibition.

To the radicals, of course, a law which allowed a saloon area to exist contiguous to antisaloon areas was no better than one which prohibited adultery in one room of a house but not in others. Their anxieties could be relieved only by world-wide prohibition. The ASL, however, wasted no time in futile ravings. It decided to get as much out of the 1909 legislature as it could before moving on toward the next evolutionary stage, and it did. After the blisters of the local option fight had begun to heal, the legislature passed a series of saloon restrictions: laws to keep minors and women out of saloons, a law making Sunday sales more serious offenses, a law to eliminate obstructions to the view of saloon interiors, a law prohibiting a wholesaler from holding an interest in a saloon. Cotterill got through a law making it a felony to sell liquor to Indians of even one-eighth blood. And his colleagues, curiously, produced two laws to protect drinking men—one prohibited any artificial flavor in whiskey and another banned the sale of whiskey less than four years old.

Acting Governor Hay had undoubtedly helped the antisaloon laws along by speaking sharply and critically of those Republican legislators who had, in the local option voting, ignored the admonitions of the dying Cosgrove and the party's pledge.[24] He could speak with growing confidence, for even during the debates in Olympia, a dry wind was blowing across the state as new townships, voting for the first time, approved town charters which prohibited the licensing of saloons. In forty-seven such elections that spring, fewer than a dozen towns voted wet.[25] And while these elections were taking place,

another revolution of which the Governor could be proud was occurring. Mrs. Emma DeVoe of Seattle and Mrs. May Hutton of Spokane
were in Olympia with their bright-plumed and full-bosomed lobby,
worrying the legislature into submitting to the people a constitutional
amendment on women's suffrage. They too were successful.

After the local option law had passed, Ernest Cherrington was
called to the national headquarters of the ASL to edit the *American
Issue*, the national antisaloon weekly, and to edit, write, and publish
the books and pamphlets which were to make him internationally famous in the prohibition movement. ASL leaders then chose Boyd P.
Doty, formerly the attorney for the Ohio League, to manage the next
stage of evolution.

Doty could rejoice in local option, in the amount of territory that
was already dry, in the antisaloon laws, and, most happily, in an
ASL governor. Governor Hay paid dues to the Anti-Saloon League
and extended to it a degree of cooperation with the governor's office
that probably no pressure group—not even the railroads—had ever
enjoyed. He conferred with Doty on the appointment of judges and
began to advise Doty on techniques for electing a legislature in 1910
that would support a stronger local option bill.[26]

But the immediate battles—those called for by local option petition
shortly after Hay signed the 1909 bill—would be the most significant:
Hay and the ASL stood up to be tested. The Governor was a true
moderate, dedicated to popular sovereignty, and he even participated
in some of these elections, which were held by the score from June to
December. Though the voting units were the smaller ones—the 30-
per-cent petitions would take longer in the cities—the campaigns
stirred up emotions and excitement that split communities apart just
as territorial local option had done for another generation. Before
the year was out, 41 localities had taken the dry option, abolishing a total of 288 saloons. By January, 1910, eight counties were
completely dry (Island, Skagit, Klickitat, Grant, Douglas, Okanogan,
Garfield, Columbia), and seven others were dry outside the cities
(Cowlitz, Clark, Pend Oreille, Spokane, Whitman, Asotin, and
Thurston).[27] Inasmuch as these were all victories without the aid of
women's suffrage, the antisaloon men had cause for their great optimism.

In the year's most virulent battle, however, the wets demonstrated
the depth of their numbers. By December of 1909, Walla Walla was

ready to be tried, the first city of major significance to present petitions. There were thirty-seven saloons in Walla Walla. The county had a total population of approximately thirty-one thousand, about 55 per cent of whom lived in the urban area. The wets in the city were led by a prominent banker and by a businessman with extensive property holdings, and they were a hard-headed lot who had fought for years to protect their right to do business in their own ways. Farmers in Walla Walla County had for at least a generation looked upon the city as a necessary evil: it robbed them with railroad rates and interest rates, then debauched their hired hands with liquor, women, and gambling, even on Sundays. Their many petitions for a Sunday closure during harvest time had met with only transitory success.[28] The lines of country-city conflict in Walla Walla County were probably as hard as those anywhere in the United States.

Both of the newspapers in Walla Walla opposed the antisaloon law. But the farmers came into town to crusade against the saloons, and there were crowds and fist fights and demonstrations throughout the business district for a full week before the election. Governor Hay had asked Joe Smith, an investigator on his staff and one of the state's leading journalists, to go to Walla Walla to take charge of the antisaloon propaganda for the campaign. The Governor himself provided dry leaders with a long letter which was read to the crowd during the climactic rally, a letter in which the Governor testified that the saloons were a "cancer in the body politic."[29] The drys employed football players from Whitman College to guard the polls during election day, but Walla Walla stayed wet: 1,008 voted for local option, and 1,630 voted against.

Dry voting was high in the residential precincts, but in only one of these was there a clear dry majority. Even Whitman precinct, which contained the college, voted wet. The ambivalence of the middle class in Walla Walla had brought a victory for the saloons. To both sides in this battle, there were obvious conclusions: a county-unit local option law would have dried up the city; the drys would have to wage more effective campaigns if they were to win any of the cities which were even then preparing for elections; and they would have to work harder among the church-going middle class in the residential areas of these cities.

Women's suffrage would make this task much easier—a thought not as obvious to people in 1910 as it might seem, for by this time the suffrage movement had to a remarkable degree disassociated itself from the antisaloon movement. The WCTU papers, for example, gave only casual reference to the referendum on the equal suffrage amendment set for November, 1910. In many local newspapers, it was local option that commanded the headlines and made the big noise; the suffrage pitch was by comparison soft and subtle. In 1910 the wisdom of Abigail Scott Duniway, who had blamed the suffrage defeats on the prohibitionists, had prevailed. The most colorful leader of the Washington suffragettes at that time was her friend, Mrs. May Hutton of Spokane, who had absorbed the Oregon leader's philosophy and campaign techniques and who therefore held for a complete separation of equal suffrage from any discussion of liquor legislation.[30] This was possible now, as it had not been in 1889, because each movement was vigorous enough to do without the other. There was apparently no effort at all to coordinate the two in 1910; the opposite, in fact, may have been true. Local option forces could have waited in pressing their cause until after the women's suffrage election in November, but they did not. The antisaloon movement took its own course.

Many of the elections were as bitter and as marked by rural-urban tensions as the Walla Walla battle had been. For example, a prohibitionist in Granger, Washington, wrote George Cotterill after the election in that town: "I am sorry to inform you that we lost in our local option election. It was, however, very close, the 'wets' winning by a majority of two votes. The farmers came in from the country and formed a long procession and marched through our streets and did all they could to influence the people to vote 'dry.' "[31]

Other elections brought forth the tensions of the cities themselves. In Everett, for example, the local option election was scheduled for November, 1910, at the same time as the suffrage referendum. In 1910, Everett was a thoroughly industrial community—a "city of smokestacks," its boosters called it—where twenty-four thousand people lived in the smoke from mills that turned out over six million cedar shingles and over a million board feet of lumber every day. It was a mill town and workers' town. Forty saloons lined Hewitt Avenue from salt water to the Snohomish River and awaited the raw anxieties charged by the hundreds of saws that had screamed twenty-four hours a day since the turn of the century. Everett was a new city, born of the railroads, for there had been nothing at all at the mouth of the Snohomish River in 1890. By 1910 it was a sort of cross-section of what the railroads had brought to the mills: city workers, immigrants, merchants, real estate promoters, people leaving the farms for urban centers. The city makes a good case study of western enthusiasms and disillusionments, especially those associated with reform.[32]

The evangelical churches had come almost with the real estate developers, so there had been organized temperance sentiment from the beginning. In 1910, the Everett Local Option League was prominent. The banner of the ASL was not waved openly, but its techniques were clearly apparent in the strategy of the Local Option League. The city precincts were divided into "prayer-meeting districts," in each of which ten families made the basic organizational unit. Meetings were held at increasingly short intervals after October 15. While these meetings rallied—or split—neighborhoods with the slogan "the cause of Local Option . . . is the cause of mankind," local option leaders downtown worked hard on both businessmen and workers.

They produced sworn affidavits from businessmen in dry communities—Edmonds was a favorite—which testified without reservation that business had improved with the drought. A typical downtown local option meeting featured a speaker to analyze saloons and "the tax situation," another to discuss "saloons and business," another to examine "the saloon and the local labor situation." There were also segregated meetings—businessmen meeting at one hour, "laboring men" at another. In such attacks the local option forces enjoyed the real advantage of being able to address themselves to specific conditions in Everett which needed changing.

The saloon men, on the other hand, could call upon no neighborhood captains, no evangelical rallies. They were embarrassed by the reality of the saloons which they had to defend. One of their principal spokesmen was a Reverend William A. Wasson, former rector of the Episcopal church in Everett. He spoke several times in early November on "personal liberty" and on the saloon as a "poor man's club" that was no way inconsistent with Christianity. He stressed that Catholic, Episcopal, Jewish, and some Lutheran churches—all of them represented in Everett—were not opposed to good saloons. Wasson was assisted by the president of the Everett Realty Company, and there was the inevitable "Taxpayers' League," the usual name for the saloon owners' front organization.

A closer approach to real zeal came from the *Labor Journal*, the Everett trade-union weekly, a sometimes bitterly class-conscious paper that stood by the brewery workers' and the bartenders' locals. The *Journal* pointed out that the life expectancy of the workingman was 60 per cent of what "rich people" might expect, and that the reasons for the difference were wages, hours, and working conditions, not booze. The local option campaign, its editor said, was controlled by "a handful of fanatics who know nothing about their cause. . . ."[33]

Saloon forces also brought Clarence Darrow to Everett to speak on personal liberty, matching the famous criminal lawyer and secularist against the Reverend Billy Sunday, who worked the city from a big-tent revival a week before the election. Apparently the saloon men gained little from this encounter.

There was ample opportunity for petty malice in boycott campaigns. Salooners boycotted certain barbers and merchants; the drys boycotted wet businessmen. There was one remarkable instance of a man and a woman from the "Riverside restricted district," disguised and richly attired, who went around the city exciting known dry merchants with pretensions of large purchases, including real estate. They would pause in the act of signing a check to inquire about the merchant's position on local option, then angrily refuse to have anything more to with him. There was street-brawling a full week before election day.

After the sermons on Sunday, November 6, some twenty-five hundred children—four abreast and stretched for seven blocks—marched through the city with banners pleading for the end of the saloon. Those in front carried a wide sign reading "A Little Child Shall Lead Them." Those following held aloft banners lettered "Purify Everett," "Repent, Ye Boozers," and "The Saloon Must Go." Antisaloon workers served coffee on the street corners so that thirsty men would not have to miss the parade.

Continuous prayer meetings were held on election day, and church bells tolled hourly for the death of the saloon. The dry newspaper concluded its exhortations in a low tone:

> . . . we know what the saloon is, how it figures in politics, tries to dictate to the candidate, and very often does so, how it violates the laws. . . . We know that the saloon has by such actions brought this

storm down upon its own head. . . . Only fanatics will claim that prohibition is an unqualified success. . . . But this alone is not a reason
for voting against it.

The men of Everett voted dry by 275 votes—2,208 to 1,933. The
Everett *Daily Herald* was quick to point out that the early returns
showed wet majorities, and that not until after working hours in the
mills did the dry votes come in numbers. The mill hands, the editor
concluded, had won the day. "It was the patent leather crowd that
double-crossed the dry poll takers," he wrote, "not the workers."[34]
He might have noted that many of the early wet votes probably came
from the saloons' daylight regulars—those not working and willing
to vote for a free drink, but it is true that Everett went dry on the
votes of millworkers.

This fact suggests a weakness in the generalizations about the prohibition movement which stress the rural-urban aspect of the conflict,
just as it challenges the presumption that the working class favored
license. In this last regard, a precinct analysis of the Everett vote is
an interesting study in class attitudes toward the saloon (table 4).

TABLE 4

SOCIAL CLASS AND LOCAL OPTION: VOTING IN EVERETT, 1910*

First Ward

1st Precinct: *wet* (203–97).	Waterfront saloon area.
2nd Precinct: *wet* (144–62).	Downtown, with some shop owners living in their shops, but mostly flats, roomers, boarders; includes saloons.
3rd Precinct: *wet* (116–85).	Same as 2nd; heavy with saloons.

Second Ward

1st Precinct: *dry* (167–158).	Mixed, though mostly business and professional class.
2nd Precinct: *dry* (193–117).	Mixed. Some working class, some business and professional. Includes Rucker Hill estates of millowners.

* Based on one hundred random samples from listings in R. L. Polk and Co.,
Everett City and Snohomish County Directory, 1910 (Seattle, Wash., 1910),
and on interviews with citizens of Everett who have lived in that city for more
than forty years, and on consultation with John A. Broussard (sociology),
Everett Junior College. Col. Hartley (7th Ward, 1st Precinct) was mayor of
Everett in 1910 and was later governor of the state.

(Table 4—*Continued*)

Third Ward

> 1st Precinct: *wet* (126–122). Commercial area. Predominantly working class. Includes "restricted district."
>
> 2nd Precinct: *dry* (162–97). Predominantly working class residences.

Fourth Ward

> 1st Precinct: *wet* (201–169). Commercial area around the bridge across the Snohomish River. Predominantly working class. Includes several saloons.
>
> 2nd Precinct: *wet* (139–77). Some business and professional residences along the river front, but mostly working class residences.

Fifth Ward

> 1st Precinct: *dry* (209–152). Predominantly workers' family residences.
>
> 2nd Precinct: *dry* (222–120). Same as 1st.

Sixth Ward

> 1st Precinct: *dry* (142–131). Seems fairly evenly mixed, working class residences and business and professional class residences.
>
> 2nd Precinct: *dry* (143–111). Mixed. Baronies to boarding houses, though mostly working class residences.

Seventh Ward

> 1st Precinct: *dry* (189–114). Rucker Avenue baronies (including Col. Hartley's) to boarding houses. Predominantly working class residences.
>
> 2nd Precinct: *dry* (109–66). Same as 1st.

Everett in 1910 was a millworkers' town, and the working class did not live in clearly segregated areas. In none of the precincts, actually, was the business and professional class or the millowners' class in a clear majority. The most obvious division which the voting illustrated was between the downtown precincts and the residential ones: only one residential precinct voted wet, but all the downtown precincts did so. Residential working class precincts voted dry, and the residential precincts in which most of the business and professional class lived also voted dry, as did those where the millowners lived. The most recently settled precincts (North Rucker and South Rucker) were dry about two to one.

Thus it seems clear that the Everett *Daily Herald* was correct in concluding that the millworkers voted Everett dry in 1910. It is probably not accurate, however, to identify these workers with the "lower" social class in American society. This "lower" class—the class-conscious proletariat—as it existed in Everett, probably lived in the rooming and boarding houses along Hewitt Avenue, close to the saloons. The great majority of the workers of Everett, however, lived in their own houses in residential areas. Many were church members. They had come only recently to the state, and their geographic mobility was often class mobility. Most of them voted against the advice of the *Labor Journal,* which attempted to define the obligations of the working class. Surely these men were—in their attitudes at least—as much a part of the American "middle class" as the merchants, the physicians, the undertakers, and the lawyers among whom they lived. They were a part of the urban middle class of a new city in a new state faced with new problems, some of which could be solved, they believed, by abolishing the saloons.

On the same election day, November 8, 1910, the city of Bellingham—the major mill and mining center north of Everett—also voted to close its saloons. In Seattle there had been no local option on saloons, but many of the same forces had clashed a few months earlier in the mayoralty election when Hiram Gill, defender of the open town, had been opposed by the reformer William H. Moore. Gill's open-town platform carried all the downtown wards and won the election, but the reformer carried most of the residential wards.[35] In 1910 there was plenty of evidence that the urban middle class was willing to see the saloon go.

This was, of course, quite clear to the state ASL and to Governor Hay. Before the November elections the Governor had argued with Doty, sometimes sharply, over the Anti-Saloon League's insistence that the local option voting unit be the county, with no exceptions. The cities, Hay had felt, were the centers of wet sentiment, and he had thought that much time and education would be necessary before the cities would submit to any dry law. He was still a moderate, still an advocate of popular sovereignty. In the November elections, however, he saw in the urban vote against saloons a major evolutionary step.

In 70 municipal elections, there were 35 dry victories; 129 saloons had been closed. And in a remarkably quiet way, the voters had approved the constitutional amendment on women's suffrage. (In Everett, there were more votes cast in the local option election than in the women's suffrage referendum.) Weighing all this, Governor Hay wrote to Boyd Doty that "owing to the action taken by the Everett and Bellingham people, as I see it there is only one thing for me to do and that is to recommend [to the legislature] a county unit without exceptions."

He had already done what he could to secure a legislature that would be receptive to this idea. Early in the campaign Hay had requested Doty and the ASL to instruct him on the attitudes of various candidates toward local option so that, as governor, he could exert pressure in the proper places. "I would be pleased," he wrote to Doty, "if you would advise me who of our friends and who of our enemies are out in the open for representative and senatorial honors. . . ."[36] The Governor, in turn, advised Doty when to press for pledges from candidates and when not to press. Insofar as they could apply the persuasions of the Republican party and the Anti-Saloon League, the two men had hand-picked a legislature as eagerly as ever a railroad had done.

When Governor Hay addressed the 1911 lawmakers, he recommended the limit of what the ASL judged the state could take at that time: county-unit local option, stronger enforcement, and—copying a Nebraska law he had read about—laws which would limit the sale of liquor in wet areas to the hours of daylight. He chose his words carefully:

> Discussion of the present local option law occupied a large portion of time of the regular legislative session of 1909. The bitterness engendered in that contest was apparent throughout the session. . . . As a result of the feeling thus aroused, the vote on many other important measures was influenced less by the merits of the measures than by the position taken on the local option question by those who fathered the bills. . . . I believe that the disagreement of the members on this question in most cases arises from a divergence of views as to the methods of minimizing the evils inherent in the liquor traffic as now conducted, and not because of the sympathy of any number of legislators for the saloon as an institution. . . .
>
> Every opportunity has been afforded the better element in the saloon

business to effect the necessary reforms from within, but, since they have utterly failed to achieve any substantial betterment, the people are determined that . . . the reforms must come from without.[37]

The reaction of the legislature, then, must have been a great shock to him and to the ASL, for both Hay and Doty had erred grievously in their evaluations of the antisaloon movement in 1911 and in their estimation of the degree to which legislators would respond to the ASL. And even though they recognized it, they had not properly appreciated the residue of bitterness from 1909. The legislators received Hay with some hostility, and they almost immediately resolved (in the House, fifty-two to forty-two, after a day's fighting) to ignore any proposed liquor legislation during the 1911 session because, they said, the local option fight of 1909 had cut wounds that affected the public interest. Their resolution read, in part: "[Local option] . . . engendered strife among the members of the legislature, created factions, coloring and interfering with the consideration of other legislation, against the best interests and common good of the whole state. . . ."[38]

Marion Hay, who in 1911 wanted very much to continue being governor, had made what was probably his worst political mistake. He would never know exactly how much this contributed to his defeat the following year. And Hay's friends in the Anti-Saloon League had been unequivocally rebuked; but unlike the governor, they could retaliate with a great wrath. Doty wrote a letter that went to every minister in the state:

This is the most notorious, cowardly, and un-American attempt at gag rule ever put through a Washington legislature . . . [he gives a list of those who voted for the resolution]. . . . Read this letter to your congregation. If possible have action taken by them . . . deluge your representatives with letters, telegrams, and telephone messages . . . demand the passage of an effective and enforceable county unit law, excepting, possibly, cities of over 50,000 people from the county unit.[39]

The legislators stood adamantly against the League, ignoring even Doty's belated attempt to compromise on "cities of over 50,000." In the 1911 session, at least, county-unit local option was dead. The ASL leaders, however, wasted no time in sullen regrets or public weeping. With almost push-button efficiency, they turned their energies down an alternate route which they had long before explored—the route of direct legislation.[40]

The initiative and the referendum were gleaming tools for political craftsmanship which could achieve the breakthrough the reformers had for years awaited. With I and R a dedicated group of voters could circumvent recalcitrant legislatures dominated by "whiskey, sawdust, and fish" and bring their reforms directly before the people on the general ballot. To people convinced that the states should have more democracy rather than less, the devices had a strong appeal. George Cotterill had for years proposed a constitutional amendment which would have given Washington the initiative and referendum. The legislature had debated the matter in every session since 1901, but each time the Grange and the labor lobbies—strongest in support of I and R—had been effectively stopped by railroad and big-business forces.[41]

By 1906, the ASL in Washington, riding the reform movement, was already committed to direct legislation. It had, for example, sponsored the Anti-Saloon Convention and Congress of Reform Forces which met in Seattle in September, 1906, to beat the drums of local option and direct legislation. During this period the forces of liquor reform and democracy were smiling partners, for the convention heard Reverend Mark Matthews condemn liquor and the saloon, then listened to George Cotterill speak on "The Reign of the People."[42]

When the legislature turned against the ASL in 1911, George Cotterill had already conferred with William S. U'Ren of Oregon, the "father" of I and R (and, incidentally, a Prohib), and written the 1911 version of the amendment which would be submitted to the legislators.[43] The amendment was pushed by a strong-minded front called the Direct Legislation League (farmers and labor) and by the ASL. Because the legislature in 1911 was quite sensitive to the ropes with which "whiskey, sawdust, and fish" had for so many years encircled it, and perhaps because organized labor gave the Direct Legislation League something the ASL could not, the amendment passed the legislature without a major struggle.

There were no clear voting patterns on I and R in the legislature—no solid opposition or support that was obviously rural or urban, business or antibusiness. It was a matter in which Republicans had no real unity, for Governor Hay had spoken against it in 1910, then reversed himself in 1911. It was, consequently, a matter open to the persuasions of pressure groups like the Direct Legislation League and the ASL.

This same haze of political ambivalence hung over I and R when the amendment was referred to the people in 1912. Few candidates chose to speak to the matter directly, and the city newspapers were noncommittal or at least not vocally opposed to the amendment. The only publications actively engaged in the campaign were the rural weeklies and the propaganda organs of the pressure groups. Thus, like women's suffrage, direct legislation came to Washington as the work of the few who could make up their minds about these matters without insisting that everyone else do so at the same time. The principal student of initiative and referendum in Washington has drawn this conclusion:

> . . . there was no general, popular demand for the initiative and referendum. Less than half the electors troubled themselves to vote on the question when it was presented to them [331,790 voted in 1912, 154,015 of whom voted on I and R] . . . it is probably safe to say that the amendment would have been long delayed, probably never adopted, had it not been for the campaign put on by the farm and labor organizations. Their constant presentation of the issue . . . and their lobbying represent one of the many triumphs of pressure politics.[44]

The initiative took from the saloon men, who might otherwise have regarded 1911 as a year of legislative peace, any security they may for the moment have enjoyed. It was by far a more formidable threat to them than local option had been. In Oregon, they well knew, local option itself had come by initiative in 1904, and state-wide prohibition had already been proposed there as a subject for direct legislation. The shape of future antisaloon measures should have been clear enough to them. They may also have known that in some cases the very votes that had protected them from county-unit local option had been turned against them in the legislative approval of I and R— craftily, one might believe, and to the gloating delight of antisaloon leaders. For example, Elihu F. Barker, a lawyer and a dry leader in Walla Walla, wrote to Cotterill in 1910 about a certain wet legislator: "He will be found voting for the 'wets' straight down the line, but . . . I believe he will stand for the initiative and referendum. . . . I am willing to sacrifice everything to get that, because after that is once secured, as you are so fully aware, we will be in a position to do things."[45]

What these "things" were the Grange made perfectly clear in 1912 when it resolved to do "all in its power" to pass I and R, "whereby, we, the people, may secure for ourselves state-wide prohibition in place of further stultifying ourselves by pleading with our servants, the Legislature, for reform measures, which they disdain to consider." The Anti-Saloon League decided to use the initiative immediately. In many ways the elections of 1912 had not gone well with the League—not because antisaloon sentiment had abated, but because the antisaloon movement had been caught in the vortex of a political revolution. The enthusiasms of the Progressive era were erupting everywhere. The ASL had lost its governor. Next to the Republican presidential electors who lost to the Progressives, Marion Hay was the state's most prominent political casualty in the Republican disintegration of 1912. (Democrat Ernest Lister 97,251 votes; 96,629 for Hay; 77,729 for the Progressive, Hodge; 37,155 for the Socialist, Maley.) J. A. Falconer, the ASL state senator, had gone over to the Progressives. In the campaigns of 1912 the realignment of forces was so delicate that candidates dared not mention the saloons at all, and none was likely to do so until his political future was a great deal more secure. In his final remarks to the legislature, Governor Hay said nothing about saloons, local option, or prohibition. His successor, Ernest Lister, avoided the topic with equal determination. Quite clearly, liquor legislation was not going to be a major concern in Olympia for a while.[46]

It had been, however, in the local option contests of November, 1912. These had created as much or more excitement and confusion than the Progressive revolution. A disturbing defeat for the drys had occurred in Everett, which turned from dry to wet by about a thousand votes. And this was—most seriously—the first election in that city in which women had voted. The Everett campaign of 1912 had been at least as vituperative as the one in 1910. One observer called it "a gangrenous wound, sapping the strength and poisoning the system of the city." The most vocal support for the return of saloon came from the *Labor Journal:*

> Among business men there is a wide-spread dissatisfaction with present conditions. . . . After two years' trial of a "saloonless" town it is apparent to those who are courageous enough to look conditions in the face that the only change has been in the mode of drinking. The saloon has been replaced by the speakeasy, the blindpig and the bootlegger.

. . . Women are drinking. . . . You can't have a dry island amid a sea of booze. . . .[47]

The Everett *Morning Tribune* was for license, the Everett *Daily Herald* was vague on the issue. On the day before the election, the Mayor and the city commissioners all endorsed the wet cause. The major factor in their action was the embarrassing crisis precipitated in city finance after the saloons had closed in 1911. The mayor, Roland Hartley, had balanced the budget by turning off street lights and allowing horse manure to pile high in the city's thoroughfares until the commissioners levied an additional property tax to cover the loss in revenue caused by the local option election of 1910.[48]

It is interesting again to examine the Everett precincts. Those that changed from a dry vote in 1910 to a wet vote in 1912 were three precincts in which numbers of the business and professional classes lived (2W2, 6W1, 6W2) and two precincts that were fairly solidly working class (3W2 and 5W1). Large increases in the number of voters—because of women's suffrage—were common. One precinct (4W2) shifted from wet to dry—a precinct of mixed business, professional, and working classes. Several precincts stayed dry—some solidly working class, some mixed. About all one can conclude from the returns is that some workers changed their minds— and that their wives voted with them.

TABLE 5

LOCAL OPTION IN EVERETT, 1910 AND 1912*

First Ward	*1910*	*1912*
1st Precinct:	wet (203–97)	wet (301–134)
2nd Precinct:	wet (144–62)	wet (246–105)
3rd Precinct:	wet (116–85)	wet (231–133)
Second Ward		
1st Precinct:	dry (167–158)	dry (147–144)
2nd Precinct:	dry (193–117)	wet (344–270)
Third Ward		
1st Precinct:	wet (126–122)	wet (266–153)
2nd Precinct:	dry (162–97)	wet (230–105)

* Everett *Morning Tribune*, Nov. 6, 1912. For a socio-economic classification of the precincts, see table 4, pp. 97-98.

(Table 5—*continued*)

Fourth Ward

1st Precinct:	wet (201–169)	wet (252–131)
2nd Precinct	wet (139–77)	dry (258–190)

Fifth Ward

1st Precinct:	dry (209–152)	wet (206–144)
2nd Precinct:	dry (222–120)	dry (280–245)

Sixth Ward

1st Precinct:	dry (142–131)	wet (274–203)
2nd Precinct:	dry (143–111)	wet (255–227)

Seventh Ward

1st Precinct:	dry (189–114)	dry (345–292)
2nd Precinct:	dry (109–66)	dry (203–177)

The reason for this change of faith was probably close to the surface. The appeal to morality by the temperance forces can be ruled out—it was a constant factor in both elections and one unlikely to change many votes between 1910 and 1912. However, in 1912 the saloon men were also using moral suasion. Drinking women, speakeasies serving minors, bootleggers in the back alleys—these were evils of another kind that could be challenged with as much righteous fury as had ever been heaped upon the saloons. Another strong factor was the concern of businessmen about taxes at a time when "the lumber mills were in the doldrums."[49] These considerations—along with the millworkers' thirst—can account for Everett's 1912 repeal movement in miniature.

But from the ASL point of view, 1912 had brought enough local option victories to compensate for the Everett defeat. Bellingham had remained dry. Six counties in 1912 were completely dry (Cowlitz, Garfield, Island, Klickitat, Mason, and San Jaun), and twenty-eight others were dry outside the cities and towns. Of the 220 local option elections in 1909-12, 140 had resulted in dry victories.[50]

By ASL calculation in 1912, the dry areas of the state included 42 per cent of the state's population. While there is no account of their analysis of the forty local option elections held that year, the leaders probably looked hard at the fairly even split—about half of the elections were won by the wets, about half by the drys. A closer look at these elections shows that a three fifths–two fifths division in the vote was a fairly standard pattern, whether in a wet or dry majority.[51] Thus in the 42 per cent (480,500) of the population living in the dry areas, there were perhaps about 288,300 dry citizens (three fifths of 480,500). And among the 58 per cent (661,490) of the population in saloon territories, there might have been about 264,596 (two fifths of 661,490) citizens equally dry. In the total population, then, of 1,141,-990, there may have been 552,896 (from the totals above) people of the dry persuasion. These, of course, are rough estimates, but they may have been strong considerations when the ASL leaders decided to go for state-wide prohibition.

Other major considerations were that women were voting in 1912 and would vote thereafter, and I and R had passed easily, and that Hiram Gill, the saloon mayor of Seattle, had been removed from office in 1911 by a vote of the people following a recall campaign led by the Reverend Mark Matthews. Furthermore, George Cotterill, probably the most widely known prohibitionist in all the West, had been elected mayor of Seattle in 1912. Indeed, just about all the evidence except the Everett vote indicated that antisaloon sentiments were increasingly strong. The time was surely propitious for a full war against the saloon.

The decision was also in line with national developments. In 1907, the people of Oklahoma had voted to abolish the saloons in a victory which, according to Cherrington, "electrified the moral forces in other states."[52] Alabama and Georgia went dry that same year. North Carolina and Mississippi voted antisaloon in 1908, Tennessee in 1909, West Virginia in 1912. The South was almost solidly antisaloon by then; one can see what Cherrington meant by "evolution." And all the while the ASL had been preparing the Far West.

States ready for the big battles between 1912 and 1916 were Oregon, Washington, Idaho, Arizona, Colorado, Arkansas, South Carolina, and Virginia. (California would have its referendum in 1914, but against the better judgment of the ASL: the Prohibition party there forced it prematurely.[53]) Thus when "World Temperance Sunday" was declared for November 9, 1913, the strategies were already well laid.

8

1914–"The Saloon Must Go"

AFTER THE legislative defeat in 1911, the national Anti-Saloon League sent George G. Conger to the state of Washington to relieve Boyd Doty as state superintendent. Conger had been trained for state-wide campaigns, and he had led the local option forces in Illinois. He prepared Initiative Measure Number 3, called the "state-wide prohibition initiative," and began the circulation of petitions through the churches.

Initiative Measure Number 3 was drawn to the ASL pattern that had been successful in other states. It was in no real sense a true prohibition measure, though it was called one. It was, instead, the step in controlled evolution that followed local option. The sequence ran from city abolition to county abolition to state antisaloon laws, then to state antidrink measures, then national and international prohibition. Number 3 was properly an antisaloon measure. It promised to end the "manufacture and sale" on January 1, 1916, and thus to destroy the liquor industry in the state—the breweries, the distilleries, and the saloons. But it was most carefully not an antidrink measure. The proposed law would allow druggists to sell alcohol on a medical prescription or a clergyman's request, or "in case of extreme illness where delay may be dangerous to the patient."[1] Even more liberally, the law would permit an individual to import into the state a generous supply of beverages for his own use. Thus the ASL could soothe its critics with the claim that the law was intended to hit the liquor traffic, not the drinker, and it had no designs against a man's right to drink peacefully in his own home. Like the local option law, Number 3 forced its critics to defend the institution of the saloon.

Conger filed 112,101 signatures with his petitions in January, 1914, and the election was scheduled for the coming November. The state superintendent let it be known that he had been approached

108

many times with offers of bribes for the destruction of the petitions.[2] The forces of corruption were abroad in the land, and the impressive strength of the national temperance organizations was marshaled for deployment all along the West Coast. The state stood ready then to suffer the great battle between saloon and antisaloon.

The Presbyterians put up $150,000 for Washington, Oregon, Idaho, and California. The Methodists sent seven hundred ministers into the field. The ASL scheduled a long list of prominent speakers for almost every town in the region. The league organized the state of Washington into ASL "precincts" which averaged 120 families, each of which were worked by a "captain" and ten canvassers. The main jobs were voter registration and the distribution of propaganda. In Seattle there were "committees of 100"—businessmen and women—sponsored by the WCTU. Churches arranged for billboard space on the lawns and yards of their friends in residential areas. The national ASL "Flying Squadron" hit the state in October to support the local churches and Granges with spectacle and color: singers, speakers, parades of automobiles, brass bands, and hundreds of young people marching through the night with torches.[3]

The battle—according to the ASL—centered naturally in Seattle, where there were over ninety thousand registered voters whose attitudes on liquor control had never been directly tested at the polls. The antisaloon forces could be relatively confident of the rural areas. They knew, however, that their chances of state-wide victory could be measured in a few thousand votes and that it was in the cities that these votes must be won.[4]

But there were enormous difficulties in Seattle. The newspapers there were solidly opposed to Number 3. Editors of the *Post-Intelligencer* did not care for initiative measures in the first place: they were an affront to the dignity of the legislature, and they were running wildly socialistic with proposals like an eight-hour working day (Initiative Measure Number 13). Number 3, they said with some detachment, was premature; the state was not ready for so radical a change.[5]

The *Seattle Times* kept the word "radical" clearly in focus. Its editor, "Colonel" Alden J. Blethen, had supported George Cotterill in 1900, but since then he had been moved from irritation to outrage by his conviction that the security of his very way of life was seriously threatened by the proliferation of wild-eyed moralists: "Seattle does not need to swallow this nauseous dose," he said in reference to Number 3. "It has already been punished enough for its red-flag mayor [Cotterill] and other freaks, without facing the calamity of state-wide prohibition." Editorials in a similar vein appeared almost daily in the *Times*. Blethen offered one thousand dollars in gold to anyone who could "reasonably contend" that Number 3 was a true "temperance" law. "Instead of destroying the saloon," he warned, "Initiative Measure Number Three will establish a saloon in every household."[6]

In the weekly *Town Crier*, which reached a much smaller audience, the prose was more sophisticated but the spirit was just as bitter. The prohibition movement, said the editor, was an attack upon individual liberty as well as upon the rights of property, and Number 3, he argued, was "anomalous. It isn't prohibitive; it isn't even corrective—it is simply and entirely destructive of existing property rights and of revenues upon which state, county, city and school district now depend." His favorite sarcasm was to propose an initiative measure designed to eliminate all evil in one sweeping abolition: prohibit money.[7]

H. A. Chadwick, of the equally sophisticated *Argus*, conducted the most searching and persistent of all the press campaigns against Number 3. Throughout most of the year his weekly carried editorials against state-wide prohibition—as an unenforceable law, as an attempt of small-minded farmers to dictate to the city, as a measure which was economically unsound and morally evasive. But Chadwick was no friend of the saloon; he took a dark view of the total problem: "The world would be better off had alcohol never been known. . . . The writer does not argue—has never argued—that there is anything to be said in favor of the sale of liquor. He does maintain, however, that it is better to have it sold legally than illegally. . . ."[8]

There was no way the people of Seattle could escape the battle. It quickly became the most anguished conflict between the evangelical churches and the business community in the city's history. The anti-saloon leaders had no major newspaper, but they did have the man called "the black-maned lion" of the West, the Reverend Mark Matthews, who in October opened his attack in a full and steady roar. Now in his maturity—six feet five inches, white-faced, red-lipped, sharp and lean—and at a high plateau of his remarkable career, Matthews was pastor of the largest Presbyterian church in the world.

A master of sensational preaching, he spoke every Sunday evening to a congregation of three thousand, 70 per cent of whom were men. After hearing him, a writer for *Collier's* commented that "it is doubtful if in the American pulpit there is a man more skillful in the arts of public denunciation than Mark Matthews. Few men can paint black blacker than he."[9] Matthews took unblushing pride in having led the movement which dumped Mayor Hiram Gill by recall in 1911 and in exercising the political power which this feat had brought to him. He was, in addition, moderator of the Presbyterian General Assembly, which had endorsed federal prohibition in 1913. He was a force to be respected both locally and nationally.

Matthews attacked the liquor traffic with the lash of his prodigious rhetoric, confident that faith could move mountains and abolish industries:

> The Congress of the United States has been dominated by the liquor interests for the last forty-two years, and the two great political parties are rum-soaked, saloon-cursed, and without conscience on the question of the abolition of this great enemy. . . . The nation cannot exist half-drunk and half-sober.[10]

He began daily revival meetings in October, each sermon leading inexorably toward election day.

Also in October the Seattle Chamber of Commerce took a stand against Number 3, announcing that its membership had voted against it in a private poll, 632-45. Erastus Brainerd, former editor of the *Post-Intelligencer*, a significant figure in the Republican party, and a principal spokesman for the commercial interests in the state, spoke almost daily for the Anti-Prohibition Association. He faced George Cotterill, for example, before the Seattle Commercial Club with the theme that alcoholism is a sickness, not a crime. He was assisted by Judge Thomas Burke, who brought his prestige as a financial leader to the economic arguments against Number 3: the state was in a depression, Burke said, and Number 3 would only make it worse by putting eighty-three hundred more men out of work, by terminating an eight million dollar payroll and a three million dollar market for barley and hops. (Unemployment was a real problem in the fall of 1914, before the war orders came.) The brewers ran full-page ads urging "moderation but not prohibition."[11]

By 1914, the United States had experienced so much antisaloon legislation that both sides in this debate were able to find all the statistics they needed. For example, in Seattle a prohibition group called the Kansas Sun-Flower Club was organized by an energetic ASL minister for the purpose of "telling the truth about Kansas prohibition." The truth was that Kansas had fewer mental patients than some other states, a fact which moved the *Town Crier* to cry that it thought Number 3 "had moral, physical, and financial sides, but . . . all that is necessary for a voter to know is how many insane people there are in Kansas."[12]

The question of Number 3 brought the nineteen thousand members of the Washington State Federation of Labor to a prolonged and painful crisis. The leadership had for a while been successful in keeping the question from arising on the floor of conventions. But in 1914 there were in the Federation fifteen bartenders' locals, six cigar makers' locals, twelve cooks' and waiters' locals, ten brewery workers' locals, in addition to all of the wagon drivers, musicians, and engineers who would be ruined if Number 3 carried the state.

The locals threatened by Number 3 joined together in the Anti-Prohibition Labor League and appealed to the executive board of the State Federation. This occasioned considerable embarrassment to the board because many union men were actively campaigning for Number 3. Among these was James Duncan, Seattle leader and member of the National AFL Executive Council. The State Federation also hoped to continue its cooperation with the farmers' organizations, all of which were radically dry. In the end, however, the board voted unanimously to support the Anti-Prohibition Labor League, just as the Spokane Central Labor Council had done, in the desperate hope that such action would "unify labor, not split it." But their worst fears were realized, and the president later acknowledged that the membership had divided with so much malice that the closing of ranks in 1915 required a major effort.[13]

On October 31, Matthews spoke on "Satan at the Polls" and then rested. The next day ASL leaders announced in the papers that they had sent out "thousands of letters" to persons whom they had cause to suspect were fraudulently registered for voting, and that 90 per cent of these letters had been returned because the post office had been unable to locate the addresses. The ASL closed the campaign with a still more sobering announcement—that their challengers would be at every polling place and that Burns detectives had been retained to run down voting irregularities. On election day the

WCTU ladies posted signs in every precinct which read "What Is Five Dollars Against a Trip to the Pen?" They retired then to the all-day prayer services held in many churches.[14]

Throughout the urban centers of the state, the course of events had been about the same. In Everett, fifteen hundred children paraded and sang, carrying banners calling for "Less Booze, More Shoes." In Spokane, the Central Labor Council had pitched itself against the churches, and the ASL-WCTU techniques were the same as those in Seattle. In the rural counties, the fires of local option were stoked into a hundred minor crusades.

At 1:00 P.M. on election day, the wets were winning, but in the end the saloons fell low. The vote for Number 3 was 189,840; against, 171,208.[15]

One of the most striking aspects of the election was the size of the vote. More people voted for Number 3 in 1914, an off-year election, than had voted for any other issue or candidate in the history of the state (see table 6). No initiative or referendum measure has yet surpassed the 94.6 per cent of the total vote that was cast for Number 3. It was a remarkably pure measure of the public mind.

TABLE 6
PROHIBITION AS A POPULAR ISSUE

Candidates and Issues	Total Vote Cast
Initiative Measure Number 3, 1914	361,048
United States Senator, 1914	345,279
President of the U.S., 1912	331,790
Governor of Washington, 1912	318,319
Initiative and Referendum Amendment, 1912	154,015

The size of the vote in 1914 reflects in part the organizational achievements of the ASL and its allied organizations—the work of captains of precincts and of canvassers, the registration drives, the meticulous attention to every possible persuasion. The vote also records the power of machine evangelism—the parades, the rallies, the songs, the calls to battle and sacrifice. But the full significance of these statistics to Washington State history is this: they show that to the people of the state in 1914, prohibition was the major issue. No other issue had caused so much political excitement, no other issue had crossed so bitterly over political, social, economic, and religious loyalties. No other issue had been so emotionally advanced. No other issue—not Progressive politics, or wage-hour reform, or railroad land grabs, or corruption in government—had so inspired the emotions of crisis which move voters to the polls with real urgency.

Some historians have regarded the shrill pitch of this urgency over prohibition as a symptom of a deep and complex rural-urban conflict which lies behind so many of the social and political tensions that have shaped American life. The Anti-Saloon League, early in its history, adopted a self-conscious role in this conflict, presenting itself as a champion of rural America in its struggle against city corruption. It was clear, of course, that the cities were the centers of wet entrenchment, and the ASL tactics reflected a deliberate and methodical attack upon the urban areas.[16] County-unit local option was the principal strategy before 1914. In the records of the Grange and of the ASL, in hundreds of speeches, sermons, books, and pamphlets, the conflict is literally a geographic one of country against city.

There is some solid statistical evidence to support this. For example, the states with the lowest percentages of urban population—in the South and the West, generally—were the first to vote for statewide prohibition. On the other hand, those states with the highest percentages of city people resisted prohibition to the last. Thus most of the states that never had prohibition laws before 1919 were those with at least 60 per cent of the population in urban areas, states like California, New York, Massachusetts, and Illinois.

But these urban states were also the states in which the old American, Anglo-Saxon stock made up less than 50 per cent of the population and where non-Protestant religious faiths claimed more than 45 per cent of the church members. In a broader view, then, the conflict was one of rural values against urban values, and "the country" and "the city" become potent symbols of two ways of life. In the literature of the conflict, "the country" is a symbol for which Anglo-Saxon racial purity and Protestant religious faith are the Urim and the Thummim and from which flow the virtues of temperance, cleanliness, thrift, and individual responsibility. "The city" is the symbol of racial amalgamation and religious pluralism which together, according to its enemies, bred sloth and hedonism, money-changing, a society dedicated to graft and greed, crime and industrial squalor.

Thus in the 1920's, Walter Lippmann drew these implications from his own experience with the prohibition movement in America: "The Pope, the devil, jazz, the bootleggers, are a mythology which expresses symbolically the impact of a vast and dreaded social change. . . . The Eighteenth Amendment is a rock upon which the evangelical church militant is founded, and with it are envolved a whole way of life and an ancient tradition. . . ."[17]

Three decades later, Richard Hofstadter was somewhat less kind to the rural tradition than Lippmann had been:

> For Prohibition was a pseudo-reform, a pinched, parochial substitute for reform which had a wide-spread appeal to a certain type of crusading mind. It was linked not merely to an aversion to drunkenness and to the evils that accompanied it, but to the immigrant drinking masses, to the pleasures and amenities of city life, and to the well-to-do classes and cultivated men. It was carried about America by the rural-evangelical virus: the country Protestant frequently brought it with him to the city when the contraction of agriculture sent him there to seek his livelihood.[18]

And in the 1960's, Andrew Sinclair, after quoting the passage by Walter Lippmann above, re-emphasized the theme:

> Great cities were the enemies of the evangelical Protestant churches of America. They fostered liberals and agnostics, saloons and Roman Catholics. Nothing seemed more dangerous to the fundamental beliefs of primitive American Protestantism than the urban millions. . . . Prohibition was the final victory of the defenders of the American past. On the rock of the Eighteenth Amendment, village America made its last stand.[19]

In this regard, the state of Washington in 1914 provides an interesting example of a prohibition state against which the rural-urban thesis can be tested. Was, in fact, the vote on Number 3 a triumph of the country over the city? To approach the answer first from the literal, geographical level, it is significant that the census of 1910 listed the state as 53 per cent urban; the national figure was 46 per cent. Fortunately, the statistics of the census and of the secretary of state's report in Washington are both rich enough to indicate specifically how the rural areas voted and how the urban areas voted and to suggest certain factors in this voting.

Of the six counties that returned wet majorities in 1914, only three were urban by at least 50 per cent (table 7). At this level of analysis, therefore, the thesis of rural-urban conflict falls short of the mark. It is true, however, that the extreme dry vote occurred in the rural

TABLE 7
Prohibition, Urbanization, and Agriculture in the State of Washington, 1914*

Counties in Order of Urbanization, 1910 (Percentage living in places of 2500 or more)	Vote Cast on Number 3, 1914 (Percentage dry and wet)		Land under Cultivation, 1910
	Dry	Wet	
King (84)		59	11%
Spokane (77)	51		more than 20%
Pierce (73)		54	14%
Chehalis (61)	54		9%
Walla Walla (61)	61		more than 20%
Kittitas (54)	53		18%
Jefferson (50)		56	3%
Whatcom (49)	56		11%
Snohomish (47)	56		9%
Thurston (40)		52	more than 20%
Lewis (37)	57		14%
Clark (36)	63		more than 20%
Yakima (34)	67		10%
Chelan (27)	63		8%
Pacific (24)	53		8%
Kitsap (17)	53		18%
Whitman (16)	68		more than 20%
Skagit (14)	66		10%
Adams	54		more than 20%
Asotin	77		more than 20%
Benton	62		more than 20%
Clallam	51		7%
Columbia	60		more than 20%
Cowlitz	62		14%
Douglas	59		more than 20%
Ferry	60		7%
Franklin	57		more than 20%
Garfield		51	more than 20%
Grant	61		more than 20%
Island	64		more than 20%
Klickitat	59		more than 20%
Lincoln	61		more than 20%
Mason		54	7%
Okanogan	61		11%
Pend Oreille	52		more than 20%
San Juan	50		more than 20%
Skamania	52		2%
Stevens	58		more than 20%
Wahkiakum	61		17%
Total	52	48	

* *Abstract of the 13th Census, 1910, with Supplement for Washington* (Washington, D.C., 1913), and "Report of the Secretary of State of Washington, 1914."

counties and that the extreme wet vote occurred in the urban counties. A rural-urban factor was operating in 1914, but it was not as significant as one might have assumed.

This significance is further obscured by the inadequacies of the census definition of "rural" and "urban," for a population density of twenty-five hundred does not measure the full connotations of these terms. One should notice, for example, that "rural" cannot mean "agricultural" in the state of Washington (see table 7). In many of the counties where fewer than 50 per cent of the people lived in "urban" areas, the amount of land under cultivation was actually small. These were the counties of logging camps or fishing towns, counties where really urban conditions might have existed among groups of people numbering somewhat fewer than twenty-five hundred. Table 7 shows that most of the wet counties were not very agricultural, but it does not indicate an accurate agrarian dimension in the dry voting.

TABLE 8

PROHIBITION IN THE CITIES, 1914*

City (Population, 1910)	Vote on Number 3, 1914 (Percentage dry and wet)	
	Dry	Wet
Seattle (237,194)	39	61
Spokane (104,402)	48	52
Tacoma (83,743)	45	55
Everett (24,874)	50.6	49.4
Bellingham (24,298)	51	49

* County Records of Snohomish County, Washington; Seattle *Post-Intelligencer*; Spokane *Spokesman-Review*; Tacoma *Daily News*; Bellingham *Herald*.

One can examine the urban vote from another approach by listing the cities of the state which had populations of more than twenty thousand in 1910 (table 8). These were the major urban centers, and 42 per cent of the state's population was included within their boundaries. They were the thoroughly urban, industrial cities with populations well above the twenty-five hundred figure used by the United States census in defining "urban." The voting in these cities supports the rural-urban thesis to the extent that the larger urban populations generally returned higher percentages of wet votes.

But how, in these terms, can one explain the dry voting in these cities and the dry victories in Everett and in Bellingham? Everett had been dry after 1910, and wet again following the election of 1912; but then it returned a dry majority in 1914 when a significant number of voters apparently felt that state-wide prohibition would succeed where local option had failed. Bellingham had been dry since the local option election there in 1910. It is unsatisfactory, surely, to assert merely that the dry votes in all these cities were from people most recently removed from the country; no firm body of evidence supports such a deduction. And it would be begging the question to contend that these voters were simply those in the cities who held rural attitudes. One might say, then, that a theory of rural-urban conflict that cannot accommodate smoky cities of mill hands and mine workers does not cast enough light on the prohibition movement in the state of Washington. The geography of dry sentiment is an important but not entirely adequate insight into the election of 1914.

One can return, however, to a further consideration of the symbolism of city and country, to the concept of two sharply differing systems of values and ways of life. Was the election of 1914 a triumph of the values symbolized by the country? There is a profusion of literary evidence to support an assertion that it was. The Grange papers are rich in choruses of hate and fear of urbanization. The sermons of Matthews and his more vocal colleagues paint the glory of agrarian ideals as they condemn the saloon. The prohibition weeklies were edited to catch the reader who remembered—or imagined that he remembered—the warmth and the purity of village life. And even more clearly, the county voting recorded in table 7 is solid statistical testimony that Number 3 expressed the values of rural life in 1914.

Because it seems clear that rural values did triumph, one must ask certain questions about the urban areas in which the outcome of the election was largely determined. Which groups in the cities supported Number 3, and which groups held those systems of values implicit in the opposition? Were there significant factors here of ethnology, religion, or social status?

One can approach these questions through a thesis recently advanced by the sociologist Joseph R. Gusfield in his book *Symbolic Crusade: Status Politics and the American Temperance Movement.* Gusfield believes that the prohibition movement reflected class and status tensions in American society and that temperance sentiment was mainly a middle-class value. He believes, furthermore, that this sentiment was an avenue into middle-class society open to socially marginal individuals who were anxious to identify themselves with this class. The appeal of the prohibition movement, he says, was the appeal of assimilation into traditional American society.

If such factors were operating in the election of 1914, the hard evidence must lie in the voting records of the urban areas themselves. City by city, and ward by ward, who was it that voted for Number 3? An identification of "lower-class" and "middle-class" areas might

TABLE 9

SOCIAL CLASS AND PROHIBITION: THE CITIES, 1914*

City (By population, 1910)	Dwellings/Family Ratio	Vote on No. 3 (Percentage Dry and Wet)	
		Dry	Wet
Seattle	.853	39	61
Spokane	.894	48	52
Tacoma	.900	45	55
Everett	.932	50.6	49.4
Bellingham	.943	51	49

* *Census, 1910*, and city newspapers.

help illuminate this aspect of the voting, and here again the census of 1910, in its fine detail, throws a good light.

The census lists, for example, the figures for "number of dwellings" over those for "number of families" by city and by ward in the larger cities. This ratio should be a reasonably serviceable index to the social status of these areas insofar as a ratio of one to one in 1910 was the middle-class ideal. When this ratio for the various areas is converted to a decimal and compared to the voting percentages recorded in 1914, the results are striking. The figures in table 9 show a correlation between the dwellings-to-families ratio and dry sentiment in the major cities. But the figures indicate, if anything, only that the larger cities had proportionally higher percentages of wet votes. Since one cannot, of course, label entire cities as "lower-class" or "middle-class," this correlation suggests rather than confirms a relationship between social status and voting on Number 3.

A much more satisfactory point of focus is the basic political unit of the city ward, for it is only at this range that one can see enough detail for a valid generalization. At this level, the ratio of dwellings to families measures something more than the population density of the unit; it becomes a sharp index to social status itself. In Washington in 1914 (it is reasonable to assume) the city wards with low ratios were those of low social status. It would be in such wards that one might have found a group of fairly class-conscious individuals living as tenants in apartments or boarding houses, people who were unwilling or unable to adopt the common denominator of middle-class status, an individual family residence. As the ratio fell, too, one would have approached the downtown wards and the saloon-oriented neighborhoods where saloons might have been "poormen's clubs" and an integral part of the ward ecology. In such wards one would naturally expect the lowest degrees of temperance sentiment.

Table 10 shows the converse also to be true: as one approached the middle-class ideal of one family per residence, one found the highest percentage of dry sentiment. In the middle-class wards, the voting shows that the values of "the country" were dominant.

The Spokane wards were probably typical of wards in the larger cities and can be analyzed in this way:

1st Ward. This can be called middle class, though it was slightly lower on the social scale than the 4th Ward because of more illiterates, Orientals, and Indians. Another factor in the wet vote—a minor one, to be sure—was probably the number of Germans and Catholics.

2nd Ward. Here is a good example of a lower-class downtown ward: low dwellings to families ratio, high illiteracy. The significant number of Indians and Orientals is a good indicator of lower-class status. The saloon probably was an important part of the ecology here.

3rd Ward. Like the 2nd Ward, this is a downtown ward, but parts of it pull away from this environment. It approaches "marginal" status.

4th Ward. This is the most nearly middle-class of them all, distinguished from the 1st Ward by the features noted above.

5th Ward. This ward is as "upper-middle" as Spokane could go in 1910. The dwellings to families ratio places it higher than the 4th Ward. The Orientals and illiterates here were probably servants of the wealthy.

TABLE 10
SOCIAL CLASS AND PROHIBITION: THE CITY WARDS*

Spokane Wards, 1910

Total	1st	2nd	3rd	4th	5th
Population	25,120	18,954	13,442	21,991	24,975
Indians and Orientals	54	468	51	8	27
Foreign-born Germans	725	502	449	506	573
Foreign-born Irish	186	302	132	152	248
Foreign-born Italians	501	588	211	36	208
Foreign-born Norwegians	641	470	152	246	365
Foreign-born Swedes	880	852	330	550	731
Total Foreign-born Whites	5,096	5,565	2,844	3,484	4,231
Number of Illiterates over ten years old	230	367	301	46	179
Dwellings/Families	.930	.670	.840	.931	.962
Percent of Dry Votes, 1914	51%	37%	40%	53%	51%

* Census, 1910, and Spokane Spokesman-Review. It would be valuable to know how these wards voted on reform (women's suffrage, I and R), progressivism (Poindexter, Roosevelt, Wilson), and class-consciousness (Debbs). Unfortunately, neither the Spokane County records nor the daily newspapers offer these data.

In these wards one finds the answer to the question of who in the cities voted for Number 3. The middle class did, and those on the margins of this class contributed a good measure of support. The dry appeal to the urban middle class had yielded the 18,632 votes which brought the state-wide dry victory. With Number 3, the middle classes of the country and of the city had united in a great effort to control their environment, and the lower classes, who lived mainly in the cities, had opposed them. The victory, however, was much more one of the middle class over the lower class than it was of rural areas

over urban areas. In 1914, the mill hands of Everett, the miners of
Bellingham, the merchants, physicians, and bookkeepers of Spokane,
Tacoma, and Seattle cast their votes with the farmers to exorcise a
social evil which they did not know how to control.

This dimension of class tension in the prohibition movement in
Washington helps one see it as a part of that widespread agitation
for reform in American society after 1900 called the progressive
movement. This movement is usually defined as a middle-class concern with the problems of progress and poverty, a middle-class attack
against the social abuses caused by the monopolies and the trusts,
against corruption and vice and social irresponsibility. It was also a
movement against the spread of class-consciousness that seemed to be
undermining the American dream after the Civil War, because the
rich were growing richer and the poor were growing more poor.

In the first years of the twentieth century, the western states stood
in the vanguard of the progressive movement. The migration of
Americans to the West by the hundreds of thousands between 1880
and 1910 was a most important aspect of the movement, for the migrants were surely fleeing the evils of the old society as eagerly as
they were responding to the opportunities of the new. The West during these years was a safety valve for the frustrations of poverty and
social immobility. The railroads—by making the journey cheap and
the relocation easy—pulled the valve wide open. To those who escaped through it, the progressive movement expressed their determination to avoid the social inequities they had left behind them.

They moved west with a faith that democracy was good, and that
evil could be legislated away if democracy could be purified. One
sees this in the sweep toward the initiative and referendum, in the
legislative regulation of monopoly, in the laws to improve the conditions of labor. These were the attempts of the new and dominant social class to force its newly acquired and still pliable environment to
conform to a fleeting image of an older, pre-industrial society—to *reform,* in the most literal meaning of this word. This is to say, almost,
that the progressive movement and the prohibition movement were,
in fact, the same.

The extent to which progressives and prohibitionists shared the
same ultimate goals—a perfect society—and were moved by the same
social concerns—the increasingly bitter class-consciousness in the
United States—has been recently examined at the national level by

James H. Timberlake in *Prohibition and the Progressive Movement, 1900-1920*. Timberlake's conclusions are drawn without equivocation:

> . . . the Progressive Movement embraced a wide variety of individual reforms, one of the more important and least understood of which was prohibition. Although today sometimes regarded as a conservative measure, prohibition was actually written into the Constitution as a progressive reform. As an integral part of the Progressive Movement, prohibition drew on the same moral idealism and sought to deal with the same basic problems. If the Progressive Movement was nourished in a belief in the moral law, so was prohibition, which sought to remove from commerce an article that was believed to despoil man's reason and undermine the foundation of religion and representative government. If progressive America's growing devotion to efficiency also reflected an optimistic belief in the desirability of material progress, the attack on alcoholic beverages as an enemy of efficiency mirrored the same faith. . . . If progressivism desired to curb the power of an industrial and financial plutocracy, prohibition aimed to remove the corrupting influence of one branch of that plutocracy—the liquor industry. Again, if progressivism represented a quickening of the humanitarian impulse, manifested in redoubled efforts of philanthropists and social workers to banish crime, poverty, and disease from the environment, prohibition was an effort to eliminate one factor that caused them. And, finally, if progressivism sought to improve the status of the lower classes by direct legislation, prohibition sought to uplift them by the same means.[20]

Timberlake's study analyzes in some detail the religious, the scientific, the social, the economic, and the political arguments for prohibition which, by 1915, most middle-class Americans believed. His work clarifies the rational foundation of the prohibition movement which one does not see in the caustic psychoanalysis of reform by Richard Hofstadter or in the motivational research of Andrew Sinclair, which is based largely on literary evidence and stresses the morbid base of prohibitionist sentiment in sexual and racial fears.[21]

Timberlake's book is, quite directly, a response to the Hofstadter thesis:

> Although the prohibition movement took on the nature of a conflict between country and city, it is better understood if viewed more as a class than a rural-urban struggle. For the movement cut across geographic lines: the old-stock, urban middle classes, which comprised about 40 percent of the urban population in 1910, tended to favor it, whereas the labor classes in the country were more often opposed.

He traces the social and ethnic character of the movement through the attempts of the urban middle class to regulate the saloon, and he shows that in state after state where prohibition was popular, it had solid middle-class, progressive support. In California, for example, the state senators who favored local option all had impressive records as progressive reformers.[22] In Boston, the middle-class wards voted "no-license" when the issue was before them in 1916. In the southern states, the urban middle class returned majorities for prohibition after it had restricted the Negroes' franchise.

There is abundant evidence from the state of Washington to support this interpretation. The analysis of social class and voting patterns in 1914 developed here provides some regional depth for such a view, just as an Anti-Saloon Convention and Congress of Reform Forces, which met in Seattle in 1906, was a perfect expression of the relationship between the leaders of the antisaloon movement and the progressive movement. These leaders were, indeed, most often the same men. One thinks immediately of George Cotterill, who helped write the women's suffrage amendment, the amendment for initiative and referendum, and the prohibition initiative; and of Marion E. Hay, who as governor of the state and as a private citizen did all he could to assist Cotterill in these achievements.

This relationship can be reinforced by the records of the state legislature, which show how dry sentiment and progressive sentiment were usually well blended.

Table 11 shows how twelve state senators of the dry persuasion voted on certain progressive measures in 1909 and 1911. Of the thirty-six votes recorded in the table, twenty-eight are progressive. A similar table for twelve wet senators present in 1909 and 1911 would show fifteen progressive votes of the total thirty-six. In the House there were twenty-one dry representatives who voted in 1909 and 1911, and in forty-two of their votes on progressive measures (women's suffrage and I and R), thirty-three were "yes."[23]

An interesting group in this regard is those senators who in 1909 and 1911 voted "no" on a majority of reform issues (table 12). These were men who with some consistency and tenacity entrenched themselves against the pressures for social change. Four of them were from urban counties and four were from rural ones. A similar listing for the House would show only six representatives of this persuasion who were present in both 1909 and 1911—this fact is itself a

TABLE 11

PROHIBITION AND THE PROGRESSIVE MOVEMENT:
THE STATE SENATE*

Dry Senators Present in 1909 and 1911 (By county)	Vote on Progressive Measures		
	Women's Suffrage	Initiative, Referendum	8-hour law for women
Arrasmith (Spokane)	YES	No	No
Bassett (Franklin)	YES	YES	No
Brown (Whatcom)	YES	YES	No
Bryan (Kitsap)	YES	YES	YES
Cox (Walla Walla)	YES	No	YES
Falconer (Snohomish)	YES	YES	YES
Fishback (Lewis)	YES	No	No vote
Hutchinson (Spokane)	YES	YES	YES
Metcalf (Pierce)	YES	YES	YES
Myers (Lincoln)	YES	YES	No vote
Paulhamus (Pierce)	YES	YES	YES
Rosenhaupt (Spokane)	YES	YES	YES

* Senate Journal of the State of Washington (1909 and 1911). The indicator used for "wetness" or "dryness" here is the vote on a motion to refer Senate Substitute Bill 121 to committee, a motion which lost, 24-18 (pp. 419-25). The indicator for women's suffrage is the vote on final passage, the only roll-call vote recorded on that issue (p. 467). The indicator for I and R is the vote on the motion to place petitions only in the office of county auditors, a provision which would surely have killed I and R. The indicator for the issue involved in the eight-hour law for women is the vote on a motion to change "8" to "9" (pp. 892-93). The I and R indicator is examined carefully in Claudius O. Johnson, "The Adoption of Initiative and Referendum in Washington," Pacific Northwest Quarterly, XXXV (October, 1944), 291-303.

TABLE 12

GENTLEMEN OF THE OLD GUARD:
STATE SENATORS WHO OPPOSED REFORM, 1909-1911

Senator (By county)	Vote on Reform Measures			
	Local Option	Women's Suffrage	I & R	8-hour law for women
Eastham (Clark)	NO	Yes	NO	NO
Nichols (King)	NO	NO	NO	Yes
Roberts (Pierce)	NO	Yes	NO	NO
Rydstrom (Pierce)	NO	NO	NO	NO
Smithson (Chelan)	NO	NO	NO	NO
Stewart (Cowlitz)	NO	Yes	NO	NO
Whitney (Spokane)	NO	NO	NO	Yes
Ruth (Thurston)	NO	NO	NO	Yes

measure of the conservatives' political misfortune. Five of these six
survivors were from rural counties.

These tables show that there was, of course, no perfect congruence
of the progressive movement and the prohibition movement, for in
complex ways each reform touched a different level of passion and
conviction in each individual. There were many men and women in
the state who were close to May Arkwright Hutton of Spokane, who,
in her easy-going tolerance and sympathies for the dispossessed, dedicated herself to charity, to the cause of women's suffrage, and to the
beauties of I and R, but all the while detested the prohibitionists.[24]
There were counties like King and Pierce that returned majorities in
perfect alignment with the sympathies of Mrs. Hutton. But on the
other hand, one can see clearly that the progressive movement—as it
is measured in these tables—usually included the antisaloon reform.

In 1914 the dominant social class struck down the saloon, which
had been a source and a symbol of the evils that this class had
feared. These evils had come from the competitive degradation of humanity in an unregulated industrial society. For the saloon there was
no Pure Food and Drug Act, no easy way to restrict its excesses, no
conceptual tools, really, for the effective control of saloon competition. So the saloon had to go. In abolishing it, the voters of course
created other problems, but they surely solved the one problem they
wanted most to solve: the "hell-soaked institution" which had stumbled out of the nineteenth century would close its doors forever.

The closing suggests that there is a broad period in American history which might be called the "Age of Evangelism," a period during
which evangelism as a quality of life permeated individual and social
being. Its components would be romantic optimism, strong emotionalism, passions for righteousness, and convictions that righteousness
could be grasped through vigorous action; hence the pledges, the parades, the speeches, the songs, the votes. This quality tapped what
Reinhold Niebuhr calls the "deep layer of Messianic consciousness in
the mind of America."[25] It included also a demand for maximum
dedication and efficiency, an eagerness to sacrifice, and a sense of
moral uplift in the sacrifices of others. There was a color here, to be
sure, that approached the discomforting shades of fanaticism, and
one could easily identify in this period a good number of fanatics in
the ranks of evangelical religion, politics, unionism, or technology.

The evangelical character of the prohibition movement expressed these qualities very well. Though it was imbued with selfish economic motives, class tensions, maybe even with subconscious racial and sexual fears—with paranoia, stupidity, and greed—the prohibition movement also urged men and women to vote with their hearts and with their sometimes desperate hope that they could restore the lost purity of the great agrarian dream and make a better world. In the prohibition movement one can see an attempt of the "Age of Evangelism" to resist what Carl Bridenbaugh has called "the great mutation"—the change in American society from a natural environment to an artificial one, from a religious faith to a secular one.[26] The age—and the movement—may end when the mutation is finally complete, when the symbol of "the country" has lost all of its reality. The dying flames of evangelism which one sees today may be, in fact, a true measure of this mutation. For when all the old Prohibs are dead—as so soon they will be—one may look vain for the old America.

9

Moderate Reconstruction and the Radical Triumph

ONE OF THE most poignant ironies of the progressive age lies in the ease with which the devices of reform could be used by the very groups against whom they were intended. I and R, designed to circumvent corrupt governments and achieve reform, could be used also to circumvent reform governments and achieve special-interest programs. In their hours of anguish, it was natural that the liquor interests should attempt direct legislation. Initiative Measure Number 18, drawn for the legislature of 1915, would have amended the prohibition law to permit the sale of liquor in hotels. Petitions for it were circulated immediately after the November election in 1914, and they quickly brought forth the righteous wrath of those who supposed that Number 3 had been a victory of some permanence. The Grange, for example, attacked Number 18 as an attempt to "make a saloon . . . a den of vice and a brothel of the hotels of the land." But the petitions were validated before the end of the year, and as an initiative to the legislature, Number 18 had, according to the constitution, precedence over all other legislation. Legislators received their instructions on this matter with proper dignity, then assigned the measure to committee where it was isolated as a piece of political leprosy and never returned to the floor. The constitution further required that initiatives to the legislature not acted upon must go before the people, and Number 18 was accordingly scheduled for the general election of 1916.[1]

This treatment by the legislature suggests political discretion as much as it does dry conviction, for there were enemies of Number 3 in Olympia in 1915. In the House, a resolution was introduced which would have prevented discussion of any measure whose purpose was

128

to amend the prohibition law, but this resolution was indefinitely postponed. Such action protected those legislators involved in a movement to call for a special referendum on "day-light saloons." Other members were behind a proposal to allow breweries to produce for export, and Senator William Wray of King County intended to introduce a bill which would have repealed Number 3 entirely. For the liquor interests, though, their hour of desperation was also an hour of political bankruptcy. When it became clear that the legislature did indeed plan to consider modifications in Number 3, Governor Ernest Lister let it be known that he would kill any such attempt with his veto.[2]

The people would have their experiment in prohibition, and it would begin as scheduled on January 1, 1916. Whatever hope the saloonkeepers may have sustained was gone by December, 1915, when the state Supreme Court upheld the validity of the dry law. Challengers had questioned both the law and the I and R amendment through which it had come, but to no avail. They had claimed that the law was discriminatory because it granted to drug stores certain privileges denied other businesses, but the court said that this was constitutional discrimination. On the next point—the constitutionality of I and R—the entire future of direct legislation in the state was at stake. The critics challenged the plurality of the initiative and the referendum which, they asserted, was improper in a single amendment to the constitution. The court, however, ruled that the amendment may be plural in form but surely singular in meaning, and that the unity of concept and intent in direct legislation precluded any consideration of the initiative and the referendum as separate or distinct.

After this decision had been registered, saloon men began the unhappy business of leasing or selling their halls and selling or storing their fixtures. In this task they were beset by yet another calamity when souvenir hunters began stripping the drink palaces with a wanton enthusiasm. As the artifacts of a dead era were torn from them, saloon men might have turned with mixed emotions to the heroic posture of the Seattle *Post-Intelligencer,* which editorialized "Going Dry—Cheer Up," or to Chadwick of the *Argus,* who urged strict enforcement as the only way the state could ever get rid of a miserable law. Ernest P. Marsh, president of the Washington State Federation of Labor, extended his best but cheerless wishes to the departing members of the Federation who had lost their jobs because of the impending drought.[3] Mail-order houses in Montana looked forward to the new year by buying full pages in newspapers to advertise prepaid shipments of beer and liquor.

The new law, of course, would burn out the saloons and the indigenous liquor industry, but not liquor. The law allowed an individual to import as much as two quarts of hard booze or twelve quarts of high percentage beer each twenty days. To get his share, the individual had to obtain an import permit from his county auditor, and the unseemly haste with which people gathered at the auditors' offices warmed the cynical hearts of those who criticized the prohibition movement. In Seattle, for example—then advertised by the ASL as the largest dry city in the world outside Russia—the auditor issued over eighteen thousand permits in the month of August. In Spokane, the auditor warned churchmen in 1917 that he had issued thirty-four thousand permits when there were but forty-four thousand registered voters in the county. Such was the distance between the antisaloon movement and the antidrink movement at this time.

Throughout the state, too, there were hundreds of ambitious entrepreneurs prepared to accommodate citizens who were unwilling to suffer the bureaucracy of the permit system. After a three or four month period of adjustment, the market for illicit liquor began a steady expansion. The demand soon surpassed the supply, and moonshine booze was selling for five dollars a quart by the end of the year. The Spokane County prosecutor complained in 1917 that the soft-drink shops which flourished in the cities were worse than the old-time saloons: moonshine was plentiful, and every crook and hooligan in the state was moving in on the business. In Tacoma, even the longshoremen demanded that police clean up the illegal practices of soft-drink shops and drug stores.[4]

Between January and March, 1916, some sixty-five new drug stores opened in Seattle. The mayor at the time was Hiram Gill, who, after his recall in 1911 because he had condoned a wicked city, had been re-elected in 1914 and 1916 on a platform of repentance and—if this was what the city wanted—rigid virtue. When he turned to the problem of bootlegging across the new drug counters, it was not really clear whether his zeal was that of a convert or that of a cynic bent upon making the worst of a bad situation. Gill enforced the law with an ax, and usually in person. The newspaper pictures of Seattle's mayor, shirt-sleeved in indignation, reducing drug stores to pulp and litter, brought cheers from the radical reformers. Gill's critics, on the other hand, concluded that the mayor's split personality had led him to confuse himself with Carry Nation.[5]

The Gill ax raids fell across the city apparently without discrimination. In October he destroyed twenty-five hundred dollars' worth of fixtures in a drug store that had sold whiskey illegally—smashing the counter and the chandelier, breaking the bottles, squashing the toothpaste. In December the Dry Squad hit two restaurants, destroying a total of twenty-two thousand dollars in fixtures. In May, 1917, the destruction at a hotel was estimated at twenty thousand dollars. Even the *Argus*, which had urged strict enforcement, cried that the raids were "the most high-handed outrages ever perpetrated in this community."[6]

One of Seattle's new drug stores was called the Stewart Street Pharmacy, a sort of family enterprise owned by Logan and Fred Billingsley. In the first months of their operation, the Billingsleys were fined several times for bootlegging, but they appealed their cases and continued their illegal business with no obvious discomfort. In May of 1916, Gill's police arrived at the store just when a carload of liquor was being unloaded. Taking firemen's axes, the police laid waste the entire establishment, leaving nothing but a heap of wreckage which an hour before had been worth ten thousand dollars. When the Billingsleys protested, Gill told reporters that he was willing to take his chances with a jury should "these fellows go into court to claim damages."[7]

The Billingsleys, though, were not likely to approach court from that direction. They were being guided through the network of Number 3 by a brilliant criminal lawyer named George Vanderveer, who a few years before had been the prosecutor of King County. Vanderveer manipulated the paper work which took the Billingsleys out of the petty business of neighborhood bootlegging and into the world of international conspiracy. He organized a mock-up company for them which, on paper, shipped liquor from Cuba to Canada. As wholesalers rather than bootleggers, they were shifting carefully toward a vast illegal market. Single shipments which reached them circuitously from the Hunt Liquor Company in San Francisco ran as high as $250,000.[8]

Such shipments brought the Billingsleys into still another world—

that of pirate capitalism. A former policeman named Jack Marquett, who had taken to rumrunning with some success, regarded Seattle's illegal trade as his own private domain. As the Billingsleys encroached upon it, competition led directly to hijacking and violence. Two men were dead, for example, after a gunfight at the Billingsley warehouse in July, 1916. That summer Seattle had a frightening glimpse into the next decade of whiskey, bullets, and bloodshed.[9]

This notoriety attending the first year's experience with the dry law was sure to stimulate the hopes of the brewers, the distillers, and the wine sellers who had been watching the state attentively, waiting for a break in public opinion that might open a way for their return. The bootlegging, the killings, the ax raids, the complaints from county prosecutors, the protests from longshoremen and newspapers that the law did not work—these were symptoms of unrest which the liquor interests eagerly overestimated when they determined to make the general election of 1916 another major battle between the wet and the dry.

Initiative Measure Number 18 (labeled the "Hotelmen's Liquor Bill") was already scheduled to go before the people, and two other initiatives aimed at the prohibition law were prepared for validation. Number 24 ("Brewers' Bill"), which would have permitted the manufacture of beer and the sale of it directly to the consumer, received enough signatures to get it on the ballot. But Number 25, which would have repealed Number 3 outright, lacked enough public support to move beyond the petition stage.

The campaign focused naturally upon the consequences of Number 3 that were apparent from its few months of practice. In its defense, the drys used some impressive statistics. Spokane police reported a 67 per cent decline in arrests for drunkenness. The Spokane County Auditor reported that the cost of running the county was significantly less in the first six months of 1916 than it had been in 1915, and, in addition, tax delinquency had been cut by 50 per cent. In Walla Walla, the Mayor said that drunkenness was down 80 per cent, arrests down 70 per cent. Bank deposits, he added, had increased; bills were being paid on time. State Highway Commissioner George F. Cotterill stated that so few convicts had entered the state prison since January, 1916, that he had to employ free labor for road construction. Even some Seattle businessmen were praising the results of the dry law.[10] In short, the chorus was, the middle-class virtues were spreading.

One remarkable feature of the campaign was the conversion of the Seattle *Times*. Its editor, Major C. B. Blethen—son of old Colonel Alden J. Blethen, who died in 1915 and was thus spared the realities of the dry state—studied the statistics of his city and announced that he had joined the drys. He told his story to the nation's press:

> My paper fought its damnedest against Prohibition. We fought it on economic grounds alone. . . . In the first three weeks of January the savings accounts in the banks of Seattle increased greatly in numbers. There was not a grocery store in Seattle that did not show an increase in business. . . . Every dry goods store . . . had a wonderful increase in business . . . it makes me sorry we did not have Prohibition long ago. . . . It is the women and children who benefit greatest from Prohibition. . . . It is just like this: When you close the saloons the money that formerly was spent there remains in the family. . . . Yes sir, we have found in Seattle that it is better to buy shoes than booze. . . .

Blethen spoke frequently, citing his figures on drunkenness, arrests, bank deposits, and retail sales. The dryer we get, he said, the better is business. He also wrote an article for *Collier's* so that the world could know what had happened in Seattle.[11]

This reversal of a leading conservative must have brought deep pain to those who held steadfast in their belief that prohibition was the work of demented farmers and weakling fanatics. Chadwick, of the *Argus*, had anticipated something of this sort when he wrote in 1915 that "All reforms breed hypocrisy. It must be expected. And Washington has started on its big spree." After several outbursts by Blethen about the glories of dry Seattle, Chadwick mocked sourly, "Come to Seattle. . . . Not only will you live longer in Seattle, but with the lid clamped down, the saloons closed . . . it will seem twice as long as it really is." But even Chadwick himself had to appraise what Blethen was saying, and despite his stinging pen, he moved perceptibly toward the moderate position. He wrote against Number 25, the repeal measure, saying that he did not want the old-time saloon ever to rise again. He favored, instead, Number 24, the Brewers' Bill, because it provided for regulated sales. The Hotelmen's Bill he regarded as too much a piece of selfish-interest legislation.[12]

Seattle's unreconstructed conservatives must have read Chadwick with growing distaste and irritations. Among men of this faith there were three who had, perhaps, more interest in the course of events than most—William E. Boeing, the airplane manufacturer; John

Carmen Eden, owner of a cement company; and D. E. Skinner, mill-owner. On the first dry day, January 1, 1916, Gill's Dry Squad had raided the homes of these gentlemen, and, to their considerable in-dignation, seized stores of wines and liquors from their private cel-lars. The raid was illegal, but the Mayor had his fun, perhaps dra-matizing his attitude toward the new law. Boeing, Eden, and Skinner saw no humor; it was rumored that they had threatened to remove their places of residence to a more civilized state.[13]

As the wet and dry forces regrouped themselves across the state in 1916, the campaigners found that prohibition had become a major issue in partisan politics. In 1914, few politicians had dared to take positions on either side of Number 3, but in 1916 the candidates spent a good part of their efforts in proving themselves more dry than their opponents. Governor Lister expected no difficulties in this regard, for he could stand on his warning to the legislature in 1915 that he would veto their attempts to modify the dry law. He also had urged appropriations for the enforcement of it, and he was, moreover, a reformer of long standing. (He had been a union leader, an official in the Populist government of 1897-1900, and, as a small businessman, always close to the progressive movement.) The Republican candidate for governor was Henry McBride, who had accepted saloon support in 1908. Democrats did what they could to keep his wet history be-fore the voters. McBride fought hard, though, campaigning explicitly against Number 18 and Number 24 and placing himself squarely against the hotel men and the brewers.

It was something of a scandal, then, when the hotel men accused Lister of having taken money from them in 1912 to beat Marion Hay.[14] Coming as it did in the last moments of the campaign, the charge seems to have been the anxious effort of hotel interests to strike at Lister for his treatment of the 1915 legislature and to reduce him to a position in the wet-dry competition at least equal to that of Henry McBride. But the choice before the people, quite clearly, was between two drys. The participation of the hotel men in the partisan contest served only to illustrate once more their consistent political incompetence.

Lister won again, and there could be no doubt about his wisdom in waging a dry campaign. Voters rejected the proposed wet meas-ures in overwhelming numbers.

TABLE 13

THE PROGRESS OF DRY SENTIMENT
1914-1920*

Direct Legislation Measures	Wet	Dry
State Prohibition Law, 1914	171,208	189,840
Hotelmen's Bill, 1916	48,354	263,390
Brewers' Bill, 1916	98,843	245,399
"Bone-Dry" Referendum, 1918	54,322	96,100

* *Washington Public Documents* (1914-20).

At the same time the people elected a legislature which would be more dry than any in the state's history. The next question on a liquor measure in the state senate—on the "bone-dry" law—returned only three wet votes. This was the afternoon of the progressive era, too bright and too dry for the old guard to find any comforts. Senator Link Davis of Thurston County, defeated in the Republican primary of 1916, was perhaps representative of those who had been pushed aside. "I have come to the conclusion," he told Chadwick, "that . . . with a railroad commission and United States Senators being elected by popular vote, the legislature is no place for a gentleman, anyhow."[15]

One of the most significant aspects of the 1916 election was the change that took place in city voting on liquor issues. In 1914 Seattle had been wet by fifteen thousand votes, but it went dry by twenty thousand in 1916; Spokane had been wet by fifteen hundred in 1914 and was dry by twelve thousand in 1916. Clearly, the city voters had changed their minds. One good reason for this was, of course, that their experience with prohibition by 1916 had generally been a happy one. Major Blethen, in heralding the glories of sobriety and prosperity —and the causal relationship between the two—probably echoed what most men and women were thinking about a dry state.

Surely the dark warnings of Judge Thomas Burke in 1914 had been exposed as unwarranted pessimism. Most fortuitously for the drys, the European war had absorbed the unemployment caused by Number 3, and the opening of the Panama Canal had brought a great surge in the economy of all the Pacific Northwest. Burke had been wrong only because he had not foreseen these developments. The causal relationship between the war and the canal and the dry prosperity was not, however, a prominent part of the drys' propaganda.

But all of Blethen's exuberance cannot be so easily criticized. The solid fact was that in 1916 the saloon was dead and many of its evils had been buried with it. There were fewer drunks on the streets, fewer arrests, and consequently less municipal and state expense in protecting society from the backwash of alcohol. There were no more saloon bosses of city wards, and the liquor interests no longer manipulated the legislature. Workers now did not cash their checks in saloons; they took them home. Wives were happier, and businessmen were delighted.[16]

And many workers had discovered that the changes in American society were sweeping them into the middle class and that the saloon was, after all, dispensable. The "poor men's club" was being displaced by institutions of more vitality and attractiveness. Even before the saloons closed in 1916, it was clear to some observers, for example, that the increasing popularity of moving-picture theaters had cut sharply into saloon attendance.[17] The technology of the progressive age was producing a machinery and gadgetry which diverted saloon regulars and to a marvelous degree accelerated the social assimilation of the working classes. Workingmen and their families found in movies and automobiles—and a little later, in radios—a new ladder into the middle class, a ladder so sturdy and so smooth because of wartime prosperity that just about anyone could give it a try. Throughout Washington, the theaters were replacing the saloons as centers of neighborhood entertainment; automobile registration between 1914 and 1918 increased over 300 per cent.[18] The saloon remained dead because the symbol of class identity it had provided no longer served a social need.

But there was an even more significant change measured by the election of 1916. In rejecting the Brewers' Bill, the voters illuminated the transition between the antisaloon movement and the antidrink movement. Chadwick was still lagging behind the public mind in 1916, when he had written against saloons—he wanted no more of them—but supported the Brewers' Bill. He did this with perfect consistency because, quite simply, it would have allowed those who wanted beer in their homes to buy it in the state rather than out, and it would have discouraged the bootlegging that thrived on the permit system. Shocked by the overwhelming vote against the Brewers' Bill, Chadwick had to conclude that the people opposed even the use of beer and that they would soon vote the state bone dry.[19] He was correct, and the factors in the antidrink sentiment are not difficult to find.

Chadwick himself had contributed to this sentiment when in 1915 he published a report on life insurance statistics which held that as few as two drinks a day would shorten the life of a robust man.[20] For the antidrink movement, like the antisaloon movement, was fed by as many conscious motives as it was subconscious ones. Scientific evidence in support of total abstinence had been widely publicized by 1915. The discoveries that alcohol does not warm the body, that it is a depressant, not a stimulant, and that it depresses the higher mental functions as well as muscular control—these had been the topics of articles in national middle-class magazines for over a decade. During this period, too, various "studies" had demonstrated to the satisfaction of intelligent men the close relationship between alcohol and insanity. It was generally believed that alcoholic parents produced degenerate children. Many scientists were radically lowering their estimates of what they regarded as harmless doses of liquor, and some of the most prominent members of the scientific community had given up the personal use of alcohol entirely. Among these were August Forel, the Swiss entomologist known for his work on the anatomy of the brain and in sex hygiene, and Emil Kraeplin, a German psychiatrist who had investigated the influence of alcohol on mental processes. American psychiatrists and neurologists, at a national meeting in 1914, declared alcohol a poison. Physicians had been prescribing less and less alcohol for their patients, and prominent educators—such as Charles Eliot, president of Harvard University—had, on the basis of scientific evidence, taken up the cause of total abstention. Investigators in the new social sciences supplied a mass of statistics to prove the existence of relationships between whiskey and crime, prostitution, and poverty. Studies in scientific management had stressed efficiency and sobriety, and some American manufacturers, even before the war, had forbidden their employees to drink at any time, on or off duty. All of these developments were products of the best scientific thought of the age. Probably even more than religion, science had prepared the public mind for complete prohibition.[21]

It was in this climate of opinion that the national preparedness program picked up momentum after 1915, coupling the emotions of self-sacrifice and national sacrifice with the concept of a healthy, sober nation. The result was that in the short period of these two or three years, the prohibition movement gained strength more rapidly than even the most wildly optimistic of the radicals could have imagined. In 1916, Oregon had passed a bone-dry law which ended the permit system in that state and prohibited any importation of alcoholic beverages. Arizona and West Virginia had taken similar action. On January 8, 1917, the Supreme Court upheld the constitutionality of the bone-dry laws by ruling that the Webb-Kenyon Act of 1913 had properly granted to the states the power to so interfere in interstate commerce. This decision was the invitation for which the drys in many states, including Washington, had been waiting. It allowed them to transform the prohibition movement—with little conflict or protest of any kind—into a movement openly dedicated to abolishing all alcoholic beverages from the land.

One symptom of the strength of the movement was that the Anti-Saloon League was outpaced by public opinion and temporarily lost its control. Early in 1917 the state legislature in Olympia took under consideration H.B. 4, a bone-dry measure aimed at ending the permit system, except for clergymen and druggists. This would close off the state from the mail-order houses and thereby bring the great drought. The bill reached the floor through channels opened independently by the Grange and the WCTU forces, and it was met there with general approval. The ASL men sat in confusion. George Conger, state president, personally opposed the bill because both he and the national leaders regarded it as too radical a move for 1917. But he could not, with any composure, make an overt effort to kill it. His position was especially awkward when, at a dramatic moment, the Speaker of the House turned to the gallery and invited Conger to the platform where he could stand for questioning about his attitudes toward the bone-dry law. When he refused the invitation without comment, the radicals were free to take the field.[22]

A move to amend the measure with a provision for a referendum was lost in the House, sixty-one to thirty-four. Despite the plea of one representative that "this bill bears the marks of passion. . . . It tears to pieces a law adopted by a direct vote of the people . . ." the vote on final passage was seventy-five to eighteen. In the Senate there were only three votes against the bill, but the three dissenters were established drys who objected only to the legislature's refusal to submit the bill to the people.[23] The radical persuasion was in complete command, and Governor Lister signed the bill on February 19, his office crowded with dry legislators, ladies from the WCTU, and ASL leaders. According to the law, the state would go bone dry in ninety days after legislative adjournment unless the people themselves demanded a vote.

The attitude of the legislature toward a referendum caused some critical editorial comment even while the debates were in progress. The *Spokesman-Review* warned:

> The arbitrary passage by the legislature over the heads of the voters of a so called "bone-dry" liquor law without a referendum attachment would be more likely to stimulate bootlegging than to diminish it . . . in Washington we have a prohibition law that has the sanction of public approval at the polls, and the legislature is now asked to overthrow the public judgment and substitute a law that may or may not be wanted by the majority of the people.[24]

With such encouragement, referendum petitions were circulated and validated by the end of the summer. The petitions, however, had been empty gestures against an established fact after the month of March, for it was during that month that federal legislation overtook the state's dry movement. The Congress of the United States had by then amended the Post Office Appropriations Bill of 1917 to forbid interstate shipments of alcoholic beverages into any state which had a dry law, whether or not these states had permit systems. (This was introduced in the Senate as the Reed Amendment, by James A. Reed, a "dripping wet" senator from Missouri, who had thought the Anti-Saloon League leaders were insincere and who wanted to harass them with a move far in advance of their own program.[25] This goal was accomplished, for the League men had their difficult moments; but the move backfired on the wets when the Reed-Randall Bone Dry Act, as is was called, passed both houses of Congress.)

After this, those who signed the referendum petitions in the state of Washington may have held a thin if unwarranted hope for a revision of the federal law, or they may simply have wanted to protest it. But referendum or no, the permit system was contrary to federal law, and Washington was bone dry.

In August of 1917, the state had a bone-dry Supreme Court as well. The court ruled that Michael Fabbri of Tacoma had been constitutionally prosecuted for making wine for his own consumption, and that the state law should be understood as prohibiting the manufacture of alcohol for any purpose whatsoever. This decision closed the last opportunity for legal boozing in the state.[26]

Illegal drinking had fared no better. Seattle's Dry Squad had captured Jack Marquett and his whiskey pirates, and before the Billingsleys could realize any advantage from this, they too were in jail. The investigation of Marquett's affairs had involved the Hunt Liquor Company of San Francisco and directed the prosecutor's attention to a rich body of Hunt-Billingsley correspondence. The Billingsleys pled guilty, but then they shocked the state with the charge that they had been double-crossed by Mayor Hiram Gill, to whom, they claimed, they had paid four thousand dollars for protection.[27]

To the leaders of the dry movement, though, the work of Gill's ax was more valid evidence than the bitter testimony of a bootlegger, and they rushed to his defense. Laurence Colman, a prominent dry who had worked for Gill's recall in 1911, supported the Mayor in 1917. Gill was indicted but acquitted. He led ax raids throughout 1917 and kept his Dry Squad after the bootleggers who swarmed around the ships in the harbor from Alaska, California, Europe, and Japan. As Chadwick had written, "There is only one thing for an intelligent man to do, and that is to climb on the water wagon and stay there."[28] Very likely, most people did just that.

By this time, too, the country was at war. By May, 1917, Congress had dried up the military, making it illegal to serve liquor to servicemen under any circumstances. If soldiers could go without liquor, the public reasoned, then surely the civilians could do no less. As the country steadied itself for the great sacrifice, conditions less than bone dry were conditions less than patriotic. A question of real immediacy in the public mind was, "Shall the many have food, or the few have drink?"[29]

Concern over the amount of grain diverted from the war effort by the liquor industry produced in September the Food Control Bill, which forbade the use of foodstuffs in the production of distilled liquors, and thus the manufacture of hard booze came to an end. On December 8, a presidential proclamation prohibited beer with an alcoholic content of more than 2.75 per cent and also sharply limited the amount of foodstuffs that could be used in brewing. And on December 22, 1917—to climax the year and perhaps the century—Congress submitted to the states a resolution to amend the Constitution in such a way as to prohibit "the manufacture, sale, or transportation of intoxicating liquors."

As the emotions of nationalism came to full flood, they even further accelerated the rapid pace of social assimilation. The tempo sometimes became a fierce and brutal thing in the persecution of Germans and in the coercion of the wealthy classes—two groups that had resisted the prohibition movement. Chadwick joined the crowd in 1917, possessed with war fever and a hatred of the "hellish Huns." In his slick, sophisticated, leisure-class journal, he turned hysterically upon German sympathizers and urged that they be summarily shot. On the other side, the Seattle *Star*, a daily newspaper of screaming headlines and pink pages, published the names of wealthy citizens who, in the opinion of the editor, had been rather niggardly in their donations to the Red Cross.[30] In the atmosphere of 1917-18, one joined the middle class or else looked for a place to hide.

Thus when the referendum on the bone-dry law went before the people in November of 1918, it had no strong backers, no promise, no hope of success. Its day at the polls was further shaded by the public anxieties over the war and the influenza pandemic which made the autumn of 1918 a grim and dismal season. Stories of "Hun atrocities" were widespread; casualty lists from the western front filled the newspapers. State law required that flu masks be worn in public at all times. The courts were closed, schools were closed, college classes were dismissed, nurses were on constant emergency call. Flu deaths averaged a shocking twelve to fifteen a day in Spokane. In Seattle, the mortality rate of 252.1 per hundred thousand for influenza in 1918 had never been exceeded by any single cause of death.[31] In this climate of fear and pathos, voting on a meaningless referendum was perhaps the least of public concerns. In 1916, some 400,000 had voted in the general election. In 1918, about 215,000 went to the polls, and of these only 150,000 bothered to vote on the liquor law. The bone-dry total was 96,000, a victory of two to one.

These diminishing statistics again emphasize the significance of the war in bringing radical prohibition to the state, but they cannot divert a conclusion that most people wanted it. The mood of 1918 was one of self-sacrifice, dedication, moral unity, frustration, intolerance, and fear, and these feelings interacted to bring the prohibition movement to its greatest triumph. But these were, after all, the very feelings that had propelled the movement throughout its history. The old Prohib E. B. Sutton, who had signed his letters "Yours, for the war . . . ," had known this very well.

There remained but one detail before the radical reconstruction of public mores could continue in total security, and that was the ratification of the Eighteenth Amendment to the federal Constitution. The state legislature voted for ratification without opposition in January, 1919. An interesting constitutional problem arose when a wet citizen, Frank B. Mullen, tendered to the Secretary of State a referendum petition on this legislative ratification. I. M. Howell, the secretary, refused to honor it, claiming that a referendum on such legislative action was not within the terms of direct legislation defined by the state constitution. The case went before the state Supreme Court, which ordered Howell to accept the petition. Mullen won his point, but it availed him nothing. When the final petitions were submitted for validation in December, 1919, they lacked enough signatures to get the referendum on the next ballot.[32]

Had it ever reached the ballot, Mullen's referendum would have been only an embarrassment to a few sullen wets on a dry day. By January 16, 1919, the required thirty-six states had ratified the Eighteenth Amendment to the Constitution of the United States, and the amendment would be proclaimed in one year. But the country was really dried up in July, 1919, when the War Prohibition Act was enforced. Passed the previous year, this law prohibited the manufacture of beer or wine until the end of demobilization and thus complemented the wartime prohibition of the manufacture of distilled spirits. These two laws would carry the dry cause until the proclamation of the next January 16. In 1919, there were no organized sentiments against prohibition, no discernible pools of wet enthusiasm from which an honest conservative might have drawn hope or solace. The old voices had been silenced, or they had been changed. The Washington State Federation of Labor, which had opposed Number 3, in 1919 criticized Sam Gompers, the president of the American Federation of Labor, for his stand against the Eighteenth Amendment. The State Federation resolved to "denounce, condemn, and repudiate the action of the American Federation of Labor on this matter." The resolution had been brought before the convention by its most urban delegation, the Seattle Metal Trades Council. The following year the convention praised prohibition as "a great benefit to the commonwealth, and especially to the working classes. . . ."[33]

After a battle of at least fifty years, the radicals had convinced the middle class in American society—which in 1920 included the working classes—and had, for a while anyway, been given a free hand. From the vantage point of the victory in 1919-20, one can see certain ironic conflicts within the prohibition movement which would threaten its future, for the dry utopia, like all utopias, was easier to fight for than to administer. First of all, the dry morale depended upon arming the dry law with penalties severe enough to deaden temptation; if prohibition did not in fact prohibit, the cause would be lost to backsliding. Yet at this time the middle class, in accepting Progressive jurisprudence, was moving away from the concepts of harsh and uncompromising justice and the practices of legal vengeance. Even in 1919, it was difficult for prosecutors to persuade juries to return convictions against violators of the dry law because the mandatory penitentiary sentences offended the middle-class conscience.[34]

This irony was complemented by a second one, which lay in the ecology of the movement. Based on agrarian values, prohibition sentiment had swept through the the middle class during an age of rapid urbanization. To adjust to urbanization would be, in part, to shed the garments of rural morality, and this surely would include liquor morality. And finally, the emotions of war which had boosted the movement through its victory had been carried to excess, and surely they could not be sustained.

10

Reconstruction, Law, and Order

DURING THE first few years of the 1920's, many Americans regarded the coming of prohibition more as a moral triumph than as a noble experiment. The Eighteenth Amendment had come to the Constitution after a long period of conflict and a remarkable revision of public attitudes. It stood as a victory for science, education, religion, and political machinery, though not in exactly balanced proportions. Leaders of the Anti-Saloon League could well assume that such an achievement, bearing all the marks of finality, would endure the petty whining of a disgruntled few who walked out of cadence with the pace of twentieth-century progress. Probably the League echoed a general sentiment when it resolved to thank "Almighty God that the people of this nation, in our day and generation, have placed in the fundamental law of the land, by means of the Eighteenth Amendment, the great principle of sobriety."[1]

Even those less given to the public display of their gratitudes seemed to share this feeling and to honor it. Contemporary writers stressed that in the beginning, most hotels, clubs, and individuals wanted to obey the law and usually did. Hosts were at times eager to observe that what they served was of pre-war purchase and, of course, not illegal. Self-respecting people respected the law—generally speaking—and illicit liquor was not in great demand.[2]

The saloon was indeed dead, and in the minds of some it had passed forever into history. The secretary of the Washington State Historical Society received the following communication early in 1920:

> When we had the saloons I used to do considerable drinking and when I saw the drought coming I took the foolish precaution to lay in a large supply of liquor and wines, but now I find I get no satisfaction of drinking at home as the bar room acquaintances are absent and I

was wondering if your museum would be willing to take my stock and make an exhibit of it that coming generations may see in bottled form what their forefathers were foolish enough to pay good money for.[3]

The writer, who signed himself "former drinker," was not entirely facetious. The Mayor of Everett said in 1921 that he had seen only one drunken man in the past year, where before such encounters would have been an hourly occurrence. Others were satisfied that the tranquility of the Seattle General Strike of 1919—remarkable for its lack of violence, riot, or destruction of life or property—was an immediate result of the prohibition laws in the city. Labor leaders agreed, and the Tacoma Central Labor Council even claimed that czarist prohibition in Russia had allowed the working classes to shake off the alcoholic stupor of the ages and rise up with clear heads to overthrow their corrupt and oppressive rulers. The Industrial Workers of the World held the "lumber barons" responsible for what bootlegging there was, because the bosses hoped liquor would obscure the truths of industrial unionism. To the rich and the poor, the weak and the strong, to capitalist and socialist alike, prohibition was the glory from which all blessings flowed. To the liquor interests of the state, it was a time more for philosophy than for hope. The aging Leopold Schmidt, founder of the Olympia Brewery, told his friends that prohibition was inevitable. "We will not fight it," he said. "It is a disease, and must run its course."[4]

And on the face of it, the prohibitionists of Washington had just about everything in their favor: a dry federal Constitution, a dry Congress, a dry state with a dry legislature. If they had anything at all to fear, it was the human frailty of those whom they had persuaded to share their ideals of the sober society. The character—and the danger—of this weakness was expressed perfectly by a Seattle editor who had given the drys his encouragement and his vote. "I voted for prohibition," he wrote in 1921, "not that I don't take a drink now and then, because I do, but because I thought it was the best thing for the coming generation. . . ." This attitude—that society can surely do without liquor so long as it knows that liquor does not exist—was probably shared by many. But living only a hundred miles from Canada, these same people were moved to contemplate the very real existence of liquor, easy to get, and to "take a drink now and then" as their hopes glowed for the future generation. It was fairly well known that even state legislators, politically dry almost to a man but

anxious about the state budget as well as about the future, steadied
themselves with smooth Canadian rye in the little room "adjoining
the upper corridor" to which distinguished members had individual
keys.[5]

There were others, though, who entered the new era in a somewhat
different frame of mind. They rejoiced that the saloon was dead, to
be sure, and that the sober forces of democracy had triumphed in
1918 by fighting on bread rather than alcohol. But the coming of
normalcy, to them, meant a release from the intensities of patriotism
and reform ideology, a freedom from the tight atmosphere of reform
and dedication, an opportunity to relax, be nonpolitical, and to "take
a drink now and then." The years of urgency were gone, and normalcy meant the easy rhythms of life before Woodrow Wilson, the
Kaiser, and the bone-dry laws. Relaxation was a great stimulus to
illicit trade.

Wet goods came down across the border in automobiles, trucks,
boats, airplanes, and railroad cars, in coat pockets, hubcaps, suitcases, and gunny sacks. Though the Eighteenth Amendment discouraged many people from an active participation in the traffic,
both the Congress and the state legislature had happily stopped short
of declaring drinking itself a serious crime. And those who really
were willing to violate the Constitution and make money at it found
the competition so keen that some of them despaired of ever making
an "honest" living—which meant competing without being forced to
"doctor" their goods.[6]

Protests against these developments came without delay from the
groups that had been the body and blood of the progressive movement—the churches, the urban middle class, the farmers, organized
labor. Many of the old voices were still loud and clear. James Duncan stood strong with state labor leaders; he was as politically liberal
as ever and as radically dry. George Cotterill, his thoughts still close
to Henry George, William U'Ren, and E. B. Sutton, was still the most
prominent Democrat in the state and close to the inner circles of the
Anti-Saloon League. The Reverend Mark Matthews, no longer "a
lion, rampant, on a crimson field" but a "quieter . . . more noble . . .
more generous soul," could be as fierce as ever when he attacked so-
cialism, defended Woodrow Wilson, or stood tall to cry out against
the sins of the flesh. The Tacoma *Church Record,* a Protestant weekly, was still progressive, supporting the League of Nations, farm re-

lief, and prohibition. The State Federation of Labor was as thoroughly committed to economic, political, and liquor reform as it had been in 1916. The state's farmers were, if anything, even more so. Grangers in their convention of 1923 noted that some of their members had a tendency to "refer to the prohibition law as a joke," and the great majority solemnly resolved against such levity and for strict enforcement of the law.[7]

Behind these voices, though, there was no unity, no strength, no social bonds, no political discipline. Within four years after the war, the progressive movement in Washington—i.e., the cooperation and confidence among the farmers, the urban middle class, the trade unions, and the churches for the achievement of reform—had come to a rather confusing and noisy end. The coalition had been strained since 1915, when farm and labor groups first opposed preparing for war. Such opposition continued to frighten and irritate the urban middle class until April, 1917; and even then, the labor organizations in Seattle and Spokane criticized Wilson's declaration of war. The middle class, smarting from the harshly anticapitalistic tone of much labor oratory, had taken about all it could. Then in 1919, the Seattle General Strike closed down the city for a week. Among farmers and urbanites alike, it was interpreted as at best an act of collective irresponsibility and at worst a dark machination of the international Communist movement. Still another crisis in this relationship occurred in 1919 when members of the American Legion in Centralia clashed on Armistice Day with a group from the Industrial Workers of the World in a riot that took several lives on both sides. The Seattle *Union Record* was the only paper in the state which defended the right of Wobblies to defend themselves from Legionnaires. The *Record*'s press was seized by federal agents, and its editor was indicted under the Espionage Act. When the *Record* published again, it suffered the boycott of middle-class businessmen and eventually sank into bankruptcy.[8]

By 1920, these fears and hysterias had critically infected the state's farmers as well. A majority of the Grange members supported a move to divorce that organization from any further relationship with the trade unions, and in 1921 the national Grange organization excommunicated the Washington State master, William Bouck, for his prolabor heresies. Bouck then led at least a third of the Grangers in the state into a secessionist movement called the Western Progressive

Farmers. After that, neither group prospered. The parent organization, deprived of the vigor of the insurgents, became limp and ineffective. Throughout the decade it was hospitable only to the shabby fanaticisms of an older generation, and it blazed with invective against drinking, smoking, and movies. It dropped its Temperance Committee and put in its place the Law Enforcement Committee. The reform spirit changed to a dry and negative nagging about the superficial aspects of rural morality while its leadership sifted the ashes of ancient discontents.[9]

The postwar economic depression precipitated these crises, and it brought the same disruption to the State Federation of Labor. Membership in trade unions fell off almost 40 per cent by 1921. Palsied by financial troubles and a poor labor market, the organization went through a bitter period of infighting among radicals, moderates, and conservatives. The rending-of-limbs came in 1922 when James Duncan and his more radical followers joined with the dissident Western Progressive Farmers under the banners of the Farmer-Labor party. When Duncan himself bid for the United States Senate, he received no support from the State Federation of Labor, from the Grange, or from any middle-class organization.[10]

Thus the united strength of farmers, union men, and the urban middle class, before so instrumental in political progress and prohibition, disintegrated by 1923. The liquor reform achieved by these groups would no longer have their unified protection. Each group was still dry, but this dryness itself, detached and alone, seemed to encourage a rash of class and sectional animosities: the churches wanted the dry laws enforced with justice and reason; the Grange wanted them enforced with absolute severity, especially in the wicked cities; the Farmer-Labor party wanted the law enforced "against the rich and poor alike" and pledged its "bitter denunciation of the present system . . . by which the wealthy are undisturbed in the consumption of liquor."[11] In this state of disarray, it was unlikely that any of the formerly progressive forces could be a significant influence upon the public tendency to slide away from the ideal of the Eighteenth Amendment.

The amendment was given its teeth by Congress in January, 1920. In the National Prohibition Act—usually called the Volstead Act, after its sponsor, Andrew J. Volstead—the Anti-Saloon League and its lawmakers had attempted to synthesize the best of the dry laws in the various states. The act defined intoxicating beverages as those containing over 0.5 per cent of alcohol. This, they assumed, would destroy the liquor industry. The law then forbade anyone to "manufacture, sell, barter, transport, import, export, deliver, furnish or possess any intoxicating liquor" so defined, and made first offenders liable to fines as high as one thousand dollars and to imprisonment for as long as six months. The purchaser, however, was not liable to prosecution for conspiracy to violate the law, and this exemption left him reasonably safe from the clutches of federal agents. These provisions, the drys acknowledged, were not calculated to abolish drinking; they authorized about as much enforcement as dry politicians thought the country would endure.[12]

In several ways, the Volstead Act was not bone dry. It allowed drinkers to possess and use liquors laid in before the date of the law, and it allowed anyone to manufacture "non-intoxicating" drinks at home. This last provision had an especially tantalizing concession: home-brewed or fermented beverages were exempt from the 0.5 per cent definition and were to be considered legal or illegal only on the basis of their being in fact intoxicating, a matter which juries could decide in individual cases. The law also made concessions for liquors used for medicinal, sacramental, or industrial purposes.

Congress handed all the problems of enforcing this law to the Treasury Department. It also excused prohibition officials from the civil service requirements, thus opening prohibition offices to patronage for senators and representatives. Those who did enforce the law suffered, as Andrew Sinclair has observed, from "administrative stupidity, political graft, the federal structure of the United States, an antiquated legal system, and the flaws in the act itself."[13]

They suffered also from "normalcy" and the character of national leadership at the time. Many people knew that Andrew Mellon, secretary of the treasury and ultimately responsible for enforcement, had invested millions of dollars in the liquor industry. And it was a rather poor secret that the President of the United States had his own private bootlegger who trucked his goods in broad daylight up to "the little green house on K Street," the brothel-speakeasy which served the friends of Warren Harding.[14]

The twentieth district of the Prohibition Service, Treasury Department, included Washington, Oregon, and Alaska. The area's most

prominent politician, Senator Wesley L. Jones, dropped this patronage plum into the lap of Roy C. Lyle of Seattle, who had served the
Senator in various political capacities for several years. Before his
appointment as prohibition administrator, Lyle had worked as a li-
brarian, then as a real-estate salesman. He would probably have been
among the first to admit that he was not equipped by training, experience, or personality to direct the pursuit of rumrunners and bootleggers throughout the Northwest. Lyle had indeed wanted a federal
job, but he had not expected this one. Somewhat dispirited by the
demands it would make on him, he nevertheless promised to "do his
best."[15]

It was generally recognized in Seattle that Lyle's principal function
was to please the Anti-Saloon League and to keep fences repaired for
Senator Jones. Only a few would have questioned his efficiency in
these areas. However, as a policeman, Lyle inspired little confidence.
For a decade he played out a pathetic and sometimes comic role for
which he was never suited. He was lavishly and mawkishly praised
by some of the dry leaders, ridiculed and despised by the wets, regarded variously as a prince of virtue, a fount of corruption, an unhappy fellow full of good will, or a fool. He was actually a rather
slow and bookish man who probably never touched a dishonest dollar. Loyal to his friends, dedicated to Senator Jones, he was seriously
concerned with serving them well and largely unaware of his public
image. When newsmen once asked him what he intended to do about
rumrunning by airplanes, Lyle quite sincerely replied that he was
"working right now on a paper to be read before the coming sheriffs'
convention, which deals with the use of airplanes in whiskey and
narcotics smuggling." At least one newspaper speculated that Lyle's
scholarship was destined to terrorize the bootleggers—then howled
with laughter. Others cursed Lyle furiously as a "weakling" and a
liability to the Republican party.[16]

While Roy Lyle went sadly about his political duties, he left the
management of his agents largely to William M. Whitney, his legal
advisor and chief assistant. Whitney too was a political appointee. A
Seattle lawyer, he had been chairman of the King County Republican
Committee in 1914, an unsuccessful candidate for Congress in 1916,
and a campaign worker for Senator Jones in 1920. While Lyle was a
dry by conviction, Whitney was so only by professional circum-

stance. He was considerably more affable than his superior, so much so, in fact, that his difficulties with a prominent lady Republican in the state legislature were favorite topics of speculative conversation. He also had much more affinity for police work than Lyle did, and because of this, perhaps, he made more enemies. Energetic and untiring, he was sometimes indiscreetly direct and ruthless. Even by 1922, he had offended so many people around Seattle by searching the automobiles and homes of solid citizens and by his ax-and-hammer methods that the Seattle *Star* urged that he be fired.[17]

It was, furthermore, a matter of general concern that Whitney's agents were frequently a disreputable lot. There were local jokes about "the flocking of good drinking men to the offices of Roy Lyle to get jobs as undercover men for the prohibition forces." But, more seriously, some of them were accused at different times of bribery, sadism, murder, and contributing to the delinquency of minors. The agent William H. ("Kinky") Thompson made the office notorious by getting drunk and consorting with prostitutes during his "undercover" activities. Thompson, only twenty-three years old, was apparently an exceedingly brutal man who beat helpless prisoners and welcomed a chance to use his fists and guns. He once drew hoots and hisses from a crowd in Port Townsend when he pistol-whipped a handcuffed man on the main street. This act, like so many others of his, seemed so unnecessarily brutal that juries soon refused to convict anyone on Thompson's testimony. Late in 1927, "Kinky" attacked a policeman during a drunken brawl in Tacoma and was shot and killed, to the satisfaction of many people across the state. Lyle dismissed another agent afte: a judge rebuked him for brutally beating an eighty-year-old man.[18]

The violence which attended Whitney's work provoked an increasing voice of protest. Senator Jones became disturbed by this in 1927 and asked Whitney for a full accounting; the list of shootings in Washington State which Whitney sent to the Senator included the following:

GEORGE WALTHERS was shot by Agent John G. Montgomery in Skamania County, on September 1, 1923, when Walthers attempted to escape from the operation of a fifty-gallon still. This shooting was accidental. Walthers, after being seen in the actual commission of the crime, was hailed by Agent Montgomery and ordered to surrender. Instead he started to run. This was a very deeply wooded and dense country. Agent Montgomery attempted to pursue Walthers, stumbled and fell, and accidentally discharged his gun shooting the defendant in the back. . . .

A man by the name of EMILY was shot and killed in May of 1921, some months before Mr. Lyle assumed office, at Keller, Washington, when he was escaping arrest for liquor violation. Involved in the shooting was a prohibition agent by the name of Vest, another by the name of Croxall, both of whom have been let out of the Service. . . .

GEORGE CASPAR on December 30, 1925, in Skagit County, Washington, was shot by Prohibition Agent W. H. Thompson who is now deceased. Caspar later recovered. Agent Thompson, together with another agent, had discovered Caspar in the commission of a felony in the operation of a large still with a large quantity of mash and had arrested him under Sections 3281 and 3283 R.S., and for which Caspar and another man were later indicted and a conviction had. On the night in question the agents had placed Caspar and the other man under arrest and Caspar asked Agent Thompson to take him to a nearby house where he could get some clothes. Caspar and Agent Thompson had to cross a small creek over a bridge. When they reached this point Caspar turned on Thompson, struck him, knocked him down, and attempted to take away Thompson's gun. A desperate fight ensued and then Caspar tried to break and run. Thompson fired out blindly with his gun, the bullet striking Caspar in the hip and severely injuring him. No proceedings, of course, were ever taken against Agent Thompson as he was clearly in the right and in the performance of his duty. This occurred in the night time.[19]

In the same report Whitney said that there had been more than seven thousand arrests in the state since Lyle took office, many of them for felonies, and that there was "hardly an agent who has served any considerable length of time who has not been shot at or upon whom assault has not been attempted." Though he did not say so, it seems clear that his agents were, for the most part, men too poorly trained in police work and too poorly paid to take many risks. They probably reasoned that the best way to stay alive was to pull the trigger frequently. But whatever their point of view and whatever the dangers of their work, they received little sympathy from the public.

To make matters even worse for Whitney, some of the agents conducted their investigations in ways indistinguishable from crime itself. In 1928 two of them pled guilty to participating in a drinking orgy near Everett which included several young girls. The judge commented that what they had done was itself a violation of the law and served no purpose other than debauchery. "If it continues," he said, "something will happen to this country if this is a fair example of the kind of men that are forced on the public."[20] He added that the testimony of such men was not worthy of consideration by a jury. To a growing number of critics, the evils of enforcement were almost those of the old-time saloon: political influence, violence, the corruption of youth.

The quality of the Prohibition Bureau reflected more than anything else the reluctance of the government to grant it any really effective power. Throughout the decade, Lyle's salary never exceeded six thousand dollars; Whitney's was about five thousand dollars, and his field agents made approximately half that amount. Even in 1929, the twentieth district had only thirty-four thousand dollars to cover a sixteen-month period of operations. Lyle seldom had more than twenty agents under his control for all of the Northwest, and during most of the decade he had no automobiles, no airplanes, no boats. There was a great deal of truth in his repeated saying that "We are doing as well as we can."

But in the face of the problems confronting prohibition enforcement in the state of Washington alone, his best was absurdly inadequate. There were probably ten thousand illegal stills in the state in 1920, and there were many more as the years went by. The hundreds of miles of the Canadian border were impossible to patrol without a huge standing army, and the waters of the Pacific Ocean and Puget Sound with their adjacent wooded beaches provided a foggy and private paradise for the rumrunners. Anyone with a small boat could enter the business. And many were equipped for large-scale business, for the risks were but slight disadvantages compared to the rewards. When the nature of Lyle's power was generally recognized, nearly one hundred bootleggers and rumrunners attended an open convention in a Seattle hotel in 1922. Under Roberts' Rules of Order, they adopted resolutions condemning narcotics smuggling, setting "fair" prices for bootleg liquor, and establishing a code of ethics "to keep liquor runners within the limits of approved business methods."[21] No wonder Lyle seldom smiled.

When Lyle's superior, John F. Kramer, took office as national prohibition commissioner, he vowed that the law would "be obeyed in the cities, large and small," and that liquor would not be sold, "nor given away, nor hauled in anything on the surface of the earth, or in

the air." Less than two years after he spoke these words, he told delegates to the national Anti-Saloon League convention that the federal
government could never do the job alone. If prohibition were to in
fact prohibit, he said, then state and local officials would have to enforce it.[22]

Delegates from Washington were not at the time discouraged.
They knew that before 1920, at least, the state's own dry laws had been
enforced with some success. State codes were even more severe than
the Volstead Act, for the bone-dry law of 1918 allowed no homemade beers or wines. In 1921, the state legislature made bootlegging
and "jointism" (maintaining a place where liquor is unlawfully
sold) both felonies, punishable by imprisonment up to five years.
The drys had reason to believe that enforcement in Washington,
backed by tradition and strong laws, would present fewer problems
than in the newly dry states.

After 1921, though, it was clear that they would be disappointed.
Governor Louis Hart (1919-25) told the 1921 legislature that prosecuting attorneys throughout the state were urging "the necessity of a
State Police to assist in the enforcement of the Prohibition Law." He
went on to say that this was agreeable to him if the highway police
could offer such assistance.[23] It was soon apparent that those officers
had enough to worry about with their regular duties and were not
often available for chasing rumrunners, but Governor Hart never
bothered the legislature with this matter again. His attitude toward
prohibition, as seen in his public papers, seems to have been one of
rather adamant indifference. Since Congress had passed the Volstead
Act and increased its own police powers, he reasoned, then Congress
could very well use those powers if it wanted the Volstead Act enforced. The law, after all, was aimed at individuals and not at state
governments. Section 2 of the Eighteenth Amendment—that "Congress and the several States shall have concurrent power to enforce
this article"—was an interesting doctrine upon which the lawyers of
the Anti-Saloon League might pontificate. But to Governor Hart, it
was surely no mandate. He had no desire to appoint a state prohibition commissioner, as some governors had done in other states. He
referred all questions and complaints about prohibition enforcement
to Lyle's office in Seattle. If his correspondents were irritated with
the inefficiency of the federal agents—their blindness, for example, to

the stores of liquor in Seattle's Rainier Club, Elk's Club, or Arctic Club—the Governor made it clear that these were matters over which he had no control. When Wayne B. Wheeler, general counsel for the national Anti-Saloon League, wrote to Hart asking if "officers of the law" in Washington State "heretofore friendly to prohibition . . . are becoming more or less hostile to it," the Governor replied that he simply did not know. Governor Hart was mainly interested in reorganizing the administrative structure of the state and in controlling the state budget, and he felt it would be singularly inappropriate to inject any moral fanaticism into these problems.[24]

His successor, Roland H. Hartley, had, if anything, even less sympathy with the dry cause. As mayor of Everett in 1911, he had allowed the horse manure to pile high in the main streets as an enduring lesson to those who had reduced the city's income by voting out the saloons. One might say that Hartley approached the reduction of public expenditures with the same fanatical zeal which the Reverend Mark Matthews took toward reducing the liquor traffic. Hartley was not actively or vocally a repealist, but for eight years as chief executive he did much to frustrate any attempts to engage the state's police powers in the enforcement of prohibition.

During the eight years of his tenure, he repeatedly angered the drys with vetoes of their efforts to make enforcement more effective. He would not increase the penalties; he would not allow state officers to seize automobiles and boats used in the transportation of liquor. In 1931, one of Hartley's appointees to the Board of Regents of the University of Washington, R. A. Balch, was picked up in a liquor raid and fined for possession. When the state PTA asked the governor to remove Balch from his position of public trust, Hartley admonished the ladies in the manner of Abraham Lincoln: if he knew what brand of whiskey Mr. Balch drank, he said, he would send some to the other regents of the university. To another complainer, he wrote that "the head of the liquor law enforcement is, I believe, Roy Lyle, Seattle, Wash." Governor Hartley would have had little sympathy for the modern public relations man. Most of the Governor's prohibition correspondence—including letters from Wayne Wheeler and Peter Odegard—was simply unanswered.[25]

Thus for fourteen years, the governors of Washington remained aloof from the real problems of either the wets or the drys. They looked after their state budgets and their political enemies. Their attitudes and actions effectively reduced enforcement to a simple matter of county and city local option.

At the county level, there were indeed some serious efforts to enforce the law. But because of the archaic structure of county governments and the overlapping state-county-city jurisdictions, it was unlikely that these efforts could be really effective. The sheriffs, as elective officials, were obliged to consider the attitudes of their constituents in just about everything they did, and most of them were careful not to offend any significant body of public opinion. They were forced to develop the delicate maneuvers of acting dry while protecting their wet voters, and this usually meant that they fell with a fury upon the politically weak—the vagrant bootleggers and lonely moonshiners. Thus one prosecuting attorney, in his annual report, noted the fate of most liquor cases in his county:

> There has been only a small amount of suits in our Superior Court. . . . The few convictions were of visitors or those to whom no jury could have had sympathy. Our own bootleggers are small retailers who, if convicted at all, the juries seem to have a feeling that the possession of intoxicating liquor of such inferior quality, is enough punishment, in itself.[26]

Much of the county work was conducted by deputies, who, of all law enforcement officials, are usually the least trained in orderly procedure and the least sensitive to civil liberties. They could, however, make the headlines, irritate the judiciary, and create a great deal of noise. For example, two deputies standing on an Everett street one afternoon looked up into the sky to see what, in the language of the court, "they were pleased to term 'a strange looking plane' . . . and thereupon they repaired to the port and watched the defendant as he landed. . . ." They searched the plane, found liquor, and arrested the pilot, charging him with bootlegging. The state Supreme Court reversed this conviction because it was based on "search and seizure . . . without a warrant and without probable cause, in violation of the Fourth and Fifth Amendments to the Federal Constitution."[27]

In 1922, another major civil liberties decision came before the court from Ritzville. A man named Fred Gibbons was driving through the town when the sheriff—apparently on a tip from a bootlegger—jumped on Gibbons' automobile, pushed a gun in his face, and forced him to drive to the County Court House, where a justice of the peace issued a warrant. Gibbons had a few bottles in a suitcase and was charged with unlawful possession. The state Supreme Court reversed his conviction, saying that "We think the most elementary principles of the law of arrest render it plain that the arrest of the appellant here in question was unlawful. . . ."[28]

Such violations of law, and of public sentiment, continued throughout the decade. When deputies in Snohomish County burned down a house in which they had discovered a still, the *Argus* asked if "distilling liquor is a worse crime than murder. . . ."[29]

When Whitney sent his chronicle of violence to Senator Jones in 1927, he included these incidents involving county officials:

ARTHUR JAHNS was shot by some deputy sheriffs of Spokane County, Washington on or about October 16, 1924, in the mountains southeast of Spokane. . . . The deputy Sheriffs signaled Jahns to stop on the road and when he did not stop, knowing that Jahns was a bootlegger and that he was known to be operating a still, a deputy sheriff fired a charge of buckshot at the tire of Jahns' car but one or two of the shots struck Jahns in the body. . . .

PAUL HICKEY was shot and killed in a terrific battle in Skamania County, Washington, on the 7th of August, 1922. Agent James Morgan and Deputy Sheriff W. E. Rorison of Clark County came upon Paul Hickey and Harold Ahola while they were in the actual operation of a still. . . . The officers called upon the two defendants to surrender. Instead of doing so Hickey at once began to shoot at the officers with a thirty-thirty rifle. The first shot was fired by Hickey. The officers then began to advance upon Hickey, he firing first at one and then at the other of the officers and Hickey killed Deputy Sheriff Rorison and shot Agent Morgan thru his right hand, permanently crippling him and again shot Agent Morgan in the head, leaving Morgan for dead. Hickey was killed by Deputy Sheriff Rorison after Rorison had been mortally wounded.[30]

In the more urban counties, the sheriffs had dry squads of deputies especially charged with prohibition enforcement. Claude C. Bannick of King County, who had been chief of police under George Cotterill in 1912 and who was highly regarded by both wets and drys, employed several dozen men on his Dry Squad throughout the decade. Petty bootleggers were never safe from him. Even the wet newspapers respected Bannick's force, for here, it seemed, was at least one sustained and intelligent program of enforcing the law. There were some shocked reactions, then, in 1932 when the *Post-Intelligencer* revealed that Bannick had been making a good thing of running bootleggers in before justices of the peace with whom he had a proper understanding. Because the sheriff's office was remitted 50 per cent of the fines in such cases, Bannick regarded a jailed offender as a poor producer of revenue; his friendly justices fined the bootleggers and released them, free to bootleg and be fined again. Critics came to call this procedure "licensing by fine."[31] Thus county enforcement frequently became either a matter of political showmanship or a profitable racket—to the bitterness of those who held to the ideals of reform.

What the county governments could not do for prohibition, the city governments seldom attempted. After the war, city governments faced a host of complex and vexatious problems which grew more demanding with each year: schools, sewers, utilities and public ownership, labor, crime, taxes, and the structure of government itself. These problems had to do with immediate municipal well-being and could not be ignored. Councilmen thus could welcome the dubious blessing of "concurrent enforcement" as an escape from the dissipations of money and time that would surely have followed any full-scale attempts to keep liquor outside the city limits. The alternative staggered even the most radical imagination. If a city wanted to stay dry, it would need an army of policemen, maybe a police state; if it expected these men to remain honest, it would have to pay them salaries high enough to discourage graft. Hardly a city councilman in the country was willing to consider methods of raising such revenue. The popular attitude was that prohibition was a moral issue, to live or die not in the city budget but in the public conscience.

It seemed clear that the fatal erosion of the prohibitionists' faith occured at the level of municipal enforcement. Repeal, like prohibition itself, rose from the local to the national conscience. Early in the decade, the chief of police in Seattle, William B. Severyns, observed that "the dry law has created an opportunity for graft in law enforcement such as never before existed, and it is surprising that no more policemen go wrong than do." Both he and the mayor, "Doc" Edwin J. Brown, were easily convinced that many of the federal prohibition agents were "crooks and incompetents"—in the words of Mayor Brown—and the clash between the two forces quickly became a major public spectacle. When the Mayor refused to allow federal agents to house prisoners in the city jail, William Whitney of the

Prohibition Bureau told the press that this was "an effort . . . to hamper federal authorities . . . because bootleggers and their attorneys have brought too much pressure to bear on local officers." Mayor Brown retorted that "I can only reply by quoting the old saying about people who live in glass houses."[32]

The Mayor's own house was, at best, made of some equally fragile and translucent material. Dr. Brown had been a practicing dentist whose advertising in Seattle papers began on a medical note and ended on a political one, usually about 20 per cent Democratic and about 80 per cent Socialist. Dr. Brown also had a lively gift for public speaking, and for years he had been a soap-box regular in the oratorical arena along the Skid Road District, where boisterous political disputes among Wobblies, Socialists, Democrats, Single-Taxers, and just about anyone who happened along had warmed many a winter's evening.

In the years of normalcy, it was perhaps natural that Seattle should elect another "downtown" mayor whose demeanor could suggest the happy days of wild politics and Klondike gold. Dr. Edwin Brown's understanding of the city's moral character came to him through his years on the soap boxes and through his deep rapport with a generation of policemen and small businessmen. In his awareness of human frailty, he was easily as cynical as Hiram Gill. In his warm response to polemics, he was wholly as high-spirited as George Cotterill. He discovered in public life a day-to-day intensity which challenged his sensitivities far more than the sculpturing of false teeth had ever done.

Dr. Brown thrived on controversy. He had the capacity to make enemies easily, and he knew how much Seattle enjoyed a good show. At one meeting of the Port Commission, for example, he presented George Cotterill with a corkscrew to keep the prohibitionist abreast of the public mood. Brown's quarrels with Roy Lyle and William Whitney were usually marked with this same search for the ironic gesture, and in 1922 the city's Dry Squad arrested three federal agents and charged them with bootlegging.

Brown was not, however, an ungenerous or vicious man. He always held Cotterill in high regard; and he appointed him to the City Planning Commission. The Mayor was probably sincere in believing, with his chief of police, that the Volstead Act was "the cause of more police delinquency than all other laws put together." The more he opposed the liquor laws, however, the greater became his notoriety, and there was soon talk of his running for governor.

He was on a first-name acquaintanceship with many city policemen, and it was generally assumed, after his election, that the mayor and the police force would be on the friendliest of terms. Brown's victory was taken as evidence that the city wanted a vacation from the moral excesses of "Holy Ole" Hanson, the closed-town, red-fighting mayor who had left the city to seek the presidency of the United States after the collapse of the Seattle General Strike. What all this meant to Chadwick of the *Argus* was that by 1923, the town had run wild again: "The crook learned to smuggle. Officials were corrupted. . . . Liquor began to pour into Seattle. . . . Saloons, in the guise of soft drink places, started up on every hand. Lewd women rented apartments and did a big business selling booze. . . . Seattle has become . . . so rotten that it stinks."[33]

11

The Rumrunner

A MONTH later, Chadwick advised his readers that good whiskey in Seattle cost only two dollars more a bottle than it did in the government stores of British Columbia. This stabilization of the liquor economy under Brown was no mean achievement. The man largely responsible for it was the city's most famous rumrunner, a former policeman named Roy Olmstead. Newspapermen in the 1920's knew him as "the king of the rumrunners" or "the booze baron" or "the good bootlegger" who "had served a social purpose."[1]

Each of these sobriquets suggests why Olmstead was one of the popular heroes of the time: he grossed over two hundred thousand dollars a month for several years while he controlled an intricate rumrunning empire, and he scrupulously guarded the integrity of his products, selling without adulteration the liquor he brought from Canada. More significantly, toward the end of his career as a rumrunner, the case of *Olmstead* v. *The United States* moved through three levels of the federal judiciary and brought before the public conscience a distinctly modern problem—that of wire tapping by federal agents.

At the age of twenty, Roy Olmstead was a large and powerful young man of keen, undisciplined intelligence and ambition. Disgusted with the labor problems in the Seattle shipyards where he had been working, he joined the Seattle police department in 1906. There he distinguished himself, in the words of Austin Griffiths, once his chief of police, as "quick and responsive . . . upright . . . bright and competent," and he advanced through the ranks during some of the most violent years of Seattle politics—the open town of Mayor Hiram Gill, the reforms of George Cotterill, then Hiram Gill again, and finally "Holy Ole" Hanson.[2] As Seattle grew from a city with a population of about one hundred thousand in 1906 to a city of more than three times that size in 1920, Olmstead learned to know it intimately.

Olmstead was a sergeant in the police force by 1910 and a lieutenant in 1916 when, after a vote by the people, the state began its experiment with prohibition. Though Olmstead was not on the city's Dry Squad, he was a personal friend of Mayor Gill and a close observer of the city's problems with the new law. Bootlegging and rumrunning had become both popular and profitable, and Olmstead watched the increasingly vicious competition between the two rival gangs, one headed by Jack Marquett, the former policeman whom Olmstead knew well, the other by Logan and Fred Billingsley. As they tore themselves apart, Olmstead learned a great deal about their organizational structures, their international connections, their successes, and their mistakes.

The demise of the Billingsleys and Jack Marquett left the rumrunning business of Seattle in an untidy situation. Marginal operations were in fierce competition, purchasing procedures were crude and inefficient, and distribution was totally lacking in sophistication—chaotic at worst and haphazard at best. Then in January, 1920—with the appointment of federal prohibition agents—the risks of entrepreneurship increased sharply, but so did the rewards. The conditions promised unlimited opportunities for someone with administrative talent who knew the business in its full scope—from the wet gunny sacks in the bottoms of dark speedboats through the garages in back alleys to the offices of law enforcement officials.

Olmstead was thirty-four years old in 1920. He had a wife and two daughters. The youngest lieutenant in the Seattle police department, he was widely respected for his intelligence, his initiative, and his responsibility. He made frequent appearances in court to recommend probation for certain prisoners, and because he reasoned well and spoke with authority, the court was pleased to accept his judgment. This was a beginning of the power and the prestige which he ambitiously sought. But in exercising his influence, he came to a great moral crisis in his life: when he discovered that his influence with the court was worth large sums of money to certain parties, Olmstead had to face the true nature of his ambition. Never a man to suffer the throes of anguished ambivalence, his decision was quick. He soon began to sell his authority, and in keeping with his character and the times, he sought high-risk investments for his money. Rumrunning was an easy choice.[3]

On March 22, 1920, at two o'clock in the morning, Olmstead and several of his associates were unloading liquor from a tugboat on the beach of Brown's Bay, near Meadowdale, Washington. Just as the unloading had been completed, there was a confusion of lights, shouts, and gunfire. Prohibition agents, who had waited for days in the woods, crouched behind a roadblock and fired wildly at the boat and the rumrunners. Olmstead leaped into an automobile and went roaring through the brush around the barrier, but the agents were able to identify him before he escaped. Behind him on the beach he left the largest shipment of liquor ever seized in the Northwest.[4]

Olmstead was apprehended easily at his home that afternoon. He was immediately dismissed from the police department and arraigned on a federal charge. Released on bail, he found that these inconveniences happily made it possible for him to give his full time to his business. After he had entered a plea of guilty and been fined five hundred dollars, he discovered that he now stood as a public figure. The newspapers had made much of the Meadowdale story, playing on the "baby lieutenant" with the "brilliant career." They had even listed the brands of captured liquor which he had intended to sell in Seattle.[5]

After Meadowdale, Olmstead had enough experience in rumrunning to form an accurate estimate of its potential. His initiation had given him a measure of the field: the easy sources of supply, the untapped markets, the exciting profits. He quickly found eleven investors who would stake one thousand dollars each. He retained an attorney and assembled a staff of boatsmen, navigators, loaders, dispatchers, bookkeepers, and salesmen—including some former Canadian policemen—and began a shrewd and vigorous economic war against his competitors in the Pacific Northwest.[6]

One device was to use the weaknesses of Canadian export law. In 1920 the dominion government influenced the price of bootleg liquor by taking an export duty of twenty dollars a case on all liquor signed for the United States. This was an undisguised determination to make the most of the Volstead Act, for Canada took no such duty on liquor cleared for any other country. United States rumrunners, of course, paid the duty without protest. Olmstead's coup was to hire ships which loaded in Vancouver, British Columbia, and cleared for Mexico, carrying two thousand to four thousand cases a load, all of it free of export duty.

In an operation that suggests those of the Billingsley brothers, the cargo was discharged on D'Arcy Island, a lonely spot of forest in Haro Strait northeast of Victoria and well out of the main steamer lane. D'Arcy was uniquely insulated from either public or private curiosity by the dangerous reefs that surround it and by the small leprosy station maintained there by the Canadian government. The station keeper became Olmstead's fast friend, and the cargo was secure until the swift boats could run it to American ports on Puget Sound.[7] Olmstead preferred the stormy, windy nights for running—nights when coastguardmen and federal prohibition agents would normally seek the warmth and shelter of quiet coves.

This neat arrangement, in addition to the discount Olmstead received in Vancouver for the large volume of his cash purchases, allowed him to undersell his competitors in Seattle by as much as 30 per cent.[8] There was soon chaos in the ranks. Many quit the business in confusion and disgust, some turned in bitterness to piracy, and others joined Olmstead. Even before Canadian revenue officials expressed their concern by occupying D'Arcy Island, Olmstead had his empire. Many of the rumrunners and bootleggers on Puget Sound were working for him; he acquired a large ocean freighter and formed an alliance with the big runners all along the West Coast. The magnitude of his operations—as later recorded by a federal judge—included refinements that any new business might envy:

> . . . scouts, transfer men, office men, salesmen, telephone operators, dispatchers, checkers . . . collectors . . . bookkeepers, and an attorney [Jerry Finch]. A farm was purchased at which to cache the liquor. A fleet of boats was chartered and numerous trucks and automobiles. . . . There was evidence of a daily delivery at Seattle of 200 cases of liquor and of transactions that each month amounted to nearly $200,000.[9]

In what the New York *Times* later called "one of the most gigantic rum-running conspiracies in the country,"[10] Olmstead was truly a "king."

By 1924 the organization functioned so well that Olmstead went almost entirely into wholesaling. He shipped out of Vancouver, British Columbia, via Discovery Island, just east of Victoria, and sold only to retailers with whom he had established a working relationship. As the money began to fill the old clothes hamper which he casually called "the safe," the king took his place in grand society. He bought a spacious colonial residence in Mount Baker, one of Seattle's high-prestige districts. He became president and owner of the American Radio Telephone Company, Seattle's first radio station, which he had backed as good public relations and as something that might prove useful should law or circumstance change his good fortune.

After a divorce in 1924, he married Elsie Campbell, a vivacious young woman with a taste for excitement, whom he had met in Vancouver. Her real name was Elise, though everyone called her Elsie, and the marriage inspired one of the most delightful myths of the decade: Elsie, a newspaper later claimed, had been an employee and protégée of the prohibition administrator of the northwest district, planted by him in Olmstead's organization as an undercover agent. This story grew out of testimony offered during the trial of 1925-26 that Mrs. Olmstead had for a while in 1922 assisted the federal agents—but the reference was to the rumrunner's first wife, not to Elsie.[11]

Olmstead dressed and entertained in princely fashion and walked the streets of Seattle with a big smile, his pockets full of money. During his walks he might hail, for example, the Reverend Dr. Mark Matthews and encourage him not to take life so seriously. He might drop a few sparkling remarks about his irregular church attendance and about the quality of the medicinal brandy used by the minister's suffering parishioners. Or Olmstead might spend a few minutes with his friend the mayor, Dr. Edwin J. Brown. Or as he strolled along, Olmstead might give personal attention to the needs of his more distinguished customers, such as a "millionaire airplane manufacturer" and the exclusive Arctic Club.[12] At night he would go out with his boats to supervise the international hide-and-seek in the Strait of Juan de Fuca and in Puget Sound. Thus he became the dapper idol of the city he knew so well.

> Public officials, professional men, merchants and bankers waved cheery greetings to him. Twenty men would speak to him in one block on Second Avenue. He had the power that goes with good liquor, easy to get, and good money, easy to give. He was the toast of parties where

popping corks warmed the gregarious spirit. . . . A bootleg king? . . .
It made a man feel important to casually remark, "As Roy Olmstead
was telling me today. . . ."[13]

Olmstead's prestige was much more than that accorded the ordinary rumrunner. His audacity touched everything he did with a
cheerful sense of excitement. He sometimes brought his boats to the
docks in downtown Seattle, unloading them in broad daylight into
trucks marked simply "Meat" or "Fresh Fish." He would roar with
laughter as time and again he eluded the law. And even more than
this, his unique code of ethics endeared him to many thirsty citizens.
He never corrupted his merchandise. People could trust it. He never
allowed his employees to arm themselves, lecturing to them sternly
that no amount of money was worth a human life. His business arrangements were conducted with a firm integrity, for he was, in his
own way, a moralist. Because Olmstead was so attractive personally
and because he scrupulously avoided the sordid behavior of others in
the same business—no murder, no narcotics, no rings of prostitution
or gambling—many people could not regard him as an authentic
criminal. The times being what they were, some felt that the Olmstead organization was in many ways the best thing that could have
happened to rumrunning in the Pacific Northwest.[14]

There were, of course, real hazards in his way of life. The pirates,
for example, Olmstead regarded as more dangerous than the police.
The hijacking was sporadic and vicious, and except for an occasional
news story based largely on hearsay, it was not open to investigation.
There were, however, enough boats around the Sound that carried
masked gunmen and hid in isolated coves to cause grave concern in
the rumrunning industry. A friend of Olmstead's named Peter Mari-
noff lost two men—killed by hijackers in September, 1924.[15]

Such dangers encouraged Olmstead to prefer the dark and stormy
nights for shipments around Puget Sound. His attitude was that he
must live with the situation and fight it not with guns, but with fast
boats, shrewd planning, and tight control over the patterns of distribution. While Olmstead was king, hijacked liquor was not easy to
sell in Seattle.

The city police were a hazard to other rumrunners, but not to
Olmstead. Olmstead could find a friend by telephoning any police
station at any hour. This convenience was clarified later in court by

the federal agent who had tapped the telephone line and who offered
the following testimony:

> Roy phoned the police station. M . . . came to the phone and said,
> "Hello, Roy, what is on your mind?" Roy said, "One of your fellows
> picked up one of my boys." M . . . replied, "Who is it?" Roy replied
> that it was B. . . . "I don't give a damn what they do but I want to
> know before he is booked." M . . . replied, "I'll take care of it for
> you, Roy."[16]

The wire tapper reported another conversation that began as a call
from a policeman to Olmstead's headquarters for instructions:
" 'Down under the Fourth Avenue Bridge is a car with seven gallons
of moonshine in it, and I was wondering if it is yours.' T . . . said,
'No . . . I don't think it is ours because we don't handle moonshine.' "[17]

Still another suggests how Olmstead spent most of his money and
why he never became really wealthy:

> Olmstead (to policeman) : You picked up one of my boys.
> B . . .: Yes, he was loaded clear to the axle. I could not do anything
> else. It was too raw. I have passed by several of your men and never
> got any thanks for it, but this is too raw.
> Olmstead: Well, what are you going to do about it?
> B . . .: What are you going to do about it?
> Olmstead: What do you want?
> B . . .: What have you been doing for the motorcycle boys?
> Olmstead: Nothing. Jesus Christ. It is split so many ways now I am
> broke. When I get through, there is nothing left.[18]

The government contended during the trial of 1925 that at least some
of the city police took care of Olmstead's men and fell relentlessly
upon his few competitors—gaily called "outlaws"—to protect the
empire. The wire tapper testified that on one occasion when police
discipline presented a problem, Olmstead had said to his men, "We
will just have to take things easy and look after our best customers
only until Doc gets back"[19] (Dr. Edwin J. Brown, the mayor, was
absent from the city).

To meet the hazards presented by the Treasury Department, Olmstead depended upon his own wit and courage and upon what he regarded as the mediocre staff in the office of the prohibition administrator. The wire tapper, himself a member of the staff, repeated
Olmstead's judgment: "McL . . . to Roy, he says, 'The Federals will

get you one of these days. . . .' Roy said, 'No . . . those sons of bitches are too slow to catch cold.' "[20]

Indeed they were slow in the beginning. Not until 1924 did Whitney learn where he could charter really fast boats, and after this the sport at night became a grim and more evenly matched contest. Olmstead was very much in the game, but it was expensive: a new runner he had built and named with some affection the *Elsie* was supercharged for greater speed, only to explode and burn in Puget Sound.[21]

At about this same time, Olmstead was approached by Richard Fryant, a free-lance wire tapper who had six years' experience in industrial espionage as a tapper for the New York Telephone Company.[22] Fryant—according to Olmstead—showed him a transcript of conversations which had been conducted on Olmstead's office telephone during a period of several weeks. The transcript was for sale, Olmstead later alleged, for ten thousand dollars. Olmstead replied that he knew something about the rules of evidence, that such a transcript could never be used in court against him, that wire tapping was against state law, and that Fryant could go to hell. He learned shortly that Fryant had gone to William Whitney, who made him a federal prohibition agent. (Another possibility is that Fryant was already an agent and that his interview with Olmstead was an attempt to seduce the rumrunner into bribery.)

Olmstead had the telephone company remove the tap—found in the ladies' room of the Henry Building—but he knew there would be others. His caution, though, was only minimal. Still trusting his understanding of the rules of evidence, he suppressed only those calls that might lead Whitney to a productive raid. The dispatching continued, and the calls to the police were undisguised, marked only by profane references to William Whitney, who was sure to receive them.

The tap even had certain advantages. Some of Olmstead's rarest moments came when he telephoned false directions to his men about the landing of his boats. Assured that the federal agents had rushed out to intercept him, he then went casually to the street and a public phone and gave correct directions, and smiled with the confidence that Whitney would spend the night on a lonely beach clutching a heavy revolver and shivering in the rain.[23] One night Olmstead's men left a lighted yellow lantern on Whitney's car as a jeering symbol of their ridicule.

But William Whitney, stalking his prey, could absorb the ridicule. In October, 1924, he had a valuable windfall when Canadian officials seized Olmstead's boat the *Eva B*, with three men and 784 cases aboard, on a customs charge. The three men talked, and Whitney began to sift the evidence. Thereafter, he kept two men on the phone tap constantly.

In November Whitney raided the office of Jerry Finch, Olmstead's attorney, and the home of Olmstead himself. There he arrested Olmstead, his wife, and fifteen guests who were entertaining themselves by reading children's bedtime stories over Olmstead's radio station. The raiders held the group in a room while they seized boxes of the organization's records and while Whitney, impersonating Olmstead, telephoned well-known bootleggers and asked them to bring liquor to the house. Whitney's wife, who was also his secretary, was a member of the raiding party and used the telephone to summon more liquor for her husband to seize. "This is Elsie," Mrs. Whitney was reported as saying. "Come on over. We're having a party."[24]

Whitney was jubilant. He was now confident that he had enough evidence for a grand jury. The next night he and Lyle took out the rumrunner's yellow lantern which Olmstead had left them to contemplate, lit it, and ran it up the flagpole that topped the federal office.

Olmstead and Finch, of course, cried loudly that their civil liberties had been violated. One measure of public reaction is the statement that Olmstead's friend Mayor E. J. Brown gave to the newspapers: "I would call this making a grandstand play. They could raid my home in the same way; come to my home and search it; find no liquor and then telephone to bootleggers who would bring it. They could raid the Rev. Dr. Matthews' home the same way."[25]

But Lyle and Whitney were accustomed to statements from Mayor Brown. On January 19, 1925, a federal grand jury returned an indictment against Roy Olmstead and ninety other defendants for conspiracy to violate the National Prohibition Act since June, 1923. The conspiracy was charged in two counts: "to possess, transport and import intoxicating liquors" and "to barter, sell, deliver and furnish" them. Among the overt acts listed were the activities of the *Eva B* and the leasing of a ranch for business purposes, these acts being "against the peace and dignity of the United States of America." This promised to be the biggest liquor trial in the history of the country under the Eighteenth Amendment.[26]

Olmstead's reaction to the indictment and to the publicity that followed was direct: he posted bail, then went back to his office, tightened up the table of organization, placed orders in Canada for more liquor, and set the boats and trucks in motion again. His affairs with the United States government he left in the hands of his attorney, Jerry Finch.

Finch, who had been included in the indictment, faced a possible jail sentence and an end to his career. He tried to convince the court that the government should force Whitney to return the records taken from him and from Olmstead, contending that the seizure was unconstitutional and that the use of these records as evidence against the defendants would violate the Fifth Amendment. These motions were denied by Judge Jeremiah Neterer, though he did assure Finch that the evidence gained from the seizure would be suppressed as to him and to Olmstead. This was small consolation to the attorney, and none at all to the other defendants.

Finch also filed suit against the Pacific Telephone and Telegraph Company for permitting federal agents to tap Olmstead's telephone lines. In this dispute the telephone company maintained that it was not legally bound to guarantee a customer the exclusive use of the lines, and again the court ruled against Finch.

At this, some of the defendants began to panic, and whatever loyalty they had displayed began to disintegrate. A few left in great haste for Canada. Some went to Whitney to plead guilty and to testify for the government in return for promises of leniency. Twelve of them left Finch and his quiet pedantry and called on George Vanderveer, the bellicose "counsel for the damned," who had a national reputation for his practice of criminal law.

Vanderveer was most widely known for his defense of members of the Industrial Workers of the World at Everett, Chicago, and Centralia, but to the rumrunners he was a crafty courtroom technician whose virtuosity could set men free. They remembered him for his association with Logan Billingsley, the pre-Olmstead bootlegger whom he had once successfully defended. Vanderveer had also served as King County's prosecutor and knew most of the defendants personally. He took their defense and began to prepare the acid rhetoric which would make a national issue of wire tapping by federal agents.[27]

Opposite Vanderveer and Finch in the courtroom would be Thomas P. Revelle, the United States District Attorney. In 1912 Revelle had quit the Methodist ministry to study law. He had been an unsuccessful candidate for the Republican gubernatorial nomination in 1924, and, like Roy Lyle and William Whitney, he owed much of his career to Senator Jones. Now the three of them had committed themselves, and their success would measure the wisdom of the Senator's appointments. This was made perfectly clear to Revelle by Millard T. Hartson, one of Jones's emissaries. As Revelle later wrote: "Colonel Hartson came to me and said I was being watched and if I did not convict Olmstead and his co-defendants, it would mean the loss of my office. . . ."[28] Under this pressure, Revelle and Whitney did all they could to encourage defection among the members of the Olmstead gang.

A windfall came to them in September when Al Hubbard, one of Olmstead's chief lieutenants, came to Whitney and offered to turn coat. His price was a federal appointment as a prohibition agent. Hubbard's talent for mechanics and electronics had first attracted Olmstead. He was hired initially to keep the boats running faster than Whitney's or the Coast Guard's, and he soon won the king's confidence. Hubbard, something of a boy wizard around Seattle, had interests which included a "vision radio machine" as well as conventional radio, and he personally built the transmitter for Olmstead's American Radio Telephone Company. (This was KFOX, later KOMO. The station was not, as myth has it, used to send boat messages disguised as children's stories, although the transmitter was located in Olmstead's home.[29])

Hubbard was also smoothly persuasive. He offered insights into the rumrunning business and demonstrated a true competence in the arts of bribery, surveillance, and mediation. He had, he later claimed, bribed even the coastguardmen at Deception Pass.[30] Olmstead trusted him with large sums of money, and Hubbard probably knew more about the organization than anyone except Olmstead and Finch.

Lyle immediately wrote to Washington, D. C., for permission to hire Al Hubbard, exulting that Hubbard could help break up "the big ring," that there were "higher-ups . . . bankers, men of finance, and, I am led to believe by Mr. Hubbard, fairly high government officials who are involved."[31]

When Jerry Finch learned that Hubbard was working for Lyle and

Whitney, he burst into tears. Olmstead, on the other hand, took the news indifferently. He had long since developed a debonair fatalism toward the erosive quality of big money on the loyalty of men. But early on Thanksgiving morning, 1925, when he was unloading a boat on Woodmont Beach—when the federals should have been home asleep—he turned from the water to find himself surrounded. Not since 1920 had federal agents been able to confront him with the evidence at his feet. "It looks like things are going very bad for Olmstead," he remarked as he raised his hands.[32]

The trial opened in January, 1926, in Seattle before Judge Jeremiah Neterer and quickly commanded wide attention. Roy Olmstead was already a public figure, always good for a smiling photograph. Elsie Olmstead was attractive and eager to testify. George Vanderveer was good copy. William Whitney was reported to be on the verge of a nervous collapse. He and Revelle had built their case on the charge that the defendants had conspired to violate the National Prohibition Act, not that they had in fact violated it; thus they did not have to prove a substantive offense. (They were saving the Woodmont Beach capture for another trial on the charge of smuggling.) Nevertheless, a case including ninety defendants was a harsh test of their intelligence and energy.

To prove "conspiracy to possess, transport, and import intoxicating liquors and to maintain public nuisances," they called Canadian officials who had overhauled the *Eva B;* they also had the crew of the boat and a group of Olmstead's dispatchers, drivers, and warehouse keepers. To prove "conspiracy to barter, sell, deliver and furnish intoxicating liquors," they called an unimpeachable customer, the airplane manufacturer William E. Boeing; they also had the steward of the Arctic Club and more of Olmstead's telephone operators and salesmen. Then to bind together all the defendants and to underline the other evidence—and to prove, as Revelle said in his opening statement, that Olmstead was unofficial chief of police in Seattle—Whitney and other agents took the stand to tell what they had heard over Olmstead's tapped telephone. Transcripts of the conversations were never offered in evidence, although the government witnesses were allowed frequent looks at "the book" to "refresh their memory" of what they had heard.[33]

George Vanderveer was furious because the court would not allow him to examine "the book." Snarling at the government witnesses, he ground hard at whatever would discredit the federal agents. He brought out that neither Boeing nor the Arctic Club had ever been charged with possession of liquor. Although he suggested that the tappers could not really distinguish one voice from another over a telephone, he was not allowed an opportunity to prove it. He found that Whitney's wife had typed "the book" from longhand notes, then destroyed the originals. When he tried to bring out that Richard Fryant, the first tapper, had attempted to blackmail Olmstead, the court denied the relevancy of this argument. He let Elsie Olmstead say that Whitney had struck her during the big raid.

But Vanderveer's principal focus was on the legality and morality of the wire tap, and he disrupted the court with increasingly caustic demands that he be allowed to examine not only the witnesses, but "the book" through which they spoke.

> Vanderveer: I want a fair, decent whiteman's chance to test the truth of this, that is all.
> The Court: Just a minute. When you address the court employ language that is fitting for the occasion.
> Vanderveer: I am.[34]

Vanderveer cited the Washington statute adopted in 1909 which made wire tapping illegal: "Every person . . . who shall intercept, read or in any manner interrupt or delay the sending of a message over any telegraph or telephone line . . . shall be guilty of a misdemeanor."[35] The law, he insisted, cannot sanction a violation of the law as a means of obtaining evidence. His points were frequently overruled, but he hammered on. In the words of an observer who was at the time a young lawyer in the courtroom audience:

> Vanderveer used his time in court to build the foundation for an appeal, seeking every opportunity to invite judicial error. His technique was not unlike that of a legal toreador, taunting and tormenting . . . while never permitting himself to get beyond the borderline of contempt.
> Judge Neterer, with equal skill, pondered his judicial rulings and took occasion to place his own substantiating arguments in the record.

This spectacle brought professors and law students from the University of Washington to the courtroom to watch "one of the classic legal battles of Northwest history."[36]

THE DRY YEARS

As the taunting continued, Thomas Revelle also became furious. He approached the bench with strained dignity on one occasion to complain that he was being hissed at by the defense. The judge had not noticed it. Colonel Hartson, seated in the audience, wrote quickly to Senator Jones that things were not going at all well.[37]

Olmstead watched and listened as his fate unwound, confident that a higher court would uphold Vanderveer. He was also impressed with the deep irony which escaped the attention of those less intimate with the proceedings than he. Olmstead roared with laughter as some of the phony telephone calls, the products of his own humor, were brought in evidence against him. He sometimes grinned at the United States Attorney's young assistant whom he had supplied, and continued to supply, with good Canadian whiskey.[38] It was all in the game.

The conclusion was never long in doubt. Of those indicted who did not flee to Canada, twenty-three were convicted and sentenced. These included Jerry Finch, but not Elsie Olmstead. Judge Neterer, on March 9, 1926, sentenced Roy Olmstead to serve four years at hard labor in a federal penitentiary and to pay an eight thousand dollar fine. He gave Olmstead a lecture the rumrunner would never forget:

> The damage . . . to organized society and to the government of this country is incalculable. It was amazing, widespread, but a short step to the undermining of those institutions which are so sacred to us. . . . As to you, Roy Olmstead, I'll say this . . . if the same constructive force, organizing ability, which was devoted to this enterprise had been used legitimately, in harmony with the laws, the final result would have been marvelous. . . . If you don't know you have erred grievously, I am sorry for you.

Those defendants who cooperated with the government received one-year sentences. On March 12 the Seattle WCTU passed resolutions lauding Judge Neterer, Revelle and his young assistant C. T. McKinney, Roy Lyle, and William Whitney. Mrs. Mabel Walker Willebrandt, assistant attorney general of the United States, had serious reservations about the legality and morality of wire tapping, but she believed that the Olmstead conviction "was a prohibition victory of no small proportions."[39]

Thus ended the case of *The United States* v. *Olmstead*. But for the next two years the case of *Olmstead et al.* v. *The United States* was very much alive. Olmstead, bailed for the appeal, sold his home, his radio station, and his household effects while he waited for Finch

Everett Saloon, 1907

Everett Saloon, 1907

Everett Saloon, 1907

Alden J. Blethen

Hiram C. Gill

Harry A. Chadwick

George F. Cotterill

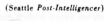
(Seattle First Presbyterian Church)

(Seattle *Post-Intelligencer*)

(Seattle Public Library)

Reverend
Mark A. Matthews

Governor Marion E. Hay

Ernest H. Cherrington

L. to r.: Bernard N. Hicks, Scott McBride, J. Ralph McGee

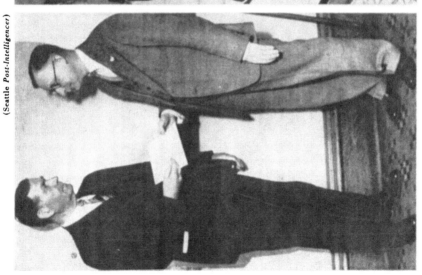

Agusta Trimble

Wesley L. Jones and Charles Allen

Roy Olmstead

Roy Lyle

Edwin J. Brown

William Whitney

(Seattle *Times*)

Ladies of the WCTU. Mrs. Lillian Vincent standing, left

(Seattle *Post-Intelligencer*)

Seattle saloon after an ax raid, 1916

Beer parade, Seattle, 1932

"Putting Liquor to Work"

and Vanderveer to argue with the government before the circuit court of appeals in San Francisco. When they arrived there, they requested abatement principally on these grounds: (1) that the indictment had been written by Whitney, who had, furthermore, coerced the foreman of the grand jury with personal threats to have the indictment returned exactly as it was written; (2) that papers taken from Olmstead's home and Finch's office were, in fact, used against them; and (3) that the use of wire-tap evidence violated the search and seizure clause of the Fourth Amendment and the self-incrimination clause of the Fifth.

The majority of the jurists found no adequate cause to reverse the lower court. Roy Lyle telegraphed Senator Jones a one-sentence message: "Olmstead now in McNeils (*sic*) Island Penitentiary."[40]

If this was jubilation, it was premature, because a dissenting opinion written by Circuit Judge Frank H. Rudkin was worded with enough eloquence to keep the discussion of the constitutional issues involved in Seattle's "whispering wires" case on a national level. Rudkin did not doubt that Olmstead was guilty. He felt, however, that the use of "the book" during the trial, to refresh lagging memories of intercepted conversations, and the tapping of telephone lines by federal agents were matters of grave significance: "the book, and not the witness, was speaking. A better opportunity to color or fabricate testimony could not well be devised by the wit of man." He continued his objections on much broader grounds.

> I think it is also a matter of common knowledge that there is a growing tendency to encroach upon and ignore constitutional rights. For this, there is no excuse. . . .
>
> Must the millions of people who use the telephone every day for lawful purposes have their messages . . . intercepted? Must their personal, private, and confidential communications to family, friends, and business associates pass through any such scrutiny on the part of agents, in whose selection they have no choice, and for the faithful performance of whose duties they have no security? . . . If such ills as these must be borne, our forefathers signally failed in their desire to ordain and establish a government to secure the blessing of liberty to themselves and their posterity.[41]

The strength of Judge Rudkin's dissent gave Olmstead's attorneys ample reason to petition the Supreme Court for a review of the case. Wire tapping was a new problem in official morality, a murky and treacherous one in no way illuminated by federal legislation. In 1924 Attorney General Harlan F. Stone, reversing the procedures of the Department of Justice, had admonished agents of the new Federal Bureau of Investigation that wire tapping was to be regarded as "unethical tactics" and would not be tolerated.[42] Directives to the FBI did not, of course, inhibit the Treasury Department's prohibition force.

Vanderveer's friend John F. Dore of Seattle—described by Lyle in a letter to Jones as a "vicious, unscrupulous bootleg lawyer"[43]— argued the petition. He was opposed by Mrs. Willebrandt of the Justice Department. The Court denied the petition in November, 1927.

In the interim Olmstead had been acquitted on a charge of smuggling based on the Woodmont Beach episode of 1925. Because the jury would not believe Al Hubbard, the government could not establish clearly just whose liquor was being unloaded on the beach. Olmstead went back to the federal prison on McNeil Island in Puget Sound, hair clipped, dressed in prison garb, commenting to newspapermen, "I'm not complaining. I violated the law."[44]

But he was unexpectedly bailed out again in January, 1928. On further petition the Supreme Court had reconsidered—in the attitude, apparently, that the issues of the case did demand clarification. The Court granted writs of certiorari with the specific qualification that its review would be limited to the question of "whether the use of evidence of private telephone conversations . . . intercepted by means of wire tapping, is in violation of the 4th and 5th Amendments. . . ."[45]

The emphasis of the qualification caused a quick re-evaluation of conscience within the Justice Department. Mrs. Mabel Willebrandt, whose "Flying Squadron" rushed around the country to take prohibition cases that might become politically explosive, had argued for the government in November. Then in January she stopped short before the total implication of the Olmstead case. "Irrespective of its legality," she later wrote of her decision on wire tapping, "I believe it to be a dangerous and unwarranted practice to follow in enforcing the law." She declined to participate in the case further. "I indicated to the Solicitor General my unwillingness to argue the case in an attempt to justify the prohibition agents' wire-tapping tactics of which I so thoroughly disapproved. Consequently, the Solicitor General . . . employed other counsel."[46]

The case was heard in February, 1928. Chief Justice William Howard Taft, in the majority opinion, denied the core of the defense's contention. "The Amendment does not forbid what was done here. There was no searching. There was no seizure. . . . The reasonable view is that one who installs in his house a telephone instrument with connecting wires intends to project his voice to those quite outside. . . ." He recognized the moral problem involved, but insisted upon a higher morality: "A standard which would forbid the reception of evidence if obtained by other than nice ethical conduct by government officials would make society suffer and give criminals greater immunity than has been known heretofore. . . ."

In dissent were Justices Louis Brandeis, Oliver Wendell Holmes, Pierce Butler, and Harlan Stone. Justice Brandeis wrote the opinion which showed that the Court was sharply divided along fundamental lines. The language of the amendments, he said, must extend protection to telephone lines if the Constitution is to be affirmed as more than an ephemeral document.

> Discovery and invention have made it possible for the government, by means far more effective than stretching upon the rack, to obtain disclosure in court of what is whispered in the closet. . . . Whenever a telephone is tapped, the privacy of persons at both ends of the line is invaded and all conversations between them upon any subject . . . may be overheard. . . . As a means of espionage, writs of assistance and general warrants are but puny instruments of tyranny and oppression when compared with wiretapping. . . .

Echoing in part the dissent of Judge Rudkin in the lower court, he interpreted the general spirit of the Constitution:

> The makers of our Constitution undertook to secure conditions favorable to the pursuit of happiness. . . . They conferred, as against the government, the right to be left alone—the most comprehensive of rights and the right most valued by civilized men. To protect that right, every unjustifiable intrusion by the government upon the privacy of the individual, whatever the means employed, must be deemed in violation of the 4th Amendment.

Regarding the agents' violating the laws of the state of Washington, Justice Brandeis concluded: "In a government of laws, existence of government will be imperilled if it fails to observe the laws scrupulously. . . . If the government becomes a lawbreaker, it breeds contempt for the law . . . it invites anarchy. . . . Against that pernicious doctrine this court should resolutely set its face."[47]

The significance of this dissent was almost immediately recognized, and it was to become a classic statement in this aspect of American civil liberties. Shortly after it was announced, the *Literary Digest* stated that some newspapers, such as the Cleveland *Plain Dealer*, supported the Taft decision: "to break it [the conspiracy] up some stretching of the Fourth Amendment is likely in the long run to do more good than harm. . . ." But the *Digest* found that a majority of press opinion was critical of the Court. To the New York *Times*, the Taft decision "made universal snooping possible." The New Haven *Journal Courier* said that, "Instead of further protecting society from the criminal, the majority opinion increases the possibility of criminal indulgence. . . ."[48]

To the editors of the weekly *Outlook*, the Olmstead case was "A New Dred Scott Decision."

> It is not too much to say that the decision in the wiretapping case will probably become the Dred Scott decision of prohibition. . . . The popular mind will regard it as an infringement of liberty growing out of prohibition . . . we must weather the devastating effects of a decision that outrages a people's sense of a security which they thought they had under their Constitution.[49]

Olmstead went back to prison. Having him there had already brought certain—though transitory—satisfactions to the men most responsible for his commitment. When, for example, Roy Lyle failed his civil service examination in 1927, Senator Jones wrote to him "in strictest confidence" that there was nothing to fear. "I had a little talk with the President . . . and he authorized me . . . to tell the Commission that he would be glad if you could be given another examination."[50]

Thomas Revelle, the prosecutor, discovered that the evidence he had sharpened against Olmstead could now be used as a political sword. He had feuded with Seattle's Democratic mayor, "Doc" Brown, over the quality of prohibition enforcement throughout his term of office. During the Olmstead trial Brown had challenged Revelle to make something of the charges of corruption in the police department, and in the spring of 1926 Brown was boasting that he would replace Wesley Jones in the United States Senate. Then Revelle did indeed make something of the charges, for booze and politics were already inextricably mixed.

12

Booze and Politics, 1920-30

WHILE governors, mayors, and policemen relaxed, the Anti-Saloon League of Washington set itself to perpetuate the broad influence it had enjoyed during the world war. George Conger, and then Bernard N. Hicks, who was superintendent after Conger's death, printed and mailed thousands of pamphlets every year. Hicks spoke each Sunday from at least one pulpit somewhere in the state, taking pledges and donations after every speech or sermon. He kept a sharp eye on candidates for state and national offices, and before each election he published lists of office-seekers "for whom every Christian should vote."[1]

Though some voters felt that the League, having slain the saloon, should itself retire and let the public have its normalcy, Hicks was relentless in his pronouncements and his political energy. Feeling that the first ten years—if not the first generation—after the Eighteenth Amendment would be the most difficult, he urged his followers to be constantly on their guard. He pointed out to them that the legions of Hell were marshaling behind those unreconstructed rebels who spoke openly about modifying the Volstead Act to allow wine and beer, or spoke even of repealing the Eighteenth Amendment. These were to be circumscribed and cut off, and their "hirelings," the rumrunners and bootleggers, were to be driven into the earth without mercy.

During these years the leading defender of the faith was the state's senior United States senator, Wesley L. Jones, whose portrait hung conspicuously in the office of the Anti-Saloon League for as long as the organization existed under that name. Jones was a tall, sincere, devout former lawyer from Yakima. He did not drink, gamble, smoke, or swear. He was dedicated to middle-class American values and to the Republican party, both of which he in many ways personified. The League could have found no more perfect champion.

Jones had gone to the House of Representatives in 1898, then to the Senate in 1908, the first year that a member of the upper chamber was elected in Washington by a direct vote of the people. In that year of the preferential primaries, Jones was clearly the reform candidate and was supported by the "conscience" wing of the party that hoped to shoot down old Levi P. Ankeny, senator since 1902. Ankeny was a Walla Walla banker who smelled of cigars, whiskey, privilege, and corruption and who, according to the most credible story, had laid down forty-nine thousand dollars of his own money to buy the votes in the state legislature which sent him to Washington, D.C.[2] While Ankeny contemplated his prestige and sought the amenities of the Rich Man's Club, Jones was working hard to bring federal money into state agricultural and reclamation projects. For the honest, intelligent young congressman, Ankeny was an easy target in 1908. After some deadly barrages from Reverend Mark Matthews in Seattle and an aggressive campaign by Jones, the Old Guard crumbled: Jones took the seat he occupied until 1932. But long before that, he had become a political institution.

Though he never identified himself as a Progressive by name, Jones's heart was close to the movement. Like the Progressives, he was eager to use the power of democratic government to abolish evil, including railroad privilege, giant trusts, and demon rum. In his quiet and businesslike manner, he worked for racial equality, for direct primaries, for the inheritance tax, for the direct election of United States senators, for eight-hour labor laws and child labor laws, and for government loans to individuals for the purchase of homes or farms. He opposed a law that would have prevented court injunctions against labor unions, but he did so only because he regarded it as a piece of class legislation. He was against immigration, for the gold standard, and for the purification of politics. In a word, during the progressive era, Jones was a thoroughly middle-class reformer.[3]

Jones's ties with the Anti-Saloon League came as easily as did his convictions. The League's Ernest Cherrington was related by marriage to Jones's close friend Charles Fowler of Seattle; Jones and Cherrington were friends of long standing before either became nationally famous. In 1914, when he was challenged by the prohibitionist mayor of Seattle, George Cotterill, and by the rabid Progressive,

Ole Hanson, Jones leaned heavily upon the League to see him through. When Cotterill brought the issue of prohibition into the campaign—this was the year of Initiative Number 3—Jones advised his people that "I am a tee-totaler . . . I will vote for all measures looking toward the elimination of the liquor traffic," but he urged them to avoid the matter if they could. By telegram, he advised his first lieutenant, Millard Hartson, to seek the advice of George D. Conger, state superintendent of the Anti-Saloon League. He outlined his proposed strategy:

> Conger . . . friendly. Talk over situation with him and decide what wise course to follow. Dinwiddie [of the national League] here will do whatever thought best for me. Can get full understanding attitude League from Conger. Believe wisest course convey word quietly along line temperance workers. . . .

To do this "quietly" was important to Jones in 1914, because he did not yet wish to commit his career to the prohibition movement. He knew that political passions were running high and that the outcome of Initiative Number 3 would be close. Nothing about the campaign worried him more than the prospect of being mauled in the climax of a local fight in which he had taken no part. But however graceful his sidesteps, he could not avoid the friendly but insistent inquiry from Erastus Brainerd, who as editor of the Seattle *Post-Intelligencer* had been instrumental in Jones's victory of 1908. In 1914, Brainerd was leading the Anti-Prohibition Association of Washington in its battle against Number 3. Jones's reply to Brainerd's questions came in labored phrases:

> No one has spoken for me in this matter . . . nor have I given any statement of my views for publication. It seems to me that the question should be settled upon its merits and as free from politics as possible. . . . I have my own personal view in regard to the matter, and yet I am not entirely free from doubt as to what is the best method to deal with what all must admit results in much evil. . . .[4]

He concluded—still uncommitted—with the thought foremost in his mind: "Unless public sentiment is very strongly behind a proposition of this kind, there is likely to be a great reaction from its enforcement." He wanted to measure public sentiment before he acted. Senator Jones's great failure in later years was that he misjudged the force and direction of the reaction which he so rightly feared.

After both Jones and prohibition won in 1914, there was no further need for reluctance. Becoming a sort of Anti-Saloon League warhorse, he was always willing to hold the line with his vote, his seniority, his voice, or his prose. He read memorials from churches into the Congressional Record and worked for the Webb-Kenyon Bill. It was Jones who achieved prohibition laws for Alaska and all the territories and possessions of the United States, and he helped override President Woodrow Wilson's veto of the Volstead Act. For his services, the ASL quickly endorsed Jones in the primary election of 1920, and in November he again won easily over George Cotterill.

Throughout the 1920's, Jones was as valuable for the defense as he had been for the offense. He became associated with the Board of Temperance, Prohibition, and Public Morals of the Methodist Episcopal church, and the public everywhere soon knew Senator Jones as a leading spokesman for strict enforcement of the prohibition laws. When the rather alarmist editor of the Spokane *Chronicle* asked Jones to have federal troops brought to the Canadian border to search automobiles for liquor, Jones immediately urged President Harding to do just that. (The President, however, felt that "there are other matters of more immediate importance at the present time."[5])

Perhaps his greatest triumph for the Anti-Saloon League nationally was the Jones Law of 1929, which raised penalties under the Volstead Act to maximums of five years' imprisonment and ten thousand dollars in fines. This law armed the government—in the words of Mrs. Mabel Willebrandt of the Justice Department, who liked the law—"for effective warfare against the type of lawbreaker whose violations are numerous, persistent, and on a large scale."[6] The law was attacked by newspapers, judges, and prominent citizens as too savage, and it brought Jones a daily bundle of mailed vituperation and fanatical acclaim from all over the country. It did much to harden the public image of the Senator as a cold, even cruel, grim, and humorless old man. Though this image unhappily arose from the acts of Jones himself and was therefore not without basis, it was not an entirely accurate one. The Jones Law showed his inability to control the issue of prohibition in the late 1920's. The issue was controlling him, sometimes to his complete frustration.

In 1921, Jones had shared the optimism of most Americans about the Volstead Act and the new, dry era. Enforcement, he said confidently, would get easier and easier. With the same confidence, he anticipated an early dismissal of the issue fom political debate.

Disillusioned in both of these hopes, he stuck with his friends in the ASL. He was shocked by the Olmstead case, harried by its political implications, and dismayed that violations so extensive and so celebrated could have occurred in his own state. Jones was grim in his determination that Olmstead and his kind should be removed from society, and he twice stopped parole proceedings for Olmstead at McNeil Island. If he sometimes feared that bootleggers were cutting at the very pillars of American life, it was because to a "conscience" and "good government" Republican, the absolute qualities of American life were law, order, and honesty. He believed, just as sincerely, that prohibition promoted personal liberty—freedom from drunkenness, from poverty, from the liquor "interests."[7] To this the ASL said "amen" loudly enough for Jones to hear it over the confusion of voices. After 1928 he found in the League, just as he did in the policies of Herbert Hoover, some security and direction through treacherous times.

For the Anti-Saloon League of Washington, Jones's most sustained service was his defense of the people in the local prohibition office. Although he received a flood of advice to the contrary, Jones persisted in his belief that adverse criticism of Lyle and Whitney could be inspired only by those who were opposed to prohibition or to Jones himself. Events later proved that he was not entirely wrong in this regard. He believed, further, that his own political future was dependent in important ways upon the support given to him by the League and its followers, most of whom were admirers of Lyle and Whitney. Bernard N. Hicks regarded the two federal agents with a feeling that approached adoration, and he brought to Jones every detail of their heroic qualities. Furthermore, Jones liked Lyle and Whitney personally, and having seen to their appointments, he was perfectly willing to take the responsibility for any reflection their actions might cast upon him.

Thus he used his considerable prestige and seniority in the nation's capital to protect his two men in Seattle. He badgered the Treasury Department and the Justice Department for years to stop their investigations of the Seattle office or to withhold the results of these investigations. When he could not do this personally, he had his friends do it for him. On one occasion he wired Senator Charles Curtis of Kansas, asking him to stop the Justice Department's move against Lyle and Whitney until Jones could get back to his office.

"Charlie," he said, "I am appealing to you as Senate leader. . . ."
He told Curtis that the removal of Lyle or Whitney would "disrupt
our prohibition force and be a severe blow to prohibition enforcement in our state. Our temperance people will resent it in no uncertain way and I certainly will. It will reelect Dill."[8] (Clarence Dill
was the state's Democratic senator.)

The deeper Jones became involved in the affairs of the Seattle
office, the deeper became his woes. When the Treasury Department
and the Justice Department moved to indict Al Hubbard and Richard
Fryant for their alleged business with bootleggers, the Senator
stepped in to stop it and thus put his office in the service of those two
rather shady characters. He was embarrassed by the actions of
"Kinky" Thompson, the agent whose brutality caused so much criticism. This criticism, in turn, caused Jones to release a blast of his
most fatuous phrases: ". . . the respectable citizen who denounces
the officers for doing their duty is sowing the seed of crime, anarchy
and Bolshevism which will bring a whirlwind of riot and disorder
that means rapine and murder."

On the other hand, an editorial in the Tacoma *Ledger* about the
brutality of another agent so outraged Jones that he ordered Lyle to
fire the man, and in doing so brought upon himself the wrath of various "strict enforcement" individuals and groups. Jones was simply
unable to control the degree of his participation in the local machinery of law enforcement. Because his patronage was almost as deep as
it was wide, his appointees were everywhere, and most of them had
something to do with prohibition. Deputies of the United States Marshal, for example, were commissioned at the request of the WCTU,
the Colored Republican Club, the ASL, and any number of Jones's
friends.[9] It was not just Lyle and Whitney, then, but all the deputies,
agents, clerks, and petty officials of the United States government
throughout the state that carried upon them the name of Senator
Jones.

Miles Poindexter, the junior United States senator from Washington until 1922, chose a posture somewhat different from Jones's total
identity with the prohibition movement. First elected to the Senate in
1910, Poindexter was a Progressive both in name and spirit during
his initial term. As an "insurgent" Republican, his attacks on the
"interests" won him the leadership of the state's Progressive party in
1912, and the electoral victory of his new party in the state that year

caused him and his closest followers to believe that the Progressive party could carry him to the presidency by 1920. During these years, he, like Jones, hoped that somehow the explosive issue of prohibition could be kept out of politics and out of the bold path of his projected career. But unlike the senior Senator, Poindexter was no "tee-total-er," and he revealed an early lack of enthusiasm for prohibitionists, even after the victory of Initiative Measure Number 3 in 1914. He did, however, give his support to the national laws which carried the country toward the Eighteenth Amendment.[10]

After he returned to the Republican party in 1916, Poindexter, like most of the Progressives, voted for the Webb-Kenyon Bill. He was careful to make it clear to his dry constituents that he had done so, and that he had supported the exclusion of liquor advertising from the mails, even adding an amendment of his own to strengthen the law. When the war ended, though, and the national conventions loomed immediately ahead, Poindexter had no intention of allowing his public image to become entangled with that of the Anti-Saloon League. "I am not extreme in the matter," he wrote of prohibition shortly before the Republican convention, "and by no means a fanatic."[11]

As his supporters came to realize, the war years had brought many changes in the attitudes of the former insurgent. In a remarkable way, the war changed the reformer into an iron-backed conservative, bringing out in Poindexter many traits of brash intolerance that had been hidden from the public since 1904 and 1905, when, as a superior court judge in Spokane, he had been known as "stern" and "severe." Poindexter after 1917 was a patriot who saw war as a glorious experience, a purification of the soul. He urged universal military training. Upon those who opposed the war he heaped the same phrases of scorn that in 1912 he had used to villify the "interests." By 1918 he regarded the Seattle labor movement as a Communist conspiracy, and he introduced a bill in the Senate to make strikes illegal. In 1920 he opposed any federal aid for farmers suffering from the postwar depression. Thus by the time he made his bid for the presidency, he had alienated the very groups that had brought him into national politics.[12]

To the old reformers, Poindexter had sold out to the big money so he could become President. Their fears were justified when it became known that Poindexter had accepted an eighty thousand dollar slush fund from big business—including one thousand dollars from William E. Boeing in Seattle—to finance his bid for the White House. They were then sure that he had abandoned labor, farmers, liberal economics, and probably prohibition.

As a candidate for the Republican nomination, Poindexter never expressed any clear approval of the Volstead Act. His standard evasion was that "the law should be enforced." After the nomination and the presidency went to Warren Harding, observers in the capital noted that Poindexter identified himself closely with the administration. As a personal friend of the President, he ran with the "drinking crowd" in Harding's inner circle.[13]

But probably as much as any other single factor, it was Poindexter's part in the notorious Newberry Case that turned his voters against him. When Truman H. Newberry of Michigan came to the Senate in 1919, it was known that he had spent two hundred thousand dollars—much of it smelling of whiskey—to defeat the prohibitionist Henry Ford in the Republican primaries of 1918. He had violated the Corrupt Practices Act, but nevertheless, in a Senate conflict which pitched the "interests" against "conscience," Newberry was seated. Jones voted against him, but Poindexter voted with his new friends.

It was the "new" Poindexter, in contrast to the old Progressive, who returned to the voters of Washington State in 1922. Though he had been more successful than Jones in keeping the prohibition issue out of his office, he had not remained entirely untouched. There were some citizens who blamed all Republicans for Lyle and Whitney, and Poindexter received his share of this. Mayor Brown, for example, thought that Poindexter should discipline the Seattle prohibition force if Jones would not. Whitney wrote to Jones that he and Lyle were hurting Miles Pointexter because the bootleggers all ran to Poindexter's friends to complain about their rough treatment. Poindexter never gave Lyle's office the dignity of his attention.[14]

He was challenged in the Republican primaries by two reformers, Mrs. Frances Axtell, prominent in Republican affairs, and Austin H. Griffiths, the prohibition lawyer who had been Hiram Gill's chief of police. In a bitter campaign, both attacked Poindexter as a traitor to reform, including the liquor reform. Mrs. Axtell told her audiences that the wets wanted Poindexter back in the Senate, and Judge Griffiths called for the election of "honest and dry" senators. In July the Bellingham *American* published an article claiming that Poindex-

ter was backed by eastern big money, and that in return for this support, Poindexter would back a beer and wine bill in Congress. Poindexter never bothered to refute the charge.[15]

When the national WCTU wrote to him in an effort to get evidence
which would stop the rumors of his wetness, the ladies received only
more evasion. Mrs. Victor Miller, chairman of the state PTA, twice
sent her questionnaire to Poindexter and was twice treated to the
Senator's vagueness and irritation. He ignored most of the questions,
including those about his personal habits regarding liquor. Poindexter would say only that he favored "enforcing the law."[16]

The *Anti-Saloon League Year Book* of 1921 published an article
by Poindexter in which he explained how "the absence of the open
saloons has brought about a very great improvement in the lives of
our people." But the state organization withheld its endorsement of
him until well after he had won the primaries.[17] George Conger then
said that Poindexter should be returned to the Senate because he had
supported all dry measures, but his words came so late, and by implication so reluctantly, that they carried little weight. Neither Mrs.
Axtell nor Judge Griffiths supported Poindexter in the general elections, and his two opponents in November were both dedicated drys.

One of these was James Duncan, labor leader and prohibitionist,
who stood on the Farmer-Labor platform. Duncan, very much the
idealist, attacked the "interests" and then lectured to his audiences
on the evils of drink.[18]

Between the "reactionary" Poindexter and the "radical" Duncan
—as they were called—stood Clarence C. Dill of Spokane, the Democratic nominee, with everything to recommend him. A farm boy who
never smoked or drank, a member of the YMCA, Dill had studied
law before he had become infected with populism, then progressivism, then with Democratic politics. After 1914, he added liquor reform to his platform, and he stood there four-square. As a United
States congressman, he had been one of the "men of peace and prohibition." Not only did he vote against the declaration of war; he
proposed that the names of all those who did be turned over to Army
recruiting officers. After such compounded irreverence, he was defeated in 1918.[19]

In 1922, however, people remembered Dill as the reformer. A
pleasant and handsome man, he was against privilege, and he appealed to the farmers and the union men, the very groups against

which Poindexter had turned his back. He had also a strong appeal to the drys, and he was introduced to the state WCTU convention as "an honorary member." Touring the state, he asked both farmers and city people what they thought of Poindexter's new friends. He always mentioned Newberry. "I based my campaign largely on the seating of Senator Truman H. Newberry of Michigan," he said after the election. "That [is what] I conceived to be the weakness in the armor of Senator Miles Poindexter."[20]

As the most scholarly student of the role of prohibition in this election has concluded, it was Poindexter's "toadying with wealth" which proved to be "the most vital factor" in his defeat, and it is principally within this context that the issue of prohibition played its part.[21] Though Poindexter's attitude toward the Eighteenth Amendment was never the hard focus of the debate, it was nevertheless a vital part of the background for the campaign. Dill had indeed found his mark, a damp spot on the armor, and he sent Miles Poindexter out of politics. As a Democratic senator without patronage, C. C. Dill opposed modification throughout the decade, and he stood up straight to be counted behind all the dry laws. After 1923, Washington State had two dry United States senators, both of them standing shoulder to shoulder with the militant drys because of conviction and because they were convinced that their voters wanted them there.

The senatorial election of 1922 was something of a bonanza for the ASL, which found its man in spite of itself. Its leaders demonstrated a certain political ineptitude in this campaign, which was more complex and subtle than the one-dimensional politics for which they had been trained. George Conger did not know what to do with Poindexter—the Senator voted right, and there was no solid evidence against him—so he endorsed him. The ASL line at the time held that the wets of the country were trying to get rid of all those who had voted for the Eighteenth Amendment (as Poindexter had done), even if they had to support drys to accomplish this.[22] At any rate, when Conger died in 1923 he left the state reasonably safe for the principles of the Anti-Saloon League, though he had at times stumbled badly. His successor, B. N. Hicks, would not be so fortunate.

Hicks took his office just when dry leaders were beginning to hear the first really serious murmurs of dissent in the state legislature. In 1923 some lawmakers were suggesting slyly that the Volstead Act had superseded the state's bone-dry law, and that the latter might as well be discarded. They were ready to support others who felt that the bone-dry provisions—more severe than the Volstead Act in their prohibitions of homemade beer and wine—were gratuitously restrictive. Hicks was quick to detect the appearance of evil, and he armed his forces with a recent decision by the United States Supreme Court which held that state dry laws passed before the Volstead Act were indeed valid, even if more harsh than the federal statute (*Vigliotti* v. *Pennsylvania*, 1922). The sermons, the letters, and the telegrams came forth at his call; the repealers and the modifiers were pushed back.[23]

The legislative session of 1923, however, was not an entirely happy one for Hicks. He had hoped for a measure to require state officials to enforce the Volstead Act, but it did not get the approval of the Senate Committee on Public Morals. The efforts of his friends in the Senate to override the committee proved futile.[24] In this setback, Hicks and the ASL experienced what was probably an accurate reflection of public sympathies—or ambiguities—at the time: a stout "no" for repeal or modification, but an equally strong refusal to pledge the state unequivocally to any responsibility for strict enforcement. This attitude, shared by the governor, was what both wets and drys labored to change.

In 1925, the ASL supported a bill which would have directed state officials to seize automobiles, boats, and airplanes used to transport liquor, but it did not pass through the Judiciary Committee of the Senate.[25] This action disturbed Hicks and caused him to take great care as he prepared endorsements for the election of 1926. As that year approached, he had a cause for serious concern, for it looked as if Senator Wesley L. Jones might be in for a difficult time.

Jones's image as "the prohibitionist" was beginning to harden to deep lines of intolerance, fanaticism, and bungling. The Olmstead conviction had certainly made it easier for him to praise the competence of his appointees, but the proceedings of the trial, insofar as they touched on the area of civil liberties, had intensified the suspicions which many people had about the prohibition office. Especially in Seattle, Tacoma, and Spokane, where the abuses of enforcement were most obvious and where the newspapers fed upon them daily, Jones could expect a surplus of political trouble. This trouble came from two directions: from the mob, as it were; and, more seriously, from the aristocracy.

Judge Kenneth Mackintosh of the state Supreme Court, a man of considerable dignity and reputation, had since 1925 been known to entertain political ambitions. Republicans who hoped to hear the last of Senator Jones's speeches on prohibition had been encouraging Mackintosh to come forward in 1926, but the judge played the game of watchful waiting with consummate stoicism. When the word reached Jones, he thought first of removing Mackintosh with an appointment to the United States Court of Appeals, but Mackintosh shortly explained himself. He would not run, he told Jones, at that time. "While there has been discussion as to the possibility of inducing me to enter the contest," he said grandly, "others who might really desire to make the effort have been deterred. . . ."[26] That was to say, his plan was to keep the rascals out of the race to protect Jones, and he offered to withhold any statement whatsoever until it was convenient to the Senator. With the shadow of Mackintosh stretched over the primary, only Austin Griffiths, generally regarded by this time as a harmless do-gooder, and an unknown hopeful named Frank Hammond, dared to file. At least in his own club, Jones would be safe.

Across the lines, Dr. Brown had left the Olmstead trial in a mood of great expectations. The federals had tried to get him, but they had missed. Never doubting that his own views were those generally shared everywhere, and feeling that the trial must have blackened the government from Al Hubbard right up to Senator Jones, Brown acted immediately. He announced his candidacy for United States senator on the Democratic ticket. Replacing Senator Jones, he commented, "may be my only means of getting access to certain reports on Bill Whitney that are on file in Washington, D.C."[27]

Chadwick of the Seattle *Argus* thought that the idea of Brown for the Senate was a brilliant one. "When we have a big joke," he said, referring to the Mayor, "we should share it with others." The Yakima *Republic* lacked this sense of humor: "In Seattle he may be considered a statesman. The requirements for office there are simple. Painless dentistry and a proper appreciation of the bootlegger's function will commend any public man highly and get him a majority. Out in the state it's different. . . ." Other friends of Jones, however, were seriously worried and advised him that if Brown should win the Seattle mayoralty again that spring, he would indeed be a threat to the Senator.[28]

By this time, though, Brown had his own backlog of troubles. For one thing, he had discovered that he was not the only showman in city politics. Mrs. Bertha K. Landes, wife of a university professor, was chairman of the city council, and she had for several years been making a career of her hostility to the wet Mayor and his chief of police. When Brown left town in 1924 to attend the Democratic National Convention, Mrs. Landes, as acting mayor, summarily fired Chief Severyns and set about closing down the town as tightly as she could before Brown returned. Her race for time—as the newspapers gloated—was also frustrated by Severyns, who one night sneaked two suitcases labeled with Brown's name into the mayor's office and caused Mrs. Landes to believe that Brown was somewhere in City Hall. When Brown did in fact return to his office and began to straighten out the affairs of Severyns and the city, Mrs. Landes had become nationally famous.[29]

Then in 1925 the Reverend Ambrose M. Bailey, pastor of the First Baptist church and an official of the ASL, entered the conflict in the role Dr. Matthews had played so well in 1910. Disguised as a logger, Dr. Bailey toured the city's lower regions and uncovered liquor and wickedness. He then began a series of lurid sermons attacking Dr. Brown and the police force. This packed his church every Sunday night and opened another of Seattle's dazzling political melodramas.[30]

When Dr. Brown answered the sermons in the newspapers, Dr. Bailey offered the Mayor the use of his pulpit at the First Baptist church for a more dignified reply. Brown accepted. Bailey responded the following Sunday, then Brown hired a hall. Before his largest audience ever, Brown accused Bailey of political conspiracy, called him "ambitious, ambiguous Ambrose," and challenged Bailey to take his case before a grand jury.

Dr. Bailey did exactly that, and the grand jury in December suggested that Brown be either impeached or recalled. Bailey, true to the role of Dr. Matthews, led the recall movement in what the newspapers called the final act of the "Brown and Bailey Circus." When Bailey failed to collect enough signatures for recall, he urged citizens to form vigilance committees to police the city. Brown, in triumph, threatened to throw Dr. Bailey, along with all such committees, into the city jail, and announced his candidacy for re-election.[31]

It was then that Thomas Revelle stepped into city politics with his

Olmstead portfolio. He spoke widely to different audiences around
the city. He claimed that seventy thousand dollars in graft was collected every month in Seattle, that the task of prohibition agents in
Seattle was a "horrible" one. "There are 500 policemen," he said,
"and most of them are used to spy on officials and to tip off advance
information on pending raids."[32] The people thought about this, and
in April of 1926 they made Mrs. Landes their mayor. Revelle expressed his satisfaction to Senator Jones: "They charged me with
having been instrumental in Brown's defeat," he wrote. "It certainly
put a crimp in his ambitions to occupy a seat in the United States
Senate."

Even so, Dr. Brown refused to get off the Senator's back. He continued to talk about Whitney and gave no indication that he had
given up his ambitions. In July when the intelligence unit of the Bureau of Internal Revenue sent a group of special agents under a man
named Alf Oftedahl to the West Coast to investigate international
smuggling and ordered Lyle to subordinate the Seattle office to the
investigators, Jones's irritation exploded privately. Two years before
Oftedahl had tried to get rid of Whitney, and it looked as if he
would try again, this time with vengeance. Jones therefore wrote to
the assistant secretary of the treasury that the Oftedahl appointment
was nothing less than a "disaster," and he accused the Treasury Department of conspiring against him.[33]

Meanwhile the ASL had laid its plans. As Dr. Brown threatened,
the League turned to its old Democratic warrior, George F. Cotterill.
Though the prohibitionist's desire for a seat in the United States
Senate had waned, his hatred for Edwin J. Brown had grown sharper
with the years. He was eager, however, to be off to London where he
was to address an international prohibition convention. Before his
departure, he gave a signed declaration of his candidacy to B. N.
Hicks to be filed if Dr. Brown did not withdraw during the summer.
Hicks felt that Cotterill could defeat Brown in the primaries, and the
plan was then that Cotterill would wage only "a formal and perfunc-
tory campaign against Senator Jones."

The plan fell to pieces when, in Cotterill's absence, his friend A.
Scott Bullitt, a wealthy and well-known Seattle Democrat, filed for
the Senate. With this, Brown had second thoughts and withdrew
from the contest. B. N. Hicks, had he been faithful to Cotterill's expressed wishes, should then have destroyed the declaration of candi-

dacy from Cotterill which he held. Instead, he conferred with ASL leaders about Bullitt, whose attitudes they distrusted because he had once spoken in favor of modifying the Volstead Act to permit light beers and wines. They feared that Bullitt was much stronger even than Dr. Brown, so they decided to split the Democrats as by the original plan. Thomas Revelle wrote a check for the filing fee, and Hicks entered Cotterill in the race. They gave him a quick ASL endorsement, thus stamping Bullitt from the beginning as the wet candidate.[34]

When Cotterill returned in August, he was furious at having been placed in this position against a friend. He quickly sat down with Bullitt, and after a four-hour interview convinced himself that Bullitt was neither a modifier nor a repealer, that he had repented his advocacy of mild beer and stood solidly behind the Volstead Act. Cotterill himself then withdrew from the race, announcing that Bullitt was dry and urging all Democrats to support him. At the same time he submitted his resignation from his post on the Headquarters Committee of the Anti-Saloon League of Washington. Along with it he sent a check—signed by Scott Bullitt—to refund the filing fee which the ASL had paid for Cotterill in July. The Headquarters Committee immediately accepted both.[35]

Cotterill, in a scathing defense of himself and Bullitt, claimed that he had been "excommunicated." The ASL, he wrote to the committee, was guilty of "the most brazen hypocrisy and falsehood, or the rankest ignorance. . . ." He accused Hicks of "bad faith and outright dishonesty," of "sheer malice" and "revengeful injury." The committee, which had never before suffered from such a lashing, blandly explained to the newspapers that Cotterill was "out of harmony" with the policy of the ASL.[36]

The "excommunication" left strong suggestions that the ASL was indeed engaged in partisan politics. Hicks had stumbled, and Bullitt might draw significantly upon dry support in his campaign against Jones. Unfortunately for the ASL, its endorsements had been somewhat tarnished. A new list of these endorsements for the general elections appeared on October 11, and the next day things were even worse for the League.

Harry M. Westfall, a prominent Democrat shortly to become chairman of the Judiciary Committee in the state House of Representatives, publicly repudiated his ASL endorsement. Westfall said that he favored modification and had never concealed his attitude. The ASL, he charged, had thrown him an endorsement as "a sop to the Democrats and to certain temperance leaders who have been criticizing Hicks for committing that organization to the partisan candidacy of Wesley L. Jones." He said further that he had wanted a modification plank in the state platform of 1926 but had not pushed it out of respect for Scott Bullitt. Against this second blast, Hicks's only defense was silence.[37]

As November approached, the Democrats had some reason to believe that Scott Bullitt might receive the backing of those who had carried Clarence Dill to victory in 1922. Bullitt hoped for the solid support of farmers and unions and for the votes of all those dissatisfied with national prohibition, including many Republicans. This last group could be crucial, for it was clear enough that to win in the state of Washington, just being a Democrat and supporting the wishes of farmers and working men was not enough. To win some of the normally Republican votes, Bullitt had to do some delicate maneuvering. To attack Jones as a radical dry would obviously have been political foolishness. Many of the farm and labor votes would be lost, and all of the anguish of George Cotterill would have been wasted. Yet Bullitt knew that Jones's blue nose was his most—and maybe his only—vulnerable spot. Jones was not antilabor and antifarm, as Poindexter had been; he had delivered wonders for agriculture in federal irrigation projects. And he was not dishonest or unduly wealthy.

Bullitt's attack was craftily indirect, if not really very subtle. He found that Jones had favored a strict Sunday closure law for Washington, D.C., so he projected this to the implication that Jones wanted to close down the entire United States every Sunday. Pushing hard along this approach, Bullitt probably found a way to the hearts of many businessmen who were grateful for the taxes which flowed into municipal treasuries from business conducted on the Sabbath. Meanwhile, the Seattle *Star* gave its readers an almost daily diet of Lyle-Whitney atrocity stories tailored to reflect upon Senator Jones.[38]

In the other camp, there was an equally realistic appraisal of the weaknesses of A. Scott Bullitt. His former association with the mild beer idea, whatever his more recent change of mind, was all the ASL needed. The League distributed over twenty-seven thousand copies of a pamphlet which identified Bullitt as a wet. The WCTU sent letters out across the state in support of Jones, and—so Bullitt later claimed —some of the ladies were being paid to go from door to door with the message that Scott Bullitt wanted to destroy the achievements of prohibition. Jones himself was perfectly willing to follow the ASL path, and he toured the state charging that Bullitt was backed by "brewery, distillery, and saloon interests." In Walla Walla, Jones coined the phrase "bourbon cash barrel" in referring to Bullitt's expenses and sources of income. Jones enjoyed the words so much that he used them frequently, and they soon inspired charges which almost created enough scandal to bring real excitement into the last weeks of the campaign.

Jones had discovered that Bullitt's father-in-law was financing an organization called the Anti-Sunday Closing League. A single-page ad in the *Motion Picture Record*, Jones charged, had cost the League seven thousand dollars. Then the chairman of the state Republican Central Committee announced that Bullitt's relatives had already spent one hundred thousand dollars on the campaign against Jones, and, his sources indicated, they were prepared to go to three hundred thousand. The same announcement reiterated that Bullitt was a wet, a very rich one. Clearly the shafts which had brought down Poindexter could be used by Republicans too.

As the charges were repeated, Senator Jones, who perhaps believed them, became so incensed that he asked the United States Senate to inquire immediately into campaign expenditures in the state of Washington.

The hearings began on October 23 in Seattle before a special investigating committee of one, Senator Charles McNary of Oregon. Bullitt represented himself during the proceedings, and McNary, perhaps to demonstrate the committee's impartiality, gave Bullitt a free hand to review the entire conduct of the campaign by questioning leaders of the ASL, the WCTU, the Republican party, and even Senator Jones himself. Seldom has a candidate had so many of his enemies before the public and under oath.

Bullitt dragged the reluctant Hicks through a recitation of the Cotterill dispute, which, surprisingly, did not sound so bad the way Hicks told it. Hicks was followed to the stand by ladies of the WCTU, and Bullitt received some grinning condolence from the chair when he found it impossible to get the ladies to say anything specific—even "yes" or "no." Jones proved to be almost as evasive, but Bullitt, a skillful lawyer, cornered his opponent long enough for Jones to admit that the charges of excess spending were, at best, "estimates," and that Jones did not have certain knowledge of any contributions which liquor interests had made to Bullitt's candidacy.[39]

When McNary left Seattle, his investigations had revealed only the hyperbole of state Republicans and the verbosity of Scott Bullitt. The scandal which Jones and his campaigners had hoped for never materialized; if anything, the Senator himself was exposed as more foggy and sloppy in his research than a senator should be. Bullitt's attempt to discredit Jones and the ASL grew repetitive and tiresome and not at all shocking. If anything, Bullitt confirmed his identification with wealth, albeit dry and unsullied wealth. But even so, among his farmer and labor groups, this may have hurt him.

Jones's margin of victory was only fifteen thousand votes, and if the seven thousand votes which went to the Socialist and Farmer-Labor candidates are counted against him, the margin was even more slim. If the image of Bullitt as wet and wealthy turned a few votes toward Jones, surely the dry machine—the workers in the many federal offices throughout the state, as well as the members of the ASL, the churches, the WCTU, and the PTA—could have accounted for the rest.

Jones lost the urban districts of Seattle-Tacoma by about eight thousand votes. This figure, however, is no measure of wet-dry sentiment in this area. Mayor Brown had been defeated in Seattle a few months earlier by a prominent dry candidate, and in a contest even more accurately marked as a wet-dry struggle, John F. Miller, the incumbent dry Republican from the First Congressional District (Seattle), won a close and emotional victory. Miller's campaign had few issues other than prohibition and personal abuse. He campaigned with Jones, and to one audience he said that he wanted to take his opponent, Stephen J. Chadwick, by the neck and drop him in Puget Sound so that he could "watch him come up, wet as usual." Chadwick matched blow for blow: "I'd come up with one of John F. Miller's dead soldiers in my hand."[40] The vote was 35,944 to 34,401.

It seems likely, then, that in this area the votes measured a fairly even division of opinion on national prohibition. Probably some voters who approved of the Volstead Act did not approve of the conduct of Lyle, Revelle, and Whitney, and for that reason voted against Senator Jones. Perhaps Jones himself might have accepted such an inter-

pretation, for several years later he filed in his private papers an editorial from the Puyallup *Valley Tribune* which reviewed the election
of 1926 by recalling the attack of federal officers on Brown and the
"host of enemies" which this attack brought against the "federal bri-
gade": "The secret of the close call of Senator Jones for re-election
in 1926, was the bitter factional contest involved in the activities
—and animosities—aroused by the Revelle-Lyle-Whitney Federal
regime."[41]

In other parts of the state, the election of 1926 caused little concern for the ASL because most of the candidates were dry. In the
Fifth Congressional District (from Wenatchee to Spokane), Jack T.
Fancher won the Republican nomination over the ASL candidate,
Arthur True, but in November Fancher lost (twenty-nine thousand to
twenty-seven thousand) to the ASL choice, Sam Hill. In the legislative contests, the ASL put the wet mark on certain candidates, especially those members of the House who had voted against H. B. 240
(seizure and forfeiture of vehicles used to transport liquor) in 1925.
Of the twenty-six who so voted, fourteen returned to the House after
the election. Eight of the marked twenty-six were from King County,
and of these, five survived.

The election of 1926, then, was at several levels a test of dry sentiment and ASL power. There were, of course, other issues and other
pressure groups, and in no single contest were the people voting exclusively for or against prohibition. Nevertheless, it seems reasonable
to say that most people in the state—perhaps about 60 per cent—still
kept their faith in the Eighteenth Amendment, but that numbers of
these were disturbed about the manner in which the Volstead Act
was being enforced. It seems certain, too, that the ASL was a political factor of considerable significance among the majority who still
favored the dry experiment, but that the League exercised less power
than it had a decade before. From the heights of 1916-18, the loss
seems great indeed.

Early in 1927 there were signs that the losses were becoming even
greater. First of all, the brutality of Lyle's agents had become something of a state-wide scandal. Then Thomas Revelle grew extremely
uneasy about rumors that agents Al Hubbard and Richard Fryant
were working more closely with bootleggers than they were with Lyle
and Whitney. Alf Oftedahl of the intelligence unit was suspicious, cu-

rious, and unfriendly. Early in the spring, a grand jury in Seattle looked into the affairs of the prohibition office, but to the disappointment of the enemy camp, the jury's report sounded as if it had been written by B. N. Hicks. "The government is very fortunate," the jury said, "to have such a person and character as Mr. Whitney in active charge of the enforcement of the national prohibition laws, because of his superior abilities, his indefatigable zeal and his unimpeachable honor."[42] In Washington, D.C., Jones was delighted. In Seattle, Lyle and Whitney were free to work out the details of their second major courtroom drama—the trial and conviction, in the fall, of fifteen leaders of a major rumrunning and bootlegging ring in Grays Harbor, including Chris Curtis, a runner second only to Olmstead in notoriety, and Elmer Gibson, the sheriff of Grays Harbor County. In Olympia, Hicks could give all his attention to the state legislature, then in session.

The attitudes of the legislature which had ruffled Hicks in the past—attitudes against both repeal and enforcement—were as unyielding and as confusing in 1927 as ever before. Both houses stopped cold before a move to memorialize Congress for the repeal of the Eighteenth Amendment, but they also avoided two important ASL bills and managed to lose them in the flurry of the last week of the session.

The first of these, the old "seizure of vehicles" bill again, passed through the Senate, though it was wounded with the amending clause "vehicles . . . transporting more than one gallon . . ." before it was lost in the House. Then H. B. 278 (to make the manufacture of liquor, with intent to sell, a felonious act) passed through the House but was ignored by the Senate.

The fate of this last bill particularly infuriated Bernard N. Hicks. He reported to national Anti-Saloon League headquarters that the House in his state was dry, sixty to thirty-seven, but that the Senate was wet, twenty-six to sixteen, and that in both chambers the wets controlled the important committees. He then called a press conference and criticized the committees which had "deliberately smothered" the ASL bills. Just as Boyd Doty had done in 1907, he announced that the ASL would attack the wet lawmakers and officials in Washington State across the entire front of government, from governor on down.[43] Because of this publicly declared war, and because the coming national campaigns promised to present the voters with the wet-dry issue in terms more clear than they had ever been presented before, 1928 was a critical year for the League and its dry friends everywhere.

In the beginning, things did not look bright for them. Mrs. Landes of Seattle was coming to realize that her goading the police force into liquor raids had cost her many valuable political friends. Early in 1928 she called at least one police officer to her office and gave him an oral reprimand for raiding homes in the University District, accusing the officer of being a party to a plot to embarrass her in her own neighborhood.[44] As a closed-town mayor, she had perhaps done too well. The number of arrests for liquor violations in the city each year had more than doubled since she took office. She found no easy way to retreat from her achievements. Seattle was tiring of reform and of Mrs. Landes.

She lost in 1928 to Frank Edwards, a businessman who had done well with a string of theaters which featured second-rate movies. Edwards' campaign showed how confident he was of moving in on a good thing: it sparkled with flashy publicity tricks but revealed nothing about his plans for the city. Even to the Seattle *Argus*, which held little love for Mrs. Landes, Edwards was an "unknown quantity." This was apparently just what Seattle wanted. When Edwards took office he ordered policemen not to drink on duty or off, but arrests fell down somewhat from the Landes heights. This degree of reform, not too much and not too little, was appropriate to the situation. Lyle, however, wrote to Jones that the election of Frank Edwards was a "calamity,"[45] for under Edwards, prohibition ceased to be a significant issue in city politics.

In the same month, a grand jury in Seattle began an inquiry into the affairs of Al Hubbard and Richard Fryant. United States District Attorney Revelle told Jones that this was another effort to embarrass them both. When the jury failed to indict, Mrs. Willebrandt of the Justice Department lost all her patience with Revelle and Whitney. Revelle himself resigned shortly thereafter.

These events, and the developments of national politics during the summer, caused many people to anticipate some climax in the wet-dry debate. Chadwick of the *Argus* said he would vote for Al Smith if it were possible for the New Yorker to do anything about the Eighteenth Amendment. Chadwick doubted that any state politician would have the courage that Smith had in opposing dry laws, and he further doubted that the issue could significantly affect the campaign. Others, however, felt that prohibition surely would be the issue. William H. Cowles, publisher of two Spokane papers (both very dry and very Republican), was sufficiently convinced to give the ASL five thousand dollars.[46] And Cowles was right: in almost every race, candidates faced the issue, sometimes squarely and sometimes obliquely, but always at length.

When Clarence Dill stood for re-election, he was more aggressively dry than he had been in 1922. "It is well known that I am opposed to modifying the Volstead Act," he said, recalling his radio debates with wets before a national audience, "except to make its enforcement more stringent. . . . The people of this state have voted dry. . . . I am their servant."[47] Nothing could be plainer. In the Republican contest for the chance to oppose Dill, Kenneth Mackintosh came forward from the state Supreme Court; Miles Poindexter resigned his ministerial post in Peru to return to his state and try again; and Austin Griffiths, undaunted by normalcy or Coolidge republicanism, once more offered his progressivism to the public. The ASL saw no cause to waste time or words—it endorsed Dill as well as all the Republicans.

The congressional races attracted only one candidate of whom the ASL did not approve—Hugh Todd in the First Congressional District—but he was defeated by the very-dry John F. Miller in November. In the gubernatorial contests, however, there were weeks of political bloodshed. At this level, the state Republicans had no unity at all; Governor Hartley had seen to that.

He had, first of all, outraged many Republicans by precipitating a legislative gang war over methods of selling state timber lands. Then many others were offended by the manner in which the Governor disposed of his most eminent enemy, Henry Suzzallo, president of the University of Washington, who was dismissed without charges and without a hearing after clashes with Hartley over educational policy and finance. Still others felt that Hartley's budgets were ruining the state's school and highway programs. The Seattle *Times*, speaking for many unhappy Republicans, had led a recall movement against the Governor, calling him the "most despised man in the state of Washington." This futile effort was also supported by the Tacoma *Tribune* and the Wenatchee *World*.[48] Even without any direct evidence, one can assume that the ASL leaders were in sympathy with such efforts, for their conflict with the Governor over law enforcement was of long standing. In the summer of 1928 the Republican split seemed so serious that it appeared likely that ASL endorsements might be decisive factors in the primaries.

Insurgents brought forth two men in 1928 with some potential for replacing the Governor. Claude Bannick, the sheriff of King County, was known throughout the state. The professionals were supporting Edward L. French of Vancouver, the owner of a fruit-packing company, a former state senator, and the runner-up in the primaries of 1924. Bannick's reputation for strict enforcement made him something of a dry hero, and French was a member of the Board of Trustees of the state Anti-Saloon League. Both were enthusiastically endorsed by the ASL. While Hartley toured the state displaying a one-hundred-dollar cuspidor from the capitol which he claimed was a symbol of irresponsible waste in government, French and Bannick attacked him and his record of neglect for roads, schools, farm relief, and public welfare. In almost every speech, though, they raised prohibition as a fundamental issue of their campaigns.[49]

If the Republicans had disharmony in their ranks, the Democrats, as befitted them, had chaos. George Cotterill had watched with increasing distress while the various candidates for the governorship maneuvered through the summer. When his friend A. Scott Bullitt filed, and was challenged by Stephen J. Chadwick, Cotterill felt fine. But when both candidates pledged themselves to Al Smith, the old prohibitionist suffered the anguish of Creon, king of Thebes. After several days he rose up to join the ranks of the "Democrats for Hoover" and announced his own candidacy for the office of governor. His initial broadside read in part:

> May I state plainly, that my campaign is made for a principle rather than an office—as a protest against the Smith-Raskob-Booze "bolt" from the Democratic platform, and in defense of Constitution and Law against the Tammany threat of nullification and eventual repeal of the 18th Amendment. I refuse to follow that road in November, and propose to remain a true Democrat while voting for Herbert Hoover— the man who helped Woodrow Wilson do world service while Tammany was crucifying him for a Smith holiday and selling democratic ideals for a mess of New York pottage. . . .
>
> There is no hope for Progressive Democracy or for Good Government in the renomination of Governor Hartley—as seems most probable. He represents the same booze trend and abuses of State Government

similar to the Tammany threat against the Nation. If renominated in September, Hartley will be defeated in November by any Democratic nominee. If defeated by his "dry" opponent, Mr. French—or by the law enforcement Sheriff Bannick—the Hartley forces, largely "wet" and worse, will flock revengefully to the Smith-Booze-Democratic standard, and elect a "wet" Tammany nominee for Governor.[50]

Thus Cotterill in 1928 found himself against Scott Bullitt and in the company of his betrayers of 1926. The ASL quickly endorsed him.

Cotterill was shortly joined in his "dry revolt" by the Reverend Mark Matthews of Seattle, who in September equated Al Smith with city corruption and wet wickedness, almost with the Devil himself. Though Cotterill and Matthews were advised by another Democratic minister that "it would be better for them to take a little wine for their stomachs' sake than to try to swallow Teapot Dome oil,"[51] they spoke and preached dry politics to the limit of their energies until November.

The ASL probably had no really stable hopes for a Cotterill victory. His reputation in the states as a do-gooder was about the same as that of Austin Griffiths. But it was counting on E. L. French to save it from hopelessness in the general elections. When Bullitt and Hartley won the primaries, it was a two-edged defeat for the ASL, and the executive board went into a painful and protracted session. Bernard Hicks, probably leaning desperately upon Hartley's sullen and consistent refusal even to discuss prohibition, favored supporting the Governor. He was overruled, though, and the ASL washed its hands of the whole dirty gubernatorial business. French urged his friends not to support Hartley. Scott Bullitt angled for these votes by stressing that he was "for the enforcement of all laws, including liquor laws," but the ASL adamantly refused to give him any attention.

Meanwhile, the races for the office of lieutenant governor brought the ASL some compensating satisfactions. The field had caused almost as much excitement as the governor's because the issues were practically the same. Among Democrats, everybody knew that the nomination would go to Harry Westfall of Seattle, who had kicked against the ASL in 1926. To stop him, then, dry leaders entered the Republican primaries in the spirit of an anxious crusade. In this contest, too, there were grave dangers, for Paul Houser of Renton promised to take all the Hartley votes. As a state senator, Houser had been the principal Hartley defender and the principal organizer of wet sentiment in Olympia. It was he who first defiantly moved to memorialize Congress for the repeal of the Eighteenth Amendment. The anti-Hartley forces supported John A. Gellatly, of Wenatchee, for lieutenant governor. Another anti-Hartley candidate, Victor Zednick, hoped that the split might turn to his advantage. The ASL chose Gellatly with real urgency, and Mrs. Landes, former mayor of Seattle, assisted in making Gellatly's campaign the dry one.[52] When Gellatly won the nomination and the election, stopping Houser and retiring Westfall from public life, the ASL could feel that it did indeed

TABLE 14

BOOZE AND POLITICS, 1928

* ASL Endorsement
(n) Nominated
(E) Elected

Office	Democrat	Non-Partisan	Republican
Mayor of Seattle		Frank Edwards (E) Bertha K. Landes* Edwin J. Brown	
President	Al Smith		Herbert Hoover* (E)
U.S. Senate	C. C. Dill* (E)		Kenneth Mackintosh* (n) Miles Poindexter* Austin Griffiths*
Congress			
1st Dist.	Hugh Todd (n)		John F. Miller* (E)
2nd Dist.	no candidate		L. H. Hadley* (E)
3rd Dist.	no candidate		Albert Johnson* (E)
4th Dist.	no candidate		J. W. Summers* (E)
5th Dist.	Sam Hill* (E)		Thomas Corkery* (n) C. E. Meyers*
Governor	A. Scott Bullitt (n) Stephen F. Chadwick George Cotterill*		Roland Hartley (E) Edward French* Claude Bannick*
Lt. Gov.	Harry Westfall (n)		John Gellatly* (E) Paul Houser Victor Zednick

State Senate: Dry, 30-8 (ASL estimate)
State House of Representatives: Dry, 68-17 (ASL estimate)

have some influence, but the Hartley victory at the same time did little to clarify just how extensive this influence might have been.

It was more clear, however, in the legislative returns. True to the promise of B. N. Hicks, the League participated in every contest, and seldom with any compromise. For example, lists of "candidates for whom all Christians should vote" did not include the name of Donald McDonald of Seattle who, for a brief period before Roy Lyle, had been prohibition administrator and who in 1928 was a trustee of Dr. Matthews' Presbyterian church. He was not endorsed by the ASL for the legislature because, it was reported, he had spoken in favor of some modification of the Volstead Act. To the *Argus* this proved the League's fanaticism, but to Hicks it proved sound politics. McDonald lost, and when the votes in the general election were counted, Hicks's score was impressive. The Senate was dry, thirty to eight, he said, with four unknowns; the House was dry, sixty-eight to seventeen, with twelve unknowns.[53] In view of his count in 1927 (Senate wet, twenty-six to sixteen, House dry, sixty to thirty-seven), his activities in 1928 had wrought a significant change.

The election of 1928 was a demonstration of prohibition sentiment throughout the state and a dry victory of considerable proportions. Voters elected dry candidates to every national office at a time when every candidate recognized prohibition as a serious issue. It was, of course, not the only issue, and the fact that it was not helps to explain the few enigmas which the year produced. Clarence Dill, perhaps no more dry than Mackintosh but better known for it, had his personal attraction, popularity, and prestige to swing against the Republican tide. Governor Hartley had this tide, as well as a split vote and his powerful machine and a demagogic flair for dramatizing his fight with "the politicians" to throw in the face of his rather pusillanimous, if dry, opposition. Other than the dampness—fog would perhaps be a better word—around Hartley, everything was dry. Hartley's man Paul Houser went down as did Hugh Todd and Harry Westfall. Politically, the state was almost as dry as it had been in 1920.

B. N. Hicks was among the first to acknowledge the complexities of the election of 1928. Al Smith, he said, had been beaten not only by prohibition, but also by Tammany, by prosperity, and by Roman Catholicism. Even before November, a minister in Everett had predicted much the same thing, though he used broader terms. The great political battle in 1928, he said, was between "Main Street and Broadway," between purity and corruption, between high ideals and cynicism.[54] One may wish to question the precision of the minister's symbolism, but it would be difficult to deny that this was an accurate reflection of how people of Main Street—generally speaking, the American middle class—thought about their voting.

It should be emphasized again that even Governor Hartley never said a word against the principle of prohibition. He refused to be squeezed into an either-or position.[55] Perhaps he knew that among the people of Washington, prohibition was still regarded as a noble expression of American values. While they had their doubts, and while many of them might themselves tarnish the ideal in their daily lives, they were not yet willing to support any politician who told them that their transgressions were right and the ideal was wrong.

13

Transition, 1929-30

EVEN AFTER ten years of prohibition, the radical drys were still not properly sensitive to the delicate balance of public attitudes implicit in the election of 1928. Most people wanted their ideology protected, but at the same time they cherished a broad tolerance for human weakness. To make enforcement more severe—to translate a misdemeanor into a cardinal sin—would surely force people to re-examine their ideological fundamentals, and this is just what the radicals did. The radical mind was not equipped to live in the world of paradox. It insisted on righteous consistency, which may be appropriate to crusades but was the very antithesis of normalcy.

It was Senator Jones's misfortune that he should represent those who forced the issue. Early in 1929 he was induced to introduce the Jones "Five and Ten" Act, which raised the federal penalties for liquor offenses to maximum sentences of five years or ten thousand dollars. In the debate which preceded its passage, the law was so forcefully identified with "the philosophy of hate" that Jones himself inserted an amendment which made it "the intent of Congress, that the courts . . . should discriminate between casual or slight violations and . . . attempts to commercialize violations of the law." Aimed then specifically at the big bootleggers, the law passed through Congress and was signed by President Hoover.[1]

The damage, however, had already been done. To many critics the original intent of the law was as significant as its final phrases. The attitude which had inspired the Jones Law was offensive enough. Then President Hoover expressed determination to make all prohibition laws effective, even if he had to build more federal prisons to do it. And when Hoover's fact-finding committee made a preliminary recommendation that liquor cases be tried without a jury—all these factors were enough to wreck the fragile compromise between law and

206

order. Senator Jones, amid many congratulatory messages, received
stones of abuse and vituperation that surpassed in size and velocity
anything in his long experience. (One letter, addressed simply "Senator Sourpuss, Washington, D.C.," was delivered to his office.) A flow
of rebukes streamed from the press and even from the courts where
his law would be administered.

For example, one judge of a United States District Court said that
the law would "retard rather than aid the enforcement" of prohibition. Jones was both hurt and angry. In Seattle, Federal Judge
George M. Bourquin was a sharp thorn in the side of William Whitney because (according to Whitney) of his "ridiculously small fines
and sentences." After the Jones Act, Judge Bourquin found occasion
from time to time to shed light upon the doctrine of strict enforcement. One day in 1930, after sentencing a man who had been arrested in possession of liquor which was destined for the Arctic Club of
Seattle, Bourquin turned to the prosecutor and asked "why it would
not be proper to obtain a roster of this club and ask a grand jury to
bring indictments against each and every member on charges of violating the prohibition law?" Everybody knew that the names of many
friends of Senator Jones—including Roy Lyle, the federal prohibition administrator—would appear on such a roster.[2]

In Olympia, too, things were not going well for the radical cause.
B. N. Hicks of the ASL was beginning to blister in frustration. The
legislature, under his watchful eye, had passed four bills to strength-
en state enforcement, each of which had been vetoed by the Governor. Over a proposed law to make the manufacture of liquor for sale
a felony, Governor Hartley had written that "observation of the situation indicates that the fault is not so much with present laws as with
the demand for intoxicating liquor and a lack of public sympathy for
law enforcement." He killed a bill to allow the search and seizure of
vehicles used in transporting liquor by charging that such a law
would "let loose an army of snoopers to harry, harass, and annoy
the traveling public. It would create conditions intolerable to a free
people." Hicks was certain that Hartley was playing to the crowd
and charting a course toward the United States Senate in 1932.[3]

Along with the troubles caused by his law, Jones suffered from the
chronic nagging of the Reverend Mark Matthews of Seattle—reformer, prohibitionist, dry Democrat, and friend of dubious loyalties. Matthews was frequently inspired to advise the Senator, often

in long telegrams sent collect, and he was insistent that such advice always be read into the Congressional Record. Jones had tried to place Matthews on President Hoover's fact-finding committee which was investigating the enforcement of prohibition,[4] but the President deliberately selected men of more moderate views than those of Mark Matthews. The minister's years had in no way softened his relentless fundamentalism, for he continued to delight Seattle with his thunder over loose morals, smoking, cosmetics, modern novels, Sunday golf, and liquor. Though he was regarded in sophisticated circles as a rather quaint and crabby character, he still had the authority of a pillar of morality and the voice of a puritan father. The law, he shouted, was sovereign, eternal, and "ought to be enforced if every street in America had to run with blood and every cobble stone had to be made of a human skull." Prohibition, as it had for thirty years, touched the deeper recesses of his personality and caused such eruptions of fanaticism that one wonders why only a few people thought him demented. One of his letters to Senator Jones is a fair example of what the *Argus* referred to as "mental constipation":

> The whiskey on the one side, the narcotic evil on the other side, the immoral question on the other side, and the false, rationalistic, atheistic, bolshevistic, damnable Russian propaganda on the other side are all combining to make a hollow square in which they are putting the youth of this land and sacrificing it with as much glee as the demons of the Roman forum sacrificed the Christians of ancient days. . . . Give me position and power and let me do something. . . .

Jones's reply to this was to stress his "confidence in the substantial people of the country" and blame everything on the newspapers. He ignored the dark plea for power.[5]

In October, 1929, Matthews became even more urgent. He warned Jones that a great and scandalous exposé was approaching which would wreck the Senator: "They will get you on the Aberdeen Radio business . . . on campaign contributions. . . . Let me take charge . . . get people to resign . . . save a great upheaval." Jones replied pointedly that he did not know what Matthews was talking about.

In November, Matthews asked Jones to write a law which would make the possession of liquor a gross misdemeanor. Just three days later—even before Jones could reply—Matthews stunned the Senator with a Sunday sermon called "Respect for the Law" which fell like a bomb upon prohibitionists everywhere. In it he flayed "fanatical drys who hold the Eighteenth Amendment above all other laws." He claimed that the prohibition laws had been "defied by the American public" and mentioned "the spectacle of Congress considering a bill to punish a man for buying liquor." Blasting heavily into the Anti-Saloon League, he declared that no law should require special pleading and that "we need a league to abolish such leagues." B. N. Hicks, likewise stunned, had no comment. The Seattle *Times* remarked that "Dr. Matthews gave the public occasion for serious thought."[6]

Perhaps the most serious thinking was done by the prohibitionists, whose unity Matthews had shaken even more than George Cotterill had in 1926. They had for some time suspected the motives and Democratic affiliations of Dr. Matthews, but they had not prepared for this blow. Newspapers across the state praised the attack—Lyle counted only two editorials which objected to what Matthews had said. Lyle soon concluded that Matthews, in attempting to split dry leadership, hoped to assume all of it for himself, that he was "deliberately betraying us," and that he was "working closely with Bullitt, Doc Brown, and others. . . ." Senator Jones could believe this, and he already knew even more: Matthews had written that he "would like to give prohibition a real enforcement test," and had asked Jones to get him the office of United States Prohibition Commissioner.[7] Jones apparently never acted upon this request.

What Dr. Matthews would do next, no one knew, but by the spring of 1930 it was clear that the sweep of events had brought the nation toward a full review of prohibition fundamentals, and in the state of Washington, the egomania of Dr. Matthews had weakened the unity with which prohibitionists might have faced such an ordeal. That spring the state heard an unfettered chorus of wet voices. Following hard upon the law and the sermon—and the criticism by judges, the newspaper articles, and the "serious thought"—the political discipline of the ASL broke wide open.

The break was apparent in February, when a meeting of high-level Democrats resolved that all federal prohibition agents in the state be dismissed. The leaders criticized the agents' being allowed "to override state laws against wiretapping" and spoke indirectly but clearly to Jones, Lyle and Whitney, Al Hubbard, and the deceased Kinky Thompson:

Confessed criminals, who turn state's evidence, should not be rewarded by appointments as federal prohibition agents. Such appointments in the state of Washington, coupled with the unrebuked brutality of federal agents toward helpless prisoners and innocent bystanders have so discredited the federal prohibition service as to make all law enforcement more difficult.

Before their convention met that summer, wet Democrats had programmed their strategy in fine detail. Knowing that the combined strength of delegations from King and Spokane counties could dominate the convention floor, and knowing also that the King County delegates were assuredly wet, Democratic leaders relied upon Mrs. Edith Dolan Riley of Spokane for the clinching maneuver. Mrs. Riley was a party regular with an impressive reputation for political skill. Though she had not crusaded in the cause of wetness, she was already working toward the election of Franklin Roosevelt in 1932, and to that end she was determined to make the Democratic party the party of repeal. As a former Spokane County chairwoman and a member of the state resolutions committee, she was in a position to select many of the delegates to the county convention. All of her choices were women pledged to repeal.

In Spokane, Mrs. Riley adroitly committed the county convention to the unit rule, then waited for the votes to fall in place. During a long evening in June, the convention was held in suspense by the delaying tactics of the drys who hoped that Mrs. Riley's ladies would sooner or later go home to cook for their families. According to fascinated masculine observers from the press, the evening began to measure in an unusual way whether wet politics was more important to these women than hearth, home, and dinner. At two o'clock in the afternoon, the vote was 259 wet to 160 dry. The drys spoke at length and demanded roll calls on each contrived amendment. But at six o'clock, there were still 105 hungry and wet women voting against only fifty-five dry and hungry defenders of prohibition. While husbands and children waited, the wets won Spokane County for repeal and guaranteed a wet Democratic platform at the state convention.[8]

These developments were mild, however, when compared to the riot of wet anger when the Republicans assembled in Bellingham that May. Some of Jones's friends thought that Hartley had dominated the convention; but the *Argus'* correspondent reported that the Governor had hoped to avoid the prohibition issue but was overwhelmed. Whatever the situation, there had been no such insurrection in Republican ranks since 1912. The real keynote for the convention had been delivered the month before by Guy Kelley of Tacoma, former speaker of the state House of Representatives who had supported every dry bill of the decade. In April, Kelley announced his apostasy:

> The time has come when Republican leadership must take the hypocrisy out of politics and assume the leadership for repeal or modification. . . . The day is past when the Anti-Saloon League can brand and politically murder a candidate for public office. . . . The machinery for enforcement of the prohibition law is permeated with the most rotten system of graft in the history of the world. . . .[9]

The similarity between 1930 and 1912 was one of structure as well as mood. Just as in 1912, the state committee allowed county chairmen to hand-pick the delegates to the convention. In King County, for example, the chairman was Ralph Horr, a very ambitious wet, and King County sent 243 delegates to Bellingham, wet to the last man. Ralph Horr was already well known to Senator Jones: Whitney had reported as early as 1927 that Horr was acquainted with Roy Olmstead and had been working with the intelligence unit men to compile evidence against the prohibition office in Seattle. Horr was on his way to a seat in Congress; in Bellingham he was official keynoter as well as unofficial key man. He criticized Senator Jones before the convention, charging the Senator specifically with smothering an investigation by the Justice Department into the affairs of Lyle and Whitney. And swinging his 243 wet votes behind the wet plank he put in the platform, he passed it, 456-448. While the Spokane *Spokesman-Review* cried "disgrace," the convention adjourned without having voiced any approval of either President Hoover or Senator Jones.[10]

The suffering was only beginning. Just a few days after the Bellingham convention voted its wet plank, the drys staggered under an equally disastrous blow when a grand jury in Seattle returned an indictment against Roy Lyle and William Whitney, against R. L. Fryant, the wiretapper, and against C. T. McKinney, who had assisted Thomas Revelle during the Olmstead trial and who was a favorite speaker among temperance groups. The charges were bribery and cooperation with bootleggers.[11]

Something had been brewing here for a long time. Besides the vague and confusing threats from Dr. Matthews, Senator Jones had for months been warned by other correspondents around the state that his defense of Lyle and Whitney was placing his career in jeopardy. Perhaps the most objective of these was H. A. Chadwick, the droll editor of the Seattle *Argus*:

> At the time of the receipt of your last letter . . . I was quite busy recovering from a slight paralytic stroke. I don't know what caused it, unless it was that rotten booze you prohibitionists have inflicted on us. . . . I believe that when Roy Lyle was appointed he was an honest man. I hope he is an honest man now. He is not smart. . . . About some of the others I do not care to express an opinion. But, Senator, if you do not watch things carefully, and be prepared to admit that you have been mistaken when, and if, it is proven, you are now serving your last term. . . .

His phrase "some of the others" probably referred most pointedly to the turncoat agent Al Hubbard, who held the key to much grief to come. Intimate with bootleggers and prohibition officials alike, he apparently played both sides to his own advantage. According to Revelle, one of Hubbard's typical moves was to join a bootlegging gang and accept money with which he was supposed to bribe the federal agents. He would turn over a small amount to Whitney for a good show, then lead Whitney and the agents to the bootleggers on a raid from which the outlaws always managed to escape at the last minute. A Grays Harbor bootlegger later told a grand jury that he gave Hubbard more than one hundred thousand dollars in 1926-27 to buy off federal agents.[12]

Finally, Thomas Revelle became so concerned about Hubbard and about similar reports of corruption among other agents—and about Whitney's refusal to become concerned—that before he resigned he asked Mrs. Willebrandt to investigate the Seattle prohibition office. Hardly had he done so when Hubbard himself appeared before Mrs. Willebrandt and offered to help the Justice Department prove that federal officials in Seattle—Lyle, Whitney, Revelle—were protecting bootleggers.

The Justice Department assigned a special investigation, and Hubbard returned to Seattle in a capacity that shocked the prohibition office: he said he was an agent of the Justice Department gathering evidence of corruption against Lyle, Whitney, and Revelle. He was joined by other special agents assigned by Mrs. Willebrandt and later by members of the Treasury Department's intelligence unit, all of whom began long conferences with bootleggers and rumrunners in Seattle and on McNeil Island. Seattle was treated to the spectacle of spies spying on the spies. As Mrs. Willebrandt later wrote:

> An intense bitterness developed between the two branches of the Treasury Department, and it was not an uncommon thing for agents of the Intelligence Unit and for special assistants to the Attorney General who had been sent to Seattle . . . to be "shadowed" by agents of the Prohibition Unit and their friends.[13]

In a maze of rumor and deceit, even William Whitney began to wonder about the intentions of his associates. He wrote to Senator Jones about United States Marshal Ed Benn: "[he is] spending his entire time stirring up opposition to prohibition and this office and is bearing the chief burden of this investigation." Whitney was also suspicious of the special intelligence agents: "During the past week the agents had a bootlegger in their office confronting him with seven of their number, trying to make him say that I sold him ten cases of whiskey . . . while the Olmstead trial was being developed." He said too that Revelle was becoming "an enigma" to him because Revelle had been in conference with Al Hubbard and Ed Benn and would tell Whitney nothing about it.[14]

Late in 1929, the newspapers began telling of a delegation from McNeil Island that would testify against those who had sent them to prison. Then early in 1930, just between the Matthews sermon and the Jones Act, the Justice Department brought testimony before a grand jury which suggested sensationally that William Whitney had at one time protected the Olmstead gang as well as other rumrunners with the authority of his office, and that he had prosecuted Olmstead only when pressure from Washington, D. C., made him choose a scapegoat to clear himself. Whitney, supposedly, had employed a platoon of thugs as federal agents with orders to "beat hell out of 'the outlaws' "—the nonpaying rumrunners and bootleggers.[15] The focus of the indictment was upon Whitney and Roy Lyle. But since the indictment had been timed neatly to fall just a few days after the state Republican Convention in Bellingham, its focus was just as clearly on Senator Jones and prohibitionists everywhere.

Jones himself chose to ignore the many warnings he had received and to see the Lyle-Whitney trial as a showdown between those who stood for prohibition and those who opposed it. His opponents, as well as some of his supporters, were outraged when Jones on the eve of the trial responded to Whitney's plea and arranged for the removal of United States Marshal Ed Benn, who was clearly part of the government's case. To replace Benn, Jones arranged for the appointment of Whitney's friend, Charles Allen, to insure that the marshal's influence on the jury could be more "fair and just." A telegram to Jones from Dr. Matthews suggests the private and public outcry: "You know Allen is Whitney's appointee and you know that the marshal picks the jury. I am not for or against Allen. I am acting in the interest of Wesley L. Jones. This situation has enough dynamite in it to ruin the state."[16] (Interestingly, the government kept from the jury all those who had strong views favoring prohibition, and the defense kept off all those with a strong antiprohibition sentiment.)

During the trial there was testimony to delight anyone who opposed the Eighteenth Amendment. Hubbard said he gave six thousand dollars to Lyle in 1926 for the campaign of Senator Jones (Lyle and Jones denied this under oath); he said further that he had given Lyle $250 for a contribution to the WCTU. Olmstead went on the stand to say that Revelle had promised him a presidential pardon in return for testimony against city and county officials. Other rumrunners and bootleggers told of bribes to Whitney through Hubbard. The government tried to prove that Hubbard, while he was a federal agent, had brought rumrunners from Grays Harbor into the monopoly for Whitney and that he had operated a radio station there for communication with boats along the coast.[17]

The defense hit hard at Hubbard, describing him as a confessed liar and criminal, and it was bitterly critical of the government's parade of felons. The government, on the other hand, had Dr. Matthews take the stand as a character witness against Whitney. After six weeks of testimony and nearly two hundred witnesses—including the leaders of the ASL and the WCTU, who testified for Lyle and Whitney—the judge advised the jury that testimony from government witnesses should be "viewed with suspicion" because these men had been sent to prison by the defendants.[18] The jury decided for the defense.

There appears to be no substantive reason to question this verdict. Olmstead today insists that Lyle and Whitney throughout the decade were never anything to him but implacable enemies. Thus there is good cause to accept Thomas Revelle's interpretation of the Lyle-Whitney trial, even in view of his obvious bias. Revelle wrote to Jones at the time of the indictment that he believed Lyle and Whitney were not guilty, but that some of the others were. His analysis, based only on personal information, was that the indictment had been engineered by these men: Ed Benn, who wanted to become United States Senator, representing the wet Republicans; members of the Department of Justice, urged on by the ambitions of Anthony Savage, who had succeeded Revelle as United States District Attorney; Al Hubbard, the bootleggers, and rumrunners, for revenge and promises of parole.

Then at the conclusion of the trial Revelle wrote:

> I have known of no more diabolical conspiracy to discredit law enforcement than that which just ended in such a miserable fiasco. . . . This conspiracy was instigated by disgruntled politicians, enemies of Senator Jones, together with convicted felons and Al Hubbard, a self-confessed perjurer. . . . In carrying out this conspiracy I have good reason to believe that truth was suppressed and perjury encouraged . . . . and resort made to blackmail.[19]

Though this interpretation is vividly conspiratorial, and though Revelle, like Lyle and Whitney, had eyes which saw villians behind every event which affected him adversely, no one was in a better position to know how much conspiracy really did leaven the political life of the decade.

The dates of the trial—August and September, normally a vacation period for federal courts—made prohibition enforcement the center of public attention during the campaigning for the primary elections of 1930. The immediate target for this maneuver was probably Congressman John F. Miller of Seattle. Miller had been mayor of Seattle in 1909, when he had opposed Governor Hay's local option. In the 1920's, though, he was a devoted dry, close to Senator Jones. He was challenged in the Republican primary of 1930 by Ralph Horr, keynoter of the wet Republican convention. The *Argus*, not usually friendly to drys anywhere, stuck with Miller because, its editor said, Ralph Horr had nothing to recommend him but his wetness. If Horr should win this contest, the editor concluded, King County would prove itself "so wet that it has become mildewed."

Miller, standing on his dry record and on the Republican national platform of 1928, lost the nomination. Chadwick of the *Argus* commented sadly that Miller, absent from the state for two years, did not realize how quickly public sentiment had changed. Voters, he wrote, not without prescience, "want a new deal."[20]

Chadwick was only slightly premature. The election of 1930 was more one of transition than of attrition. King County got its wet congressman, but nobody else did. Horr's victory, even after the conventions and the Lyle-Whitney trial, was a singular one. According to Hicks, the state legislature elected that year was dry by a two-thirds majority. (The year before it had been dry by about four to one.) ASL discipline was broken, but the League had not yet considered retreat.[21]

Hicks continued to badger the men in Olympia, but nobody seemed to listen. People were waiting for something new, and his voice was the babble of a false prophet. There were other, more serious things to think about. The markets for lumber, fish, and wheat had almost disappeared. The mills were closing down, the fishing fleets did not go out, and banks were closing their doors. In some areas, especially west of the mountains, whole communities were without work. The skid roads began to fill with drifting men. As they joined the gloomy lines of the unemployed, their mood was ugly and impatient. That bootleggers were hiding in the alleys became less and less important, but that public officials would worry about prohibition and be paid for it—this became more and more intolerable.

Another great change had taken place, and the signs, for the prohibitionists, were everywhere. Roy Lyle was quietly moved into the office of the supervisor of industrial alcohol permits. William Whitney returned to his private law practice, bitter over a wasted decade, and found some satisfactions in defending bootleggers. Thomas Revelle sold real estate, but as he looked backwards, his Methodist conscience was painfully aroused. Almost as a valedictory for these years, he wrote to Jones a melancholy confession:

> I have always felt that much of the testimony that resulted in the convictions of a number of men who I tried was at least colored, if not perjured. . . . The thing that is concerning me today is the amount of injustice perpetrated upon these men whom I convicted. . . . Feeling as

I do, had I my way, I would go to McNeil's penitentiary and unlock the doors and let every such man walk out. . . . If these men have been done a wrong, I would at least like to feel in the closing hours of my life that I have done what I could to remedy the same.

Jones advised against writing the Attorney General about this matter; he told Revelle to forget it, and Revelle did.[22] They both turned fearfully toward the years of the great depression.

14

The Voices of Repeal

EVEN THOUGH the year 1930 brought signs that the prohibition era had come to its time of troubles, hardly anyone could have predicted the scope of the disasters which were to befall the drys during the next two years. In the churches and the legislative halls, the labor temples, and the chambers of commerce, the shifts in public attitudes since 1920 had done little to diminish the confidence of the drys in their ultimate victory. Nor had they lifted the vision of the wets beyond some slow, eventual compromise or modification of the Volstead Act. To most people it seemed that the Eighteenth Amendment would survive the generation.

This thought was poignantly expressed in May, 1931, when Roy Olmstead was released from McNeil Island federal prison. As he crossed the waters of Puget Sound again, the Seattle *Post-Intelligencer* made the dreary comment that "Olmstead will find little change" except that his place had been filled by others.[1] And there were indeed still rumrunners and hijackers, bootleggers and federal agents, both honest and dishonest. Dry politicians were still in a majority, and there was still much contempt for the law.

Olmstead found all these, but he found also a very great change: the depression had come, and his friends and enemies had almost all gone into its shadows. The parties, the adventure, the big money, the great good humor—these were all gone. Gone too, he discovered, were the old certainties of right and wrong, of truth and error, of wet and dry. Change sometimes rides on sly ironies, and at this juncture there was a particularly engrossing one: the rumrunner, after years in a prison library, returned to his home dedicated to the principles of the Church of Christ, Scientist, and to the proposition that liquor is bad for man and society. He was surprised to discover that in his absence even the most faithful of his enemies had begun to feel the tremble of confusion. If conditions were superficially the same, there were deeper manifestations of change which foretold the end of an epoch.

The Lyle and Whitney trial, for example, had only increased the criticism of the prohibition office. Lyle wrote to Senator Jones that Dr. Matthews felt "very vindictive over the results of the trial" and that the clergyman was making no effort to conceal his belief that, whatever the verdict, William Whitney was guilty.[2] Many others felt the same way. The correspondence to Senator Jones after the trial was mostly from dry leaders supporting Lyle and urging that he be reinstated in his office, but few of these writers had anything positive to say about Whitney. Shortly after the trial, Lyle was back in office, but in the shuffle of the Justice Department's taking over prohibition enforcement from the Treasury Department, Jones found himself unable to do anything for William Whitney.

Rightly or wrongly, Whitney had come to represent all that was ill-advised or downright malicious about federal enforcement in the state of Washington. The ax raids, the violence, the killings, the bribery and corruption, the contempt for civil liberties—for all of these Whitney was to some degree responsible. And the public derived certain rich satisfactions from blaming Whitney because of his aggressive personality. He had provided the newspapers with steady fodder which could be used against dry enforcement and which brought to the state a measure of notoriety that was difficult to dispel. For example, in 1933 Dr. Nicholas Murray Butler, president of Columbia University and a leading critic of prohibition, said that among the "moving influences which hastened repeal" were bootlegging, corruption among officials, and the Court's decision in the Olmstead case upholding federal agents in wire tapping—a decision, he said, which brought "revulsion and revolt."[3] Many people in Washington thought that the "revulsion and revolt" was largely Whitney's doing, and they could link it to all that they knew about Izzy Einstein, the St. Valentine's Day Massacre, and Al Capone. It was too seldom that they could find between the extremes of farcical circus and grim destruction any honest and dignified pursuit of law and order.

Many of these people could also conclude that the politics of the dry decade had been only slightly more clean than the politics of the saloon era. B. N. Hicks had disciplined the state legislature in quite the same way that the old saloon barons had done before 1907. Political appointments had been handled with the same expediency, and it was just as clear that special interests were privileged to use public agencies for their own private purposes.

In April, 1931, for example, B. N. Hicks sat smiling in an easy chair of an Olympia hotel when federal agents burst into the lobby and raced through the rooms above. Most observers thought that the raid had been carefully designed to catch the Governor, who—it was charged—escaped arrest only because he knew more of the hotel's geography than did the agents.[4] The public's tolerance for this kind of crazy enforcement had limits which Hicks failed to recognize.

By 1931, Ralph Horr, the Republican congressman from the state of Washington, was calling the Jones Law "sadistic." At about the same time, federal agents in Seattle terrified apartment owners with their wanton destruction of the furnishings in one apartment where they discovered liquor. Hotel men joined the protest after they had been warned that they were liable for any liquor found in their hotels.[5] Thus it was not at all unusual for those opposed to prohibition to oppose it with the same words the ASL had used against the saloon: crime and corruption.

In a similarly ironic twist, the repeal movement (just as its opposite had) rode hard upon the prestige of scientific findings which were widely circulated through the middle-class magazines. During the 1920's, only the disgruntled had listened to Professor Raymond Pearl of Johns Hopkins University, who claimed his studies showed that moderate drinkers lived longer than abstainers; or to Dr. Samuel Lambert, who insisted that alcohol was valuable in treating pneumonia; or to Dr. S. H. Church of the Carnegie Institute of Technology, who spoke warmly of liquor being "one of the greatest blessings that God has given to men." In the early 1930's, though, repealers reminded everyone of these voices, and they called others: Professor Yandell Henderson, physiologist at Yale, who somehow thought that 4 per-cent beer was no more intoxicating than an equal amount of coffee; Dr. Martin Dewey, president of the American Dental Association, who said that beer in the diet of pregnant women helped build strong teeth in children; Dr. W. G. Morgan, past president of the American Medical Association, who testified that as much as four glasses of 4 per-cent beer would not impair a drinker's physical or mental equilibrium. That these spokesmen of science were perhaps no closer to truth than their prohibitionist predecessors had been in 1916 was not a matter for public analysis at the time. They were no less highly regarded.[6]

In the same magazines and newspapers, the testimony of scientists was complemented by dazzling economic statistics which supported the cause of repeal. The National Association of Manufacturers called for beer to boost markets, put men to work, and relieve businessmen of tax burdens. Pierre S. DuPont wrote that the liquor tax "would be sufficient to pay off the entire debt of the United States . . . in a little less than fifteen years." Ralph Horr, seeking the repeal of the state bone-dry law in 1931, said that "Grain growers of Eastern Washington should realize what repeal of the dry law would mean to them." Chadwick of the *Argus* voiced the fears of automobile owners that the state would tax them more heavily unless it could somehow get at wine and beer.[7] Sharpened almost daily by the hard realities of the depression, the economic arguments for repeal cut across just about every thread that held the Eighteenth Amendment together. They undoubtedly raised the cause of repeal to the stature of a political movement.

The major efforts toward bringing the issue into politics were led by the people who had the most to gain and who could best afford it—the very well to do. The Association Against the Prohibition Amendment was by far the most significant organization working for repeal, and it was directed by several dozen millionaires, among whom the principals were the DuPonts from the chemical industry, General Atterbury from railroads, H. B. Joy from automobile manufacturers, Charles Sabin from investment trusts and glass, and E. S. Harkness from oil. These men in turn organized several millionaires in each of the forty-eight states who, like themselves, were sensitive to the potential that liquor taxation held for reducing their own obligations to state and national treasuries. In Washington State they enlisted, among others, Charles H. Bebb, known as "dean of architects"; Edward I. Garrett, chairman of the board at Garrett and Shafer Engineering Works; C. B. Fitzgerald, manager of the Federated Industries of Washington; and William E. Boeing.[8] (Some of these had a backlog of unpleasant experiences with prohibition: Boeing had been raided on the first day of dryness in 1916; in 1928 Fitzgerald's room in the Marcus Whitman Hotel of Walla Walla had been raided while he was there asleep.[9])

The backgrounds of officials in other repeal organizations similarly suggest their anticipations. The president of the Washington State Repeal Association was James Crawford Marmaduke, a wealthy Seattle man engaged in the promotion and operation of hotel properties. The Republican Repeal League was organized in 1933 at the Arctic Club of Seattle.[10]

Dry leaders were quick to point out the rather obvious motives of such men. Among the most eloquent of these critics was Representative John W. Summers of Washington, who spoke bitterly against the friends of the Association Against the Prohibition Amendment who had taken seats in Congress:

> You talk of revenue. I know and you know that this is not the sound, unselfish judgment of the American people, but the hue and cry of paid propagandists. This is the culmination of a deep-laid plot of heartless millionaires to shift the tax burden from their pockets to the cravings of the helpless.[11]

Repeal organizations, however, suffered only mildly from such attacks. They drew upon the rich prestige of their own officers and upon the support given them by outstanding members of the nation's business and intellectual communities. Widely publicized repeal statements came from such men of distinction as General John Pershing, Alfred P. Sloan, Jr., of General Motors, Harvey S. Firestone, Nicholas M. Butler, Walter Lippmann, and John D. Rockefeller, Jr. Rockefeller's stand was particularly significant inasmuch as he had been a leading prestige figure in favor of prohibition before the war.[12]

And the repealers, in a brilliant move, enlisted their wives as well. In 1929, Mrs. Charles H. Sabin organized the Women's Organization for National Prohibition Reform, which enrolled a large group of wealthy society women and moved dramatically into the repeal movement. Although ridiculed as "Sabin's sob sisters," or "cocktail-drinking women," or even more luridly as "Bacchantian maidens, parching for wine," they blended a colorful measure of dedication and intelligence into a major political force. Mrs. Sabin's lieutenant in Washington State was Miss Agusta Ware Webb Trimble, recently returned from London where, in a twenty thousand dollar gown, she had met the Queen. Miss Trimble's advisory board included Mrs. William E. Boeing, Mrs. Clarance B. Blethen, Mrs. Stephen F. Chadwick, and Mrs. Joshua Green.[13]

Against these sparkling arrays of economic and social eminence, the prohibitionists had little, save their sarcasm, to offer. The newspapers were all wet or silent. The state Grange in 1930 presented the appearance of pinched-nosed puritans and aging farm wives, embittered by a decade of poverty and political defeat, nagging its members with remembrances of a forgotten morality. The State Federation of Labor—before so proudly parading for the dignity of labor in a sober society—was in 1930 as silent as stone. It would shortly favor repeal because beer would create jobs. Twenty years before, the WCTU had attracted the wives of prominent physicians, lawyers, and men of commerce. In 1930, it could list only the wives of morticians, chiropractors, tradesmen, and ministers of minor distinction.[14] The principal dry voices were either small or tired: Laurence Colman, James Duncan, George Cotterill, Austin Griffiths, the Reverend Mark Matthews—pace-setters and taste-makers for a world that no longer existed.

Though the prestige of its heroes contributed a great deal to the success of the repeal movement, its power must be explained in terms of the combined length and depth of the issues that were raised so strongly after 1929: corruption, violence, personal freedom, scientific evidence, economic factors, and the character of its leadership. The polemics of repeal were distinctly political. And it is as a political movement—as distinct from a social movement—that repeal differed from prohibition. In all the literature of repeal, in the speeches, debates, and sermons, and in all the political strategies and the voting statistics, one can search in vain for any significant expression of class-consciousness or any of the subtle enticements toward class identification that were so prominent in 1914. Those who opposed prohibition in 1931 did not appeal to middle-class aspirations. They urged the middle class to regard its own best interests and to change its mind.

In the previous decade, the prohibitionists had been favored by a world war which bound together the virtues of patriotism, sacrifice, and purity. In 1930, the repealers could splice their arguments to the nation's troubles: repeal went with relief, recovery, and reform.

15

The Politics of Repeal

THE "big issue of the day," Chadwick wrote in the *Argus* in 1931, "is prohibition. . . . It is more talked of than any other subject. It is believed by many to be quite as important as was the slavery question eighty years ago. . . . In some sections of the country pretty nearly every other consideration is lost sight of. . . ."[1]

He went on to say that both political parties were "filled with cowards" and expressed his hope that one of the major political denominations would oppose prohibition and the other support it so the people could have a clean choice. Though his comments clarify the power of the political movement, his hope was no better founded than his historical analogy. The simplicity he hoped for had disappeared from American politics. Though prohibition was "more talked about than any other subject," the talk was more like that given to reconstruction in the 1870's than to slavery in the 1860's. The issue was whether or not prohibition had been a failure. The saloon, like slavery, had been abolished. No one denied this. But the experiment in regulating liquor morality outside the saloon, some were saying, had not worked at all. The cure was more dangerous than the disease, they contended, and it was time to give the whole thing up.

This sentiment was indeed so strong that no major political party would dare to stand with the hard-core reconstructionists. Like prohibition, repeal was too broad a movement for partisanship. In 1931, a group of Republicans and Democrats, led by State Senator Paul Houser of Renton, had again asked the state legislature to memorialize Congress for the repeal of the Eighteenth Amendment. Most of the legislators, however, were unwilling to be counted behind this proposal at that time. Another small group was urging modification to allow the sale of beer and wine, and these would have supported the repeal of the state bone-dry laws in anticipation of a national

224

move to remodel the Volstead Act. But they, too, lacked a majority, and when the session ended nothing had changed at all except the patience of repealers in both parties, who were more determined than ever to carry this issue before their conventions in 1932.

They drew confidence from the national meeting of the American Legion in the fall of 1931, which resolved in support of a national referendum on the Eighteenth Amendment. By January, 1932, it looked as if the people themselves would move against legislative recalcitrance, just as they had done in 1914. Initiative Measure Number 61—to repeal all the state's liquor laws save the prohibition against sale to minors—was filed in Olympia. The reception it received almost immediately was called "astonishing," for word had it that the petitions picked up twenty thousand signatures before the end of January.[2] While the American Legion encouraged repealers, Initiative 61 offered some hope to hesitant politicians that a mandate from the electorate might spare their parties the devastations of intraparty fratricides.

But the movement was already too strong to await such a mandate. Before February, the state's Democrats met in county conventions, many of which were fierce conflicts between the wets and the drys. In the counties of Grays Harbor, Whatcom, and Pierce, insurgent drys rebelled against the authority of their county chairmen and held independent conventions to select dry delegates to the forthcoming state convention. Most of these insurgent groups were from the ranks of "new" Democrats who had rushed the party in anticipation of a Democratic landslide in November. In Snohomish County there was peace only because regular Democrats wanted to avoid the issue to please Lloyd Black of Everett, who was a county leader, a candidate for the United States Senate, and a dry. Several eastern counties followed this road toward tranquility. But in King County the delegates were almost unanimously wet, and their numbers made them the strongest influence when the state convention met in Tacoma on February 6.

The first battle in Tacoma was over the seating of disputed delegations, and in this the drys were defeated by the older, more seasoned professionals who had stood by Al Smith in 1928. These leaders, though, had no intention of allowing party discipline to slip away from them again as it had done in 1928, and they directed the loyal and the faithful in their brigades toward some happy compromise that would satisfy all but the most radical prohibitionists. When the Seattle delegates moved to force a naked repeal plank into the state platform, they were stopped cold by the professionals. The majority, they had decided, would accept an appeal for a national referendum on prohibition and no more. King County finally yielded to prevent political mayhem, and the convention endorsed the compromise plank.[3] Even George Cotterill supported it. Democrats everywhere rejoiced in their unity.

When Republicans met at Seattle in May, a well-turned but inaccurate rumor was abroad that Initiative Measure 61 already had over two hundred thousand signatures.[4] Faced with such adversity, the ASL shuffled uncomfortably for a tenable defensive position. B. N. Hicks saw no chance of a dry plank from the Republicans; his greatest hope was to defeat a wet one before it reached the floor of the convention.

He was fortunate in that the Republican Committee on Resolutions, which would write the various planks, consisted of one delegate from each county, and most of these delegates were dry. Wet delegates—many of them from the cities—had of course foreseen this and had made careful plans for confusion. They quickly moved a resolution which demanded strict support of the prohibition laws and called upon the federal government to appropriate funds for "effective enforcement." This plank, they knew, was so uncompromising that it would have no future at all on the convention floor. They assumed that their dry colleagues, led by former Governor Marion Hay, would realize this and be caught in the embarrassment of opposing a dry resolution.

The dry delegates, however, voted with more enthusiasm than analysis and approved the resolution for the state platform. In some discomfort, then, the wet committeemen saw the necessity for some delicate explanations. They faced the situation like honest men and patiently instructed Marion Hay on the proper parliamentary procedure for rephrasing the resolution in such a way as to assure party unity. In its final form, the proposed plank endorsed the Constitution of the United States and called for "enforcing the laws," but it made no direct mention of the Volstead Act or of the Eighteenth Amendment.[5]

Even so, there were many uncompromisingly wet delegates on the floor, and the proposed plank met a hostile reception. The opponents of prohibition had counted their numbers. Confident of a majority, they turned the convention into a riotous battleground by ignoring the Committee on Resolutions and moving immediately to have delegates approve the resubmission of the Eighteenth Amendment. Debate raged amid cries of "vote as you drink" and fighting which reminded one correspondent of "an old-time bar-room brawl." When the votes were finally counted, everyone was shocked almost beyond belief. And only then did they realize how deeply the party had been wounded by the savage power-struggle between those who followed and those who opposed Governor Roland Hartley.

Hartley men controlled the delegates from Pierce County (Tacoma) and their eighty-seven votes. When the King County delegates had refused to allow a Hartley man to chair the convention, Pierce County threatened revenge at any cost. Their chairman was quoted as saying, "We're going to show those double-crossing Seattle delegates we mean what we say." They did indeed. Though dripping wet almost to a man, Pierce County delegates voted against the wet resolution in a "sulky reprisal" against Seattle. The drys carried the floor, 499-421. The dry plank, as rephrased and approved earlier by the committee, went into the platform.

Ralph Horr arrived at the convention too late to help the wet cause. The blame for his absence at the critical moment, said Horr, lay especially with the President of the United States and the state's senior Senator. Horr did not make it on time because Jones had arranged for him to receive a "command" invitation to the White House which he could not ignore and which delayed his departure from Washington, D. C.[6] The lack of his influence may or may not have been decisive. At any rate, it seemed clear that the Republicans were seriously divided, and that few of them would be bound by what took place on the convention floor.

After May, the ASL could expect a massive deterioration in the influence it had exercised for twenty-eight years. Hicks went through the traditional ceremonies of questioning candidates about their attitudes and their personal habits, but his most crucial tactical necessity was to attack Initiative Measure Number 61, which would repeal all the state liquor laws. The initiative was ostensibly an antisaloon repeal measure, for it provided that "the repeals herein . . . shall not be construed . . . to revive . . . the licensing and operations of saloons." This clause did not in any way soften the fact that Number 61 would destroy every achievement of the Anti-Saloon League, for the absence of all laws would surely encourage all the evils of the old-time saloon. Hicks called the initiative a "bootleggers' bill" and began work on a campaign which for him and his League meant survival itself.[7]

His workers were the Prohibs of the old-line orthodoxy, people like Laurence Colman of the business community, James Duncan from labor, Mark Matthews and other ministers, Mrs. Lillian Vincent from the WCTU. In speeches and in sermons, in thousands of small colored leaflets that were scattered across the state, the arguments were the traditional ones: the horror of drunken women and alcoholic crime, the menace of drunken drivers. In addition, there was a legalistic argument which held that a state had no right to impede the federal government by abolishing state laws which upheld a federal enactment. There was also a heavy emphasis on the economics of repeal—those who buy booze cannot buy shoes and the shoe factories will shut down. In some of the literature, Hicks argued coldly that Number 61 would deprive the state of almost a million dollars a year in fines levied against bootleggers—a thought so curiously opposed to prohibitionist theory that it suggests a lapse of judgment in an hour of desperation.[8]

The organized opposition which Hicks assembled against Number 61 came principally from the state's women's clubs, the Grange, the WCTU, the "Christian churches," the PTA, and the Washington Education Association. This last one, the state teachers' organization, participated only in November, when its board of directors finally voted with some reluctance to commit its prestige to the fight against repeal. It advised teachers that Number 61 would be contrary to public education:

> It would mean less education for many children because of the inability of the father to pay for their schooling. . . . It would mean the birth of many physically weak children to drinking parents. . . . It would rob the public treasury and state school fund of $725,000 because all fines would be paid to the federal treasury. . . .[9]

These arguments are worth noting mainly because of their rather dated fanaticism. They suggest the heavy hand of an older, even antique Prohib, and this was indeed the case. The executive secretary of the Association, Arthur L. Marsh, was a power in the Methodist church. The directors' resolution was probably written by him and approved by the board more in consideration of his position than in any crusading zeal.[10] If this same motive were also a factor in other antirepeal organizations, Hicks's marshaling of forces was largely an illusion.

The initiators of Number 61 had no fear of Hicks. They fought, understandably, almost entirely with economic arguments: the measure would reduce taxes, provide jobs and payrolls, restore agricultural markets, and generally contribute to prosperity. In one stroke, they suggested, the voters could solve the problems of the depression and still prevent the return of the saloon. An organization called the Washington State Modification Association printed a leaflet to this effect and ran large newspaper ads in November, but not without rather surprising difficulties. When Number 61 was validated in July, its supporters could not raise the five-hundred-dollar printing fee to pay for an official publication of its arguments in the voters' pamphlet issued that year. In the pamphlet, the ASL arguments against Number 61 were published without a challenge.[11]

One can only surmise—as the *Argus* did at the time—that this was a matter of poverty and not of timing or of incompetence. Where, then, was the big money? Where were the millionaires and their militant wives? Though the Association Against the Prohibition Amendment listed Boeing, Bebb, Fitzgerald *et al.* among its national board of directors, the organization never had an official affiliation in the state of Washington, as it did in other states, and the AAPA apparently took no part in the campaign for Number 61.[12] The Women's Organization for National Prohibition Reform did not have a state affiliate until July, 1932, and it did not begin a membership drive until October, when it put some "Flying Squadrons" in the field to publicize the cause of repeal. There is no evidence, however, that they spent much money or much effort on Number 61. Apparently the considerable resources of repeal leaders were pumped into the national effort on the assumption that this would carry state-level repeal movements in 1932 without much special attention. Apparently, too, the people in Washington who wanted Number 61 to pass assumed the same thing.

The sponsors of Number 61 did stage a "beer parade" in Seattle in September, the main feature of which was State Senator Paul Houser's bottle of pre-Volstead beer, allegedly the only one in the state, mounted in the center of a float, insured for ten thousand dollars, and flanked by armed guards.[13] But this was only local, if rather noisy, publicity, not a serious effort for money or disciplined commitment. On the eve of the election, Chadwick of the *Argus* said that he had received not one letter or circular boosting Number 61.[14]

Thus what efforts there were specifically in behalf of Number 61 came late in the campaign, and then they were modest. In October, the group called the State Modification Association pulled itself together. Its treasurer attempted to solicit donations of from five to ten dollars from "a thousand citizens . . . who would like to have the freedom to drink beer and wine in their own home." Even then, the response he received was hardly enthusiastic, and refusals came from unexpected quarters. For example, Stephen J. Chadwick, who had run in the primaries for the United States Senate on a repeal ticket, contributed nothing more valuable than his regrets that he had spent all his money on his own campaign.[15] Implicit in his reply, it seems, was the assumption that Number 61 could not possibly fail.

This assumption illustrates that Number 61 was, in fact, at the very heart of the campaign of 1932. Its function as a political instrument was beautifully realized; in the fulfillment of a political purpose, Number 61 stands among initiative measures with a sort of classic purity. Coming at a time when the issue of prohibition was almost certain to shatter the integrity of the two-party system, the initiative removed the issue from partisan politics and allowed the more properly partisan issues to carry their own weight. The candidates could therefore pledge themselves to honor a mandate from the people on prohibition and avoid forcing the voters to consider them as wet or dry. Number 61 allowed the campaign of 1932 to turn without restriction on the grave economic crisis that demanded an unequivocal political decision.

One can read this significance of Number 61 in the fates of candidates who chose to ignore its function. Stephen J. Chadwick was one of these. In his declaration of candidacy he described himself as a "dedicated repealist" who had always opposed prohibition as "the crowning mistake of this generation." In July, he thought that the Democratic nomination and election to the Senate would surely be his. His prestige and popularity as a lawyer and a regular Democrat would, he thought, take him easily through the opposition. He wrote to James Farley that Doc Brown—trying again in 1932—was considered "an amusement." Lloyd Black of Everett, he said, was "making an appeal for the Protestant dry vote" but presented no real threat. Congressman Homer T. Bone, former Republican, former Socialist, trying for the Senate as a Democrat in 1932, Chadwick regarded as an opportunistic intruder from the Unemployed Citizens' League and not a legitimate Democrat. Moreover, Chadwick resented Bone's straddling the Eighteenth Amendment: he was, Chadwick thought, playing games with the ASL and the WCTU by telling audiences that prohibition should not be an issue in the senatorial campaign. Chadwick saw only cowardice in Bone's promise to regard the vote on Number 61 as a mandate from the people.[16] Chadwick, so involved in the repeal of prohibition, simply failed to appreciate how Bone's speeches on depression relief and public power were striking home. People were not so thirsty that they would forget the depression. The intruder from the Unemployed Citizens' League won the nomination.

Senator Jones understood this. He was ready to admit in 1932 that "prohibition and prohibition enforcement have not been satisfactory to our people generally," but he did not think that people really wanted to bring back pre-Volstead conditions. He was even willing to support a referendum, if that was what the people wanted, but his real choice was not to talk about it at all. "The main proposition that confronts us today is the economic one," he wrote to Thomas Revelle, who had asked about the liquor issue.[17]

But many of his own party did not want the liability of Jones's public image in 1932, and they prevailed upon Justice Adam Beeler of the state Supreme Court to attempt the purge. Beeler, no friend to prohibition, made "waste" and "lawlessness" the sharpest points of his attack. There were, however, plenty of regular Republicans who stood by the Senator, and the old machine was still a powerful force. Even the *Argus*, almost an official antiprohibition journal, supported Jones as a proper conservative who would "straighten out" on prohibition.[18]

Jones took the nomination again. Aging and in poor health, he struggled bravely toward the general elections under the weight of his Republican and prohibitionist past, all of which would shortly fall heavily upon him. There was really no escape from either. He was everywhere the friend of Herbert Hoover, and he had only Hoover's pallid remedies for the condition of the nation. And he was everywhere the "Great Dry," the stern and blue-nosed puritan. One

evening in Olympia he was greeted by a torchlight parade and a high
school band which, by some sad and cruel circumstance, played the
sarcastic phrases of "How Dry I Am."[19]

In other primary campaigns, the issue was effectively muted and
candidates stood wisely by their party platforms, waiting for the returns on Number 61. John F. Miller, defeated as a dry in 1930, told
the voters in 1932 that he would stand by Number 61 whatever the
results, as an expression of the public's will. Thus converted, he took
the nomination away from wet Congressman Ralph Horr. Congressmen Lindley H. Hadley and Albert Johnson had abandoned their
dryness and the ASL when, in the spring, they had voted in Congress
for repeal. They easily won renomination. Congressman John W.
Summers also won renomination, perhaps, like Senator Jones, more
for his republicanism than for his dryness. John Gellatly took the
nomination for governor from Roland Hartley, probably more because he had captured all the anti-Hartley votes than because he had
been a friend of the ASL. Detailing the Republican battles of 1932,
however, is probably irrelevant. In November the Republicans all
lost, for the state was tired of the Grand Old Party. Everyone knew
the Democrats would hasten the repeal of the Eighteenth Amendment.

Initiative Measure Number 61 won in a landslide of the same
magnitude; 62 per cent of the vote cast on the initiative was wet. The
county statistics provide an accurate measure of how attitudes on
prohibition had changed since 1914 (table 15). A comparison of the
vote on Number 3 in 1914 and Number 61 in 1932 brings some interesting conclusions.

All the counties except Garfield (population 3,362) were more wet
in 1932 than in 1914. In these counties, wet sentiment increased generally from 10 to 20 per cent, 1914 to 1932. In 1932 as in 1914, the
cities were more wet than the rural areas. But in 1932, most of the
urban counties were very wet, and some of the rural counties 'were
also very wet. Only about one third of the rural counties in 1932
were dry. (It is worth noting that there had been no great change in
urbanization throughout the state between 1914 and 1932: according
to the census, 53 per cent of the population was urban in 1914, and
56 per cent was urban in 1932.)

TABLE 15

INITIATIVE MEASURES ON PROHIBITION AND REPEAL
1914 AND 1932*

Counties in Order of Urbanization, 1910 (Percentage living in places of 2,500 or more)	Initiative Measure No. 3 1914 (Percentage of total vote cast for and against)		Initiative Measure No. 61 1932 (Percentage of total vote cast for and against)	
	Wet	*Dry*	*Wet*	*Dry*
King (84)	59	41	70	30
Spokane (77)	49	51	60	40
Pierce (73)	54	46	66	34
Chehalis (Grays Harbor) (61) ...	46	54	67	33
Walla Walla (61)	39	61	49	51
Kittitas (54)	47	53	69	31
Jefferson (50)	56	44	74	26
Whatcom (49)	44	56	57	43
Snohomish (47)	44	56	64	36
Thurston (40)	52	48	64	36
Lewis (37)	43	57	55	45
Clark (36)	37	63	47	53
Yakima (34)	33	67	51	49
Chelan (27)	37	63	51	49
Pacific (24)	47	53	60	40
Kitsap (17)	47	53	71	29
Whitman (16)	32	68	39	61
Skagit (14)	34	66	58	42
Adams	46	54	56	44
Asotin	23	77	47	53
Benton	38	62	41	59
Clallam	49	51	72	28
Columbia	40	60	42	58
Cowlitz	38	62	57	43
Douglas	41	59	46	54
Ferry	40	60	63	37
Franklin	43	57	52	48
Garfield	51	49	42	58
Grant	39	61	51	49
Island	36	64	56	44
Klickitat	41	59	44	56
Lincoln	39	61	48	52

* "Election Division," *Washington State Public Documents* (1932).

(Table 15—*continued*)

Mason	54	46	68	32
Okanogan	39	61	52	48
Pend Oreille	48	52	54	46
San Juan	50	50	60	40
Skamania	48	52	48	52
Stevens	42	58	50.1	49.9
Wahkiakum	39	61	53	47
	—	—	—	—
Total	48	52	62	38
Number of votes	171,208	189,840	341,450	208,211

Senator Jones, with 197,450 votes, failed even to win all the dry votes. He lost in every county. However, there seems to be more than a coincidence in the fact that the dry vote (on Number 61, 208,211) was very close to the Hoover vote (Republican elector Reno Odlin, 208,645 votes). In many cases those who did not want repeal did not want Franklin Roosevelt. Apparently, in many instances, those who voted against state repeal were the very people who voted for the Republican elector. They were unaware, perhaps, of the exquisite irony of their position: Reno Odlin, according to S. J. Chadwick, was a part of the State Modification Association and no friend of the drys (table 16).[20]

The repeal movement, successful at the state level in November, 1932, had clear sailing on toward the national enactment. All it needed was skillful hands, and there were plenty of these, willing and able. The directorate of the Association Against the Prohibition Amendment listed leading industrialists, bankers, lawyers, and scientists, and its president boasted, with reason, that his organization in 1933 had 428 of "the most influential men of America."[21] In June of 1932 these men had brought forth the United Repeal Council, which included the AAPA, the Women's Organization for National Prohibition Reform, the Voluntary Committee of Lawyers, and the American Hotel Association. Though not a part of the Council, the American Legion and the American Federation of Labor had by this time joined the movement.

Well before Congress met in January, 1933, the Council had its plan. Its goal, of course, was the Twenty-first Amendment which would repeal the Eighteenth, but the repealers hoped to do this in such a way as to circumvent the various state legislatures, where, they feared, the power of rural delegates might become a serious barrier to ratification. They had estimated that in existing legislatures, 132 state senators in 13 states would have the power to defeat ratification. To prevent this exercise of rural power, the Council's constitutional lawyers proposed—for the first time since the Constitution itself was ratified—that Congress should call for ratifying conventions in each state of the union to consider the Twenty-first

TABLE 16

VOTE FOR THE STATUS QUO, 1932: TEN COUNTIES

County	Dry Vote on Initiative Number 62	Hoover (for elector Reno Odlin)
King	47,951	63,346
Pierce	19,704	19,006
Clallam	1,838	1,870
Spokane	24,610	24,848
Snohomish	9,716	9,310
Whatcom	8,793	9,254
Yakima	11,460	11,137
Grays Harbor	5,407	5,200
Chelan	6,226	5,584
Clark	6,953	4,905
State Total	208,211	208,645

Amendment. This plan would not be at variance with the pledges of either political party and would, the Council carefully pointed out, allow the people themselves to pass for the first time "upon a question which so closely affects them. . . ."

When Congress met, a repeal resolution embodying these ideas and approved by the leaders of the AAPA went before both chambers. The immediate action repealers had hoped for, however, was stopped in the House, where the resolution failed by only six votes. Then in the Senate Judiciary Committee, a group of western progressive prohibitionists—among them Borah of Idaho, Ashurst of Arizona, Walsh of Montana, and Clarence Dill of Washington—tried to frustrate the AAPA by insisting upon ratification by state legislatures. They were in a majority, and it was a resolution calling for legislative ratification that went to the floor of the Senate.

But even in the face of a prolonged congressional battle, the Council's lawyers and the AAPA leaders were working on the mechanics of victory. In January they drew up a general measure which the various states could, with appropriate local changes, use to call the anticipated ratification conventions. Jouett Shouse, president of the AAPA, sent the proposed bill to friends of the AAPA in each state so that legislatures then in session might prepare for conventions even while Congress debated.[22]

The avenues of communication on this matter to Washington State are, because of scant evidence, not very clear. Shouse sent his proposal to the chairmen of the AAPA state divisions, but in Washington there was no such formal affiliation of the AAPA. It seems likely that Shouse worked through local members of his national Board of Directors—men like William E. Boeing, Charles H. Bebb, C. B. Fitzgerald, or J. C. Marmaduke. Because it was Marmaduke, president of the New Washington Improvement Company and a leader of hotel groups, who later organized the Washington State Association for the Repeal of the Eighteenth Amendment, he may well have taken the responsibility for legislative liaison. In the legislature, the AAPA plan was sponsored by state senators Paul Houser and Evert Arnold and by Representative Warren Magnuson, a newly elected Democrat. All of these men were close to Marmaduke and the repeal campaign of 1933.[23]

When Congress approved the convention resolution on February 28, the convention bill in the Washington legislature was almost ready. It passed in March and provided for an election of convention delegates the following August. About the same time-schedule was worked out in other states, and it beat the clocks of legislative adjournment. The coordination of national and local efforts may have advanced repeal by as much as two years.

The Washington bill called for each legislative district in the state to elect as many delegates as it had representatives in the legislature. Delegates would vote according to the majority vote in their districts, and in the convention a majority would rule. Candidates could campaign from March to August, and these months saw the last great duels among the heroes of prohibition and repeal. The names of those who filed for candidacy promised the final conflict. The list read like an honor roll which could span the last thirty-three years: Henry McBride, George Cotterill, Laurence Colman, James Duncan,

Agusta Trimble, Warren Magnuson. Two of the candidates had attended the state Constitutional Convention in 1889.

Some few campaigned extensively, and the month of August was
enlivened by motor caravans which carried prominent socialites from
the women's organization across the state, speaking, parading, and
distributing repeal literature. Marmaduke's repeal organization
printed leaflets and paid for newspaper ads which stressed that prohibition was costing the American taxpayer "just about $1,000,000,-
000 per year."[24] Except for a few candidates, however, nobody
worked very hard. The motorcades were usually one-day excursions
out of Seattle, and the repeal organization rested on one big ad
which was printed only once in most of the state's newspapers. Real
enthusiasm was not easy to find, for everyone knew that battle had
already been won. Congress, by modifying the Volstead Act, allowed
beer to flow in April, a spectacle which was covered nation-wide by
the Columbia Broadcasting System. Cities and states made eager prep-
arations to use the forthcoming revenue. In Seattle, where public
school teachers had faced pay cuts up to 20 per cent, the immediate
yield to the city from beer licenses was a welcome thirty thousand
dollars.[25]

An emergency committee to fight repeal was organized in Yakima
and led by Marion Hay, Laurence Colman, and James Duncan. It
enlisted the ASL, the WCTU, the YMCA, the PTA, the WEA, the
Grange, and the Salvation Army. Its keynoter was Mark Matthews,
who after the repeal vote in 1932 had announced that "We will not
modify the Volstead Act. . . . The country will recover from its insanity. . . . God is on His throne and righteousness shall prevail. . . ."
But before election day in August, other states had set a pattern of
twenty-three repeal votes, and no one expected Washington to break
it. On the eve of the voting, the Hearst papers bannered that it was
now "Washington's turn."[26]

The vote on repeal emphasizes again that more people responded
to prohibition than to any other issue of the time. In 1932, about
614,000 citizens of Washington State voted in the presidential election. In 1933, a total of 698,294 voted for repeal-convention delegates. They selected the wets by more than two to one (490,088-208,-
206). The urban areas were most heavily wet (Seattle, 78 per cent;
Spokane, 66 per cent; Tacoma, 72 per cent), but the remainder of

the state was also wet (52 per cent). As the president of the AAPA pointed out, the state of Washington would have voted wet even without the cities listed above.[27] The state's wet vote in 1933 (70 per cent) was significantly higher than it had been the year before (62 per cent)—a signal of how the vitality of the repeal movement increased with the spread of the depression.

When the state Repeal Convention met in the House Chambers in Olympia on October 3, 1933, ninety-four of the delegates voted for the repeal resolution and four opposed it. During long hours before the vote, delegates elected Augusta W. Trimble their secretary, then encouraged each other to join in joyously verbose celebration:

> Delegate A. O. Burmeister: Mr. Chairman, we are assembled here today under this inspiring dome to answer to the edict enacted in these sacred halls for a solemn and dignified purpose. . . . this momentous proposition . . . will go down as a monument, in my opinion, in the annals of the history of this State. . . .

> Delegate Howard J. Burnham [*asking delegates to recall the unseemly results of the shotgun wedding of the Eighteenth Amendment to Mr. Patriotic Citizen*]: Marriage bonds, in common with all other bonds, have a weaker trend during times of depression. . . . Mrs. Citizen is consorting indiscriminately with speakeasy proprietors, federal agents, bootleggers, coast guardsmen and gangsters. The bride may have been pure as snow, but, like snow, she has drifted. . . . In times that try the hearts of men, a far-seeing Providence always sends a leader to guide his people . . . Franklin Roosevelt . . . the other Roosevelt . . . the martyred Lincoln; Thomas Jefferson; and the . . . Father of his Country for whom this State is named. Consider the greatest leader of them all, the Galilean, Jesus Christ. Did you ever pause to ponder how he would handle the liquor traffic?

Among those nominated to chair the convention were State Senator W. W. Connor ("as a citizen and a patriot, he is one of the finest men in the State of Washington"); General Robert Alexander ("whose escutcheon is unsullied . . . who has protected this country and this State in peace and in peril"); Edwin M. Connor ("a warrior . . . newspaper editor . . . an outstanding citizen" who ultimately won a majority); and E. F. Blaine ("the father of irrigation in the State of Washington"). The delegates extended to Mrs. Trimble a standing vote of thanks before they adjourned.

The most enduring words, however, were those of the Right Reverend Arthur S. Hustan:

> and when we shall have finished the work which has been given to us to do, let it not be that we depart with the feeling that we have solved a problem but

rather that we have created a new one, for the solution of which we shall need Thy constant guidance and direction.[28]

In one of his last letters to Senator Jones, Thomas Revelle in 1932 poured out his despair in rueful phrases which carried with them the mood of his city and state:

> I think the Governor is somewhat dispirited at this time because what he claims to be the representative of his life's work, one large lumber plant in Everett, is to be sold at auction on May 19. . . . Banks are closing . . . refusing old ladies their deposits . . . their life's savings. . . . Businesses are closing. . . .
> I feel it more keenly at this time than ever before because while I have had sympathy for all suffering people yet when I anticipate my boys closing the doors of their business, with every dollar I have saved to be lost, my sympathy for other suffering people is comingled with a growing bitterness. I am not going red myself (my secretary just said she was), but many people are, and you can't blame them. You can't argue against hungry stomachs, broken women, starving children in a country like the one we live in. . . . I am praying to God that either a Moses may be found or discovered who can lead the people out of the slough of despond in which they are hopelessly floundering and crying for help and no help seems near.
> Don't answer this letter[29]

Wesley L. Jones did not answer it. He himself was in a slough of despond, and he died a few days after his defeat in November. Revelle sold real estate for a few years, then he, like Whitney, died before the outbreak of war. In 1941, Roy Lyle was put in charge of the Washington State Liquor Control Board's warehouse. Ed Benn, the United States Marshal, went to the legislature in the 1930's and sponsored bills to make wire tapping a more serious offense.

Roy Olmstead, after joining his family and taking a job in a credit bureau—refusing lucrative offers from a liquor distributor and a night club manager—sought out the friendship of Roy Lyle and Judge Jeremiah Neterer, to joke occasionally, but mostly to talk seriously about man and nature. On the day of his release from McNeil Island prison, he had told newsmen, "I won't be back on that island—ever." But he was soon crossing Puget Sound again, this time to do Christian Science work among the prisoners. When asked by them if he was really Roy Olmstead, the king of rumrunners, he would reply, "No, not any more. The old Roy Olmstead is dead."[30]

His old friend Dr. E. J. Brown continued to run for office, content in the 1930's to serve now and then on the Seattle City Council. Al Hubbard went to California to apply his many talents and was convicted on a smuggling charge and sent to prison in 1936. Richard Fryant, the wire tapper, died of a heart attack while under indictment on a liquor charge in 1932.[31]

The Reverend Mark Matthews, who withstood the years with some grace and dignity, would not be silenced by repeal. In 1934, still a thorn to the liquor men, he dug up an old 1909 blue law and began campaigning for Sunday closure. He caused a group of beer dealers to have their attorney—a young man named Albert Rosellini—plead before the courts that the Sunday Closure Law be enforced uniformly so that honest dealers might make an honest living.[32] When Matthews died, Seattle erected a statue to his memory in a public park. Some of his friends would live to see the sculpture, like George Cotterill, who was alive until 1949, and Austin Griffiths, who completed his memoir called "Great Faith" before he died in 1952. But Matthews' most friendly and unrelenting critic— the most intelligent, and persistent, and unselfish of all the wets—Harry A. Chadwick, editor of the Argus, died shortly after repeal in 1934.

In that year, Paul Houser, for a decade the political strategist of repeal, was defeated in the November elections. But even then there remained ghosts of the past in the shadows of the legislative halls. In 1935, Bernard N. Hicks, still superintendent of the ASL, cut a lonely and impoverished figure as he passed among legislators arguing for country-wide options.[33]

In 1937, his organization—two thousand dollars in debt and without funds to pay either rent or salaries—merged into a new temperance group sponsored by the Seattle and State Council of Churches. In an effort to create a new public image for temperance forces, a new generation of leaders erased the identity of the old Anti-Saloon League. Their purpose, however, was the same: "to seek the elimination of the liquor traffic" through "education, information, and research." Called for a while the Washington Temperance Association, it later merged with the Alcohol Problems Association, the national organization that lobbied in Olympia for several decades against any effort to relax the strict antisaloon legislation that controlled the sale of alcoholic beverages in 1934.[34]

16

Booze and Politics, 1933-83

FOLLOWING the repeal of state liquor laws at the polls in 1932, most county and city governments dismissed their dry squads in a rush to cut expenses. While a small band of federal agents sometimes justified their salaries with routine raids on the most notorious "parlors," they for the most part left vendors free to enjoy the ethics of those who had a century before sold "blue ruin" to the Indians.

There was beer available across the street from public schools. Free lunches appeared on the polished mahogany, as did "whisky-flavored tonics" with an alcoholic content in excess of 40 per cent. There were taxi dancers, service to minors, and shootings. Roadhouses were wide open, attractive to drunks and to prostitutes. Moonshine booze under fake labels was a standard item in many drug stores. Chadwick of the *Argus*, noting the three hundred or more "parlors" downtown selling hard booze, remarked that "we are in for about fifteen months of liquor wildcatting."[1] It was like an old-fashioned whiskey feast that even some cynics found depressing.

When by federal decree the beer taps opened legally at midnight, April 4, 1933, the great billows of suds flushed a deluge of problems upon the state and its municipalities. Some city councilmen were happy to find in retail licenses the traditional sources of city revenue and—amid rumors of bribery in broad daylight—the traditional methods of rewarding their friends. Several weeks after the national proclamation of ratification in December 1933, attorneys for the beer parlor owners approached the Seattle City Council with a candid proposal: "We would prefer to have bars where liquor could be sold by the drink," a spokesman said. "You don't need to call them 'saloons.' They might be called 'dispensaries.'" In the ensuing discussion, a motion to have the city attorney define the word *saloon* failed for lack of a second.[2]

The spree could be stopped only by the legislature. Governor Martin, harried by relief rolls and threats of violence from the dispossessed and the unemployed, wanted action on the liquor question, but only after time for consideration. He had appointed an advisory commission, but their recommendation did not reach him until November. He then called for a special session of the legislature to meet on December 5, the first day under the Twenty-first Amendment. By that time, an extended interim of chaos was inevitable, for a vast lobby of brewers, distillers, wholesalers, and retailers had already gathered in Olympia.

For lawmakers the point of departure was the majority report from the governor's commission. This report, written by Alfred J. Schweppe, former dean of the University of Washington Law School, attempted a careful definition of modern temperance:

> Your Commission in approaching the problems of liquor control has accepted as substantially sound, the view that the solution of the question is not prohibition, which has proved a complete failure, and is not the open saloon, to the return of which public opinion is strongly opposed, but that true temperance is best promoted by making widely available intoxicating beverages of low alcoholic content such as beer and light wines, but limiting so far as humanly possible the promotion of the sale of intoxicants of heavy alcoholic content through making them available in Government dispensaries. . . . The sale and drinking of hard liquor in public places should be prohibited.[3]

This definition was vigorously challenged in Olympia, where some dreaded the idea of a state monopoly even more than they did prohibition. Governor Martin himself favored the monopoly—which, it seemed to him, worked well enough in Canada and which might contribute handsomely to the revenues then so desperately needed by the state. He welcomed Alfred Schweppe's proposals for Senate Bill 7 (to be known as the Steele Act, presented by Senator Earl N. Steele, a dry Democrat from Thurston County), most of which, after a month's debate, the legislature accepted.

The Steele Act was, as Schweppe had indicated, an effort to solve both the problems of prohibition and of repeal, literally an organic act to legitimize drinking within the context of an antisaloon state. It allowed cities, and counties outside the cities, a local option to prohibit public drinking, a clause which pleased the rural areas. But the bill gave to the state complete power to license the manufacture, wholesaling, retailing, and distribution, a clause which infuriated many mayors and councilmen from cities which, before prohibition, had raised as much as one-half of the city revenues from the license fees paid by saloons. The bill tried to separate wholesale function from the retail function, in so far as that was possible, by denying one to have an interest in the other. The basic premise was that the state must impose severe restraints on the energies of competition. To exercise this vast and radical authority, the bill created the Washington State Liquor Control Board of three executive members to be appointed by the governor for nine-year terms.

Besides regulating the manufacture and distribution of all alcoholic beverages, the Board could license restaurants and hotels to sell beer and wine by the glass, in a ratio of food/beverage sales that the Board would determine. Taverns could sell beer by the glass, and an early amendment allowed them to add wine—so that they would not be tempted into the food business and competition with restaurants. But there was, without exception, to be no public consumption of hard liquor, and no saloons. The Steele Act even proscribed any signs or advertising that used the words *bar*, *barroom*, or *saloon*. The Board could license grocery stores to sell packaged beer and wine, subject to the Board's regulations and the state's Blue Laws. The Act allowed the sale of hard liquor only in state-owned package stores where, the governor believed, price policy could eliminate bootlegging. The monopoly's profits would be divided equally between the state general fund and the counties (and, after 1935, the cities).

Under the Steel Act, the LCB (Liquor Control Board) was empowered to "make such regulations . . . as are deemed necessary and advisable," such regulations having the same force and effect "as the organic law itself." Thus Board members had extraordinary powers to control the comportment of public drinking and the sale under any circumstances of all beer, wine, and hard liquor. They could suspend a license for any violation of law or of their own regulations, and their decisions were not subject to executive review, not even judicial review. (The State Supreme Court overruled this exemption in 1965.)

On January 23, 1934, Governor Martin greeted the new Board with a small sermon: "The importance of the Washington State Liquor Act is that it is supposed to be conducive to temperance. . . . Unlike other businesses, you are not expected to promote sales. Instead of promoting the sale of liquor, your function is only to make good liquor available to people under proper conditions."[1]

Board members began to codify policy and to write regulations that would have the force and effect of law regarding such economically and politically volatile matters as banking procedures, as employment in state stores and warehouses, state purchasing procedures (including use of the state's credit to acquire inventories, the selection of some brands and the exclusion of others), pricing, advertising, license fees, individual purchasing permits (to include a description of the individual eligible to buy bottles from state stores), the hours of sale wherever alcoholic beverages were sold, the ratio of food-sales income to drink-sales income in restaurants, the location of state stores, the leasing of properties, the form and the style of acceptable bottles or packages.

They had then to choose among ten thousand applicants for state jobs with the LCB, establish a state-wide system of state-owned stores, determine brands and prices, approve or reject thousands of applications for licenses from wholesalers, restaurants, taverns, grocery stores. In all of this they were sure to attract a great deal of enduring interest—from brewers, distillers, owners of taverns, restaurants, hotels, grocery stores, and real estate, from temperance advocates, assorted legislators, mayors, and, indeed, from governors and courts. With a sort of somber finality, the Steele Act subjected Board members to periodic temptation, continuous litigation, and constant criticism. Since 1934, the LCB has been the object of nervous alarm and calculated outrage from the predictable interest groups—economic, religious, social, political. The more decisions members made, the more likely they were to offend.

These first members were men of independent incomes and unchallenged integrity: a retired rear admiral, Luther Gregory; a former state assistant attorney general, William J. Lindberg; a prosperous Republican businessman, Henry Gregerson. With remarkable administrative expediency, and remarkable freedom from serious political interference, they had the new system in place by April. To the governor's great satisfaction, free-enterprise booze and its bootleggers had disappeared, and the state boasted the lowest prices on bottled liquor in the nation. Revenues were gratifying: the LCB reported in 1936 that "starting with nothing, the Board has made over $8,600,000 for the people of the state."[5]

This $8.6 million brought warm nourishment to the state treasury during the period of coldest budgetary famine. Revenues from state taxes that year were about $50 million. Governor Martin estimated that at this point in the Depression the total costs, including general relief and various pensions, of all governmental services was about $100 million each year, but much of this came from federal matching monies. That the LCB could produce such an attractive fraction of these totals was a happy signal to the legislature: it increased the LCB profit markup from 25 per cent to 35 per cent in 1937, then to 40 per cent in 1938, and to 45 per cent in 1940, when it shifted the distribution ratio to give a full 65 per cent of the profits to the cities and counties. During the same period it increased the state tax on LCB sales to 13 per cent. Thus of the $176 million biennial budget (including federal funds) that Governor Martin submitted for 1939 – 41, LCB profits contributed about $4 million (2 per cent), liquor sales taxes another 2 per cent, while the LCB distributed another $7.6 million to city and county governments (see Appendix).

Another measure of the importance of the LCB is that while state appropriations for the public schools across three budgetary bienniums (1935 – 41) totaled $95.5 million, the LCB during that period distributed about $38.5 million in profits and taxes. Although the LCB yield, compared to such budgets, would fall dramatically after the Depression (5 per cent of the state General Fund in 1967– 69, then 2.1 per cent in 1983 – 85) as the legislature solved problems by regularly jacking up the general retail sales tax, it was obvious enough to the Depression legislatures that the state could afford neither free-market booze nor prohibition (see Appendix).

While the financial success of the state liquor system pleased almost everyone, still the refusal of the legislature to allow hard liquor in taverns and restaurants—then the focus of an anti-saloon heritage—was almost impossible to police. To the Board's distress, the blatant wildcatting did not end. The reason, primarily, was that many city officials—some of them resenting their loss of a power to license, all of them with depression-struck budgets and inadequate police departments—would not or could not assign manpower to enforce the laws against liquor by the drink. The LCB, though it had a few "special investigators" handling license applications, had no real enforcement division of its own. (There would be none until 1939.) George Vanderveer, representing beer retailers, warned the saloonkeepers that they must clean up or face prohibition all over again. The mayor of Seattle, John Dore, claimed that the law could not be enforced, though he would try it anyway. "We'll probably satisfy some of the clergymen," he said, "some of the short-haired women and long-haired men. But that's all."[6]

At the same time, hotel men, restaurant men, and druggists were sponsoring Initiative Measure Number 79 to repeal the Steele Act outright. They had the support of the State Federation of Labor. In this counterrevolution, Board members could see the utter ruin of their careful efforts to build up, as they had been instructed to do, a lasting structure of compromise and temperance. Should this initiative measure pass—and apparently there was a real chance that it would—it would bring the evils of the saloon, the influences of liquor on politics, the excesses of vice and corruption, all over again, as if the state were forever doomed to internecine struggles between the wet and dry. Board members could set themselves against the measure; or they could conclude that the Steele Act, as an instrument of peace and compromise, was still too blunt a tool for so delicate a task, that it needed further modification.

The only evidence of their decision lies in the subsequent events themselves and in a rumor surrounding them. Chadwick of the *Argus*, so often correct, told his readers in May, 1934, that the hotel and restaurant interests had withdrawn their support of the initiative measure in return for a promise from Board members that they would recommend a bill to the next legislature which would authorize liquor by the drink in hotels and restaurants. By June, the initiative measure died a very private death.

That fall, in its first report, the Liquor Board announced that it would "be pleased to cooperate in the preparation of such amendments to the law" as would be required to allow hotels and restaurants to serve hard liquor—if the legislature so desired. The following February, the Board submitted such a bill to the Senate Liquor Control Committee.[7] The bill died in committee, and it is precisely at this point that one can again use the phrase "temperance movement" with some accuracy. The "interests"—and maybe even the Liquor Board itself—had been so impressed with the events of repeal and the chaos immediately thereafter that they had failed to appreciate the substantial body of moderate opinion which produced the Steele Act and was quite happy with it. Excesses are always spectacular, and those of 1933–34 may have led restaurants to misjudge the strength of moderate attitudes; the excesses may even have encouraged such attitudes. People wanted their taverns, their beer and wine in public places, but there was no substantial political support for the public consumption of hard liquor. During the bottom years of the Depression, there may even have been no market for such consumption. In any event, restaurateurs apparently lacked confidence that whatever market there might have been was worth a major political effort. To most people, the Steele Act seems to have been a happy compromise between prohibition and total repeal of any control. In what might be called the "moderation decade" or the "transition decade," hotels and restaurants lived with moderate alcoholic drinks while the Liquor Board improved its defenses against the return of the saloon.

This solution endured without open protest until the wartime industries of 1941–45 brought their great waves of migrants. The population of the state increased by almost 40 per cent between 1940 and 1950, and most of this increase was in men and women hired to produce aircraft, aluminum, ships, and plutonium. Suddenly affluent and liberated from Depression psychology, they brought attitudes and experiences that almost at once began to clash with the Steele Act's principles of moderation. As wartime social pressures rose alarmingly—new cities, new military bases, overcrowded urban areas with no strong structure for public service or social control—the LCB reported "serious problems." These included public consumption of hard liquor, public drunkness, "social diseases" traced to taverns near military bases; then shortages, black markets, and bootleggers.

The illicit trade began when the Federal War Production Board ordered all distilleries to convert to industrial alcohol and produce no beverage alcohol after October 1942. The LCB then turned to rationing, issuing a ration card for each of the individual purchasing permits required by the Steele Act. This ration card allowed the permit holder to buy one quart of whiskey a week, an allowance that seemed perfectly equitable and easily enforceable, but suddenly the whiskey was disappearing much more rapidly than the rationing plan had projected. To their dismay LCB planners soon realized that the Steele Act had not prohibited individuals from possessing more than one permit. This embarrassing problem was quickly solved by the Legislature.[8]

The LCB then found a clever way to avert what in other states became a crisis of supply and demand. In partnership with the Oregon Liquor Control Agency, the LCB purchased two properties in Kentucky, the Waterfill and Frazier distillery and the Shawhan Distilling Company. Possessing their warehoused stocks, the LCB immediately sold the physical plants and other assets, thereby acquiring a half-million cases of easily marketable bourbon. Because the state lost nothing in the transactions, this was a quick and widely admired master stroke of good business. But other strokes of crisis management were less satisfying: in anticipation of continuing shortages, other LCB purchases were, at best, excessive, including a decision to take 12,000 cases of Mexican wine, a business judgment that under other circumstances would surely have been con-

demned as either oddly naive or perversely corrupt. The liquid found
favor nowhere. As late as 1951, despite desperate price adjustments,
LCB stores were moving only about two cases of Los Amigos a year.[9]

Even when the end of the war solved most problems of supply, other
problems grew more serious. By 1946, the Liquor Board reported 599
raids and 705 arrests by its Enforcement Division and acknowledged that
"bottle clubs" had become a "major problem." Such clubs, if chartered
by the secretary of state as private fraternal or social organizations, were
allowed under the Steele Act to serve mixed drinks to members who supplied their own liquor. During the war the number of bottle clubs increased sharply to almost three hundred. Many of them required only
nominal qualifications for membership and operated in ways scarcely dis-
tinguishable from the barrooms of California and Nevada. All the Board
could do about them was to attempt to ascertain that the bottles from
which their customers were so freely served had been purchased in a state
store and brought to the club by the persons who intended to drink from
them. The Board had a few difficult years, especially after the war when
many veterans' clubs opened and the population continued to increase
rapidly.[10]

A law to authorize the public sale of hard liquor by the drink was
before the voters in 1948. Initiative Measure Number 171 was drawn to
allow the Liquor Board to license hotels, restaurants, clubs, trains,
boats—any establishment where serving full meals was a principal business—with a "Class H" license to sell hard liquor by the drink. It was
called by its supporters "The Common Sense Bill," but these people (they
included lobbyists and public relations experts, along with several
wealthy investors, who persuaded Alfred Schweppe to write the measure)
had no intention of reopening the entire issue of prohibition. They
stressed the importance of liquor with meals to the tourist trade, which
was indeed becoming a major industry—the "hospitality industry." Their
arguments were carefully phrased in conservative, antisaloon tones. Initiative 171 did not permit the serving of women "except when seated at
tables"; it prohibited licenses in residential areas or near schools. Revenues from the new licenses were marked for medical research at the University of Washington and Washington State College. There were no official arguments in opposition to Initiative 171 when the secretary of state
printed the voters' pamphlet in the summer of 1948.

But the drys of 1948 had their own bill. Initiative Measure to the Legislature Number 13 would have prohibited the sale of wine and beer except in the state liquor stores. Its supporters—identified as the Washington Temperance Association—claimed that the tavern system of Washington was unsuccessful, that taverns produced crime, violence, alcoholism, depraved women, and drunken drivers. With all the old Prohib arguments, they called for the abolition of what was to their minds the modern saloon. Number 13 was opposed in the voters' pamphlet by sheriff's organizations, veteran groups, and the State Federation of Labor.

The election of 1948, then, was another eventful measure—like 1914, 1918, and 1932—of public attitudes toward liquor control. It came, as did the others, after significant social changes had demanded a revaluation of public morality. It recorded, in the case of the anti-tavern Number 13, an overwhelming approval of Steele Act temperance; Number 13 failed in every county and lost the state, 602,141 to 208,337. The voters would clearly go no farther than the Steele Act toward prohibition, and they gave a solid endorsement to the beer-wine tavern as an institution.

In the case of Number 171, a majority chose to change the Steele Act enough to allow hotels and restaurants to serve liquor by the drink. With this change, though, there was no overwhelming endorsement; it passed, 416,227 to 373,418. Though returning veterans of the war surely contributed significantly, it is quite clear that the winning margin came from the war workers who had flooded the state since 1940. (The counties in 1948 which had received most of this migration were Benton, where the Hanford Plutonium Project increased the population by 326 per cent; Franklin, also in the Hanford area; King, with its Boeing plants and extensive shipyards; Kitsap, because of the Bremerton shipyards; Pierce, for shipbuilding; Spokane and Clark, for aluminum and shipbuilding. All of these but Clark supported Number 171 by significant majorities.)

Building this majority for liquor by the drink was at least in part the result of its authors' care in presenting the measure as antisaloon and pro-moderation. Although in 1947 the LCB had sent a representative to Yale University to consult with the nation's foremost researcher in alcohol studies, E. M. Jellinek, the law began the first allocation of state funds for the purpose of studying and combating alcoholism. The distribution of funds from Class H license fees ($100,000 a year to each school in the beginning, rising to $500,000 in 1967) was a durable commitment. On this clue the LCB entered alcohol education with a plan "to combat the purchase and use of liquor by minors" and in the 1950s with a public information officer who spoke for moderation, echoing the liquor industry's own pronouncements, before various civic groups. At the urging of Governor Albert D. Rosellini, the legislature in 1957 required the LCB to put $250,000 each biennium into an alcoholism program to be conducted by the State Department of Institutions.

In the 1960s the LCB was distributing pamphlets that encouraged moderation and discouraged drunken driving, and the legislature, at the request of Governor Daniel J. Evans, required that most fees from all liquor licenses each year go to the alcoholism programs of the newly organized Department of Social and Health Services—an amount that rose from $800,000 in 1969 to $4.8 million by 1985.

Initiative Measure 171 also recorded in part the passing of regionalism in American society. Besides the return to prosperity, war workers had brought with them an impatience with narrowly regional institutions and, as we shall see time and again, a determination to prevent such institutions from interfering with their daily lives, especially when they were determined to enjoy their unprecedented affluence. They brought the cocktail room. And because Americans were mobile and articulate, the natives would have to live with the changes that the initiative wrought. Direct legislation, once more, had allowed the state to respond rapidly to social change—more rapidly, perhaps, than the prohibitionist fathers of the initiative and referendum would have desired, for in 1948, their own weapon was again used against them.

But the "room" defined by Initiative 171 was certainly not the saloon (the word was still proscribed) of former days. Neither was it merely a modified tavern. As shaped by the Liquor Board, it was a thoroughly middle-class institution. Class H licenses went to those restaurants least likely to harbor dangers to the social equilibrium and most likely to provide clean and proper evidence of middle-class stability. The "room" was not a place where the working man was likely to be served in his dirty clothes, or where he could cash a pay check, gamble, or expect to find a variety of available women. The LCB saw to that. By 1955, the Board had issued fewer than half the number of liquor-by-the-drink licenses (set at one per 1,500 of population) authorized by Initiative 171. Policy and action, then, created the "room" as something the saloon had never been. And once created, the institution had an interest in its own survival: cooperation among "rooms" was coordinated to keep hard liquor out of the taverns, and competition among them after 1948 was for middle-class respectability.

In protecting itself, the "hospitality industry" presented a series of new problems to the LCB. The first and most persistent of these was the Board's requiring Class H-licensed restaurants to sustain a food-to-drink ratio, in gross sales, of 60/40. To most restaurateurs the conception here was the very essence of commercial prudence: allow the sale of hard liquor by the drink only in legitimate restaurants. Even so, the arithmetical rigidity of 60/40 seemed to them a rather arbitrary and ungenerous constraint upon honest entrepreneurship and hospitality, and their pressures on the LCB were polite but relentless.

The Board watched and listened, then changed the ratio to 50/50 in 1954, then to 40/60 in 1971. While in no way seeking a total elimination of the ratio principle, the "industry" was nevertheless dissatisfied, complaining that the high costs of liquor its members had to buy from the LCB in the 1980's made drinks so expensive that the ratio was difficult to sustain. However, the "industry" was eager to support the LCB in 1985 when a Seattle restaurateur's defiant 15/85 ratio provoked the suspension of his license. The case went before a Superior Court judge who alarmed the "industry" by ruling that the LCB's practice of setting ratios was itself "arbitrary and capricious" and therefore unconstitutional. The ghost of the saloon seemed very real during the months while the LCB, with the assistance of the Hotel and Restaurant Association, anxiously appealed this ruling. To the gratification of the appealing parties, the State Supreme Court in 1986 reversed the lower court's decision, emphasizing the antisaloon character of Initiative 171, which, the court unanimously agreed, was intended to prevent restaurants from becoming what in other states were simply barrooms or saloons.[11]

Another problem played out from 1933 until 1976 was that of the hours and days during which a "room" or tavern could remain open to the public. As early as 1936 the LCB asked the legislature to do something about the 1909 "Blue Laws" which required Sunday closure and which many city officers seemed to ignore. Through the 1940's and 1950's the Board's enforcement teams continued to insist that licensed premises close at midnight Saturday, and even the anguished cries during the Seattle World's Fair in 1962 did not relax this insistence. The plight of visitors to the state—and the plight of restaurateurs—did, however, cause a general reconsideration, and the "hospitality industry" moved to an easy victory with Initiative Measure 229 in 1966 (604,096 for; 333,972 against), which repealed the "Blue Laws" outright.

What the "industry" wanted next was specific authorization for liquor sales on Sundays—a matter that the Alcohol Problems Association's marshalling of church groups had stopped in the legislative session of 1967. Following legislative adjournment, however, concerned parties took their case before the LCB, whose members were willing to recognize that the blue laws were indeed dead: a new regulation allowed drinking on Sundays, but not until after church services, when it accommodated a full eight-hour shift for bartenders, without overtime, setting the hours at 2 P.M. to 10 P.M. The "industry" accepted this until 1970, when it defeated the moribund Alcohol Problems Association by impressing the Board with the importance of Sunday lunches, with drinks, to many restaurants, and with the embarrassment caused by Sunday dinner guests reluctant to surrender their wine glasses at 10 P.M. The Board ruled in favor of noon to midnight. Then in 1976 the Board recognized that Sunday professional football had created a large brunch clientele that could not reasonably be denied, and it dropped all Sunday restrictions. [12]

Such changes illuminated the very considerable amount of money at stake in any matter regarding the state's hotels and restaurants. Those who held Class H licenses were not often eager to see their number increase. The law limited the number of licenses to one for each 1,500 residents, and because the board had not issued more than about 900 in 1964—still fewer than half the number allowed by the Steele Act—sums of money might conceivably attach themselves to any consideration of who should or should not have the next one. In the 1960's there were rumors that the current rate for a new Class H was a bribe of five thousand dollars. [13]

About this time, too, the activities of some of the agents for beer and wine wholesalers and some of the sales representatives for distilleries were causing both irritation and anxiety. (These "agents" were subject to licensing and LCB regulation, but the distillery sales "reps" were not, though with later changes in the liquor law, "reps" could become "agents.") These men, some of whom were paid on commission, often had annual incomes higher than that of the governor, which was then $22,500. There had long been rumors that their jobs were virtually patronage positions used by some governors to reward their friends, and that the generosity of these friends was at times the "single biggest source" of funds for gubernatorial campaigns. [14]

Moreover, these agents and representatives were often conspicuous in Olympia. Some legislators active in the 1950's and 1960's routinely received a mixed case of beer each week from a wholesaler, and some recall that cases of hard liquor entered into many a legislative equation: there were House bills or Senate bills referred to as "two-case" bills or even "four-case" bills, and trucks regularly delivered these considerations to the Legislative Office Building. Accordingly, many legislators came to expect someone to supply the bar at their campaign fund-raising receptions, and distillers shipped large quantities of liquor into the state marked for their "reps'" political obligations. In the 1950's, about a thousand cases would carry a legislative session, served by seventy-four sales representatives. Thus a perceptible melding of interests among members of the legislature, LCB executives and their employees, the governor's office, state and county party chairmen, agents, and sales representatives was creating fateful opportunities for scandal.[15]

Governor Martin had inadvertently prepared the ground. The first three LCB executives, according to the Steele Act, were appointed in 1934 for terms of three, six, and nine years, with all future appointments to be nine years—and Martin could live with this. But Schweppe and others who helped draft the Steele Act, hoping to remove the LCB from political influences, had wanted the members subject to removal only by mandate from the state Supreme Court. Martin had complained that, given such tenure, members "would stand . . . responsible to nobody . . . with their human frailties unfortified against temptations . . . they might stand so independently as to become disdainful and arrogant toward the people and the Governor." Moreover, he predicted that people would hold the governor responsible under any circumstances for the Board's actions. For these reasons, and using his power of item veto on the Steele Act, he had deleted Schweppe's design to keep the Board "out of politics." Members, whatever their terms, were then to serve "at the pleasure of governor."[16]

Despite Schweppe's objection that Martin was inviting liquor money "to support candidates for governor in the next election," and a general concern over the possibility of governors' adjusting the inventory of state stores to reward their friends, Democratic legislators accepted Martin's wishes. But in 1937, when Martin was out of favor with a large part of his own party, and before Martin had the opportunity to make his next appointment, Democratic legislators modified his powers of appointment under the Steele Act by adding the phrase "with the consent of the Senate." The politicization of the LCB, with an uneven rhythm, continued thereafter.

In 1945, when Democrat Mon Wallgren became governor, a Democratic legislature, "by executive request," dropped Senate approval. Then in 1948, the designers of Initiative 171 took the opportunity to eliminate old Admiral Gregory who in the 1940's had effectively opposed their efforts to win "liquor by the drink" in the legislature: the measure included a requirement that the governor appoint a new Board on January 15, 1949 "with the consent of the Senate." Republican Arthur Langlie, who took the governor's office in January, 1949, was happy enough to control the three appointments, but he was also eager to remove himself from liquor-related problems. With his approval, the legislature in 1949 returned to Schweppe's original intention to keep LCB members "out" of politics and revised the law to authorize their removal only by order from the court.

These maneuvers kept the LCB fairly close to the governors. Though Mon Wallgren served only one term (1945–49), he managed to appoint two members. Arthur Langlie's terms (1941–45; 1949–57) gave him ample opportunity to appoint all three, and the same was true of Democrat Albert Rosellini (1957–65) and Republican Dan Evans (1965–77). Then as soon as Evans left office, some Democrats sponsored a bill (HB 853, April, 1977) which, in a blatantly greedy grab for power, would have abolished the LCB and created in its place something to be called the Alcohol Administration Board of three members to be appointed by Governor Dixie Lee Ray. The bill died in committee. The next governor, Republican John Spellman, explored the possibility of abolishing the entire state monopoly, but decided that the state could not afford the loss of nearly $27 million a year that would result. Then in 1986, Democratic Governor Booth Gardner, convinced that nine-year tenures left them too remote from public influence, signed a bill reducing the terms of LCB members to six years.

Clarence Martin's decision to keep Board executives "in" rather than "out" of politics—a decision to which, he indicated, he had given a great deal of thought—was rewarded in 1939 when a Thurston County grand jury opened investigations of state agencies, investigations which, by 1940, touched rumors that the LCB had been issuing licenses exclusively to the governor's friends. Even though the jury found no cause for indictment and took care to praise the executives for their efficiency, critics claimed that the investigations had been politically motivated and had contributed to the defeat in the primary of Clarence Martin. Then, with less threatening intent, a House investigating committee in 1943 looked into the Board's wartime rationing system but found no problem. A third investigation—again, during the gubernatorial campaign—brought a Republican-dominated legislative committee in 1948 to examine the alleged abuses of the state monopoly during the administration of Democratic Governor Mon Wallgren. This committee found nothing of substance before the general election, which Wallgren lost to Republican Arthur Langlie, but which returned a Democratic legislature that discontinued the investigation.

In 1963, the legislature—and then following adjournment, the Legislative Council, established to be a bipartisan investigative group but clearly controlled by Republicans—began picking through allegations and facts regarding the conduct of the LCB and its employees during the administrations of Democratic Governor Albert D. Rosellini. The private and public hearings of the Legislative Council during the spring months of 1964 were broad enough in substance and dark enough in rumor to bring into question again the mercurial role of liquor control in a democratic state government. [17]

Ross Cunningham of the *Seattle Times*, who had been Langlie's special assistant and his Republican patronage chief in Olympia, and who was not often wrong when he revealed what he knew about state politics, wrote that Rosselini had indeed demanded a free hand in LCB "policies." (He was referring daintily to power and patronage: employment practices, the appointment of agents and sales representatives, the purchasing decisions, and LCB enforcement.) The fighting became intense, according to Cunningham, and Rosellini had exercised his right to change the LCB chairmanship, removing Don G. Abel, with whom he did not agree, and replacing him with F. Garland Sponburgh, with whom he did. Cunningham carefully avoided any mention of corruption—he left the impression that this was business as usual in Olympia. He also took care to note that the members of the Board at the time, including Sponburgh, were men of untarnished reputations. [18] And according to their own account of an astonishing episode, the three Board members had discussed the hearings with a principal investigator, who had informed them privately that in this election year it was the governor and the Democrats that the Legislative Council wanted to target—not the executive members of the LCB. [19]

A fascinating political contest quickly developed. As the Legislative Council hearings continued, Rosellini vetoed the legislative appropriation of funds necessary to their work, declaring the Council was unconstitutional because it was clearly partisan. Yet the attorney general, John

O'Connell (who himself had hope of becoming governor), provided the investigators with legal counsel; and a prominent enemy of the governor in organized labor, Arthur T. Hare, president of a Building Employees' local, sponsored efforts to provide private fundings. As these stumbled forward, the chief of the State Patrol, a Rosellini appointee, refused to serve subpoenas.

The drama raised eyebrows almost everywhere because the principal investigators were all serving what appeared to be obvious self-interests. State Representative Dan Evans was seeking the Republican nomination for governor, and he had announced not only that he favored abolishing the state liquor monopoly but that the scandals uncovered by the Council would be enough to "drive a nail into the coffin of this administration."[20] Republican State Senator Albert C. Thompson, Jr., had been critical of the LCB since 1961, when, for reasons never quite clear, the Board moved the state store—which generated a brisk flow of commercial traffic—from its location next to Thompson's Drug Store in Bellevue to another part of that city. State Representative Robert A. Perry was a turncoat Democrat then working for the Goldwater Republicans.

The investigative hearings eventually faded away during the summer— because of lack of funds, because of the primary election campaigns, because all the publicity had yielded no evidence with which to indict anyone important. The Democrats were happy with an editorial comment:

> I have known several members of the State Liquor Board over a period of years, and their honesty and rectitude are above reproach. . . . Some time ago I lunched with the president of a large liquor company, and when questioned he said that the State of Washington was one of the cleanest states in the nation as far as his company was concerned. (Bailey in the *Argus*, April 1964)

Even so, the hearings did bring before the public certain realities about politics and liquor control that many people had suspected but politely ignored since 1933. At least one governor had circumvented the nine-year tenure of his LCB appointees by accepting from them signed-but-undated letters of resignation. Some governors wanted to control the LCB and others did not. Nevertheless, LCB decisions could have immediate political implications. After some gubernatorial elections, several friends of the new governor had become agents or sales representatives, whose subsequent contributions to campaign funds could be significant. One such "rep" had sold the LCB enough cases of one brand of whiskey to stock the stores for fifteen years. After each gubernatorial election, county chairmen of the victorious party had usually put pressure on the new administration to give them control of patronage over the LCB jobs throughout their counties, and this patronage had sometimes delivered an unfortunate lot of investigators, store managers, and clerks. At least one investigator had indeed solicited a bribe payable when the applicant received his Class H license. Some other inspectors had been extremely partisan, herding licensees to $100-a-plate campaign-fund-raising dinners and selling tickets to events such as "Governor's Appreciation Day." Managers of some liquor stores had indeed solicited campaign funds from their employees.[21]

There were cynics who found no surprise in these revelations, nothing that was really new in the mechanics of state politics since 1934. But others not so cynical validated Clarence Martin's fear that voters would place the blame for any flaw in liquor control directly upon the governor. Republican Dan Evans made effective use of the alleged liquor scandals to bring about his remarkable victory in 1964. (Rosellini, twice elected governor, received only 548,692 votes while the Democratic presidential candidate received 779,881.)

There was every reason to suppose that the young, ambitious, reform-minded, "straight arrow" governor was then eager both to avoid contamination himself and to destroy the baneful influence of liquor interests upon state political life. His first effort was to reduce the political influence of the distillery sales representatives, a group for whom he had little respect. Their incomes, he thought, were indecently inflated, their lobbying insidious, and he asked the legislature for a bill requiring public disclosure of their incomes and their political contributions. The problem with this request was one commonly painful to Washington governors: the opposition controlled the legislature, and the Democrats caused this bill to die in committee.

Evans next urged LCB members to impose public disclosure upon sales representatives through their power to write regulations. But in this he was frustrated by the attorney general (John O'Connell, who had earlier frustrated Rosselini), who ruled that the board lacked such powers. Even so, Evans was not totally defeated. Apparently the distillers themselves were much disturbed that their representatives had offended a popular governor whose policies could do them great harm, and they found it possible to have these men lower their visibility in Olympia. Appar-

ently, too, the "reps," after 1965, often chose to present themselves as
advisors rather than as sponsors of legislation and of political personali-
ties.[22]

Another move by Evans was to appoint a new chairman of the LCB,
Robert L. Hagist, with a mandate to rid the LCB (now grown to 716
employees bringing in $126,153,345 a year) of its partisan political
blemishes. Hagist began what he called an "18 month reform program"
that included revised warehouse procedures and measures to prevent the
leakages, shortages, cronyisms, and politicking attributed to the managers and clerks of the various stores. He took Evans' wishes seriously and,
before the legislature—which he advised to mind its own business while
he minded the Liquor Board's—perhaps too self-righteously. Again the
political consideration: when Hagist's appointment came up for confirmation, the Democratic state Senate denied it. Evans angrily concluded that the Democrats were refusing to allow him to weed out corruption. Hagist's comment was, "They got me before I got them."[23]

While the role of agents and "reps" was still uncertain and the extent to
which a governor might reform LCB practices was at least in doubt, the
legislature locked itself in battle over what became an unpredictably divisive issue: the state's monopoly in the sale of out-of-state wine.

After a 1935 amendment to the Steele Act, the laws regarding the sale
of wine by the LCB had advanced both the principles of temperance and
of protectionism. When major retailers of wine, such as grocers, bought
wine produced in Washington (called "domestic"), they could bypass the
monopoly and deal directly with the wineries or their wholesalers. But
when they wanted out-of-state wines, the law restricted them to an un-
imaginative inventory at the state liquor stores, where they had to pay the
LCB's retail prices, which included the added protection of a markup that
ranged as high as 71 per cent. For grocers to mark up a profit on California wine or French wine was sure step out of competition with the state,
for consumers who cared at all about cost bought their "non-domestic"
wines at the same state stores and at the same prices. Grocers and wholesalers endured this situation sullenly until the 1950's, when American
affluence was moving tastes toward the more elegant light wines of California, and when finally California wineries brought suit against the state
of Washington, claiming unfair trade practices. In November, 1958, the
United States Supreme Court ruled in favor of Washington, thus promis-
ing unrelieved frustrations to grocers, wholesalers, and to the growing

number of people in the state to whose newly acquired sophistication in table wines the monopoly was so crankily unresponsive. What had for years been only a minor irritation—if a glaring economic discrimination—was becoming major public controversy.

The dispute gathered both color and energy from the public jokes about the ghastly quality of what was being protected. State winemakers then produced fewer gallons of grape wine than of fruit and berry wines, 35 per cent of which were fortified with brandies to yield a strong, sweet domestic liquid dismissed by most wine drinkers as simply garbage for the "wino" trade. The LCB, itself embarrassed by this reputation, had early made arrangements with the University of Washington College of Pharmacy to submit domestic products to a systematic testing, the singular purpose of which was to disprove "the alleged toxic qualities of certain types of Washington-made wines."[24] University scientists had never identified any toxicities, but many consumers found their work unconvincing.

Thus several factors contributed to the decision in 1967 by consumer groups and sales representatives that the time was right to break the state's protectionist policies. Their instrument was called the "California Wine Bill" (to allow licensed wholesalers to carry out-of-state wines, which licensed retailers could buy at wholesale prices), and it divided the legislature into bitterly opposed bipartisan camps. Those sympathetic to the small state wine industry strongly insisted that an honorable local tradition and economy would perish without the state's protection. Others argued against the state's losing revenues by diminishing the state monopoly. And there was indeed—if one looked at all into the future—a great deal of money at issue. Wineries, wholesalers, retailers, and their various allied legislators attacked with so much thoughtless determination—so much open vote buying—that their excesses were self-defeating. In an early April confrontation, the California Wine Bill failed in the House by a single vote. This vote was cast by the Speaker of the House, Republican Representative Don Eldridge, because, Eldridge said, he was so disgusted by the outrageously arrogant and bullying tactics of the lobbyists.[25] (Governor Evans, at the first opportunity, appointed Eldridge to the LCB.)

The lobbyists, however, knew that if they exercised a seemly restraint, the bill could pass easily on its own merits. An urban population saw no reason to pay unreasonably high prices for respectable wines—or to be denied them—only to subsidize a few backward vintners whose pretentions most people still found either grossly humorous or grossly offensive. With a sort of quiet dignity, the bill met the approval of the committees and the legislature in 1969—the LCB did not protest—and the governor signed it. During the following year, the sale of California wines increased by about 150 per cent. And just as its defenders had warned, the old state industry almost perished: the domestic share of the state market fell from about 60 per cent to about 20 per cent a few years later.

Even this 20 per cent figure is misleading in that it does not represent the old wino beverages. In a remarkable development, a new generation of vintners and investors was discovering the extraordinary potential of eastern Washington hillsides for dry wines of really serious oenological significance. As this new industry began to capture public attention, it found a friendly legislature. In 1970 its friends offered an amendment to the state's wine tax (then 10 cents a gallon, plus a 26 per cent sales tax on retail price of each bottle) that promised the new wineries some advantage. Because they were so new, their wines, compared to California products, were relatively expensive. What their friends wanted in 1970 was to set the gallon tax at 75 cents and to eliminate the sales tax entirely—a change that promised a happy drop in the price consumers would pay for many wines, especially the more expensive.

But Governor Evans objected, estimating that the proposal would cost the state almost 6 million dollars in tax revenue, an amount which would threaten a state budget then only precariously in balance. However, into the next biennial budget period he was persuaded that the state should indeed extend assistance to what was becoming a most attractive new industry (the wines were winning national recognition for their quality), and in 1973 he signed a similar measure. The production of Washington table wines began a period of dramatic growth almost immediately thereafter.[26]

The debates over the California Wine Bill and the tax laws revealed that new lawmakers and LCB members were quite receptive to a revision in a wide range of liquor-related rules and policies. With very little agitation, they removed several restrictions on cocktail rooms that a growing population of well-educated and well-paid younger people living in the cities and enjoying professional theater, symphony, and sports, found quite incomprehensible: the rules that women could not sit at the bar, that drinkers could not move their drinks from bar to table, that taverns must leave their interiors visible from the street, that beer and wine could not be advertised on radio or television before 8 P.M. For a moment it seemed as though Dan Evans might avoid the exasperation that liquor control had brought to other governors. His appointees reflected a thoughtful and business-minded response to new public moods and wishes. Self-service stores made monopoly more attractive, and colorful "specialty tables" encouraged customers to feel that a more cosmopolitan and at least a pseudo free-enterprise sort of marketing was possible. In the sale of California and European wines, there might actually be competition among grocery stores, the new wine stores, and the monopoly stores. Inventories changed quickly in reaction to national trends, especially to the increasing popularity of light wines and vodka, and there were even occasional LCB "sales." No one seemed to find it odd that the LCB, in apparent contradiction to its original mandates to promote "temperance," might be vigorously engaged in what it called "merchandising." Prices were rising—to an average of 50 cents more for a fifth-sized bottle of hard liquor than in Oregon or Idaho—and people were grumbling about this, but revenues were rising also. Evans welcomed them to his often delicately balanced state budgets. (For 1971–73, state General Fund revenues were $2,414 million, of which about $30 million (1.3 per cent) came from liquor profits and about $94 million (4 per cent) from liquor taxes, and the LCB was sending another $30 million to the cities and counties; the total Evans budget for the biennium was in balance by only $18 million.) The governor himself was no longer talking about free-enterprise liquor, and for a while the state monopoly seemed beyond the reach of destructive criticism.[27]

It was soon clear, however, that there were few significant issues before state government from which the LCB could remain remote. Both before and after the Federal Civil Rights Act of 1964, Evans had issued executive orders (1963 and 1966) forbidding the practice of racial discrimination in any state agency. These supplemented a State Public Accommodations Law of 1909, which forbade the denial of "full enjoyment of accommodation" on the basis of race, creed, or color in "places of public resort." And as early as 1949 the state Anti-Discrimination Law created a State Board Against Discrimination, which, in 1957, took a special interest in places of "public accommodation." But none of these acts addressed the problems presented by the non-public accommodations of private clubs.

In April, 1968, a civil rights group asked the United States District

Court to enjoin the LCB from honoring liquor licenses held by any organization, public or private, that practiced racial or religious discrimination (Gerber *et al.* v. WSLCB). Meanwhile, other groups—an advisory committee to the United States Civil Rights Commission and the State Board Against Discrimination—asked for a report on how many clubs licensed by the LCB had discriminatory membership rules, then pointedly questioning the legality of a state agency's granting licenses to such organizations.

The LCB, unsure of how to proceed without violating someone's rights, mailed a questionnaire regarding membership restrictions to all private clubs holding Class H licenses. Of the 283 clubs—enrolling nearly 300,000 people—most of which realized most of their revenue from liquor by the drink, only 49 answered the questionnaire, and some of these answers were so vague as to be contemptuous.

Neither the governor nor the attorney general could find a legal way to revoke Class H licenses held by hundreds of fraternal or veterans' private bars. The problem was that both state and federal precedent protected private groups from the "public accommodation" clause. When the Gerber case was dismissed by the U.S. District Court in 1973, Evans said that although the LCB clearly lacked the power to revoke licenses on the basis of discrimination, the legislature could give the LCB such power, and he asked the attorney general to draft such legislation. The legislature found this an easy matter to postpone. (Private clubs, however, did not, and most of them dropped their "whites only" clauses early in the 1970s.)[28]

The matter of race and liquor control in the 1970's had yet another dimension. The federal government, following World War II, began an unsteady retreat from its central role in the lives of native American Indians. After more than a century of rigid proscriptions, Indians could at last purchase and possess liquor without interference. Then as the energies of the Indian Rights movement encouraged tribal governments toward self-assertion, members on nine reservations in the state opened liquor stores, ignoring the LCB by buying out of state and cheerfully selling without regard either to state taxes or to tribal membership. The state government was at that moment unprepared to recognize this degree of tribal sovereignty, and LCB enforcement officers began intercepting shipments of liquor and arresting bargain-seeking whites who left the reservation with untaxed booze, charging them with illegal possession. In

1979, the state sought court rulings against the nine tribes in a case filled with a charming historical twist: the government was accusing Indians of selling illegal booze to whites.

After a series of decisions and appeals—at a time when federal courts had taken from the state its right to regulate Indian fishing and when federal decisions in such matters were usually running against the states—both parties determined to live with several ambiguous court decisions. The U.S. Ninth District Court in 1982 ruled that the state did not have "licensing and distribution authority" over liquor on Indian reservations. But the U.S. District Court ruled in 1984 that Indians had "no independent sovereignty" regarding liquor regulation and no authority to bring liquor into the state and sell it to whites without LCB regulation. With this suggestion of concurrent jurisdiction, the LCB and the state attorney general began negotiating agreements whereby the LCB might appoint governments of "qualified Indian tribes" as vendors required to buy from the LCB but authorized to sell untaxed liquor to tribal members and taxed liquor to non-members.[29]

This, the parties reasoned, was better than endless litigation, endlessly expensive, but it pleased fewer whites than it did Indians. It meant, in one instance, that the state liquor store in Marysville closed its doors, and the Indian store on the nearby Tulalip Reservation established itself as the only retail outlet in the area. Non-reservation customers forced to drive from Marysville to Tulalip were at first vocal in their resentment, but there was little public discussion of the matter after 1984.

In the early 1970's some observers began to feel that Dan Evans had actually been effective in changing the very character of state government. Civil service for state employees, carried by initiative measure in 1961, had helped his efforts considerably. Then environmental controls, the public disclosure of political campaign funding, the registration of lobbyists, an Open Meetings Act, the hiring of professional staff for the legislature, even a new generation of lawmakers—along with a growing, increasingly cosmopolitan population—had contributed to a new and buoyant mood in Olympia. As the state's population approached four million, some observers even felt that the old-time lobbying practices—cash in hand, open threats, cases of booze, the alleged movement of prostitutes into the Legislative Building, the tactics that had so offended Speaker Don Eldridge in 1967—were themselves no longer probable.[30]

During this period, the focus of attention upon issues related to liquor control had shifted from the moral or philosophical or social to the clearly economic. Evans had early retracted his criticism of state monopoly, and no recent legislature had seriously debated free-enterprise liquor—i.e., had not seriously debated the loss of maybe fifteen to twenty million dollars a year from an anemic state budget. And in their own quiet ways, the LCB and the legislature had become more willing to accommodate hotels and restaurants; to "merchandise" liquor and wine; to question distillers whose bottles might be included in the state inventory about the proposed vigor of their advertising.

During the adjustments of the 1960's Dan Evans had reason to believe that he had at last found three seasoned and dependable executives— Jack Hood, Leroy Hittle, Don Eldridge—who were business-minded enough and politically sensitive enough to contain the treacherous problems that had threatened liquor control since 1933. But then in September, 1971, to Evans' dismay and open frustration, a King County grand jury returned an indictment of his three board members and of one former Rosellini appointee, Garland Sponburgh. The four appeared in Superior Court to plead "not guilty" to what Leroy Hittle called "ridiculous" criminal charges of "grand larceny and fraudulent appropriation of alcoholic beverages."

The charges grew from the state auditor's claim—picked up eagerly by the Democratic prosecutor of King County—that the LCB could not account for thousands of bottles of liquor that had passed through the state warehouse. Accounting for them was indeed a matter of some delicacy. The bottles in question—it became a sensational question—had cost the state nothing. Many were bottles not commonly stocked in state stores but they had in fact been in the warehouse, shipped by distilleries to their sales representatives for their own "sales" purposes and to members of the Board for a determination of their salability through a routine of sampling and testing. The focus of public attention fell naturally upon the LCB executives, whose immediate comments could not have pleased the governor. Jack Hood, the chairman, said curtly that the bottles withdrawn by Board members—a practice since 1934—were simply "samples" and that what individual Board members did with them was "nobody's business." (According to newsmen curious about such matters, what individual members had often done with many of them, through a long-standing courtesy, was to bring them to rest in the governor's mansion, where—except during the twelve years under Arthur Langlie, a

devout dry—they had helped control the costs of official entertainments.)
Don Eldridge offered that the bottles were for "tasting."[31]

Thus the "straight-arrow" image of the Evans administration became
the target of easy sarcasms, and what might have been dismissed as a
frivolous matter became an ordeal of painful proportions. After a King
County Superior Court judge dismissed the case as improperly prepared
and presented, the prosecutor won a request that he be permitted to share
with the newspapers the evidence he had intended to use during the trial.
LCB members then appealed what they called this "trial in the streets"
that would give them no opportunity for a properly sworn defense. The
Supreme Court ultimately ruled for them, saying that the evidence could
not be made public, but then saying that it could go to the governor, the
attorney general, and the Thurston County prosecutor. When after a while
none of these parties seemed interested, Attorney General Slade Gorton
seemed happy to announce that the whole affair had ended.

Instead, it became even more nasty. In 1976, the auditor issued a new
report in which he claimed again that the LCB members named earlier
should still be called to account for quantities of liquor which they had
withdrawn from the state warehouse. Attorney General Gorton then found
himself threatened with charges of malfeasance if he refused to act. (The
threat was from Karl Herrmann, a Democratic holdover from the Rossel-
lini era who was still attacking Republicans from his position as state
insurance commissioner.) Gorton finally filed a civil suit against the
Board members, seeking recovery of costs ($2,933 in booze, $945
in "collectors" bottles), plus penalties, of the liquor that was allegedly
missing.

The allegation was based upon an untested axiom—that warehoused
booze, whatever its source or purpose, by state law immediately became
state property; thus the Board members, in withdrawing it without paying
for it, had taken state property for personal use. The logic impressed the
Superior Court judge as impossibly specious, and he had harshly critical
words for Gorton when the court dismissed the case in 1979. Gorton
appealed this dismissal to the Supreme Court, where his defeat in 1980
was even more humiliating—a 9-0 decision against him.

All the while, Hittle, Eldridge, Hood, and Sponburgh sustained a remarkable stoicism. There was never any great editorial or political outcry
against them. The newspapers waited, Evans often expressed his confidence, and the state Senate, when Hittle's second nine-year term came

up for debate in 1976, gave him lavish praises for integrity and a 44-0 vote for confirmation. In 1981 the legislature, reminded of the ten years' litigation, reimbursed the accused for expenses "incurred in the defense of court actions brought against them while performing their duties as members of the state liquor board." They each received about $15,000, the out-of-pocket cost of an episode that finally revealed less about the nature of liquor control than it did about the constant vulnerability of LCB members—even the best of them—to political mugging.[32]

17

The Ineffable Saloon

DURING the critical years following repeal, the success of the new liquor laws would almost surely depend upon the character of public drinking, which in turn would most surely depend upon the character of a new institutional arrangement, the beer-wine tavern. In what now seems an odd conception, Alfred Schweppe, in his draft of the first liquor control law for Governor Martin, had not used the word *tavern* or proposed anything resembling it; in his view of post-repeal, beer would be sold by the glass only in restaurants, drug stores, and soda fountains. But as it took shape in the Steele Act, despite the syntax of lobbyists and committees, the tavern was defined as an "accommodation for sale by the glass and for consumption on the premises of beer." (The wine would come later.) With this legitimacy, taverns became the place where drinkers came to drink—loggers with their boots, fishermen with their aprons, sawyers with their frayed nerves—to lift a glass and laugh and tell stories and raise their voices in expectation of at least some slight freedom from middle class proprieties. If the old-time saloon had a legacy, it fell here upon the 6,470 taverns which by 1938 were licensed to do business.[1]

And Admiral Luther E. Gregory, United States Navy, Retired, chairman of the Liquor Control Board, was there to make sure that it fell very lightly. Determined to halt the lawlessness and "rowdyism" that wildcatters had brought upon the state, Gregory was perhaps the right man for the times. He was described as an executive of heroic integrity, of obvious command presence, a man forever ready to sustain the hard-eyed vigilance necessary to regulate away any ambiguous signal that the saloon might be born again. Because he was impatient with rogues or fools and sometimes with newspaper reporters and legislators, he impressed people as both arrogant and self-righteous. And, as befitted his earlier career, he was stern, confrontational, and relentlessly militant. Indeed, it was he who demanded that the Washington State Administrative Codes for Liquor

Control be cast, from the very beginning, in phrases that in both tone and diction suggest the strictures of Naval law and of The Articles of War.[2]

Taverns would close at 1 A.M.—earlier if a concerned town or city council so requested, and many did. There would be no service to minors or Indians or any "disorderly, boisterous, or intoxicated person." Tavern owners were not to allow any "profane or vulgar language" or any conduct that was in any way "indecent." No advertising sign or poster in the tavern would be "of an obnoxious, gaudy, blatant or offensive nature."[3]

Even in the late 1940's these and many other regulations were sternly enforced. Tavern owners posted notices pleading "No Credit" and "No Checks Cashed" and "Our License Depends on Your Good Behavior." The interiors of the taverns had to be visible from the streets outside. It was against the law for a customer to drink while standing or for a barkeeper to serve a customer who was not seated at the bar or a table. There could be no booths, and the height of partitions separating tables was restricted to a maximum of 42 inches. The LCB inspector—upon whose word a license could be suddenly revoked—took a stubbornly Puritanical view of violence or gambling, or of the presence of drunks or prostitutes. There was no hard liquor, no free food, no drinks on-the-house, no happy hours of reduced prices. Just as the 3.2 beer from the new barrels was but an impersonal echo of the old-time stuff of 8 or 10 per cent, so the new tavern was but a meek and emasculated version of the "hell-soaked institution."

Even when the 1948 Initiative Measure authorized the LCB to license restaurants for liquor by the drink, the same ghost of the saloon haunted—or confused—the regulators. Unlike taverns, the interiors of the new "rooms" could *not* be visible from the street. But, as in taverns, drinkers were not allowed to stand while drinking, nor were they allowed to carry their drinks from bar to table or from one table to another. Women might be seated at tables but not at the bar. There was no service after midnight and none at all on Sundays.

Given these bewildering constraints, many a sullen drinker might have abandoned the room or the tavern in disgust or disappointment. Yearning for a drink, or even two, in an atmosphere in which relaxed drinking might be possible, he might have resorted finally to what the antisaloon state apparently expected—drinking in his own home.

In search of a bottle, then, he might have traveled several miles to one of the few state liquor stores in his city, not easy to find when there was no ready sign or signal of identity and when the hours of service were set from noon to 8 P.M., with nothing, of course, on Sunday. If he found one, he might have stood in line for a while to approach what appeared for all the world to be a bank teller's cage and high counter that separated him from the bottles beyond. There he had to present his individual liquor-purchase permit (renewed annually for a fee) to the scrutiny of a languidly indifferent beneficiary of patronage or cronyism who, schooled in proce-dures of primitive antisaloon salesmanship, would have suppressed any suggestion of enthusiasm for either sales or merchandise.

The clerk would not have advised a customer regarding the merits of various brands or even genres. He would probably not even have informed the customer about what brands the store carried. (Printed lists were available—back at the end of the line.) He might have quoted a price, one which seemed calculated to punish the drinker for his folly while returning to the state each year a more and more ruthless pirate's profit. (The markup on hard liquor had risen in 1949 to 49.5 per cent, which, added to state and federal taxes, made the prices of some of the most popular items the highest in the nation.) If the customer somehow named a brand and a bottle size, the clerk, pen in hand, on the state forms printed for this purpose, recorded the code numbers for this information along with the price and the number of the customer's permit. He re-quired the customer to sign this form, which was presumably to be kept forever in the state archives. After taking the customer's money, the clerk began his search for the bottle, which, if he found, he placed in a brown paper bag of a shape and texture that everyone in the state could identify. He finally presented this bag to the customer.

We have noted that people new to the state after World War II were in-creasingly impatient with provincialisms, especially those designed to abridge or even to insult historic individual dignities that somehow, his-torically, had become mixed up with the enduring determination to pro-tect families, churches, and governments from an institution that had disappeared from the state in 1916. The LCB and the legislature, caught at times between the impatience and the older determination, have struggled into compromises that—with the exception of rising profits—have a surprisingly straight-lined chronology. They begin to move clearly in 1948, when the Initiative Measure 171 required the LCB to license the sale of liquor by the drink. As the Class H licenses began to change the system, so, as we have noted, the public mood was changing across the state and in Olympia. In 1956, the town of Albion, the last municipality to hold out against public consumption, finally, by local option, allowed a tavern for the farm hands of Whitman County. After 1958, the LCB allowed taverns and barrooms to stay open until 2 A.M. In 1959, persons buying bottles in state stores no longer needed to present individual permits. In 1960, the word *cocktail* could be used in advertising. Initiative Measure 229 in 1966 and LCB action in 1970 ended Sunday Closure.

During the next few years, legislators and the LCB—then happy to assist the "hospitality industry"—eliminated much of the dry area around the campus of the University of Washington. They also allowed women to sit at bars, where, if they chose, drinkers could also stand with drinks in-hand or even walk about from table to table. They removed wines from the state monopoly and repealed the prohibition of sales on election days. They permitted the sale of beer in professional sports arenas, and they erased the law requiring tavern interiors to be visible from the street. They allowed liquor in state parks and permitted liquor advertising in college newspapers.

During the 1970s all Sunday restrictions were gone, the food/booze ratio dropped to 40/60, and the University of Washington Faculty Club was allowed its own barroom. In 1980, the tourist-directed "western" barrooms in the city of Winthrop became the first since 1915 to be allowed to use the word *saloon*.

At that moment, more than half a century removed from the society that had so feared the saloon, the old connotations of the word were almost beyond public memory. And the LCB, more eager to please than to displease, would sustain but few gestures of its original purpose. When the awkward occasion arose in the early 1980's, it adopted a rule already enforced in California and approved by the United States Supreme Court that in taverns and barrooms the breasts of all employees except entertainers must be covered. Like California, the LCB ruled that such "topless" entertainers must perform at a distance of at least six feet from the customers. And keenly aware that all of its decisions were then subject to being declared "arbitrary" in judicial review, the LCB dropped its proscription against entertainers using profane language.

There were other ironies: in 1983, when 8 per cent beer was legal again and Indians could sell whiskey to whites, the LCB agreed to allow its stores to sell state lottery tickets—i.e., to "merchandize" gambling just as with their specialty tables and special sales the self-service stores "merchandized" drinking. In 1984, the LCB allowed itself to take into consideration "special circumstances" (such as festivals, conventions, meetings) when enforcing the 40/60 food/booze ratio. In 1986 the governor, in the presence of a "hospitality industry" lobbyist, signed a bill authorizing LCB to license hotels to sell not only liquor by the drink, but—in the context of "room service"—liquor by the bottle. By this time, few people in the state could have explained why restaurants should ever have had a food/booze ratio or why hotels had ever been prohibited from selling bottles.[4]

Thus a tableau after half a century of movement: in 1986, the public drinker, male or female, charging drinks with a credit card, his or her pockets stuffed with lottery tickets purchased at a state liquor agency operated by Indians, could stand, sit, or move around the barroom without restraint, amused, perhaps, by the breasts swaying with breath-taking regard for the six-foot rule and by the gratuitously bawdy language of the entertainers. In 1916, most people believed that forbidding such comportment was the most important issue before state government. In 1936, most people thought it was at least very important. But by 1986 many people apparently felt that it would be absurd to suppose—so long as they involved only the personal choices of freely consenting adults—that the state government should intrude in these matters at all.

This is not to suggest that the saloon had finally returned. The barkeeper in 1986 was not the debt-slave of a brewery, hounded by competition to hustle customers so he could pay his bills. To protect his license, and, increasingly, his liability insurance, he had a clear economic interst in *not* being a part of a drunkard-making business that in earlier times had in raw, anxiety-ridden towns pushed thousands of drunks out onto the streets. The barroom in 1986 was hardly ever the exclusively masculine "putrid fester spot" (in the words of the Grange Master) where lonely, transient men crowded to the bar eager to blur the memory of a day's brutal labor. It was not the place where the drunken fight was a nightly occurrence. It was a place where the real drunks were few, and where even these few need not expect to be "rolled" or murdered. Prostitution was seldom a vital adjunct—and if it were, the LCB would probably hear about it. The new barroom was to be the natural environment of the conspicuously sophisticated and disciplined middle class, not of the whore, the tramp, or the criminal.

Then nearly three-quarters of a century beyond 1916, it seemed unlikely that even without Prohibition or the Liquor Board the saloon could have survived much longer than it did. Social change in the state and nation would soon deny it the sources of its strength (a Victorian sort of masculine fellowship, a Victorian sort of welfare, casual information, neighborhood entertainment) as well as the sources of its corruption (public drunkenness, general debauchery, paid political favoritism). Very soon after 1916, the armies of transients that had moved across the mountains, building railroads and factories and cities, would diminish, and the polite community of families on what had been a social frontier would feel more and more secure. Soon people in the new state would see themselves as members of a mature, national community in which the function of automobiles, suburbs, telephones, radios, movies, motels, television, and exalted individualism had virtually displaced the function—and destroyed the threat—of the saloon. For the personal and political relationships necessary in the world of the late twentieth century, the saloon could serve no vital individual, economic, sexual, political, or social purpose. It has been disestablished, not only by law but by assembly lines and electronics and new definitions of individual and family life.[5]

When this was the new social reality, why then did voters in the state still tolerate the infringements on personal liberty implicit in the antisaloon purport of the Washington State liquor laws and the state monopoly? The idea had been around for some time that the people should *not* tolerate them. In 1960, Initiative Measure 205, aimed straight at the antisaloon codes by proposing that taverns be allowed to sell "spirituous liquors, including mixed drinks." The Washington State Licensed Beverage Association advertised it as a way to "increase state revenue without additional individual tax burdens." Standing against it in the official Voters' Guide, the Alcohol Problems Association, the Citizens Committee for Moderation, and the minister of the Plymouth Congregational Church of Seattle presented the appearance of utter weakness, but the "hospitality industry" knew where to find its friends. The measure failed dramatically, 357,445 for but 799,643 against. The next effort, Initiative Measure 261, which was on the ballot in 1972, aimed directly at the monopoly itself by proposing the sale of hard liquor in grocery stores. It was sponsored by the "Citizens Against Liquor Monopoly," who wanted to "bring an end to the state abuse of the monopolistic liquor system" and who hoped to gain momentum from the growing public resentment, even outrage, over the legislature's determination to take all it could get from liquor prices and taxes. The markup of 49.9 per cent on hard liquor, plus a 15 per cent liquor sales tax, plus a 4-cent per ounce special tax (only recently up from 2 cents) was again provoking cries against the nation's highest prices. When an effort by some legislators to lower prices had failed in Olympia, even Alfred Schweppe, author of the Steele Act, had indicated that he might favor an end to the monopoly.[6] But the measure failed, 634,973 for, but 779, 568 against.

In 1974, Initiative Measure 290 proposed to reduce the price of a fifth of hard liquor by an average of 52 cents, but it failed to attract enough signatures to place it on the ballot. Then Initiative Measure 332, which would have removed the state from the liquor business entirely in 1976—and similar measures in 1980 and 1982—failed for the same reason.

TABLE 17

POST-REPEAL ISSUES AT THE POLLS*

Number	Provision (Date)	For	Against
148	Abolish LCB, establish new liquor commission, new regulations (1940)	No signatures	
150	Liquor by the drink (1942)	No signatures	
165	Liquor by the drink (1946)	Insufficient signatures	
13 (to the legislature)	Sale of beer and wine in state stores only (1948)	208,337	602,141
171	Liquor by the drink with certain restrictions (1948)	416,277	373,418
205	Taverns to hold spirituous liquor licenses (1960)	357,455	799,643
261	Abolish state monopoly (1972)	634,973	779,568
326	Grocery stores to hold retail liquor licenses (1976)	No signatures	
332	Abolish state monopoly (1976)	No signatures	
366	Abolish state monopoly (1980)	No signatures	
390	Abolish state monopoly (1980)	No signatures	
78 (to the legislature)	Abolish state monopoly (1982)	No signatures	
487	Abolish state monopoly (1986)	No signatures	

*From a list by Jean Womer, Office of Secretary of State Ralph Munro, Olympia, 1986. A total of 42 initiative measures have been filed since 1933, of which 38 did not reach the ballot because of no signatures or insufficient signatures.

Although they obviously found it difficult to hold an audience, those who sponsored these most recent efforts were reluctant to retreat. John Spellman, in 1981 the newly elected Republican governor and a politician again uncomfortable with the state-owned enterprises, asked his Director of Financial Management to investigate "The Desirability of Continuing Retail Liquor Sales by State Government." A report with that title reached the governor in 1983. It advised him, first of all, of evidence available to the director indicating that a return to free enterprise would "stimulate" consumption, a development most people would not find "desirable." More urgently, the governor was asked to consider that the state system, with its 368 stores, had in 1981 delivered over $125 million in profits and taxes. An open-market system, the director conjectured, would probably deliver 22 per cent less, i.e., produce about a $27 million shortfall in state revenues. Spellman found this discomforting. Already acutely embarrassed because he had broken a major campaign promise by asking the legislature to raise taxes, he accepted the report's conclusion that, all in all, there were real advantages to "retail sales of liquor by the state government."[7]

Most editorial opinion and most voters supported this conclusion. When in 1986 the "Committee for Sensible Liquor Reform" presented Initiative Measure 487, proposing again to give the retail liquor business to large grocery stores, voters again defeated the proposal by refusing to sign the necessary petitions.

As their efforts continued to fail so regularly, the entrepreneurs who so coveted LCB profits were opposed by the "hospitality industry" with its claim that the measure would deprive state government of revenues vital to its essential functions. It was certainly true that the voting public had been grateful for revenues the monopoly delivered to state and local treasuries. But not since the Great Depression have LCB profits alone been reason enough to overcome serious free-market objections—if there have been any—to the enduring presence of a state-owned business. Loss of LCB profits would have created an inconvenient budgetary problem, not a budgetary disaster. In any philosophical confrontation, not even the most diffident legislator could accept the argument that an amount of money representing only 0.6 per cent of the state's General Fund (the state's share of LCB profits in 1985 was $23.5 million) could justify sustaining a conspicuous monument to state socialism. The total LCB profits that year of $47 million (combining distributions to state, city, and county governments) were but a fraction of the $202 million dropped into General Fund revenues by the state lottery and only 1.0 percent of the $4,081,954,000 total of Department of Revenue collections.

Far more significant than profit per se has been the transcendental aggregate of marginal profit linked with a vital social discipline. What the record must indicate is that the voting public has found an enduring satisfaction and security in the LCB's controlling and regulating circumstances that, were there no Steele Act, might have presented unacceptable potentials for social distress. Since 1934, when it was clear that the people of the state wanted neither the saloon nor prohibition, the Steele Act has defended major tenets of an antisaloon heritage while allowing the legislature to adjust these tenets to meet the newer anxieties of the late twentieth century. The record has indeed been impressive. Washington is among the eighteen states that after Repeal adopted programs of monopoly and strict control and have steadfastly refused to abandon them. This refusal has been a remarkable demonstration of confidence in a state agency that for fifty years has been at considerable risk of abusing its considerable powers but has nevertheless functioned effectively in open rebuke of the free enterprise system.

Appendix

THE historical significance of liquor revenues to state budgets defies precise statistical summary. What one would like to know, simply, is to what extent balancing the budget has depended upon revenues realized from the sale of alcoholic beverages. But comparing LCB profits and tax collections to other sources of revenue is a slippery business: the bases shift, the rates slide, the state's share of LCB profits moves with the political winds. The profits enter the state's General Fund, but the component sources of revenue that made up the General Fund in 1936 do not compare well with those in 1986. The data here and in chapters 16 and 17 come from the state budgets printed in the *Session Laws of the State of Washington*, from the *Message of Clarence D. Martin, Governor of Washington, to the Legislature, January 11, 1939*, from the annual reports of the state Office of Financial Management, the Department of Revenue, the State Auditor, from OFM's *Washington Data Book, 1985*, from Revenue's *1985 Tax Statistics*, and from data prepared by the present WSLCB controller, James E. Hoing.

TABLE A

PROFIT ON MONOPOLY STORE SALES
LCB MARKUP (% OF COST) AND DISTRIBUTION OF PROFIT, SELECTED YEARS

Fiscal Year	Hard Spirits %	Dry Wine %	Sweet Wine %	Whiskey Price	Profit ($ million) To state	(To counties and cities)
1935	25	25	25	$4.20	0.8	0.8
1937	35	35	53	$3.60	3.2	1.4
1938	40	40	53	$3.60	1.7	1.7
1940	45	45	53	$4.20	1.8	3.4
1941	40	40	53	$4.74	2.3	4.2
1949	49.5	58	71	$5.58	6.0	7.0

TABLE A (continued)

Fiscal Year	Hard Spirits %	Dry Wine %	Sweet Wine %	Whiskey Price	Profit ($ million) To state	Profit ($ million) (To counties and cities)
1951	45	53.6	66.3	$5.58	8.5	8.5
1959	45.9	53.6	66.3	$6.75	9.7	9.7
1972	45.9	53.6	53.6	$8.10	15.7	15.7
1973	45.9	45.9	45.9	$8.10	14.9	14.9
1982	45.9	60	60	$10.65	28.0	28.0
1985	39.2	50	50	$11.05	23.5	23.5

The "whiskey price" above includes markup, with state and federal taxes, on a quart, then fifth-gallon, then 0.75 liter size of Seagram's V. O. Canadian, the only item of hard liquor to remain in the state inventory for fifty years. From the modest markup of 25 per cent—calculated only to drive bootleggers out of business—the first increase in profit (1937) was designed to give local fruit and berry wines, none of which were sold in monopoly stores, a protected market. But the legislatures soon realized (1937, 1938, 1940) what state liquor stores could do for depression budgets. In 1941, the federal tax on beverage alcohol jumped from $3 to $4 a proof gallon, and the drop in LCB markup shown for that year was an effort to hold prices at their 1940 level. Such principles faced overwhelming temptations. In 1943 the legislature was pleased to impose a 10 per cent "war tax" (see Table B below), which had become a humorless euphemism by 1949 when the legislature dropped the tax but not the revenue by simply increasing the markup on both spirits and wines. When in 1951 the federal tax moved up from $9 to $10.50 a proof gallon, the state adjusted the markup slightly downward, but at the same time it pushed the tax on LCB sales up to 10 per cent (Table B).

In 1959 the legislature abolished the requirement that each customer purchase an annual permit—and then used this action to justify increasing both the markup and the liquor sales tax. The next session of the legislature (1961) discovered how the fluid-ounce tax could help balance the state budget (Table B). By 1972, protecting local sweet wines was a lost cause (most of the wineries had disappeared), and thereafter all wines bore an equal burden of markup. In 1982 that burden increased, and this was also a year of two tax increases (Table B). The apparent downward revision of markup on spirits in 1985 was actually an accounting adjustment that for the first time included the operational cost of the state liquor stores (salaries, rent, supplies) in the markup base, which before had been simply the cost of the beverage at delivery. The adjustment did not change profits. The adjusted markup on wines was a decision that the prices of wine should be more competitive with those of hard liquor.

One might wish to compare these matters with those in other monopoly states, but the results are not often satisfying. For example, Oregon in 1985 had a monopoly markup of 99 per cent on a base that included the cost at delivery but no operational expenses, and the state stores collected no sales taxes on liquor or wine; the cost of a bottle of Seagram's V.O. was $11.05.

The drop in actual profits recorded since 1982 (and recorded also in Oregon) has been attributed in various measures to the economic recession of the early 1980's, to the higher prices caused by rising federal liquor taxes, to a shift in consumer preferences toward lower-priced items, especially light wines and lower-proof vodkas, and to more severe penalties for driving while intoxicated. However, the reasons why Americans should decide in any year, or in any short cycle of years, to drink more or to drink less or to drink different beverages are more open to speculations than to convincing explanations.

TABLE B

State Tax on WSLCB Store Sales and Annual Tax Yield to the State General Fund, Selected Years ($ million)

Fiscal Year	Spirits	Wine	Tax Revenue to General Fund
1935	10%	10%	$0.374
1939	10% + 2%	10% + 2%	1.5
1941	10% + 3%	10% + 3%	2.3
1943	10% + 3% + 10%	10% + 3% + 10%	5.9
1949	3%	3%	5.2
1951	10%	10%	1.5
1959	15%	15%	5.01
1961	15% + 1.1¢/oz.	15%	7.9
1965	15% + 2¢/oz.	15%	14.4
1969	15% + 2¢/oz.	26%	25.4
1971	15% + 4¢/oz.	26%	27.7
1973	15% + 4¢/oz.	75¢/gal. + 4.5%	42.01
1981	15% + $1.72/liter	5.5% + $0.2025/liter	63.6
1982	15.6% + $1.788/liter	5.5% + $0.2106/liter	
	17.1% + $1.9608/liter	5.5% + $0.2167/liter	72.7
1984	17.1% + $1.9608/liter	5.5% + $0.2167/liter	77.3
1985	17.1% + $1.9608/liter	6.5% + $0.2167/liter	74.4

The State Revenue Act of 1935 introduced a tax of 2 per cent on most retail sales. At the time, however, these did not include LCB sales, for which the legislature fixed a discreet 10 per cent "liquor sales tax." This distinction allowed the legislature to impose the general retail sales tax in addition to the "liquor sales tax" during the 1937 session. The retail sales tax climbed to 3 per cent in 1941. During World War II the legislature imposed a discreet 10 per cent "war tax" on top of all other taxes, a tax that endured until 1949, when lawmakers removed all taxes on LCB sales except the general retail sales tax of 3 per cent. However, it sustained revenues by simply increasing the markups (Table A). In 1951 the legislature released the LCB from the general retail sales tax, but it found new merit then in the old 10 per cent "liquor sales tax" and reimposed it. This tax was increased to 15 per cent by 1959.

The legislature then discovered the concept of a fluid-ounce tax for distilled spirits and set this new tax at $0.011 for 1962, then at $0.02 for 1965, then $0.04 for 1971. Drawing leverage from the California Wine Bill (see Chapter 16), the legislature in 1969 increased the wine tax from 15 to 26 per cent. This increase worked a real hardship on the newer but more expensive Washington table wines just then entering the competition with California, and the legislature obliged domestic wineries by replacing the ad valorem tax with a $0.75 gallon tax to make the more expensive wines more attractive. But at the same time the legislature again added the general retail sales tax to wine, set that year at 4.5 per cent.

In 1981 the legislature went metric, changing the tax on spirits to $1.72 per liter and on wine to $0.2025 per liter. That year the retail sales tax, applicable to wine, rose to 5.5 per cent. In 1982–the year Governor Spellman had to call the legislature into special session to raise revenue—lawmakers hit all state taxes on liquor and wine with a 4 per cent surcharge in May, then in August increased this surcharge to 14 per cent on spirits and to 7 per cent on wines. In 1985 the retail sales tax rose to 6.5 per cent. Table B does not reveal how very useful the per-ounce/per-liter tax proved to be: by 1985, the liter taxes brought in 73 per cent of the total liquor-tax revenues.

TABLE C

LIQUOR REVENUES AND THE STATE GENERAL FUND, RECENT PERIODS *($ million)*

Biennium	Total G.F. Revenues	LCB profits (not including license fees) to the G.F. shown as percentage of G.F. revenue	Liquor taxes to the G.F. shown as percentage of total G.F. revenues
1963–65	1,018	$22.1 million (2%)	$27.5 million (3%)
1965–67	1,322	25.8 (2%)	44.1 (3%)
1967–69	1,685	29.9 (1.7%)	49.1 (3%)
1969–71	2,214	29.4 (1.4%)	54.1 (3%)
1971–73	2,414	30.5 (1.3%)	81.7 (3%)
1973–75	3,131	37.2 (1.2%)	89.8 (3%)
1975–77	4,296	39.1 (0.9%)	99.3 (2%)
1977–79	5,618	45.0 (0.8%)	112.3 (2%)
1979–81	6,864	47.7 (0.7%)	124.1 (2%)
1981–83	8,299	53.5 (0.6%)	150.8 (1.8%)
1983–85	9,913	46.5 (0.5%)	151.7 (1.6%)

The state's General Fund receives revenues from most taxes, fees, profits, and grants. Although it is but one of several funds used in state bookkeeping, it is the fund from which most appropriations are made and is thus central to most state finance. If not comprehensive, it is nevertheless the best single indicator of state revenues. But as state accounting procedures change, so do the sources of revenue that are channeled into the General Fund change, and there are irregular episodes of transfers, shifts, delayed payments, and long or short fiscal years.

Revenue recently moored to the General Fund ledger include state lottery profits of over $200 million a year and, from another fund, tuition money from state colleges and universities. Federal grants to the General Fund in the 1980's ranged from about 16 to about 20 per cent of total revenues. LCB contributions to the General Fund since 1963 have been 50 per cent of liquor store profits (the other 50 per cent going to counties and cities), plus taxes and license fees. Considering the many difficulties in historical coherence, it may be that all one can conclude about Table C is that a return to prohibition would cause unusual anxiety in legislative finance committees. But the table is useful also in arguing a hypothesis suggested in Chapter 17: that since the Depression, liquor profits alone have not been impressive enough as a source of revenue to paralyze political philosophy. Were the state suddenly to be overcome with a total devotion to the doctrines of free-market capitalism (a possibility even more remote than a return to prohibition), there need be no loss of tax revenues, and the transfer of liquor profits from the General Fund to private enterprise would mean a loss of what the Office of Financial Management itself calls a "minor revenue source." While it is true that financial officers find the LCB useful in balancing complex budgets, the enduring vitality of the LCB must spring more from its antisaloon heritage of strict control than from the "minor revenues" of its biennial profits.

Notes

CHAPTER 1

1. Meriwether Lewis, *The Lewis and Clark Expedition*, 1814 edition, ed. Archibald Hanna (Keystone Western Americana ed.; New York, 1961), II, 534-35.

2. Edwin M. Lemert, *Alcohol and the Northwest Coast Indians* (University of California Publications in Culture and Society, Vol. 2, No. 6, Berkeley, 1954), p. 305. Dorothy Johansen and Charles M. Gates, *Empire of the Columbia: A History of the Pacific Northwest* (New York, 1957).

3. Samuel Eliot Morison, *The Maritime History of Massachusetts, 1783-1860* (Boston, 1941), p. 57. Erna Gunther has noted that "There was considerable argument between the early traders whether to give the Indians guns or intoxicating drink." Erna Gunther, "A Re-evaluation of the Cultural Position of the Nootka," *Selected Papers of the First International Congress of Anthropological and Ethnological Sciences* (Philadelphia, 1956), p. 271.

4. Paul C. Phillips, "The Fur Trade in the Northwest," in William S. Lewis and Paul C. Phillips (ed.), *The Journal of John Work* (Cleveland, Ohio, 1923), p. 42.

5. Gabriel Franchère, *Narrative of a Voyage to the Northwest Coast in the Years 1811, 1812, 1813, and 1814*, ed. Reuben G. Thwaites (Cleveland, 1904), in Charles M. Gates (ed.), *Readings in Pacific Northwest History* (Seattle, Wash., 1941), p. 30.

6. Ross Cox, *The Columbia River*, ed. Edgar I. Stewart and Jane R. Stewart (Norman, Okla., 1957), p. 173.

7. Frederick Merk (ed.), *Fur Trade and Empire: George Simpson's Journal, 1824-1825* (Cambridge, Mass., 1931), p. 109.

8. Lemert, *Alcohol and the Northwest Coast Indians*, p. 325; Cox, *The Columbia River*, p. 173; Ruth Benedict, *Patterns of Culture* (New York, 1949); Ruth Underhill, *Indians of the Pacific Northwest* (Riverside, Calif., 1945); Philip Drucker, *Indians of the Northwest Coast* (New York, 1955).

9. Herbert C. Taylor, "Aboriginal Population Estimates for the Lower Northwest Coast," *Pacific Northwest Quarterly*, LIV (October, 1963), 158-64.

10. Lemert, *Alcohol and the Northwest Coast Indians*, p. 330. Lemert recorded this and translated it in his field work.

11. *Ibid.*, pp. 310-11. This excess has been attributed, in part at least, to the value placed on ecstatic experience in the original culture of the Indians, whose religious experience was strongly mystical. "Temporary loss of sanity or physical control would appeal subconsciously as a desirable end rather than as a condition against which will power should fight." G. A. Pettitt, *The Quilieute of La Push, 1775-1945* (Berkeley, Calif., 1950), p. 76. Quoted in Lemert, p. 353.

12. Lemert, *Alcohol and the Northwest Coast Indians*, p. 345. While Lemert's study is concerned primarily with the Indians of Vancouver Island, his conclusions have considerable validity for all of the Northwest Coast aborigines, whose societies had a high degree of cultural unity. Lemert writes at one point (p. 349) : "So far as it is possible to generalize for the whole cultural area of the Northwest coast, it is probably correct to say that in ordinary social situations sober persons avoided aggressive behavior and had a strong feeling against violence in interpersonal interaction. In consonance with this ethic of nonaggression in personal behavior, the cultures of this area had few or no formal mechanisms for using force to deal with nonconformists, and no methods of penalizing them. Ridicule, anecdotal gossip, and occasional direct reprimands from high-ranking persons were some of the controls directed at deviants. . . . However, where drunkenness . . . was an issue, such controls were apt to have a hollow ring. . . ."

13. William Todd (a Hudson's Bay Company employee) to Edward Ermatinger, July, 1829. Published in "Documents," *Washington Historical Quarterly*, I (July, 1907), 256-58.

14. *Minutes of Council Northern Department of Rupert Land, 1821-31*, ed. R. Harvey Fleming (Toronto, 1940), pp. 309-10.

15. Merk (ed.), *Fur Trade and Empire*, pp. xx, 110; *Minutes of Council*, p. 349.

16. Merk (ed.), *Fur Trade and Empire*, p. 110.

17. E. E. Rich (ed.), *Part of Dispatch from George Simpson, Esqr., Governor of Rupert's Land To the Governor & Committee of the Hudson's Bay Company London, 1829* (Toronto, 1947), p. 80.

18. Phillips, "The Fur Trade in the Northwest," p. 42; Burt Brown Barker (ed.), *The Letters of Dr. John McLoughlin Written at Ft. Vancouver, 1829-1832* (Portland, Ore., 1948), p. 216.

19. E. E. Rich (ed.), *The Letters of John McLoughlin From Ft. Van-*

couver to the Governor and Committee First Series, 1825-1838 (London, 1941), lxxxvii.

20. Barker (ed.), The Letters of Dr. John McLoughlin, p. 291; Merk (ed.), Fur Trade and Empire, p. 17.

21. Thomas E. Jessett (ed.), Reports and Letters of Herbert Beaver (Portland, Ore., 1959), p. 17.

22. John Allen Krout, The Origins of Prohibition (New York, 1925), pp. 66, 104, 108, 125-56.

23. "The Diary of Jason Lee," Oregon Historical Quarterly, XVII (1916), 113, 253.

24. Bernard DeVoto, Across the Wide Missouri (Cambridge, Mass., 1947), p. 79.

25. Hubert Howe Bancroft, History of Oregon (San Francisco, Calif., 1886), I, 66; "Diary of Jason Lee," p. 264.

26. Daniel Lee and J. H. Frost, Ten Years in Oregon (New York, 1844), pp. 140-41; Bancroft, Oregon, I, 97-99; John E. Caswell, "The Prohibition Movement in Oregon," Oregon Historical Quarterly, XXXIX (September, 1938), 235-61.

27. Clifford M. Drury (ed.), The Diaries and Letters of Henry H. Spalding and Asa Bowen Smith Relating to the Nez Perce Mission, 1838-1842 (Glendale, Calif., 1958), pp. 247-51.

28. Rich (ed.), The Letters of John McLoughlin, pp. 29, 72.

29. According to "Minutes of a Meeting of the Governor and Council of Rupert's Land, Red River Settlement, June 10, 1845," the English "fur traffickers" were forbidden to import liquor except for their own use. Quoted in James Edward Fitzgerald, An Examination of the Charter and Proceedings of the Hudson's Bay Company with Reference to the Grant of Vancouver's Island (London, 1849), p. 211; Rich (ed.), Letters, p. 183.

30. Lee and Frost, Ten Years in Oregon, p. 322; Bancroft, Oregon, I, 273.

31. Lee and Frost, Ten Years in Oregon, pp. 140-41; Cornelius J. Brosnan, Jason Lee, Prophet of the New Oregon (New York, 1932), p. 286.

32. Bancroft, Oregon, I, 196; Jesse Applegate, "Views of Oregon History" (1878 MS in the Bancroft Library); Sydney W. Moss, "Pictures of Pioneer Times at Oregon City" (1878 MS in the Bancroft Library), p. 3; Bancroft, Oregon, I, 263; Moss, "Pictures of Pioneer Times," p. 3; Caswell, "The Prohibition Movement in Oregon," p. 240.

33. Bancroft, Oregon, I, 281-82. Bancroft compliments White for his efforts to stop the liquor traffic among the Indians but considers him overzealous in his still-smashing activities.

34. *Ibid.*, I, 302.

35. E. E. Rich (ed.), *The Letters of John McLoughlin*, p. 242.

36. Caswell, "The Prohibition Movement in Oregon," p. 240.

37. The nearly perfect expression of this tone is Jason Lee's diary, which includes the poems written to him by his wife.

38. Joseph Watt, "First Things, Starting of the First Oregon Woolen Mills and First Direct Shipment of Oregon Wheat" (1878 MS in the Bancroft Library), pp. 10-11; Moss, "Pictures of Pioneer Times," p. 56; Watt, "First Things," p. 11; Elijah White, *A Concise View of Oregon Territory, Its Colonial and Indian Relations, Compiled from Official Letters and Reports, Together with the Organic Laws of the Colony* (Washington, D.C., 1846), p. 40.

39. White, *A Concise View of Oregon Territory*, p. 40; Watt, "First Things," p. 11.

40. Bancroft, *Oregon*, II, 37.

41. *Ibid.*, I, 537-38.

42. Moss, "Pictures of Pioneer Times," p. 55.

43. *Ibid.*, p. 56; Bancroft, *Oregon*, II, 37. There is some indication of the public reaction in "Correspondence of the Reverend Ezra Fish," *Oregon Historical Quarterly*, XVII (March, 1916), 49.

44. This is Moss's free translation of the song:

> Hallo! friend, give me some whiskey,
> I want whiskey, plenty of whiskey,
> Very thirsty; give me some whiskey.

Moss, "Pictures of Pioneer Times," p. 56; Bancroft, *Oregon*, II, 37.

45. Lemert, *Alcohol and the Northwest Coast Indians*, p. 310.

46. Bancroft, *Oregon*, II, 37.

47. Jesse Applegate, "Views of Oregon," pp. 41-42; Bancroft, *Oregon*, II, 37; Joseph Schaefer, "Jesse Applegate: Pioneer, Statesman, and Philosopher," *Washington Historical Quarterly*, I (July, 1907), 217-33.

CHAPTER 2

1. John E. Caswell, "The Prohibition Movement in Oregon," *Oregon Historical Quarterly*, XXXIX (September, 1938), 246.

2. Olympia *Pioneer and Democrat*, Dec. 30, 1854, Jan. 13, 1855.

3. Harvey K. Hines, *An Illustrated History of the State of Washington* (Chicago, Ill., 1893), p. 257; Wilfred J. Airey, "A History of the Constitution and Government of Washington Territory" (Ph.D. thesis, University of Washington, 1945), p. 265.

4. Steilacoom *Puget Sound Courier*, June 14, Sept. 7, Oct. 12, 1855.

5. Edmond S. Meany, *History of the State of Washington* (Revised

ed.; New York, 1946), pp. 163-64; Steilacoom *Puget Sound Courier,* Aug. 17, 1855; Jan. 4, 1856.

6. James G. Swan, *The Northwest Coast, or Three Years' Residence in Washington Territory* (New York, 1857), p. 347; Steilacoom *Washington Republican,* June 6, 12, 1857. Ezra Meeker also said that Stevens was an alcoholic: Ezra Meeker, *Pioneer Reminiscences of Puget Sound* (Seattle, Wash., 1905), p. 259.

7. Steilacoom *Puget Sound Courier,* Aug. 24, 1855.

8. Richard Oberländer, *Von Ozean zu Ozean* (Leipzig, 1884), p. 138; A. S. Mercer, *Washington Territory* (Seattle, Wash., 1865), p. 40; Steilacoom *Puget Sound Courier,* Sept. 14, 1855.

9. Theodore Winthrop, *Canoe and Saddle* (Portland, Ore., Nisqually Edition of the 1862 printing), p. 2.

10. Meeker, *Pioneer Reminiscences of Puget Sound,* pp. 42-78.

11. Robert C. Hill, "The Murder of Colonel Ebey," WPA Writers' Program, Washington State, *Told By The Pioneers,* II, 115-17.

12. Hubert Howe Bancroft, *History of Washington, Idaho, and Montana* (San Francisco, Calif., 1890), p. 237.

CHAPTER 3

1. George F. Cotterill Papers (MSS in the University of Washington Library), "A History of the International Order of Good Templars," dated 1920, probably written by Cotterill.

2. *Ibid.,* "Interview with George F. Cotterill."

3. Olympia *Washington Standard,* Nov. 30, 1867; Dec. 7, 1878.

4. John E. Caswell, "The Prohibition Movement in Oregon," *Oregon Historical Quarterly,* XXXIX (September, 1938), 235-61; Olympia *Washington Standard,* May 16, 1874.

5. Olympia *Washington Standard,* June 6, Aug. 13, 1874.

6. Murray Morgan, *Skid Road* (2nd ed.; New York, 1960), pp. 90-92; Robert C. Nesbit, *"He Built Seattle": A Biography of Judge Thomas Burke* (Seattle, Wash., 1961).

7. Dorothy O. Johansen and Charles M. Gates, *Empire of the Columbia: A History of the Pacific Northwest* (New York, 1957), p. 404.

8. Edmond S. Meany (ed.), "Washington's First Constitution, 1878, and Proceedings of the Convention" (Reprinted from the *Washington Historical Quarterly,* 1918-19).

9. Johansen and Gates, *Empire of the Columbia,* p. 406.

10. Lora E. Maxwell, "History of Liquor Legislation in the State of Washington" (Honors thesis, Washington State University, 1917), p. 8.

11. Olympia *Washington Standard,* Feb. 2, 1878; Jan. 4, June 20, 1879; July 8, 1881.

12. *Ibid.*, July 8, 1881.

13. Ernest H. Cherrington, *The Evolution of Prohibition in the United States of America* (Westerville, Ohio, 1920), p. 207; Maxwell, "History of Liquor Legislation in Washington," p. 10.

14. Charles M. Gates (ed.), *Messages of the Governors of the Territory of Washington to the Legislative Assembly, 1854-1889* (Seattle, Wash., 1940), pp. 242-43.

15. Seattle *Mirror*, Nov. 10, 1883; Jan. 19, 1884.

16. Meany, *History*, p. 270; Clarence B. Bagley, *History of Seattle from the Earliest Settlement to the Present Time* (Chicago, Ill., 1916), II, 487; *Laws of Washington* (1879), pp. 39-40.

17. Maxwell, "History of Liquor Legislation in Washington," p. 15. Miss Maxwell interviewed Mrs. Carrie M. Barr, president of the state WCTU.

18. *Session Laws, Washington Territory* (1885-86).

19. William Whitfield, *History of Snohomish County, Washington* (Chicago, Ill., 1926), I, 109; Lottie R. Roth, *History of Whatcom County* (Chicago, Ill., 1926), p. 400.

20. Seattle *Mirror*, Feb. 9, 1884.

21. Susan B. Anthony and Ida Husted Harper (ed.), *The History of Woman Suffrage* (Indianapolis, Ind., 1902), IV, 968; Adella M. Parker, "How Washington Women Lost the Ballot," in Linda Deziah Jennings (ed.), *Washington Women's Cook Book* (Seattle., Wash., 1909), p. 204.

22. *Ibid.*, p. 206; *Bloomer v. Todd* (1888), 3 Wash. Territory, p. 599.

23. Bagley, *History of Seattle*, II, 489.

24. Abigail Scott Duniway, *Pathbreaking: An Autobiographical History of Equal Suffrage Movement in Pacific Coast States* (Portland, Ore., 1914), pp. 193-97; Whitfield, *History of Snohomish County*, I, 111.

25. *Washington Territorial Reports*, III, 494. Quoted in Airey, "History of Constitution and Government of Washington Territory," p. 266.

CHAPTER 4

1. *Ballinger's Code* (1909), p. 1047.

2. Wenatchee *Daily World*, Jan. 27, 1909.

3. Olympia *Washington Standard*, June 8, 1888.

4. *Ibid.*; *Prohibition Party Campaign Book for the State of Washington, 1892* (Tacoma, Wash., 1892).

5. E. B. Sutton, *Prohibition Seed Thoughts or Thoughts Gone to Seed* (Seattle, Wash., 1893), pp. 1, 2, 3, 5, 69.

6. *1888 Statistical Report of the Secretary of the Territory of Washington* (Olympia, Wash., 1888), p. 8.

7. William Whitfield, *History of Snohomish County, Washington* (Chicago, Ill., 1926), I, 114.

8. Sutton, *Prohibition Seed Thoughts*, pp. 8, 9.

9. *Ibid.*, p. 10.

10. Charles M. Gates, forward to Beverly Paulik Rosenow (ed.), *The Journal of the Washington State Constitutional Convention, 1889* (Seattle, Wash., 1962), p. 879.

11. *Ibid.*, p. 637. The quotation is a summary of newspaper articles included in the analytical index of this book.

12. *Ibid.*, p. 882.

13. *Ibid.*, p. 881.

14. Olympia *Washington Standard*, July 28, 1889; see Harvey K. Hines, *An Illustrated History of the State of Washington* (Chicago, Ill., 1893); Herbert Hunt, *Washington, West of the Cascades* (Chicago, Ill., 1917); and Clarence B. Bagley, *History of Seattle from the Earliest Settlement to the Present Time* (Chicago, Ill., 1916).

15. Seattle *Leader*, August-October, 1889.

16. *Ibid.*

17. *Proceedings of the Washington State Grange* (1889), pp. 10-11. See also Harriet Ann Crawford, *The Washington State Grange* (Portland, Ore., 1940); Crawford, *Washington State Grange*, pp. 16-57. The Grange sent a questionnaire—quoted in Crawford—to each candidate.

18. Seattle *Leader*, Oct. 24, 1889; and Sutton, *Prohibition Seed Thoughts*, p. 10.

19. Adella M. Parker, "How Washington Women Lost the Ballott," in Linda Deziah Jennings (ed.), *Washington Women's Cook Book* (Seattle, Wash., 1909). See also C. H. Bailey, "How Washington Women Regained the Ballot," *Pacific Monthly*, XXVI (July, 1911), 1.

20. Sutton, *Prohibition Seed Thoughts*, p. 13; E. H. Cherrington (ed.), *Standard Encyclopedia of the Alcohol Problem* (Westerville, Ohio, 1924), VI, 2801.

21. Seattle *Leader*, Oct. 10, 1889.

22. Sutton, *Prohibition Seed Thoughts*, pp. 10, 16, 32, 58, 69.

23. *Ibid.*, p. 22.

24. Seattle *Leader*, March 13, 1890.

25. *Ibid.*, Oct. 10, 1889; Oct. 31, 1891.

26. *Proceedings of the Washington State Grange* (1891), pp. 23-25.

27. *Prohibition Party Campaign Book for the State of Washington, 1892.*

28. "Second Report of the Secretary of State," *State Documents* (1892), p. 329.

29. Sutton, *Prohibition Seed Thoughts*, p. 57.

30. Olympia *Washington Standard*, Aug. 19, 1892.

31. Austin Edward Griffiths, "Great Faith: Autobiography of an English Immigrant Boy in America, 1863-1950" (MS in the University of Washington Library), pp. 119-36.

32. Seattle *Post-Intelligencer*, Feb. 21, 1922.

CHAPTER 5

1. John Allen Krout, *The Origins of Prohibition* (New York, 1925), p. 14.

2. *The Liquor Problem: A Summary of Investigations Conducted by the Committee of Fifty, 1893-1903* (Boston, Mass., 1905), pp. 126-49.

3. Jim Marshall, *Swinging Doors* (Seattle, Wash., 1949), pp. 8, 14, 19, 167.

4. Spokane *Spokesman-Review*, Jan. 8, 1894; for a rhapsody on the national institution, see Andrew Sinclair, *Prohibition: The Era of Excess* (Boston, Mass., 1962), pp. 73-74.

5. E. H. Cherrington (ed.), *Standard Encyclopedia of the Alcohol Problem* (Westerville, Ohio, 1924), VI, 2800.

6. The industrial history by Stanley Baron, *Brewed in America* (Boston, Mass., 1962), discusses the importance of railroads to competition. Will Irwin, in "The Saloon—Past and Future," Portland *Oregonian*, Sept. 25 and Oct. 2, 1932, is more comprehensive as well as more caustic about the same relationship. The regional patterns of competition—and the nature of this competition—are revealed in depth in the papers of the Spokane Brewery and of the Galland-Burke Brewing and Malting Company of Spokane. These are at the library of Washington State University. For the British venture, see Archives of the Great Britain Board of Trade, Companies Registration Office, 1844-1951, microfilm, Bancroft Library.

7. *Ibid.*

8. Seattle *Argus*, Dec. 26, 1914; *Report of State Advisory Liquor Control Commission* (Olympia, Wash., 1933).

9. "Master's Report," *Grange Proceedings* (1918); Austin Edward Griffiths, "Great Faith: Autobiography of an English Immigrant Boy in America, 1863-1950" (MS in the University of Washington Library), pp. 147-48.

10. Seattle *Leader*, June 19, 1890; Portland *Oregonian*, Feb. 17, 1907; Spokane *Spokesman-Review*, Aug. 27, 1907.

11. Cherrington, *Standard Encyclopedia of the Alcohol Problem*, VI, 2800; Yakima *Republic*, Feb. 8, 1902; May 31, 1907; Delmar H. Caryl, *With Angels to the Rear: An Informal Portrait of Early Meadowdale*

(Edmonds, Wash., 1960), p. 135; Spokane *Spokesman-Review*, March 1, 1909.

12. William Whitfield, *History of Snohomish County, Washington* (Chicago, Ill., 1926), I, 109; Wenatchee *Daily World*, Feb. 3, 1909; Spokane *Spokesman-Review*, Oct. 4, 1888.

13. Spokane *Spokesman-Review*, Nov. 12, 1901.

14. Griffiths, "Great Faith," p. 229; Marshall, *Swinging Doors*, p. 179; Spokane *Spokesman-Review*, Feb. 7, 1909.

15. Seattle *Leader*, Oct. 10, 1889; Spokane *Spokesman-Review*, Oct. 6, 1909; Jan. 10, 1909.

16. Portland *Oregonian*, Sept. 4, 1908; *Senate Journal of the State of Washington* (1909), p. 34.

17. *Washington State Governors' Messages to the Legislatures, 1909-1925* (Olympia, Wash., 1925), p. 11.

18. Wenatchee *Daily World*, July 1, Aug. 21, 1908.

19. Spokane *Spokesman-Review*, Jan. 23, 1914.

20. Baron, *Brewed in America*, p. 267; Herbert Hunt, *Washington, West of the Cascades* (Chicago, Ill., 1917), III, 97; Archives of the Great Britain Board of Trade.

CHAPTER 6

1. John Allen Krout, *The Origins of Prohibition* (New York, 1925), p. 153.

2. Wenatchee *Daily World*, Aug. 20, 1908. Jimmie Durkin, a prosperous saloonkeeper, allowed the minister to have his way, apparently with no loss to the saloon. Durkin later ran for governor. He also offered Theodore Roosevelt a salary of $25,000 a year as advertising manager for Durkin's saloons.

3. E. B. Sutton, *Prohibition Seed Thoughts or Thoughts Gone to Seed* (Seattle, Wash., 1893).

4. *Ibid.; Prohibition Party Campaign Book for the State of Washington, 1892* (Tacoma, Wash., 1892); Harvey K. Hines, *An Illustrated History of the State of Washington* (Chicago, Ill., 1893), p. 720.

5. Seattle *Leader*, Sept. 12, 1889.

6. Sutton, *Prohibition Seed Thoughts*, p. 32.

7. This parallel is explored by Joseph R. Gusfield, "Social Structure and Moral Reform: A Study of the Women's Christian Temperance Union," *The American Journal of Sociology*, LXI (November, 1955), and in *Symbolic Crusade: Status Politics and the American Temperance Movement* (Urbana, Ill., 1963). The exception would be the Washingtonian movement of the 1840's which enlisted reformed drunkards in a temperance crusade. See also Krout, *Origins of Prohibition;* Everett

Daily Herald, Nov. 7, 1910; Seattle *White Ribbon Bulletin,* November, 1909, and April, 1909.

8. Mark A. Matthews, "Sermons" (MS in the University of Washington Library).

9. *Ibid.; Proceedings of the Washington State Grange* (1916), p. 137; *Grange Proceedings* (1919); Andrew Sinclair, *Prohibition: The Era of Excess* (Boston, Mass., 1962), p. 26.

10. Seattle *Mirror,* March 22, 1884; Seattle *Sun,* April 6, 1914. The Seattle *Argus* commented that "it is rather amazing to find a man of the calibre of Dr. Matthews making such an unmitigated ass of himself as to attach his name to such a mess of rubbish." *Argus,* April 11, 1914; Matthews, "Sermons."

11. *Grange Proceedings* (1890), p. 7.

12. Will Irwin, "The Saloon—Past and Future," Portland *Oregonian,* Oct. 2, 1932; Spokane *Spokesman-Review,* Feb. 15, 1917.

13. Seattle *Town Crier,* April 8, 1911; Spokane *Spokesman-Review,* April 28, 1911.

14. Gusfield, *Symbolic Crusade,* and by the same author, "Status Conflicts and the Changing Ideologies of the American Temperance Movement," in David J. Pittman and Charles R. Snyder (ed.), *Society, Culture, and Drinking Patterns* (New York, 1962); J. Joseph Huthmacher, "Urban Liberalism and the Age of Reform," *Mississippi Valley Historical Review* (September, 1962). Both of these works implicitly emphasize that status is not necessarily exclusive—the middle class can welcome recruits.

15. Matthews writing in the Seattle *Citizen,* July, 1907; a symbol of middle-class status that one finds recurring again and again is that of well-leathered feet. Of course, it rhymed well, too. Matthews used it when he thundered that the saloon changes a man into a "heartless wretch, and makes him steal the shoes from his starving babe's feet to find the price of a glass of liquor" (Matthews' "Sermons"). The saloons responded with their own poets: "Don't buy booze, / If your baby needs shoes!" (sign seen by Jim Marshall).

16. Gusfield, "Social Structure and Moral Reform," p. 221.

17. An even fifty case studies are readily available in the biographical sections of the subscription histories (Bagley, Whitfield, Hines, Hunt) and from the *Campaign Book, 1892.* The composite here is based upon the assumptions that those who ran for office on the Prohibition ticket in 1892 and those who felt strongly enough about their Prohibition affiliation to list it in the subscription histories were probably representative. This composite does not include the principal radicals—Sutton,

Cotterill, Erskine—who certainly fit the generalizations above. The fifty used here were run-of-the-mill Prohibs.

18. Austin Edward Griffiths, "Great Faith: Autobiography of an English Immigrant Boy in America, 1863-1950" (MS in the University of Washington Library), p. 137.

19. Ernest H. Cherrington, *The Evolution of Prohibition in the United States of America* (Westerville, Ohio, 1920), p. 169.

20. Robert Chase Erskine, Seattle, interview with the author, 1962.

21. George F. Cotterill Papers (MSS in the University of Washington Library) ; Clarence B. Bagley, *History of Seattle*, III, 25-30; and Seattle newspapers, 1912-14 *passim.*

22. Griffiths, "Great Faith," p. 251.

23. Everett *Daily Herald*, Nov. 1, 1910.

24. Ernest H. Cherrington (ed.), *The Anti-Saloon Year Book* (1909), pp. 208-9.

25. Portland *Oregonian*, June 2, 1910.

26. Joe Smith Papers (MSS in the University of Washington Library), Hay to Joe Smith, Dec. 2, 1909.

27. John A. Gellatly, *A History of Wenatchee* (Wenatchee, Wash., 1958), p. 355.

28. Bruce Mitchell, "Rufus Woods: Man of Vision" (M.A. thesis, University of Washington, 1962), p. 35; Erskine interview.

29. Pearl M. Mahoney, *Prosser—The Home Town* (Prosser, Wash., 1950), p. 56.

30. *Labor Proceedings* (1919), p. 130.

31. Harvey O'Connor, *Revolution in Seattle* (New York, 1964), *passim.*

32. For example, the stand of Protestant and Catholic ministers of Spokane on the wine rooms. Spokane *Spokesman-Review*, Nov. 12, 1901.

33. *ASL Year Book* (1909), p. 113. Cites Seattle.

34. Cherrington, *Evolution*, p. 250.

35. Seattle *Post-Intelligencer*, Nov. 1, 1914.

36. Marion E. Hay Papers (MSS in the Eastern Washington State Historical Society Museum, Spokane), Hay to I. H. Amos, Dec. 27, 1909; Hay to E. A. Bryan, March 17, 1910.

37. S. C. Roberts, "Reminiscences of a Pedagogue" (1935 MS in the Washington State University Library), p. 230; *Labor Proceedings* (1915), pp. 11-13.

38. *Post-Intelligencer, Times, Town Crier,* Everett *Morning Tribune,* October-November, 1914 *passim; Washingtoner Staats-Zeitung*, Dec. 31, 1915; Wesley L. Jones Papers (MSS in the University of Washington Library), Brainerd to Jones, Aug. 12, 1914.

39. Reprinted in the Seattle *Argus,* June 27, 1914; *ibid.,* March 21, April 25, Sept. 5, 1914.

40. *ASL Year Book* (1909), pp. 165-66.

CHAPTER 7

1. Peter H. Odegard, "Anti-Saloon League," *Encyclopaedia of the Social Sciences* (New York, 1948), I, 118-19. Also Odegard, *Pressure Politics: The Story of the Anti-Saloon League* (New York, 1928).

2. Seattle *Times,* Feb. 24, 1900.

3. Seattle *Post-Intelligencer,* Feb. 26, 1900.

4. George F. Cotterill Papers (MSS in the University of Washington Library), Cotterill Scrapbooks.

5. Odegard, *Pressure Politics,* p. 222.

6. Ernest H. Cherrington, *Evolution of Prohibition in the United States of America* (Westerville, Ohio, 1920), p. 278.

7. *Proceedings of the Washington State Grange* (1905), p. 115; Cherrington, *Evolution,* p. 288; the *Citizen,* June, 1907. The Anti-Cigarette Law received a degree of national notoriety in 1908 when the labor leader Big Bill Haywood, touring the country after the Boise Trials, was arrested in Yakima for smoking cigarettes. This, he said later, was his first conviction for any criminal act, and the publicity he gave the law hastened its repeal. William D. Haywood, *Bill Haywood's Book: The Autobiography of William D. Haywood* (New York, 1929), p. 228.

8. Spokane *Spokesman-Review, passim.* The index prepared by the W.P.A. Writers' Project (microfilm in the University of Washington Library) is very useful here.

9. The *Citizen,* December, 1906.

10. *Ibid.,* February, 1907; *Grange Proceedings* (1907), p. 51.

11. Wenatchee *Daily World,* May 16, 1908.

12. *Ibid.,* May 19, 1908.

13. C. Brewster Coulter, "John L. Wilson, Erastus Brainerd, and the Republican Party of Washington," *Idaho Yesterdays,* IV (Summer, 1960), 11-16.

14. *Historical Highlights of Washington State* (Olympia, Wash., no date), p. 45.

15. Wenatchee *Daily World,* Aug. 20, 21, 1908; *Historical Highlights,* p. 45, and Portland *Oregonian,* Sept. 4, 1908.

16. "Biennial Report of the Secretary of State," *State Documents* (Olympia, Wash., 1908); *American Issue* (Washington edition), January, 1908.

17. *Senate Journal of the State of Washington* (1909), p. 34.

18. *House Journal of the State of Washington* (1909), p. 151.

19. Spokane *Spokesman-Review*, Jan. 31, Feb. 5, 1909.

20. Erastus Brainerd Papers (MSS in the University of Washington Library), Hay to Brainerd, Sept. 22, 1908; and *Historical Highlights*, pp. 46-47.

21. *House Journal* (1909), p. 286ff.

22. Spokane *Spokesman-Review*, March 2, 1909.

23. Cotterill to Maxwell, quoted in Lora E. Maxwell, "History of Liquor Legislation in the State of Washington" (Honors thesis, Washington State University, 1917), pp. 23, 25; Spokane *Spokesman-Review*, March 5, 1909; *Proceedings of the Washington State Grange* (1909), p. 30.

24. Tacoma *News*, Feb. 20, 1909.

25. Spokane *Spokesman-Review*, March 3, 1909.

26. Marion E. Hay Papers (MSS in the Eastern Washington State Historical Museum), Hay to Doty, Oct. 14, 1910, and 1910 *passim*.

27. Ernest H. Cherrington (ed.), *Anti-Saloon League Year Book* (Columbus, Ohio, 1910), p. 81.

28. Calvin F. Schmid and Vincent A. Miller, *Population Trends and Educational Change in the State of Washington* (Seattle, Wash., 1960); Spokane *Spokesman-Review*, July 12, 1901; June 20, Aug. 27, 1902; Dec. 20, 1909.

29. Hay Papers, Hay to Joe Smith, Nov. 19, 1909; Spokane *Spokesman-Review*, Dec. 20, 1909.

30. Lucile F. Fargo, *Spokane Story* (Minneapolis, Minn., 1957), p. 235. Interestingly, both the suffrage movement and the prohibition movement owed a good deal to bonanzas from the mines. Mrs. Hutton's money came from the Hercules Mine in Idaho and was a significant factor in the program of the Washington Equal Suffrage Association. The state ASL, about the same time, received a gift of $25,000 from Tom Lippy, millionaire from the Klondike, according to Pierre Berton, *The Klondike Fever* (New York, 1958), p. 419.

31. Cotterill Papers, David Rankin to Cotterill, July 25, 1910.

32. Everett *Daily Herald*, Everett *Morning Tribune*, *Labor Journal*, September-November, 1910 *passim*, and Max Miller, *Shinny on Your Own Side* (New York, 1958), p. 52ff.

33. *Labor Journal*, Oct. 7, 1910.

34. Everett *Daily Herald*, Nov. 7, 9, 1910.

35. Keith Alexander Murray, "Republican Party Politics in Washington During the Progressive Era" (Ph.D. thesis, University of Washington, 1946), p. 106.

36. Hay Papers, Hay to Doty, May 2, Dec. 17, 1910.

37. *Washington State Governors' Messages to the Legislature, 1909-1925* (Olympia, Wash., 1925), p. 11.

38. Quoted in Maxwell, "History of Liquor Legislation," p. 40.

39. Spokane *Spokesman-Review*, Jan. 17, 1911.

40. Doty to Maxwell, quoted in Maxwell, "History of Liquor Legislation," p. 51.

41. Fred J. Chamberlain, "Progress of the State Grange in Legislation," *Washington Grange News*, June 10, 1939; Claudius O. Johnson, "The Adoption of Initiative and Referendum in Washington," *Pacific Northwest Quarterly*, XXXV (October, 1944), 291-303.

42. The *Citizen*, May, June, July, September, 1906.

43. Cotterill Papers, William S. U'Ren file.

44. Johnson, "The Adoption of Initiative and Referendum in Washington." Johnson does not mention any influence of the ASL in achieving direct legislation. Though the ASL did not pledge legislators specifically on I and R, the support it gave to the constitutional amendment was undoubtedly an important factor in its success.

45. Cotterill Papers, Elihu F. Barker to Cotterill, Oct. 15, 1910.

46. *Proceedings of the Washington State Grange* (1912), pp. 149-50; "Report of the Secretary of State (1912); *Washington Governors' Messages to the Legislature, 1909-1925*, p. 44ff.

47. Everett *Morning Tribune*, Oct. 23, 1912; *Labor Journal*, Nov. 1, 1912.

48. Everett *Morning Tribune*, Nov. 5, 1912; Everett *Daily Herald*, Jan. 6, 1911. Interview with David Hartley, Everett, 1963.

49. Charles M. Gates, "A Historical Sketch of the Economic Development of Washington Since Statehood," *Pacific Northwest Quarterly*, XXIX (July, 1948), 222.

50. *ASL Year Book* (1913), pp. 229-32.

51. For example:

Olympia: 1,687–1,071 (wet)   Rockford: 114–101 (dry)
Centralia: 1,546–947 (wet)   Medical Lake: 151–127 (dry)
Edmonds: 280–184 (dry)   Asotin: 220–154 (dry)
(Everett *Daily Herald*, Nov. 6, 1912)

52. Cherrington, *Evolution*, p. 281.

53. Gilman M. Ostrander, *The Prohibition Movement in California, 1848-1933* (Berkeley, Calif., 1957), p. 120.

CHAPTER 8

1. *The State-Wide Prohibition Initiative Measure No. 3: Official Arguments For and Against* (Seattle, Wash., 1914).

2. *Proceedings of the National Convention of the Anti-Saloon League of America* (1915), p. 182.

3. John E. Caswell, "The Prohibition Movement in Oregon, 1904-1915," *Oregon Historical Quarterly*, XL (March, 1939), 77; *ASL Proceedings* (1915), p. 184; Lora E. Maxwell, "History of Liquor Legislation in the State of Washington" (Honors thesis, Washington State University, 1917), p. 43; Spokane *Spokesman-Review*, Oct. 30, 1914.

4. *ASL Proceedings* (1915), p. 184.

5. Seattle *Post-Intelligencer*, Oct. 22, Nov. 1, 1914.

6. Seattle *Times*, Oct. 22, Nov. 1, 1914.

7. Seattle *Town Crier*, Oct. 17, 24, 1914.

8. Seattle *Argus*, Oct. 31, 1914.

9. "The Black-Maned Lion of Seattle," *Collier's*, L (Dec. 28, 1912), 21.

10. Mark A. Matthews, "Sermons" (MS in the University of Washington Library).

11. Seattle *Post-Intelligencer*, Oct. 14, 19, 27-31, 1914.

12. *Ibid.*, Oct. 28, 1914; Seattle *Town Crier*, Oct. 24, 1914.

13. *Proceedings of the Annual Convention of the Washington State Federation of Labor, 1915* (Olympia, Wash., 1915), pp. 11-13.

14. *ASL Proceedings* (1915), p. 184; Maxwell, "History of Liquor Legislation," p. 44.

15. Everett *Daily Herald*, Nov. 2, 1914; "Report of the Secretary of State," *Washington Public Documents, 1914* (Olympia, Wash., 1914), p. 55.

16. D. Leigh Colvin, *Prohibition in the United States* (New York, 1926); Ernest H. Cherrington, *Evolution of Prohibition in the United States of America* (Westerville, Ohio, 1920); Peter H. Odegard, *Pressure Politics: The Story of the Anti-Saloon League* (New York, 1928); Richard Hofstadter, *The Age of Reform* (New York, 1955); William E. Leuchtenburg, *The Perils of Prosperity* (Chicago, Ill., 1958); John D. Hicks, *The Republican Ascendancy, 1921-1933* (New York, 1960); Andrew Sinclair, *Prohibition, The Era of Excess* (Boston, 1962); Ernest H. Cherrington (ed.), *Anti-Saloon League Year Book, 1913* (Columbus, Ohio, 1913), pp. 5-7.

17. Walter Lippmann, *Men of Destiny* (New York, 1927), pp. 28-31.

18. Richard Hofstadter, *The Age of Reform* (First Vantage ed., New York, 1960), pp. 289-90.

19. Sinclair, *Prohibition*, pp. 64-65.

20. James H. Timberlake, *Prohibition and the Progressive Movement, 1900-1920* (Cambridge, Mass., 1963), pp. 1-2.

21. Hofstadter, *Age of Reform*, p. 290; Sinclair, *Prohibition*, pp. 9-172.

22. Timberlake, *Prohibition and the Progressive Movement*, pp. 152, 167; this is based on Franklin Hichborn, *Story of the Session of the California Legislature of 1911* (San Francisco, Calif., 1911).

23. *House Journal of the State of Washington* (1909 and 1911). "Drys"—those who voted against amending H.B. 29 to read "two percent" instead of "one-half of one percent" (pp. 219-20). Women's suffrage: vote on adoption of majority committee report (pp. 166-67). I and R: vote on accepting the minority report from committee; this too is examined by Johnson.

24. Lucile F. Fargo, *Spokane Story* (Minneapolis, Minn., 1957), pp. 224-42.

25. Reinhold Niebuhr, *The Irony of American History* (New York, 1952), p. 69.

26. Carl Bridenbaugh, "The Great Mutation," *American Historical Review*, LXVIII (January, 1963).

CHAPTER 9

1. *Proceedings of the Washington State Grange* (1916), p. 137; *House Journal of the State of Washington* (1915); *Senate Journal of the State of Washington* (1915); and "Election Division," *Washington Public Documents, 1915-1916*, p. 6. Claudius O. Johnson ["The Initiative and Referendum in Washington," *Pacific Northwest Quarterly*, XXXVI (January, 1945), 55] is in error when he states that Number 18 was passed by the legislature.

2. *House Journal* (1915), p. 86; *ASL Proceedings* (1915), p. 185ff.

3. Spokane *Spokesman-Review*, Dec. 11, 31, 1915; *Proceedings of the Washington State Federation of Labor* (1916).

4. Spokane *Spokesman-Review*, Jan. 1, April 9, 1916; Jan. 27, March 31, 1917.

5. Seattle *Argus*, April 8, 1916; Lowell S. Hawley and Ralph Bushnell Potts, *Counsel for the Damned* (New York, 1953), p. 161.

6. Spokane *Spokesman-Review*, Oct. 23, 1916; Dec. 15-19, 1916; May 27, 1917; Seattle *Argus*, May 13, 1916.

7. Westerville, Ohio, *New Republic*, June 9, 1916.

8. Hawley and Potts, *Counsel for the Damned*, p. 167ff., for a full account of Vanderveer and the Billingsleys.

9. *Ibid;* Seattle *Argus*, July 29, 1916; Spokane *Spokesman-Review*, July 25, 1916.

10. Spokane *Spokesman-Review*, May 3-5, Oct. 8, 1916; Westerville, Ohio, *New Republic*, June 9, 1916.

11. Westerville, Ohio, *The National Daily*, July 12, 1916; C. B. Blethen, "One Year Dry," *Collier's* (March 24, 1917).

12. Seattle *Argus*, Jan. 23, 1915; May 20, Sept. 23, Nov. 4, 1916.

13. Blethen, "One Year Dry."

14. Seattle *Argus*, Sept. 30, Nov. 4, 1916.

15. *Ibid.*, Sept. 20, 1916.

16. Will Irwin, "The Saloon—Past and Future," Portland *Oregonian*, Sept. 25, 1932.

17. Seattle *Argus*, Dec. 18, 1915.

18. That is to say, 30,000 to 103,000. "Report of the Secretary of State," *Washington Public Documents, 1915-18*, pp. 6-7.

19. Seattle *Argus*, Nov. 11, 1916.

20. *Ibid.*, March 13, 1915.

21. James H. Timberlake, *Prohibition and the Progressive Movement, 1900-1920* (Cambridge, Mass., 1963), pp. 39-67. The paragraph above summarizes a chapter of Timberlake's study of the conscious motives in the prohibition movement.

22. Spokane *Spokesman-Review*, March 4, 1917; *House Journal* (1917), p. 146.

23. *Senate Journal* (1917), p. 255ff.

24. Spokane *Spokesman-Review*, Jan. 25, Feb. 20, 1917.

25. Andrew Sinclair, *Prohibition, the Era of Excess* (Boston, Mass., 1962), p. 156. Herbert Asbury, *The Great Illusion: An Informal History of Prohibition* (New York, 1950), p. 125.

26. Spokane *Spokesman-Review*, Aug. 30, 1917.

27. Hawley and Potts, *Counsel for the Damned*, p. 169; Spokane *Spokesman-Review*, Jan. 28-29, 1917.

28. Austin Edward Griffiths, "Great Faith: Autobiography of an English Immigrant Boy in America, 1863-1950" (MS in the University of Washington Library), p. 184; Spokane *Spokesman-Review*, Jan. 29, 1917. The alleged guilt of Hiram Gill has become something of an issue in Seattle historiography. His corruption is implied strongly in Murray Morgan, *Skid Road*, in Hawley and Potts, *Counsel for the Damned*, and in several journalistic treatments. Against these implications, however, one should consider Austin Griffiths, who ran against Gill in 1914 and then was appointed by Gill as chief of police. Griffiths regarded Gill as a man too thoroughly convinced of the necessity of evil, but never a corrupt man. Roy Olmstead, a police lieutenant under Gill for years and later "king of the rumrunners" (see chapter 11), holds exactly the same opinion of Gill's civic morality: he condoned vice because he thought it could never be suppressed, but he did not profit from it personally; memoranda of October, 1917, in the Port of Seattle Papers (MSS in the University of Washington Library); Seattle *Argus*, Feb. 24, 1917.

298   NOTES

29. Timberlake, *Prohibition and the Progressive Movement,* p. 174.
30. Seattle *Argus,* April-December, 1917; Seattle *Star,* June 1, 1918.
31. Spokane *Spokesman-Review,* November, 1918; Calvin F. Schmid, *Social Trends in Seattle* (Seattle, Wash., 1944), p. 194.
32. *Mullen* v. *Howell,* May 24, 1919; Spokane *Spokesman-Review,* Dec. 18, 1919.
33. *Proceedings of the Washington State Federation of Labor* (1919), p. 130; *ibid.,* (1920), p. 94.
34. Spokane *Spokesman-Review,* March 6, 1919.

CHAPTER 10

1. *Proceedings of the Twenty-Third National Convention of the Anti-Saloon League of America* (Westerville, Ohio, 1927), p. 22.
2. Lawrence Lowell, "Reconstruction and Prohibition," *Atlantic Monthly,* CXLII (February, 1929), 145-51; Seattle *Argus,* April 20, 1929.
3. Wesley L. Jones Papers (MSS in the University of Washington Library), Jones to Washington State Historical Society, March 23, 1932.
4. Ernest H. Cherrington (ed.), *Anti-Saloon League Year Book* (Columbus, Ohio, 1921), pp. 308, 309; Miles Poindexter Papers (microfilm in the University of Washington Library), Tacoma Central Labor Council Resolution, June 5, 1919; Seattle *Industrial Worker,* Oct. 28, 1922; Seattle *Argus,* Jan. 16, 1932.
5. Quoted in Seattle *Argus,* Aug. 13, 1921; Maude Sweetman, *What Price Politics: The Inside Story of Washington State Politics* (Seattle, Wash., 1927), p. 98.
6. Seattle *Argus,* March 12, 1921.
7. *Ibid.,* Aug. 20, 1921; *Proceedings of the Washington State Federation of Labor* (1922), p. 77; *Proceedings of the Washington State Grange* (1923), p. 93.
8. Hamilton Cravens, "A History of the Washington Farmer-Labor Party, 1918-1924" (M.A. thesis, University of Washington, 1962), pp. 92-141.
9. Harriet Ann Crawford, *The Washington State Grange, 1889-1924* (Portland, Ore., 1940), p. 236; Cravens, "History of the Washington Farmer-Labor Party, 1918-1924," p. 156; *Proceedings of the Washington State Grange* (1926).
10. *Proceedings of the Washington State Federation of Labor* (1923); Cravens, "History of the Washington Farmer-Labor Party," p. 141.
11. *Proceedings of the Washington State Federation of Labor* (1922), p. 77; Cravens, "History of the Washington Farmer-Labor Party," p. 163; Seattle *Union Record,* June 5, 1922.

12. Andrew Sinclair, *Prohibition: The Era of Excess* (Boston, 1962), pp. 166-70; James H. Timberlake, *Prohibition and the Progressive Movement* (Cambridge, Mass., 1963), pp. 181-83.

13. Sinclair, *Prohibition*, p. 182.

14. William E. Leuchtenburg, *The Perils of Prosperity, 1914-32* (Chicago, Ill., 1958), p. 92.

15. Poindexter Papers, Lyle to Poindexter, Aug. 5, 1921.

16. Seattle *Argus*, June 27, 1925; Poindexter Papers, J. G. Johnson to Poindexter, March 18, 1922.

17. Mary Lou Krause, "Prohibition and the Reform Tradition in the Washington State Senatorial Election of 1922" (M.A. thesis, University of Washington, 1963); Papers of Governor Louis F. Hart (MSS in the State Archives, Olympia), J. W. Johnson to Hart, March 18, 1922; Seattle *Star*, April 10, 1922.

18. Seattle *Union Record*, Jan. 28, 1927; Seattle *Post-Intelligencer*, March 12, 1927; Jones Papers, Thomas Revelle to Jones, March 26, April 9, 1927.

19. Jones Papers, William Whitney to Jones, Nov. 3, 1927.

20. Seattle *Post-Intelligencer*, Aug. 11, 1928.

21. Portland *Oregonian*, March 10, Aug. 22, 1922; Nov. 11, 1923.

22. Quoted in Herbert Asbury, *The Great Illusion* (Garden City, N.Y., 1950), p. 143; *ASL Proceedings* (1921), p. 43.

23. *Washington State Governors' Messages to the Legislatures, 1909-1925* (Olympia, Wash., 1925).

24. Hart Papers, Prohibition file; Wayne B. Wheeler to Hart, March 6, 1922; Hart to Wheeler, March 11, 1922.

25. J. H. Brown, "Under the Capitol Dome," Seattle *Argus*, April 11, 1931; Governor Roland Hartley Papers (MSS in the State Archives, Olympia), Prohibition files. Some of the folders in the Hartley papers are marked "Prohibition" but are completely empty: the files have been destroyed, or the folders have never been used.

26. Hart Papers, A. F. Appleton to Hart, Dec. 31, 1922, in file of "Annual Reports of Prosecuting Attorneys."

27. Majority opinion by Judge J. Beeler, *State of Washington* v. *John Kinnear* in *Washington Reports*, CLXII (April 23, 1931), 214-27.

28. *State of Washington* v. *Fred Gibbons, Washington Reports*, CXVIII (Jan. 4, 1922), 171.

29. *Periscope*, III (August, 1927), 9. (Antiprohibition monthly published in Fox, N.Y.)

30. Jones Papers, Whitney to Jones, Nov. 3, 1927.

31. Seattle *Argus*, Feb. 20, 1932.

32. *Periscope,* III (December, 1926), 27; Jones Papers, undated clippings from the Seattle *Star.*

33. Seattle *Argus,* Nov. 24, 1923.

CHAPTER 11

1. "Olmstead Will Find Little Change," Seattle *Post-Intelligencer,* May 16, 1931.

2. Austin Edward Griffiths, "Great Faith: Autobiography of an English Immigrant Boy in America" (MS in the University of Washington Library), pp. 217-18.

3. Roy Olmstead, interviews with the author, Seattle, 1958-60 (hereafter cited as Olmstead interviews).

4. Seattle *Union Record,* March 22, 1920.

5. Seattle *Times,* March 22, 1920.

6. "Bill of Exceptions" in the file of *U.S. v. Olmstead,* Records of the United States District Court, Western District of Washington, Northern Division, November, 1924, Term, p. 25.

7. Seattle *Post-Intelligencer,* April 2, 1924.

8. *Ibid.*

9. 19 F. 2nd 849 (9th Cir., 1927).

10. New York *Times,* May 26, 1930.

11. "Bill of Exceptions," p. 85; "Mrs. Olmstead in Blue," Seattle *Post-Intelligencer,* Jan. 20, 1926.

12. Olmstead interviews; Seattle *Post-Intelligencer,* Feb. 19, 1926.

13. Undated newspaper clipping from a file kept by Mrs. Roy Lyle, Seattle.

14. Ralph Bushnell Potts, *Seattle Heritage* (Seattle, Wash., 1955), pp. 79-83.

15. Seattle *Argus,* Feb. 5, 1926.

16. "The Government's Proposed Amendment to the Proposed Bill of Exceptions," file of *U.S. v. Olmstead,* pp. 217-18.

17. Seattle *Post-Intelligencer,* Feb. 12, 1926.

18. "The Government's Proposed Amendment to the Proposed Bill of Exceptions," p. 227.

19. "Bill of Exceptions," p. 256; Seattle *Post-Intelligencer,* Feb. 12, 1926.

20. "The Government's Proposed Amendment to the Proposed Bill of Exceptions," p. 74.

21. Seattle *Post-Intelligencer,* April 3, 1926.

22. "Bill of Exceptions," p. 121.

23. Olmstead interviews.

24. Seattle *Star,* Nov. 18, 1924.

25. Seattle *Times,* Nov. 19, 1924.

26. Seattle *Post-Intelligencer,* Jan. 21, 1925.

27. Lowell S. Hawley and Ralph Bushnell Potts, *Counsel for the Damned* (New York, 1953), pp. 299-302.

28. Wesley L. Jones Papers (MSS in the University of Washington Library), Revelle to Jones, May 27, 1930.

29. Olmstead interviews; for the myth, see Potts, *Seattle Heritage,* pp. 79-83.

30. Jones Papers, Al Hubbard to Whitney, Nov. 12, 1925.

31. *Ibid.,* Roy Lyle to Roy A. Haynes, Sept. 5, 1925.

32. Olmstead interviews.

33. "Bill of Exceptions" *passim.*

34. "The Government's Proposed Amendment to the Proposed Bill of Exceptions," pp. 122-23.

35. "Bill of Exceptions," p. 109.

36. Hawley and Potts, *Counsel for the Damned,* p. 301.

37. Seattle *Times,* Feb. 11, 1926; Jones Papers, Hartson to Jones, Feb. 10, 1926.

38. Olmstead interviews.

39. Seattle *Times,* March 8, 12, 1926; Mabel Walker Willebrandt, *Inside of Prohibition* (Indianapolis, Ind., 1929), p. 237.

40. Jones Papers, Lyle to Jones, Nov. 30, 1927.

41. 19 F. 2nd 849 (9th Cir., 1927).

42. William S. Fairfield and Charles Clift, "The Wiretappers," *Reporter,* VII (Dec. 23, 1952), 8-22.

43. Jones Papers, Lyle to Jones, Aug. 22, 1927.

44. Seattle *Times,* Nov. 17, 30, Dec. 8, 1927.

45. *United States Supreme Court Reports,* 72 L. Ed., 945-53.

46. Willebrandt, *Inside of Prohibition,* pp. 231-32.

47. *United States Supreme Court Reports,* 72 L. Ed., 945-53.

48. "Wiretapping Held Legal," *Literary Digest,* XCVII (June 16, 1928), 10.

49. "New Dred Scott Decision," *Outlook,* CXLIX (June, 1928), 293.

50. Jones Papers, Jones to Lyle, Nov. 29, 1927.

CHAPTER 12

1. The best account of ASL activities during the 1920's is in the testimony of B. N. Hicks before Senate Investigating Committee; U.S. Congress. Senate. Special Committee Investigating Expenditures in Senatorial Primary and General Elections. Hearings, 69th Cong., 1st sess., part 5

(Washington, D.C., 1927). Hearings held in Seattle, Washington, Spokane, Washington, and Portland, Oregon, Oct. 23, 25, 26, 27, 28, and 29, 1926.

2. C. Brewster Coulter, "John L. Wilson, Erastus Brainerd, and the Republican Party in Washington," *Idaho Yesterdays,* IV (Summer, 1960), 11-16.

3. William Stuart Forth, "A Political Biography of Wesley L. Jones" (Ph.D. thesis, University of Washington, 1963).

4. Wesley L. Jones Papers (MSS in the University of Washington Library), Jones to Fowler, April 6, 1914; Jones to Hartson, Dec. 23, 1913, Oct. 8, 1914; Jones to Brainerd, Aug. 17, 1914.

5. *Ibid.,* Spokane *Chronicle* to Jones, Aug. 8, 1922; Jones to Harding, Aug. 8, 1922; Harding to Jones, Aug. 10, 1922.

6. Mabel Walker Willebrandt, *Inside of Prohibition* (Indianapolis, Ind., 1929), p. 257.

7. Jones Papers, Jones speech dated Oct. 7, 1928.

8. *Ibid.,* Jones to Curtis, undated telegram, probably 1927. The Jones Papers contain a large body of correspondence between the Senator and the Justice Department and the Treasury Department on the subject of Lyle and Whitney. See especially Jones to Andrews, July 17, 1926, and Blair to Jones, July 17, 1926.

9. *Ibid.,* Jones to Lowman, Aug. 20, 1927; Jones press release, 1927; Lyle to Jones, March 24, 1927; Benn to Jones, Dec. 5, 1927.

10. Howard William Allen, "Miles Poindexter: A Political Biography" (Ph.D. thesis, University of Washington, 1959), pp. 448-49.

11. Miles Poindexter Papers (microfilm in the University of Washington Library), Poindexter to A. Garborg, March 10, 1917; Poindexter to R. M. Pickens, March 9, 1917; Poindexter to William C. Lewis, March 11, 1920.

12. Allen, "Miles Poindexter: A Political Biography," pp. 14, 326-431.

13. Mary Lou Krause, "Prohibition and the Reform Tradition in the Washington State Senatorial Election of 1922" (M.A. thesis, University of Washington, 1963).

14. Jones Papers, Whitney to Jones, July 11, 1922.

15. Bellingham *American,* July 17, 1922; Krause, "Prohibition and the Reform Tradition," p. 140.

16. Poindexter Papers, Mrs. Victor D. Miller to Poindexter; Poindexter to Miller, September, 1922, cited in Krause, "Prohibition and the Reform Tradition," p. 117.

17. Portland *Oregonian,* Nov. 5, 1922.

18. Hamilton Cravens, "A History of the Washington Farmer-Labor

Party, 1918-1925" (M.A. thesis, University of Washington, 1962), p. 182.

19. Ray T. Tucker and Frederick R. Barkley, *Sons of the Wild Jack-ass* (Boston, Mass., 1932); Edgar I. Stewart, *Washington: Northwest Frontier* (New York, 1957), II, 225.

20. Everett *Daily Herald*, Nov. 10, 1922, and Krause, "Prohibition and the Reform Tradition."

21. Krause, "Prohibition and the Reform Tradition," p. 176.

22. Portland *Oregonian*, Nov. 5, 1922.

23. Ernest H. Cherrington (ed.), *Anti-Saloon League Year Book* (Columbus, Ohio, 1923), p. 190.

24. S.B. 18, *Senate Journal of the State of Washington* (1923).

25. H.B. 259, *House Journal of the State of Washington* (1923).

26. Jones Papers, Kenneth Mackintosh to Jones, April 8, 1926.

27. Seattle *Post-Intelligencer*, June 25, 1925.

28. Seattle *Argus*, Feb. 7, 1925; Jones Papers, Yakima *Republic*, undated clipping; John P. Hartman to Jones, Dec. 17, 1925.

29. Bertha K. Landes Papers (MSS in the University of Washington Library); interview with John H. Thomas, retired police captain, Seattle, 1960.

30. Seattle *Argus*, Oct. 31, 1925.

31. G. O. Williams, "History of the Seattle Police Department: The Prohibition Era in Seattle," *Sheriff and Police Reporter* (February, 1951); Seattle *Argus*, Dec. 19, 1925.

32. Spokane *Spokesman-Review*, March 3, 1926.

33. Jones Papers, Revelle to Jones, March 10, 1926; Jones to L. C. Andrews, July 17, 1926.

34. Special Committee Investigating Expenditures, Hearings, p. 2994.

35. George F. Cotterill Papers (MSS in the University of Washington Library), Cotterill to J. Ralph Magee and Associates, Oct. 11, 1926.

36. *Ibid.*; Seattle *Post-Intelligencer*, Sept. 25, 1926.

37. Seattle *Post-Intelligencer*, Sept. 12, 1926.

38. Jones Papers, Horace Kimball (Spokane Republican Central Committee) to Mrs. Nancy Coffin, Oct. 21, 1926; Revelle to Jones, Oct. 4, 1926.

39. Special Committee Investigating Expenditures, Hearings, pp. 2961, 3159.

40. Jones Papers, file labeled "Politics, 1926" *passim*; undated newspaper clipping in file labeled "Politics, 1926."

41. *Ibid.*, Puyallup *Valley Tribune*, Oct. 10, 1930, clipping.

42. Seattle *Post-Intelligencer*, March 12, 1927; Jones Papers, Revelle to Jones, March 26, May 5, 1927; Seattle *Argus*, April 2, 1927.

43. *ASL Year Book* (1927), p. 154. Perhaps Hicks would have excluded from his condemnation the Senate Committee on Public Morals, Senator Joseph A. St. Peter, chairman. One hopes this gentleman was acquainted with Mrs. Noble Hightower of Seattle who led an antitobacco campaign against teachers of that city who smoked; Portland *Oregonian*, June 12, 1927.

44. Interview with John H. Thomas, Seattle, 1960.

45. Seattle *Argus,* March 10, Aug. 25, 1928; Jones Papers, Lyle to Jones, March 14, 1928.

46. Jones Papers, Revelle to Jones (telegram), March 17, 1928; Whitney to Jones, Aug. 17, 1928; Lyle to Jones, March 14, 1928; Seattle *Post-Intelligencer,* Sept. 12, 1928.

47. Everett *Daily Herald,* July 11, 1928.

48. Stewart, *Washington: Northwest Frontier,* II, 275; Seattle *Argus,* Nov. 3, 1928.

49. Everett *Daily Herald,* Sept. 8, 1928; Seattle *Post-Intelligencer,* July 4, Aug. 29, 1928.

50. Cotterill Papers, campaign material.

51. Seattle *Post-Intelligencer,* July 11, 1928.

52. *Ibid.,* Sept. 19, 1928; Everett *Daily Herald,* Aug. 20, 1928.

53. Seattle *Post-Intelligencer,* Sept. 11, Nov. 12, 1928; Seattle *Argus,* Sept. 15, 1928.

54. Seattle *Post-Intelligencer,* Nov. 12, 1928; Everett *Daily Herald,* Oct. 29, 1928.

55. Negative evidence supported by an interview with David Hartley of Everett, 1963; Mr. David Hartley accompanied his father on each of the Governor's campaigns.

CHAPTER 13

1. Andrew Sinclair, *Prohibition: The Era of Excess* (Boston, Mass., 1962), pp. 353-54.

2. Wesley L. Jones Papers (MSS in the University of Washington Library), "Politics" file; Washington *Post,* May 3, 1929, clipping; Whitney to Jones, Nov. 24, 1929; Associated Press clipping, Feb. 27, 1930.

3. *Senate Journal of the State of Washington* (1929), p. 754; Jones Papers, Hicks to Jones, March 23, 1929.

4. Seattle *Post-Intelligencer,* March 14, 1929.

5. Mark A. Matthews, "Sermons" (MS in the University of Washington Library); Seattle *Argus,* Sept. 12, 1925; Jones Papers, Matthews to Jones, June 13, 1929.

6. *Ibid.,* Jones to Matthews, June 20, 1929; Matthews to Jones, Oct.

28, 1929; Matthews to Jones, Nov. 1, 1929; Seattle *Times*, Nov. 5, 1929; Senator Sheppard of Texas had proposed in October that purchase be made a felony, and perhaps Matthews had this in mind when he wrote his sermon.

7. Jones Papers, Lyle to Jones, Nov. 20, Dec. 13, 1929; Matthews to Jones, Feb. 13, 1930.

8. Everett *Daily Herald*, Feb. 2, 1930; Edith Dolan Riley, "Development of Political Parties in the State of Washington" (MS in the University of Washington Library), Part II, pp. 20-23.

9. Jones Papers, John S. McMillin to Jones, May 31, 1930; Seattle *Argus*, Oct. 4, 1930; Seattle *Star*, April 29, 1930.

10. Jones Papers, Whitney to Jones, Nov. 4, 1927, April 20, 1930; Levi H. Lassen to Jones, May 12, 1930; Spokane *Spokesman-Review*, June 2, 1930.

11. New York *Times*, May 26, 1930.

12. Jones Papers, Chadwick to Jones, June 23, 1930; Revelle to Jones, May 5, 1927; Seattle *Post-Intelligencer*, May 21, 1930.

13. Jones Papers, Revelle to Jones, May 5, 1927; Whitney to Jones, Sept. 4, 1929; Mabel Walker Willebrandt, *Inside of Prohibition* (Indianapolis, Ind., 1929), p. 235.

14. Jones Papers, Whitney to Jones, June 12, 1930.

15. New York *Times*, May 26, 1930.

16. Jones Papers, Whitney to Jones, June 1, 1930; Matthews to Jones, June 16, 1930.

17. Seattle *Star*, Seattle *Post-Intelligencer*, Seattle *Times*, August-September, 1930 *passim*.

18. Seattle *Post-Intelligencer*, Sept. 19, 1930; Seattle *Times*, Sept. 22, 1930.

19. Jones Papers, Revelle to Jones, May 27, Sept. 25, 1930.

20. Seattle *Argus*, Sept. 6, 18, 1930.

21. Seattle *Post-Intelligencer*, Jan. 5, 1931; the vote in the Senate in 1931 on a motion to postpone SJM 1 (memorial to repeal) was twenty-six dry to fourteen wet. This was the only significant legislative expression in either chamber of wet-dry sentiment in 1931.

22. Jones Papers, Revelle to Jones, Oct. 31, 1929; Jones to Revelle, Nov. 11, 1929.

CHAPTER 14

1. Seattle *Post-Intelligencer*, May 16, 1931.

2. Wesley L. Jones Papers (MSS in the University of Washington Library), Lyle to Jones, Dec. 13, 1930.

3. Seattle *Times*, Dec. 26, 1933.

4. Seattle *Post-Intelligencer*, March 4, 1931; Seattle *Argus*, July 4, 1931.

5. Jones Papers, Ralph Horr press release, Dec. 4, 1931; Seattle *Argus*, Dec. 12, 1931; Feb. 20, 1932.

6. Ernest Gordon, *The Wrecking of the Eighteenth Amendment* (Francestown, N.H., 1943), pp. 80, 81, 181, 183.

7. *Ibid.*, pp. 86, 97; Tacoma *Times*, Jan. 9, 1931; Seattle *Argus*, Dec. 26, 1931.

8. *Annual Report of the President of the Association Against the Prohibition Amendment for the Year 1933*, p. 46.

9. Seattle *Post-Intelligencer*, Oct. 20, 1928.

10. *Ibid.*, June 14, 1933; April 22, 1933.

11. *Congressional Record*, Feb. 20, 1933, p. 451, quoted in Gordon, *Wrecking of the Eighteenth Amendment*, p. 205.

12. *Ibid.*, p. 189.

13. Grace C. Root, *Women and Repeal: The Story of the Women's Organization for National Prohibition Reform* (New York, 1934).

14. This statement is based primarily on Joseph R. Gusfield's study of WCTU leadership in thirty-eight major cities, 1888-1950 ("Social Structure and Moral Reform: A Study of the Women's Christian Temperance Union," *The American Journal of Sociology*, LXI [November, 1955], 221-32). Gusfield shows that the percentage of the husbands in "professional" occupations dropped from 23 per cent in 1885 to 12 per cent in 1925, while leaders' husbands in unskilled occupations rose from 6 per cent to 20 per cent. In 1933, in Snohomish County, Washington (which was neither too urban nor too rural), the husbands of the president, vice president, and secretary of the county WCTU were, respectively, a salesman, a clerk, and an "engineer." (Everett *News*, Sept. 23, 1933, and *Polk's Directory of Everett and Snohomish County, 1933*.)

CHAPTER 15

1. Seattle *Argus*, March 14, 1931.

2. *Ibid.*, Jan. 27, 1932.

3. Everett *Daily Herald*, Jan. 23, 31, Feb. 2, 5, 6, 7, 1932.

4. Seattle *Argus*, Feb. 20, May 28, June 11, 1932.

5. Everett *Daily Herald*, May 6, 7, 1932; Seattle *Argus*, May 14, 1932.

6. Everett *Daily Herald*, May 9, 1932; Seattle *Argus*, May 14, 1932.

7. Seattle *Post-Intelligencer*, April 5, 1932.

8. "Campaign Literature, 1932" (scrapbook in the Seattle Public Library).

9. "Education Opposed to Prohibition Repeal," *Washington Education Journal*, XII (November, 1932), 60.

10. Interview with Dr. Staynor Brighton, Washington Education Association, Seattle, 1963.

11. Seattle *Argus*, July 23, 1932; *Washington State Voters' Pamphlet* (1932).

12. *Annual Report of the President of the Association Against the Prohibition Amendment for the Year 1933.*

13. Seattle *Post-Intelligencer*, Sept. 7, 1932.

14. Seattle *Argus*, Nov. 5, 1932.

15. Stephen F. Chadwick Papers (MSS in the University of Washington Library), Chadwick to Reno Odlin, Oct. 29, 1932.

16. *Ibid.*, press release, July 7, 1932; Chadwick to Farley, July 15, 1932; Chadwick to an unidentified correspondent, undated.

17. Wesley L. Jones Papers (MSS in the University of Washington Library), Jones to Theodore R. Terwilliger, July 19, 1932.

18. Seattle *Argus*, May 7, Sept. 10, 1932.

19. *Ibid.*, Oct. 29, 1932.

20. Chadwick Papers, Chadwick to Odlin, Oct. 29, 1932.

22. *Ibid.*, pp. 11, 14, 18.

23. Seattle *Post-Intelligencer*, Nov. 22, 1932; June 14, 1933.

24. Everett *Daily Herald*, Aug. 25, 1933.

25. Seattle *Post-Intelligencer*, April 6, 1933.

26. Seattle *Argus*, Nov. 19, 1932; Seattle *Post-Intelligencer*, Aug. 29, 1933.

27. *Annual Report of the AAPA*, p. 27.

28. *Washington State Ratification Convention: Repealing the 18th Amendment* (Olympia, 1933), *passim.*

29. Wesley L. Jones Papers, Revelle to Jones, May 3, 1932.

30. Olmstead interviews.

31. Seattle *Post-Intelligencer*, Sept. 22, 1936; Seattle *Argus*, April 9, 1932.

32. Seattle *Argus*, Nov. 17, 1934.

33. Seattle *Post-Intelligencer*, Jan. 25, 1935.

34. Anti-Saloon League of America Papers (MSS, Library of the Ohio State Historical Association, Columbus, Ohio), W. Herwig to E. H. Cherrington, June 8, 1937.

CHAPTER 16

1. Seattle *Argus*, May–September, 1933, *passim.*

2. *Ibid.*, Nov. 3, Nov. 4, Nov. 11, Nov. 18, 1933; *First Report of the Washington State Liquor Control Board (1934)* (Olympia, Washington, 1934), p.35.

3. *Report of the State Advisory Liquor Control Commission* (Olympia, 1933).

4. *Minutes of the Washington State Liquor Control Board*, I, 2 (bound, typed MSS, Washington State Archives, Olympia).

5. *Third Report of the WSLCB* (1935–36).

6. *First Report of the WSLCB*; Seattle, *Argus*, April 28, May 5, May 12, 1934.

7. Seattle *Argus*, May 26, 1934; *First Report*, p. 46; *Second Report of the WSLCB*, p. 6.

8. *Tenth Report (1942–43); Eleventh Report (1943–44); Twelfth Report (1944–45)*.

9. *Reports*, 1942–51.

10. *Thirteenth Report (1945–46); Fourteenth Report (1946–47)*.

11. *Reports*, 1949–50, 1984–85, 1985–86; Seattle *Post-Intelligencer*, July 26, 1986.

12. Interviews in Olympia and Everett, April–August, 1986: Robert A. Seeber, Don Eldridge, Leroy M. Hittle, Lewis Holcomb, John Martinis, Dick King, George Scott, Malachy R. Murphy; *Minutes of the Washington State Liquor Control Board*, XII, Nov. 13, 1970; Seattle *Times*, May 13, 1976; *Thirty-eighth Report (1970–71)*.

13. Seattle *Post-Intelligencer*, June 2, 1964.

14. Interviews; James Halpin, "Who Killed Cocky Robin?" *Seattle Magazine* (May, 1967), p. 22.

15. Halpin, "Who Killed Cocky Robin," p. 22.

16. *House Journal of the State of Washington, Special Session, 1933–34* (Olympia, 1934), p. 430; Seattle *Argus*, Jan. 13, Jan. 27, 1934.

17. Seattle *Times*, Oct. 9, Oct. 10, Oct. 19, 1963; Portland *Oregonian*, Oct. 20, 1963: Citizens for Government Control of Liquor Distribution, "Liquor Investigations" (typed, photocopied report, 6 pp., in Northwest Collection, University of Washington Library, and in Albert D. Rosellini Papers, State Archives, Olympia).

18. Seattle *Times*, April 21, 1963; George William Scott, "Arthur B. Langlie: Republican Governor in a Democratic Age" (Ph.D. thesis, University of Washington, 1971), pp. 92–98.

19. "Liquor Investigations"; see also Rosellini Papers, "WSLCB" file, *passim*.

20. Daniel J. Evans Papers (MSS, State Archives, Olympia), news release in "1964 Campaign" file.

21. Evans Papers, files labeled "Liquor Control Board," "Legislative Council—Liquor Control Board Study," "1964 Campaign," "Legislative Council"; Seattle *Times*, April 22, May 18, May 24, 1964.

22. Seattle *Times*, June 27, 1967; Halpin, "Who Killed Cocky Robin?"

23. Halpin, "Who Killed Cocky Robin?"

24. *Eleventh Report (1943–44)*, p. 9.

25. Interviews; Seattle *Times*, March 23, April 8, 1963.

26. *Thirty-fifth Report (1967–68); Forty-sixth Report (1978–79)*; Seattle

Times, Feb. 13, 1970; April 29, 1973; Seattle *Post-Intelligencer*, March 12, 1972; April 22, 1973.

27. *Reports*; Interviews.

28. Jay Higbee, "Discrimination, Private Clubs, and the State Liquor License" (typed, bound 1968 MSS in the University of Washington Library).

29. *Reports*, 1981–85.

30. Interviews.

31. Seattle *Times*, Sept. 24, 1971.

32. Interviews; Seattle *Times*, Sept. 24, Sept. 30, Oct. 18, Dec. 2, 1971; June 26, 1973; Aug. 8, Aug. 9, 1974; March 16, Nov. 14, Dec. 23, 1978; Feb. 13, 1979; Everett *Herald*, July 10, 1976; Bremerton *Sun*, Feb. 21, 1973; Olympia *Daily Olympian*, Feb. 13, 1979; Vancouver *Columbian*, Feb. 13, 1979; Seattle *Post-Intelligencer*, May 23, 1980; *1981 Session Laws of the State of Washington*, II, 1680 ("Sundry Claims") (Olympia, 1981).

CHAPTER 17

1. *Report of the State Advisory Liquor Control Commission* (Olympia, 1933); *Washington State Liquor Act* (Olympia, 1934); *Fifth Report of the WSLCB (1937–38)*, p. 9.

2. Tacoma *News-Tribune*, Aug. 15, 1976.

3. Washington State Liquor Control Board, Bulletin No. 6, *Rules and Regulations: Retail Beer and/or Wine Dispensaries* (Olympia, 1934); Bulletin No. 12, *Advertising* (Olympia, 1934).

4. *Reports, passim.*

5. Norman H. Clark, *Deliver Us from Evil: An Interpretation of American Prohibition* (New York: W. W. Norton Co., 1976); Paul Aaron and David Musto, "Temperance and Prohibition in America: A Historical Overview," in Mark H. Moore and Dean R. Gerstein, eds., *Alcohol and Public Policy: Beyond the Shadow of Prohibition* (Washington, D.C.: National Academy Press, 1981).

6. Seattle *Post-Intelligencer*, Feb. 20, 1972.

7. Office of Financial Management, Joe Taller, Director, *The Desirability of Continuing Retail Liquor Sales By State Government* (Olympia, 1983).

Bibliography

UNPUBLISHED SOURCES

Archival

Alcohol Problems Association. Records. Arcade Building, Seattle.

Brainerd, Erastus. Papers. University of Washington Library.

Chadwick, Stephen F. Papers. University of Washington Library.

Cotterill, George F. Papers. University of Washington Library.

Galland-Burke Brewing and Malting Company (Spokane). Records. Washington State University Library.

Hart, Louis. Correspondence and Official Papers. State Archives, Olympia.

Hartley, Roland H. Correspondence and Official Papers. State Archives, Olympia.

Hay, Marion E. Papers. Eastern Washington State Historical Society Museum, Spokane.

Jones, Wesley L. Papers. University of Washington Library.

Landes, Bertha K. Papers. University of Washington Library.

Martin, Clarence D. Correspondence and Official Papers. State Archives, Olympia.

Matthews, Mark Allison. Sermons. Typed manuscript, University of Washington Library.

Poindexter, Miles E. Papers. Microfilm, University of Washington Library.

Portland and Seattle Breweries, Ltd. Registration and Dissolution Papers; in Great Britain Board of Trade, Archives of the Companies Registration Office, 1844-1951. Microfilm, Bancroft Library.

Port of Seattle. Records. University of Washington Library.

Smith, Joe. Papers. University of Washington Library.

Snohomish County, Washington. Records. County Courthouse, Everett.

Spokane Brewery. Records. Washington State University Library.

United States, The. *U.S.* v. *Olmstead* (Records of the United States District Court, Western District of Washington, Northern Division, November, 1924, Term.) Federal Records Center, Seattle.

Washington Education Association. Records. Seattle.

311

Washington State Federation of Labor. Records. University of Washington Library.

Theses and Dissertations

Airey, Wilfred J. "A History of the Constitution and Government of Washington Territory." Ph.D. thesis, University of Washington, 1945.

Allen, Howard Wilson. "Miles Poindexter: A Political Biography." 2 vols. Ph.D. thesis, University of Washington, 1959.

Cravens, Hamilton. "A History of the Washington Farmer-Labor Party, 1918-1924." M.A. thesis, University of Washington, 1962.

Forth, William Stuart. "Wesley L. Jones: A Political Biography." 2 vols. Ph.D. thesis, University of Washington, 1962.

Gunns, Albert Francis. "Roland Hill Hartley and the Politics of Washington State." M.A. thesis, University of Washington, 1963.

Krause, Mary Lou. "Prohibition and the Reform Tradition in the Washington State Senatorial Election of 1922." M.A. thesis, University of Washington, 1963.

Lawrence, Joseph John. "Alcohol and Socioeconomic States in the State of Washington." M.A. thesis, Washington State University, 1955.

Maxwell, Lora E. "History of Liquor Legislation in the State of Washington." Honor's thesis, Washington State University, 1917.

McClintock, Thomas C. "J. Allen Smith and the Progressive Movement: A Study in Intellectual History." Ph.D. thesis, University of Washington, 1959.

Mitchell, Bruce. "Rufus Woods: Man of Vision." M.A. thesis, University of Washington, 1962.

Murray, Keith Alexander. "Republican Party Politics in Washington During the Progressive Era." Ph.D. thesis, University of Washington, 1946.

Sleizer, Herman August. "Governor Ernest Lister: Chapters of a Political Career." M.A. thesis, University of Washington, 1941.

Other

Applegate, Jesse. "Views of Oregon History." 1878 manuscript. Bancroft Library.

Brighton, Staynor. Interview. Washington Education Association, Seattle, 1963.

Erskine, Robert Chase. Interview. Seattle, 1962.

Griffiths, Austin Edward. "Great Faith: Autobiography of an English Immigrant Boy in America, 1863-1950." Typed manuscript. University of Washington Library.

Hartley, David. Interview. Everett, 1963.

Moss, Sydney W. "Pictures of Pioneer Times at Oregon City." 1878 manuscript. Bancroft Library.
Olmstead, Roy. Interviews. Seattle, 1959-63.
Olmstead, Mrs. Elise. Interview. Seattle, 1963.
Riley, Edith Dolan. "Development of Political Parties in the State of Washington." Typed manuscript. University of Washington Library.
Roberts, S. C. "Reminiscences of a Pedagogue." Typed 1935 manuscript. Washington State University Library.
Thomas, John H. Interview. Seattle, 1960.
Tolmie, William Fraser. "History of Puget Sound and the Northwest Coast." 1878 manuscript. Bancroft Library.
Watt, Joseph. "First Things, Starting of the First Oregon Woolen Mills and First Direct Shipment of Oregon Wheat." 1878 manuscript. Bancroft Library.

PUBLISHED SOURCES

Books

Asbury, Herbert. *Great Illusion.* Garden City, N.Y.: Doubleday, 1950.
Austin, B. F. (ed.). *Prohibition Leaders of America.* St. Thomas, Ont., 1895.
Bagley, Clarence B. *History of Seattle from the Earliest Settlement to the Present Time.* 3 vols. Chicago: J. Clarke, 1916.
Bancroft, Hubert Howe. *History of Oregon.* 2 vols. San Francisco, Calif.: History Company, 1886.
———. *History of Washington, Idaho, and Montana.* San Francisco, Calif.: History Company, 1890.
Barker, Burt Brown (ed.). *Letters of Dr. John McLoughlin Written at Ft. Vancouver, 1829-1832.* Portland, Ore.: Binfords & Mort, 1948.
Baron, Stanley. *Brewed in America: A History of Beer and Ale in the United States.* Boston: Little, Brown, 1962.
Beaver, Rev. Herbert. *Reports and Letters of Herbert Beaver,* ed. Thomas E. Jessett. Portland, Ore.: Champoeg Press, 1959.
Benedict, Ruth. *Patterns of Culture.* Sentry Edition. New York: Houghton Mifflin, 1961.
Berton, Pierre. *Klondike Fever.* New York: Alfred A. Knopf, 1958.
Breuere, Martha B. *Does Prohibition Work?* New York: Harper, 1926.
Brosnan, Cornelius J. *Jason Lee, Prophet of the New Oregon.* New York: Macmillan, 1932.
Caryl, Delmar H. *With Angels to the Rear: An Informal Portrait of Early Meadowdale.* Edmonds, Wash.: Dilemma Press, 1960.
Cherrington, Ernest Hurst (ed.). *Standard Encyclopedia of the Alcohol*

Problem. 6 vols. Westerville, Ohio: American Issue Publishing Co., 1925.

————. *Evolution of Prohibition in the United States of America.* Westerville, Ohio: American Issue Publishing Co., 1920.

Colvin, D. Leigh. *Prohibition in the United States.* New York: George Doran, 1926.

Cox, Ross. *Columbia River,* ed. Edgar I. Stewart and Jan R. Stewart. Norman: University of Oklahoma Press, 1957.

Crawford, Harriet Ann. *The Washington State Grange, 1889-1924.* Portland, Ore.: Binfords & Mort, 1940.

DeVoto, Bernard. *Across the Wide Missouri.* Boston: Houghton Mifflin, 1947.

Dobyns, Fletcher. *Amazing Story of Repeal.* Chicago: Willett, Clark, 1940.

Drucker, Philip. *Indians of the Northwest Coast.* New York: McGraw-Hill, 1955.

Drury, Clifford M. (ed.). *Diaries and Letters of Henry H. Spalding and Asa Bowen Smith Relating to the Nez Perce Mission, 1838-1842.* Glendale, Calif.: A. H. Clark, 1958.

Duniway, Abigail Scott. *Pathbreaking: An Autobiographical History of the Equal Suffrage Movement in the Pacific Coast States.* Portland, Ore.: James, 1914.

Fargo, Lucile F. *Spokane Story.* Minneapolis: Northwestern Press, 1957.

Fitzgerald, James Edward. *An Examination of the Charter and Proceedings of the Hudson's Bay Company with Reference to the Grant of Vancouver's Island.* London: Trelawney Saunders, 1849.

Fleming, R. Harvey (ed.). *Minutes of Council Northern Department of Rupert Land, 1821-31.* Toronto, Ont.: Champlain Society, 1940.

Flexner, Eleanor. *Century of Struggle: The Women's Rights Movement in the United States.* Cambridge, Mass.: Harvard University Press, 1959.

Franchère, Gabriel. *Narrative of a Voyage to the Northwest Coast in the Years 1811, 1812, 1813, and 1814,* ed. and trans. J. V. Huntington. New York: Redfield, 1854.

Gates, Charles Marvin (ed.). *Readings in Pacific Northwest History: Washington, 1790-1895.* Seattle, Wash.: University Bookstore, 1941.

———— (ed.). *Messages of the Governors of the Territory of Washington to the Legislative Assembly, 1854-1889.* Seattle, Wash.: University of Washington Press, 1940.

Gellatly, John A. *History of Wenatchee.* Wenatchee, Wash. (bound and mimeographed), 1958.

Gordon, Ernest. *Wrecking of the Eighteenth Amendment.* Francestown, N.H.: Alcohol Information Press, 1943.

Gray, William Henry. *History of Oregon, 1792-1840, Drawn from Personal Observation and Authentic Information.* Portland, Ore.: Harris & Holman, 1870.

Gusfield, Joseph R. *Symbolic Crusade: Status Politics and the American Temperance Movement.* Urbana, Ill.: University of Illinois Press, 1963.

Hawley, Lowell S., and Ralph Bushnell Potts. *Counsel for the Damned.* New York: Lippincot, 1953.

Hichborn, Franklin. *Story of the Session of the California Legislature of 1911.* San Francisco, Calif.: James H. Barry, 1911.

Hicks, John D. *Republican Ascendancy, 1921-1933.* New York: Harper, 1960.

Hines, Harvey K. *Illustrated History of the State of Washington, Containing Biographical Mention of its Pioneers and Prominent Citizens.* Chicago: Lewis, 1893.

Hofstadter, Richard. *Age of Reform.* First Vintage Ed. New York: Vintage Books, 1960.

Hunt, Herbert, and Floyd C. Kaylor. *Washington West of the Cascades.* 3 vols. Chicago: S. J. Clark, 1917.

Jennings, Linda Deziah (ed.). *Washington Women's Cook Book.* Seattle, Wash.: Washington Equal Suffrage Association, 1909.

Jessett, Thomas E. (ed.). *Reports and Letters of Herbert Beaver.* Portland, Ore.: Champoeg Press, 1959.

Johansen, Dorothy, and Charles M. Gates. *Empire of the Columbia: A History of the Pacific Northwest.* New York: Harpers, 1957.

Krout, John Allen. *Origins of Prohibition.* New York: Alfred A. Knopf, 1925.

Lee, Daniel, and J. H. Frost. *Ten Years in Oregon.* New York: J. Collord, 1844.

Lemert, Edwin M. *Alcohol and the Northwest Coast Indians.* Berkeley: University of California Press, 1954.

Leuchtenburg, William E. *Perils of Prosperity, 1914-32.* Chicago: University of Chicago Press, 1958.

Lewis, Meriwether. *Lewis and Clark Expedition.* 1814 Edition. 3 vols. (Keystone Western Americana Series). New York: Lippincott, 1961.

Lippmann, Walter. *Men of Destiny.* New York: Macmillan, 1927.

McLoughlin, John. *Letters of Dr. John McLoughlin Written at Ft. Vancouver, 1829-1832,* ed. Burt Brown Barker. Portland, Ore.: Binfords & Mort, 1948.

———. *Letters of John McLoughlin from Fort Vancouver to the Governor and Committee,* ed. E. E. Rich. 3 vols. London: Champlain Society, 1941-44.

Marshall, Jim. *Swinging Doors.* Seattle, Wash.: Frank McCaffrey, 1949.

Meany, Edmond S. *History of the State of Washington*. New and rev. ed. New York: Macmillan, 1946.

Meeker, Ezra. *Pioneer Reminiscences of Puget Sound*. Seattle, Wash.: Lowman and Hanford, 1905.

Mercer, Asa Shinn. *Washington Territory, The Great Northwest, Her Material Resources and Claims to Emigration*. 1865 ed. (Dogwood Press Series of Western Americana). Seattle, Wash.: Frank McCaffrey, 1939.

Merk, Frederick (ed.). *Fur Trade and Empire: George Simpson's Journal, 1824-1825*. Cambridge, Mass.: Harvard University Press, 1931.

Merz, Charles. *Dry Decade*. New York: Doubleday Doran, 1931.

Miller, Max. *Shinny On Your Own Side*. Garden City, N.Y.: Doubleday, 1958.

Morgan, Murray. *Skid Road: An Informal Portrait of Seattle*. Rev. ed. New York: Viking Press, 1960.

Morison, Samuel Eliot. *Maritime History of Massachusetts, 1783-1860*. Boston: Houghton Mifflin, 1941.

Nesbit, Robert C. *"He Built Seattle": A Biography of Judge Thomas Burke*. Seattle: University of Washington Press, 1961.

Niebuhr, Reinhold. *Irony of American History*. New York: Scribners, 1952.

Oberländer, Richard. *Von Ozean zu Ozean: Kulturbilder und Naturschilderungen aus dem fernen Westen von Amerika*. Leipzig: Otto Spamer, 1884.

O'Connor, Harvey. *Revolution in Seattle*. New York: Monthly Review Press, 1964.

Odegard, Peter H. *Pressure Politics: The Story of the Anti-Saloon League*. New York: Columbia University Press, 1928.

Ostrander, Gilman M. *Prohibition Movement in California, 1848-1933*. Berkeley: University of California Press, 1957.

Phillips, Paul Chrisler. *Fur Trade*. Norman: University of Oklahoma Press, 1961.

Potts, Ralph Bushnell. *Seattle Heritage*. Seattle, Wash.: Superior, 1955.

Rich, E. E. (ed.). *Letters of John McLoughlin from Fort Vancouver to the Governor and Committee*. 3 vols. London: Champlain Society, 1941-44.

——. *Part of Dispatch from George Simpson, Esqr., Governor of Rupert's Land to the Governor & Committee of the Hudson's Bay Company London, 1829*. Toronto: Hudson's Bay Record Society, 1947.

Root, Grace C. *Women and Repeal: The Story of the Women's Organization for National Prohibition Reform*. New York: Harper, 1934.

Rosenow, Beverly Paulik (ed.). *Journal of the Washington State Constitutional Convention, 1889*. Seattle: University of Washington Press, 1962.

Roth, Lottie R. *History of Whatcom County*. 2 vols. Chicago: Pioneer Historical, 1926.

Rowntree, Joseph, and Arthur Sherwell, *Temperance Problem and Social Reform*. 7th ed. New York: Thuslove Hanson and Comba, 1900.

Schmid, Calvin F. *Social Trends in Seattle*. Seattle: University of Washington Press, 1944.

———, and Vincent A. Miller. *Population Trends and Educational Change in the State of Washington*. Seattle: Washington State Census Board, 1960.

Sellers, James Benson. *Prohibition Movement in Alabama, 1702 to 1943*. Chapel Hill: University of North Carolina Press, 1943.

Simpson, Sir George. *Part of Dispatch from George Simpson, Esqr., Governor of Rupert's Land to the Governor & Committee of the Hudson's Bay Company London, 1829*, ed. E. E. Rich. Toronto: Hudson's Bay Record Society, 1947.

———. *Fur Trade and Empire: George Simpson's Journal, 1824-1825*, ed. Frederick Merk. Cambridge, Mass.: Harvard University Press, 1931.

Sinclair, Andrew. *Prohibition: The Era of Excess*. Boston: Atlantic, 1962.

Snowden, Clinton A. *History of Washington: The Rise and Progress of an American State*. 6 vols. New York: Century History, 1909-11.

Snyder, Charles R., and David Pittman (ed.). *Society, Culture, and Drinking Patterns*. New York: J. Wiley, 1962.

Spalding, Henry H., and Asa Bowen Smith. *Diaries and Letters of Henry H. Spalding and Asa Bowen Smith Relating to the Nez Perce Mission, 1838-1842*, ed. Clifford M. Drury. Glendale, Calif.: A. H. Clark, 1958.

Stanton, Elizabeth C. *et al.* (ed.). *History of Women Suffrage*. 6 vols. New York: Fowler & Wells, 1881-1922.

Stewart, Edgar I. *Washington, Northwest Frontier*. 2 vols. New York: Lewis Historical, 1957.

———, and Jan R. Stewart (ed.). *Columbia River*. Norman: University of Oklahoma Press, 1957.

Sutton, E. B. *Prohibition Seed Thoughts or Thoughts Gone to Seed*. Seattle, Wash.: Acme, 1893.

Swan, James G. *Northwest Coast, or Three Years' Residence in Washington Territory*. New York: Harper, 1857.

Sweetman, Maud. *What Price Politics: The Inside Story of Washington State Politics*. Seattle, Wash.: White & Hitchcock, 1927.

The Liquor Problem: A Summary of Investigations Conducted by the Committee of Fifty, 1893-1903. Boston: Houghton Mifflin, 1905.

Timberlake, James H. *Prohibition and the Progressive Movement, 1900-1920.* Cambridge, Mass.: Harvard University Press, 1963.

Trotter, F. I. *et al.* (ed.). *Told By the Pioneers: Tales of Frontier Life as Told by Those Who Remember the Days of the Territory and Early Statehood of Washington.* 3 vols. Olympia(?): W.P.A. Writers' Project and the Secretary of State, 1938(?).

Tucker, Ray T., and Frederick R. Barkley. *Sons of the Wild Jackass.* Boston: L. C. Page, 1932.

Underhill, Ruth Murray. *Indians of the Pacific Northwest.* Riverside, Calif.: Sherman Institute Press, 1945.

Warren, Sidney. *Farthest Frontier: The Pacific Northwest.* New York: Macmillan, 1949.

White, Elijah. *Concise View of Oregon Territory, Its Colonial and Indian Relations, Compiled from Official Letters and Reports, Together With The Organic Laws of The Colony.* Washington City [D.C.], 1846.

Whitener, Daniel Jay. *Prohibition in North Carolina, 1715-1945.* Chapel Hill: University of North Carolina Press, 1946.

Whitfield, William. *History of Snohomish County, Washington.* 2 vols. Chicago: Pioneer Historical, 1926.

Willebrandt, Mabel Walker. *Inside of Prohibition.* Indianapolis: Bobbs-Merrill, 1929.

Winthrop, Theodore. *Canoe and Saddle.* Nisqually ed. Portland, Ore.: Binfords & Mort (n.d.).

Woodward, Walter C. *Rise and Early History of Political Parties in Oregon, 1843-1868.* Portland, Ore.: Gill, 1913.

Work, John. *Journal of John Work,* ed. William S. Lewis and Paul C. Phillips. Cleveland: A. H. Clark, 1923.

Articles and Pamphlets

Annual Report of the President of the Association Against the Prohibition Amendment for the Year 1933. (n.d., n.p.).

"Black-Maned Lion of Seattle." *Collier's,* L (Dec. 28, 1912), 21-23.

Blethen, C. B. "One Year Dry." *Collier's* LIX (March 24, 1917).

Bridenbaugh, Carl. "The Great Mutation." *American Historical Review,* LXVIII (January, 1963).

"Campaign Literature, 1932." File. Seattle Public Library.

Caswell, John E. "The Prohibition Movement in Oregon." *Oregon Historical Quarterly,* XXXIX (September, 1938), and XL (March, 1939).

Coe, Earl (comp.). *Historical Highlights of Washington State.* Olympia: Secretary of State (n.d.).

Coulter, C. Brewster. "John L. Wilson, Erastus Brainerd, and the Republican Party of Washington." *Idaho Yesterdays,* IV (Summer, 1960), 11-16.

"Diary of Jason Lee." *Oregon Historical Quarterly,* XVII (1916), 253-65.

"Education Opposed to Prohibition Repeal." *Washington Education Journal,* XII (November, 1932), 60.

Fairfield, William S., and Charles Clift. "The Wiretappers." *Reporter,* VII (Dec. 23, 1952), 8-22.

Fish, Ezra. "Correspondence of the Reverend Ezra Fish." *Oregon Historical Quarterly,* XVII (March, 1916), 49-59.

Gates, Charles M. "A Historical Sketch of the Economic Development of Washington Since Statehood." *Pacific Northwest Quarterly,* XXXIX (July, 1948), 222.

Gusfield, Joseph R. "Social Structure and Moral Reform: A Study of the Women's Christian Temperance Union." *American Journal of Sociology,* VI (November, 1955), 221-32.

Hulbert, W. D. "Experiences of a Dry Town." *Outlook,* XCVIII (July 15, 1911), 594-95.

Huthmacher, J. Joseph. "Urban Liberalism and the Age of Reform." *Mississippi Valley Historical Review,* XLIX (September, 1962), 321-41.

Irwin, Will. "The Saloon—Past and Future." Portland *Oregonian,* Sept. 25, Oct. 2, 1932.

Johnson, Claudius O. "The Adoption of Initiative and Referendum in Washington." *Pacific Northwest Quarterly,* XXXV (October, 1944), 291-303.

————."The Initiative and Referendum in Washington." *Pacific Northwest Quarterly,* XXXVI (January, 1945), 29-63.

Kerr, William T., Jr. "The Progressives of Washington, 1910-1912." *Pacific Northwest Quarterly,* LV (January, 1964), 16-27.

Lowell, Lawrence. "Reconstruction and Prohibition." *Atlantic Monthly,* CXLIII (February, 1929), 145-51.

Mahoney, Pearl M. *Prosser—The Home Town.* Prosser, Wash., 1950.

Meany, Edmond S., and John T. Condon (ed.). "Washington's First Constitution, 1878, and Proceedings of the Convention" (Reprinted from the *Washington Historical Quarterly,* 1918-19).

"New Dred Scott Decision." *Outlook,* CXLIX (June, 1928), 293.

Odegard, Peter H. "Anti-Saloon League." *Encyclopaedia of the Social Sciences* (1948), I, 118-19.

Prohibition Party Campaign Book for the State of Washington, 1892. Tacoma, 1892.

Report of the State Advisory Liquor Control Commission. Olympia, 1933.

Schaefer, Joseph. "Jesse Applegate: Pioneer, Statesman, and Philosopher." *Washington Historical Quarterly,* I (July, 1907), 217-33.

State-Wide Prohibition Initiative Measure No. 3: Official Arguments For and Against. Seattle, 1914.

Taylor, Herbert C., Jr. "Aboriginal Populations of the Lower Northwest Coast." *Pacific Northwest Quarterly,* LIV (October, 1963), 158-64.

Todd, William. Letters to Edward Ermatinger, Hudson's Bay Company, 1829, published as "Documents." *Washington Historical Quarterly,* I (July, 1907), 256-66.

Walker, Anna Sloan. "History of the Liquor Laws of the State of Washington." *Washington Historical Quarterly,* V (April, 1914), 116-20.

Williams, G. O. "History of the Seattle Police Department: The Prohibition Era in Seattle." *Sheriff and Police Reporter,* (February, 1951).

"Wiretapping Held Legal." *Literary Digest,* XCVII (June 16, 1928), 10.

Official Proceedings, Serial Documents, and Separate Government Publications

Abstract of the 13th Census, 1910, with Supplement for Washington. Washington, D.C.: Government Printing Office, 1913.

Abstract of Votes Polled in the State of Washington. Olympia: State Printer, 1889————.

Anti-Saloon League Year Book, ed. Ernest H. Cherrington. Columbus, Ohio: American Issue Publishing Co., 1909-33.

Everett City and Snohomish County Directory. Seattle: R. L. Polk, 1910-34.

Federal Reporter. Second Series. St. Paul, Minn. West Publishing Co., 1925————.

House Journal of the State of Washington. Olympia: State Printer, 1889————.

Proceedings of the National Conventions of the Anti-Saloon League of America. Westerville, Ohio: American Issue Press, 1909-33.

Proceedings of the Annual Conventions of the Washington State Federation of Labor. Olympia, 1911————.

Proceedings of the Annual Sessions of the Washington State Grange. Place of publication varies, 1891————.

Remington and Ballinger's Annotated Codes and Statutes of Washington. Seattle, Wash., and San Francisco, Calif.: Bancroft-Whitney, 1907-14.

Reports of Cases Determined in the Supreme Court of the State of Washington. Olympia: State Printer, 1889————.

Reports of Cases Determined in The Supreme Court of the Territory of Washington. San Francisco, Calif.: Bancroft-Whitney, 1880-89.

Senate Journal of the State of Washington. Olympia: State Printer, 1889————.

Session Laws of the State of Washington. Olympia: State Printer, 1889
————.

Session Laws, Washington Territory. Olympia: Public Printer, 1885-89.
State of Washington Voters' Pamphlet. Olympia: State Printer, 1914
————.

Statistical Abstract of the United States, 1906. Washington, D.C.: Government Printing Office, 1907.
Washington Public Documents. Olympia: State Printer, 1889————.
Washington State Governors' Messages to the Legislatures, 1909-1925.
Olympia: State Printer, 1925.
U.S. Congress. Senate. Special Committee Investigating Expenditures in Senatorial Primary and General Elections. Hearings, 69th Cong., 1st sess., part 5 (Washington, D.C., 1927). Hearings held in Seattle, Washington, Portland, Oregon, and Spokane, Washington, Oct. 23, 25, 26, 27, 28, 29, 1926.
United States Reports: Cases Adjudged in the Supreme Court. Vols. 276 and 277. Washington, D.C.: United States Government Printing Office, 1928.

Newspapers and Periodicals

Bellingham *American*
Bellingham *Herald*
Everett *Daily Herald*
Everett *Labor Journal*
Everett *Morning Tribune*
Fox, N.Y., *Periscope*
New York *Times*
Olympia *Pioneer and Democrat*
Olympia *Washington Standard*
Portland *Oregonian*
Portland *Oregon Journal*
Puyallup *Valley Tribune*
Seattle *Argus*
Seattle *Citizen*
Seattle *Industrial Worker*
Seattle *Leader*
Seattle *Mirror*
Seattle *Post-Intelligencer*
Seattle *Star*
Seattle *Sun*
Seattle *Times*

Seattle *Town Crier*
Seattle *Union Record*
Seattle *White Ribbon Bulletin*
Spokane *Chronicle*
Spokane *Spokesman-Review*
Steilacoom *Puget Sound Courier*
Steilacoom *Washington Republican*
Tacoma *News-Tribune*
Tacoma *Times*
Washington Grange News
Washingtoner Staats-Zeitung
Wenatchee *Daily World*
Westerville, Ohio, *National Daily*
Westerville, Ohio, *New Republic*
Yakima *Republic*

Index

Printed in the United States
204800BV00002B/55-87/P